DEDICATION

To my wife
who launched our 'ship-on-wheels', but then found herself having to serve her watch in manning the helm, and in helping to bring the vessel safely to port.

FOLK DANCE OF EUROPE

Nigel Allenby Jaffé

First published 1990

Published by
FOLK DANCE ENTERPRISES
Lambert's Halt, Kirkby Malham, Skipton,
North Yorkshire BD23 4BT, England.

Typeset in Great Britain by
Chippendale Type Limited,
Otley, West Yorkshire, England.

Printed and bound in Great Britain by
Smith Settle, Otley, West Yorkshire, England.

British Library Cataloguing in Publication Data

Jaffé, Nigel Allenby, *1938-*
Folk dance of Europe.
1. European folk dancing, history
I. Title 793.3194

ISBN 0-946247-14-5
ISBN 0-946247-15-3 pbk

CONTENTS

Illustrations

FOREWORD

Please let us not get drawn into a discussion on what is, or is not, the most suitable and appropriate title for this book. Folk, Traditional, Ethnic, People's, National, Regional, Peasant, Social, each one of these does up to a point, though not one of them entirely fits the bill. Suffice it to say that I know what I mean by Folk Dance, and let's leave it at that. Hopefully all will become clear as we go along, though there may be moments when you will begin to wonder where all this is leading. At times like these I can only ask you to trust me, hang on to my hand, and let me be your Theseus and guide you along the more abstruse passages of this labyrinth, which I rather than Daedalus have constructed. At journey's end, when the Minotaur has safely been laid to rest, we can join hands in a chain and dance in celebration and in honour of those gods and goddesses, among them the fair Ariadne, who gave us the dance to enjoy in the first place.

INTRODUCTION

As regards ancient dances, I can tell you only that either the passing of time, the indolence of man, or the difficulty in describing them, has resulted in their being lost. Besides, there is no need to trouble yourself about them, as such manners of dancing are no longer in fashion. Even those that were to be seen in the time of our fathers are no longer the dances of today which will always be so since men are such lovers of novelty.

Thoinot Arbeau: Orchésographie (1589).

Thoinot Arbeau was quite right, if somewhat negative and pessimistic. Dance has ever been subject to the influence of fashion, and has developed and changed generation by generation. That is the way it was and always will be, for folk dance is not some fossilized relic to be consigned to the dusty vault of a museum. It lives and breathes; it changes and adapts itself, and, just as the social dance of the nineteenth century has been incorporated into the folk dance repertoire of today, so in all probability will the present social dance become the folk dance of tomorrow.

Yet, having said that, one should not ignore the historic evolution of our dance heritage. Indeed, there is every justification for studying its background. Without it there is little valid purpose or reason in performing these dances, especially those from the international repertoire, for so much of the enjoyment is lost. Of course, we can derive great pleasure from getting up and joining in without this knowledge, but how much more meaningful does it become when we understand something of its origins. It is the same with music - one can listen with enjoyment to a piece of music, but that joy is immeasurably enhanced by an understanding and appreciation of musical composition.

Apart from all else, a study of our traditional dance seems to the author to be the most effective and illuminating way in which to draw together the various strands of mythology, history (both social, cultural and political), and geography - almost a complete curriculum in a compact and digestible form - as well as promoting international appreciation and understanding, the very things which rid us of mutual mistrust and fear. Through the dance the world comes together in friendship and peace, for if we are dancing together how can we fight each other?

Dance was an integral and essential part of the rites which early Man observed at each season of the year, and on every important occasion: birth, puberty, marriage and death, the hunt, at the times of sowing and harvesting, war and victory, as well as when any sudden, inexplicable or frightening event affected the community; all were celebrated in dance. Celebration need not necessarily imply joy - Man lived in a constant state of anxiety, and perpetual magic rites were required to keep such uncontrollable aspects of life at bay.

The two most important elements in Man's life were (and still are) the sun and the rain. He needed the rain to make his crops grow, and the sun to ripen them. On the correct balance between these being achieved depended his well-being, because too much of either spelt ruin. In order to endeavour to influence the elements to be benevolent towards him, Man invented various rituals. Through sympathetic magic he hoped to ensure the prosperity of his community, his animals and produce, in fact, his entire way of life.

Out of these rituals emerged folk dance. This book tries to explain its origins and development through the ages, until court dance took over. Thereafter, any growth of folk dance was attributable to the development of the court and subsequently social dance. These heavily influenced the dance: the lower classes of society were always willing to ape the manners of the upper levels, and borrowed as much from them as the latter had formerly borrowed from the folk dance. This book does not ignore this aspect of history, but a more detailed description from late medieval times must await a companion volume on the history of social dance, to bring the study of folk dance up to the present day. The subject matter is vast, and a truly comprehensive study would fill several volumes. Gaps will inevitably appear, but the broad outlines have been sketched and filled in as much as time and space allow.

One of the problems the folk-dance researcher faces is in knowing whether or not a dance is 'authentic'. Writers in the past (a few references by Greek and Roman authors excepted) have hardly found it necessary to describe in any detail the dances which, since everybody knew them, did not require elaboration. Urbanization, industrialization and wars have disrupted the continuity of the traditional dance. As the young men have forsaken their villages to seek work in the towns, or as they have gone off to war, often for years at a time, sometimes never to return, there have not always remained enough people behind to keep the old traditions alive. Today, in many countries, especially those worst ravaged by war, many of the dances we see are revivals based on the memories of a few aged folk, and may or may not resemble the dances of old. Certainly much was lost in the last war.

In western Europe, the upsurge of interest in folk dance started just before the First World War, and we have many detailed descriptions, even some film, of dances and games which are no longer performed, or if done at all today, now lack many of the elements which used to be considered essential if the performance were to have any meaning. Eastern Europe has preserved its continuity much better, not that they have been spared the ravages of war, but because firstly they were predominantly agricultural countries where traditions live on more successfully than in the town, and secondly because here industrialization, when it did come, arrived later, and not before the Romantic Nationalist movement of the mid-nineteenth century had prompted a more conscious awareness of their folk-cultural heritage. After this, great efforts were made to record songs and dances for posterity, and now the people themselves ensured that this heritage would be preserved. The success of this is uneven, country to country. The central European countries of Poland, Czechoslovakia and Hungary, despite urbanization and industrialization, have preserved their folk culture to a high degree, so much so that there is even a danger of going to the other extreme, and turning it into pure 'theatre' and professional performance, and thereby losing its very roots, its *raison d'être*. Sometimes the dances were still there at the beginning of the twentieth century for the researchers to write down, but only too often these remnants were ignored. In Finland, for example, because they were considered too sexually explicit. But they had existed, and were originally regarded as playing an important part in the agrarian calendar.

For all that, it is not everywhere apparent that urbanization and industrialization killed off folk dance or had any catastrophic effect on the traditional way of life and amusements. On the contrary, as may be shown in certain places, these very factors stimulated a widening participation in those popular customs which belonged to a previous age. Often the guilds incorporated particular dances into their ceremonial, and preserved them in an urban environment. In the industrial north of England, clog and morris dancing have flourished, and the widening participation in sword dancing gives the lie to the belief that industry and folk dance are mutually antipathetic.

Where the incidence of folk dance dwindled, and in some rare cases ceased completely, one must look for additional reasons, for, travelling around Europe, one can only be aware of how much countryside and country life have remained, little affected by urban development. Religion played a part in discouraging dance at different times and in different places. In Wales, for example, the strongly puritanical Methodism stamped out any practices which smacked of the devil's work, and Calvinism played a similar part in regions of the Netherlands, Switzerland, France and Germany where it took root. Plagues and epidemics were other causes, but perhaps the greatest single factor, much more influential than the growth of towns and the spread of industry, was war.

Wars have plagued Europe for millenia. Some have confined themselves to comparatively small areas, whilst others have embroiled the whole continent. The Thirty Years' War of the seventeenth century left vast areas of north-central Europe devastated, and greater expanses still were laid waste in the two great wars of the twentieth century. With millions dying and further millions refugees, fleeing their ravaged homelands, there was little room in their lives for dance. Hence the hiatus in the history of folk dance in some countries and the need for a revival. Yet in other countries there was no break at all, and children learnt the dances from watching their elders. If the break was only of a few years, then researchers could re-create the dances, based on the memories of those old people who partially remembered how they themselves had danced them in their youth. When the gap exceeded one human life span, then the recreation had to rely totally on written references, which were more often than not quite inadequate on which to base a revived repertoire. Fortunately this rarely happened, and enough could be salvaged from the wreckage to resurrect dances which were in danger of being lost for ever.

The other thing which could adversely affect the traditional dance was the desire always to adopt the latest fashions, as Thoinot Arbeau observed. New dance crazes elbowed out the older dances which were often, though not always, discarded. Sometimes it was the misguided revivalists themselves who regarded existing (and traditional) dances as dispensible in favour of adopting 'authentic' (but not always indigenous) old dances, as happened in Ireland.

The basic formal groups of dances which were most widely performed at different times, and whose appearance and spread was conditioned by ethnic movements, wars, trade, and fashion, are the old chain and round dances, men's, women's, and group dances, and couple dances which were both regularly structured and irregular. Many of these dances are of a communal nature, some having the features of individual display, and others being of a transitional form with elements of both. Most widespread, during the earlier periods of history, were the communal dance forms. They did not allow any great opportunity for the dancers to display individual creativity or initiative; modern informal dance is the complete opposite, as free scope is given to each individual. Somewhere between the two, the peasants of western and central Europe, as they became more urbanized, and as they acquired urban middle class habits, adapted a form of dance which regulated and formalized individual activity within the customs of the towns and those arbiters of fashion, the courts. A new kind of dance with a formal framework came to the fore. The ancient chain and round dances have been especially preserved and developed in the Balkan countries, whilst the regulated couple dances, country dances, and certain processional dances found greater favour in western and central European countries. Eastern Europe has something of both these, but it is the free dances which are mainly performed. Another factor which may have played its part in this region is the different pattern of social development from that of the west. In the east, there are still many instances of separate dances for men and women, and this in itself inhibits outside influences and the whims of fashion.

Naturally, this is an over-simplification of a far more complex picture, because not all types performed at one particular period necessarily lose popularity, to give way to more favoured forms, and new and old can exist side by side. So whilst chains preponderate in the Balkans, one finds also couple and solo dances, and whilst all can be found in the central Danubian countries, it is the unregulated solo and couple dances which are most popular.

Court dance basically shared the same origins as country or peasant dance. These two categories each developed their own styles, manners and steps, especially as court dance was more open to influences from abroad and from dancing masters. The two were a world apart until, in Tudor England, the dancing of the country people became positively fashionable. Now the rounds and squares, longways and contras were established as part of the court's repertoire and became the fashionable 'ballroom' dancing of the time of James I, through the Commonwealth, Restoration and Hanoverian eras, right up to the present.

Yet again, however, the streams of development took different directions. The fashionable couple dance from Europe, the valses and polkas, mazurkas and varsoviennes, swept the community dances out of the ballrooms and back into the countryside. However, all this spanned a long period, during which there was a great deal of cross-fertilization. Before, and for some time after, the Industrial Revolution, the gentry were landowners, living much of their lives on their estates. Dancing was, alongside hunting, one of the favourite pastimes, and balls were held at the manor houses and stately homes. Naturally the latest dances from the capital or the royal court would be introduced. Dancing masters became indispensable. In England we had the Playford dances; in Sweden in the nineteenth century, the dancing master A. Selinder choreographed new dances, in this case for the theatre - his 'Daldans' is today performed as a 'traditional' dance in the same way that the Norwegian song-dances which Hulda Garborg invented in the early years of the twentieth century have been incorporated into the Norwegian folk-dance repertoire.

Much of today's repertoire is a wonderful patchwork of dances both ancient and modern. How, why and when these dances evolved is the purpose of this present study, and we shall endeavour to see how they emerged from the mists of time and developed into the form we now recognize as folk dance.

— 1 —

ETHNIC AND HISTORICAL BACKGROUND

The dancer's principal task is to draw upon his unfailing memory of ancient story. He must know the history of the world from the time when it first emerged from chaos down to the days of Egyptian Cleopatra.

Lucian: On the Dance (2nd century A.D.)

At least since the retreat of the glaciers at the close of the final Ice Age over 10,000 years ago, the peoples of Europe have been in a constant state of flux. Some of their movements can be traced by the things they left behind. For instance, from their so-called kitchen middens we can see what they ate. These can tell us, if they were hunters, what animals they ate, or, if they were farmers, what cereals they grew and what domestic animals they raised. Their burials can be dated, and the form they took helps trace the spread of their tribes, or at least their influence. So, for example, if they buried their dead in barrows, or cremated them and buried their ashes inside urns, or if they raised huge megaliths like those found in Brittany, Britain, Denmark or Sweden, or interred their kings in richly furnished graves, we can begin to draw lines and place dots on the map showing probable migration routes and areas of colonization.

Back in the early days, much of Europe was uninhabitable. As climatic conditions became more favourable, men began to filter into the continent from Asia and North Africa. Since then, there has been an unending coming and going. Adverse weather conditions, wars, invasions, natural disasters, have sent people scurrying across the face of the continent in search of more tolerable living conditions. This movement still has not ceased. In the last 150 years, probably more people have been uprooted from their homes than during the rest of Man's existence on earth.

Palaeolithic Man lay thinly spread over the habitable parts of Europe. During the Mesolithic Age, the time gap lasting nine thousand years between the end of the glacial period and the Neolithic, the indigenous people obtained their food by hunting, fishing, and gathering wild fruits and vegetables. With the retreat of the last ice cap, the fertile grasslands of the Sahara and of southwestern Asia began to dry, game became scarce, and the rain belt moved westwards and northwards. Movements of peoples across the Straits of Gibraltar and through the Caucasus and southern Russia into Europe took place. At the same time a population of Upper Palaeolithic derivation moved northwards from Spain and the Pyrenees to western France and Germany. In eastern Europe it is possible that the older Palaeolothic race was reinforced in early post-glacial times by peoples from the Near East.

During the third millenium B.C., peoples of a Neolithic culture spread across Europe in search of new lands for farming and grazing their animals. They came as a result of the desiccation of their homelands in Asia, the eastern Mediterranean and beyond. Crete and Greece and the lands near the Bosphorus were reached early in this period; eventually these agriculturalists spread into all the northern Mediterranean lands by sea. Meanwhile, other Neolithic farmers (who came to be known as Iberians) had been moving along the coast of North Africa, and had crossed over into Spain. From there they migrated northwards and eastwards as far as the Swiss lakes and the Rhine. These people may have introduced a new religion which required the building of megalithic structures such as those found at Carnac in Brittany and Stonehenge in England, and many other stone circles to be found scattered across France, the western Baltic and western Britain. Their agriculture, and their pig, sheep and cattle husbandry, spread gradually over most parts of Europe, including Britain. However, one has to be a little tentative in making these statements, because, through a correction of Carbon 14 dating by dendrochronology, the Breton tombs on the Île Carn have been dated as being 6000 years old, whilst in the Orkneys a farming people apparently independently erected stone monuments before Stonehenge was built. Still other farmers from Anatolia or southern Russia were moving up the Danube, and eventually established themselves in the fertile valleys of Moravia and Bohemia, and even further westwards, until they met the stream coming northwards over Gibraltar.

These movements brought a new agricultural population into Europe. Later there were other movements of a different character. The Corded-ware or Battle-axe people, so called on account of the decoration on their pottery and the distinctive shape of their battle-axes, came from some point in southern Russia or the steppes of western Asia, and were probably less dependent on farming than on pastoral nomadism and trade.

From the Baltic to the Urals stretched a belt of forest and swamp, crossed by many rivers, which long formed a shelter for primitive hunters and fishers, while the steppes to the south were overrun by successive groups of farmers and pastoral nomads from the earliest Neolithic until modern times. This northern cultural backwater has since early pre-Slavic days been the home of various tribes of Finns.

The Bronze Age witnessed renewed shiftings of population on a scale at least comparable with those of the Neolithic. The earliest copper and bronze objects were carried by traders to all parts of Europe which could offer something in exchange. Trade came to affect everyone, for the metal with which ordinary tools and weapons were made came from relatively few places. Copper came from Spain, the Carpathian region, and the Caucasus. Tin was found in Bohemia, Cornwall, and again in Spain. Extensive trade necessarily arose to bring the products of the mining regions together. Climatic changes brought drought to many parts of the north European plain, and fostered tribal migrations, while political disturbances in Mesopotamia and Anatolia, in the early part of the second millenium B.C., indicate that widespread movements of economic origin were prevalent at that time.

The age of metal began in Egypt and Mesopotamia early in the fourth millenium B.C., and by 3000 B.C. it had spread to the Aegean and to Anatolia. Crete probably received metal-age influence from Palestine and Egypt before Anatolia. Cyprus, which bears the same name as copper, was another early centre. In the diffusion of early metal-age culture westwards along the Mediterranean and northwestwards up the Danube, the peoples of Asia Minor, Cyprus, Crete, and the Aegean, played an important rôle, acting as transmitters of impulses which had originated in Egypt and Sumeria.

The European Bronze Age found its home in Crete and began a century or two before 3000 B.C. The metal age was introduced by immigrants from two directions: from the Egyptian delta and from the mainland of Asia, perhaps Palestine.

During the Neolithic Age, Greece was culturally connected with North Africa and the rest of the Mediterranean basin. In the early metal age, immigrants from the Cycladic Islands introduced copper into Greece along with the Mother-goddess cult. In the meantime Painted Pottery peoples of Danubian cultural origin arrived in Greece, driven south by Corded-ware people.

Between 2000 B.C. and the period of Homer, Greece was invaded three more times: by Corded-ware people from the north, who may have brought with them the Indo-European basis of Hellenic speech; by Minoans from Crete; and by invaders from across the Aegean, who established themselves as an aristocracy, in the same way as the Normans were later to impose theirs on Saxon England.

The Irish have an ancient tradition that their island was colonized three and a half thousand years ago by the Milesians, a Greek race who had been forced out of their homeland by invaders, and certainly the striking similarities between Irish and Greek mythology make this readily believable.

In the early metal age, influences from Crete and the Aegean spread westwards to Sicily, Sardinia, Italy, and Spain. This maritime diffusion was probably carried out by sea-farers in search of new sources of metal, as well as markets for their products.

During the early Copper Age in Spain, the distinctive Bell-Beaker culture arose, which was soon to spread northwards and eastwards into central Europe, and eventually to Britain, where it found its most important and enduring home.

Three non Indo-European speaking peoples: the Basques, the Phoenicians, and the Etruscans, came to colonize parts of Europe during the Bronze Age. The area occupied by the Basques is rich in metal ores, and had long attracted migrants, and the Basques may well have been one such people who came from Asia in large enough numbers to become a permanent factor in the local population. The Phoenicians, who established their principal colony at Carthage at the end of the second millenium B.C., and posted trading garrisons at various points on the North African coast, also settled along the eastern coast of Spain, where they founded the city of Cartagina. Except for the Greeks, they formed the last of the groups to migrate westwards from the eastern Mediterranean by sea. The Etruscans probably came to Italy towards the beginning of the first millenium B.C. Another wave is said to have arrived in the eighth century B.C. Their homeland, according to classical tradition, was Lydia in Asia Minor.

While the earliest metal-age culture was being carried westwards through the Mediterranean by sea, other agencies conveyed it overland into central Europe. As before, the main highroad was the Danube Valley. Concurrently, a counter-movement of the Bell-Beaker culture travelled eastwards from the Rhine to the Danube, and as far as Poland and Hungary.

The late Bronze Age was a time of considerable shifting and expansion of peoples. In most of Europe, climatic change brought an increase in cold and dampness, and fostered the growth of forest on former grasslands. The area of soil suitable for cultivation grew smaller, while the number of people had increased; these factors alone were enough to cause displacements of population. Across the plains of Asia as well as Europe, large movements took place.

Trade, even at this early date, was extensive. Amber found in Jutland and along the Baltic coast has been unearthed in the beehive tombs of Mycenae in Greece; pearls from Egypt have been found in England, as also artifacts from Mycenae, while axes of Irish provenance have been unearthed in Denmark.

The Urnfield culture, so called because the dead were cremated and their ashes interred in urns, expanded southwards from the Middle Danube to Bohemia, Poland and central Germany, western France and northern Spain. The Veneti and Illyrii had much in common with the Urnfield culture.

The civilization of ancient Greece grew up around the Aegean Sea in the eastern Mediterranean, and centred on Troy on the seabord of Asia Minor, Knossos on Crete, and Mycenae in the Peloponnese. The island of Crete is like a stepping stone between Europe, Asia and Africa, and her prosperity was built upon sea-borne trade. 6000 years ago, her ships sailed down the Nile, and her merchants brought back Egyptian religious customs and social habits, which the islanders adapted and modified. A thousand years later, Crete entered the Bronze Age, and another thousand years after that, they were building up a flourishing civilization, with magnificent multi-storey buildings. The ruins of King Minos's great palace at Knossos, which cover an area of nearly six acres, inspire wonder and admiration in every visitor to the island. It is hardly surprising, therefore, that many scholars saw in the complex of corridors and courtyards, the labyrinth of the Minotaur.

Sadly, Cretan civilization did not survive the endless wars which, by c.1200 B.C., had left Knossos in ruins, and were soon also to destroy Troy, the political leadership passing to the Mycenaeans who made themselves masters of the Aegean. Towns sprang up on the mainland, the forerunners of the later Greek city-states, and colonies were established on the coasts of Asia Minor and Syria.

The next incursion by Indo-European peoples brought the Dorians violently onto the scene. They were a warlike people, and their possession of iron weapons soon brought the destruction of Mycenae, sending many of the inhabitants fleeing eastwards into Attica, where some settled in Athens, while others sailed to Asia Minor and settled a strip of land which became known as Ionia. The next 400 years were marked by violence and conflict.

The great classical phase of Greek civilization spanned the eighth to the fourth centuries B.C., and its principal centre was Athens. The very nature of the geography of the Greek peninsula and Asia Minor with their jagged coastlines and innumerable islands, stimulated seagoing trade, while the numerous mountain ranges which crisscross the peninsula made internal communications difficult. Also the poverty of the land and the resulting problems of ensuring an adequate food supply for a growing population, prompted the Greeks to embark on large-scale colonization schemes. Settlements sprang up on the islands of the Aegean and on the shores of the Black Sea. Eastern Sicily and southern Italy were colonized so extensively that the region became known as Great Greece. Colonies were also planted further west, in present-day France – at Massilia (Marseilles), Spain, and on parts of the North African coast.

The fifth century B.C. saw war with the Persians, led by Xerxes, who annihilated the Spartans and burned Athens, but the Greek fleet destroyed Xerxes's ships, and the tide of victory was turned in favour of the Greeks. With the Persians routed, the rivalry between the Greek city states erupted into war. In 413 B.C., the Spartan League attacked Athens. The Peloponnesian War dragged on, in two phases separated by a five-year interval, until 405 B.C., when the last Athenian fleet was defeated and Athens capitulated. Not only was Athenian power ruined, but all the other Greek city-states went into decline.

In 338 B.C., the Macedonians invaded, and the Hellenic phase of Greek history came to an inglorious end. The son of Philip II of Macedonia who invaded Greece was Alexander the Great. He created an empire which stretched from Greece to Persia in the east, and to Egypt in the south, but he died of a fever in 323 B.C., while planning a campaign to the western Mediterranean, and his empire collapsed. Greece had, however, developed a high level of culture, and this was spread by empire and colonization to the far corners of the known world. Rome

1. Women dancing around a male lyre-player. Crete, Late Minoan.

was to assimilate this legacy and pass it on to the peoples of western Europe. In fact, Rome's indebtedness to Greece was acknowledged by the Roman educator, Quintilian (c. 35-95 A.D.) thus:

> *With so many teachers and with so many examples has antiquity furnished us that no age can be thought more fortunate in the chance of its birth than our own age, for whose instruction, men of earlier generations have earnestly laboured.*

It was the Celts who created the first civilization north of the Alps. They were a group of tribes related by language, culture and religion, and first emerged as a distinct people about 800 B.C. They it was who were the first in northern Europe to use iron, and thus provided themselves with tools and weapons, even chain armour, stronger and more efficient than bronze. The Celts were expert warriors and horsemen, driving two-wheeled chariots wildly into battle, and using their superior technology to subjugate the indigenous peoples with whom they came into contact, imposing their language and above all their culture. Their horses' hooves were iron-shod, and they put iron rims on their wheels. Their iron ploughshares greatly improved agriculture. By the year 200 B.C., they had spread out from their original homelands in Bohemia, Germany, Austria, Switzerland and eastern France, to extend their sway from Cape Finisterre in Spain to the Black Sea, and from the North Sea down to the Mediterranean. The map of Europe is strewn with Celtic place and river names: Ankara, Belgrade, Bonn, Budapest, Coimbra, Geneva, London, Lyon, Strasbourg, and Vienna; the Danube, Rhine, Seine. Shannon and Thames; the Parisi gave their name to Paris, the Remi to Rheims, the Helvetii to Helvetia (Switzerland), the Belgae to Belgium; the Boii crossed into Italy and founded Bologna, and settled down in Bohemia. The Celts and the Gaels were closely related: modern France was called Gaul by the Romans, the Gaels went to Ireland and Scotland, and also gave their name to Galicia in northwest Spain, and Galicia in Poland; some 20,000 are reputed to have crossed into Asia Minor where they settled in the area to which they gave their name Galatia.

For all that, the Celts never managed to forge an empire, nor even an absolute ethnic unity, but they did lay the social, economic and artistic foundations of north European civilization, and their religious beliefs and rituals were to be of vital importance to the heritage of folk culture in the lands they settled.

The prehistoric cemetry at Hallstatt (800-500 B.C.) in the Salzkammergut region of Austria has given its name to this first north European Iron-Age culture. The cemetry has yielded swords, daggers, axes, and jewellery with striking geometric and animal motifs. A superb miniature bronze cult waggon, with men and horses hunting stags, unearthed in Strettweg, Austria, belongs to this period. These Celts traded the salt they extracted from the mountains far and wide. Celtic grave goods have revealed Etruscan flagons and Greek wine vessels, as well as their own beautiful brooches and jewellery. They levied tolls on the tin traders bringing Cornish tin by river and packtrain over Alpine passes, and down the river Rhône to Marseilles, and further into Italy. La Tène in Switzerland gave its name to a later Iron Age (500 B.C.).

The Celts were formidable warriors, and their love of warfare is reflected in the ornate ceremonial shields, helmets, and swords, unearthed in all the countries where they settled. A male child was given his first food on the tip of the father's sword, the mother vowing he should find no death but in battle, while kings would demand to be buried upright, sword in hand, facing the foe. (Thus when the god Bran died, his head was set on top of the White Hill – the site of the present Tower of London – so that he could look out over the Channel, and protect his people). In 387 B.C., the Gauls sacked Rome, while others crossed the Balkans and, in 279 B.C., pillaged Delphi, the famed Greek sanctuary. Bands of adventurers even reached Sicily and Egypt.

Celtic hegemony was destroyed by the Roman Empire which expanded to incorporate all Europe north of the Alps and west of the Rhine. The Romans, as has been mentioned, borrowed profusely from the Greeks, and, as the Roman Empire expanded, it carried Greek civilization westwards throughout Europe. With the Roman legions went engineers and architects, so that today, scattered throughout those lands which once formed a part of this mighty empire, are still to be seen the remains of roads, walls, baths, basilicas, amphitheatres, aqueducts and temples.

Greeks and Romans were off-shoots of a common Indo-European stock, and these peoples settled their respective peninsulas at roughly the same time. Sometime after 2000 B.C., invaders skilled in copper and bronze settled the Po Valley. They were followed, about 1000 B.C., by Italic tribes who were equipped with iron weapons and tools. These people spread throughout the peninsula, one of the tribes, the Latins, settling the lower valley of the River Tiber. By the ninth century, immigrants from Asia Minor, the Etruscans, settled on the west coast of the peninsula, and a century later, as we have seen, the Greeks began to establish colonies in the south of the peninsula and on Sicily. Founded at about this time in North Africa was the Phoenician colony of Carthage.

But it was to be the Latins, living in the shadow of the Etruscan expansion, who were destined to rule the ancient world. The Romans, as the Latins came to be known, received Greek culture initially through the Etruscans, who were, for a time, their overlords, and their early kings were of Etruscan origin. In 509 B.C., the nobles, led a revolt against a despotic Etruscan king, and set up Rome as a republic. Rome grew from a small settlement to a dominant power in the Mediterranean in less than 400 years. By 270 B.C., Rome had conquered both the Etruscans and the Greeks of Great Greece. Unlike the geography of Greece whose mountains constituted a barrier to unification, Rome's geography positively aided unification. Italy is not as rugged a terrain as Greece, and the Appennines, which run like a backbone down the length of the peninsula, do not act as a barrier, unlike the Alps to the north, which served to protect Rome from all but the most intrepid of invaders.

Only Carthage remained as Rome's rival. Carthage was both wealthier and more populous than Rome, and, moreover, possessed a magnificent navy, which controlled the western Mediterranean. Their domain included the northern coast of Africa, Sardinia, Corsica, Sicily, and parts of Spain. The war which broke out between the rivals in 264 B.C. (the First Punic War), lasted 23 years, and resulted in a triumph for the Romans, who now annexed Sicily, Sardinia and Corsica. Carthage now concentrated her efforts on enlarging its empire in Spain, but the Carthaginian general, Hannibal, precipitated the Second Punic War by attacking a Spanish town

2. Round dance with musician. Boetian, 6th century B.C.

allied to Rome. In 218 B.C., Hannibal made his famous trek with a convoy of elephants across the Alps and entered Italy. Initially successful, Hannibal, after 15 years on Italian soil, was forced to return home, and suffered an overwhelming defeat at the hands of the Roman legions who had been sent across to North Africa. In 201 B.C., Carthage was forced to turn Spain over to the Romans.

After this (the Second Punic War), Rome was free to turn her attention eastwards, and now successfully attacked Macedonia. Further victories against the Seleucids, who had ambitions in Greece and Asia Minor, followed. In 168 B.C., Egypt allied itself with Rome, and most of the Mediterranean came under Roman sway. By 146 B.C., the Greek city-states had come under Roman rule, and in the same year the Romans burned Carthage, ploughed the ruins under, and spread salt onto the fields to destroy the fertility of the soil. Annexation of Asia Minor and lands in the Near East, in 133 B.C., extended Roman power all around the Mediterranean. Sicily, Sardinia, Corsica, Spain, Illyria, Macedonia, North Africa and Asia Minor, were organized as provinces of the Roman Republic. Further acquisitions came when Julius Caesar conquered Gaul, extending Roman frontiers to the Rhine, and, in 55 B.C., the Romans even crossed the Channel to have a brief look at Britain, though that country would not be conquered for another hundred years.

Under Augustus, the Roman Republic became the Roman Empire, and control was extended to the Danube. The occupation of Britain began in 43 A.D., and lasted until 410 A.D., when the remaining legions were withdrawn. The Roman Empire was, however, too vast to rule from one capital, especially as civil unrest and economic hardship made governing ever more difficult. Diocletian divided the Empire into two virtually equal halves, retaining the administration of the eastern half for himself, and a co-emperor was created to rule the west. Constantine reunited the Empire but moved his capital to Byzantium at the crossroads of Europe and Asia. He dubbed his capital New Rome, but soon it became known as Constantinople (today's Istanbul). After Constantine's death, the unity of the Empire was preserved by the rule of two joint emperors, one in the east and one in the west, but when, in 395 A.D., Theodosius divided the Empire between his two sons, a definite separation between the two halves was acknowledged. The fall of the Roman Empire, when it came, was the western half. The eastern half lived on, sometimes gloriously, often shakily, for another thousand years, but within an ever tightening hostile circle. Even as barbarian tribes parcelled out the western half of the Empire, so Goths, Huns, Lombards, Bulgars, and Slavs, penetrated deep into the Balkan peninsula, and settled in considerable numbers as far south as the Peloponnese.

The western half of the Roman Empire collapsed for a variety of reasons. It had become a rotten edifice, undermined by civil war and economic and social decline, and when the so-called Barbarians pressed hard against it, it fell down. Germanic tribes had long been settled east of the Rhine, covering Europe from the Rhine to southern Russia, and from the Baltic to the Danube. From the Franks in the west to the Goths in the east the Germanic peoples were grouped into tribes. They had for many years cast covetous eyes on the Roman Empire, and longed to share in all the good things they felt the Empire had to offer. But what prompted them to sweep westwards and to carve out kingdoms for themselves was pressure from other peoples to their east. These were the Huns, Mongolian nomads from central Asia who were superb horsemen and fighters. In 372 A.D., they crossed the Volga and conquered the easternmost Germanic tribes, the Ostrogoths. This set in motion a mass westwards movement of all the various Germanic tribes, and towards the end of the fourth century they began streaming across the Rhine. The once mighty Roman Empire tried to resist but failed.

Attila led his Huns across Europe as far as Châlons in Gaul, but there, in 451, he was defeated in the battle of the Catalonian Fields and forced to withdraw. For a time he threatened to take Italy, but he died in 453, and the Huns withdrew to settle outside the Empire in Hungary. In the year 410 the Visigoths sacked Rome, and in 455 the Vandals, having crossed through Gaul and Spain into North Africa, sent a seaborne raiding party across the Mediterranean to sack Rome yet again. The last emperor of the western Roman Empire was overthrown in 476. Before the end of the century, the Visigoths had established themselves in Spain and western Gaul, the Ostrogoths in Italy, the Franks in northern Gaul, the Burgundians (from their reputed homeland of Bornholm) in the Rhône Valley, the Alamanni in Alsace, the Swabians or Suevi in northern Spain, the Vandals in North Africa, and the Angles, Saxons and Jutes in Britain.

The mass folk wanderings (named by German historians as the *Völkerwanderung*) were still far from over. The Byzantine emperor, Justinian, won back Italy in 554, only to have the Lombards, a new wave of Germanic invaders, pour into north and central Italy, where they held sway until they, in turn, succumbed to the Franks in 774. Towards the close of the seventh century, the Muslim Arabs, made confident by their easy triumphs in Syria and Egypt, swept across North Africa, and, in 711, taking advantage of the weakened Visigothic defences, invaded Spain. Within seven years, they held most of the Iberian Peninsula.

In eastern Europe, a great movement of Slavic peoples from the densely forested basin of the Pripet River, northwestern Ukraine, and southeastern Poland, got under way, and in the centuries between 500 and 900, the Slavs fanned out in all directions. The western Slavs posed the gravest threat to the newly formed Frankish kingdom, itself the most easterly of the Germanic kingdoms. However, the German people themselves soon went through a period of eastwards expansion, during which they Germanised many of the new Slavic groups, either by force or by peaceful assimilation. A few islands of Slavic speech and culture survived this movement, notably that of the Wends in Saxony. Poles settled the basin of the Vistula, Czechs took possession of Bohemia and Moravia. Other Slavonic peoples moved south-westwards, colonizing the valley of the Danube, and penetrating far into Thrace, which had originally been within the old Byzantine Empire. Bulgars, Serbs, Croats and Slovenes settled the Balkan peninsula. The Slavs who remained in the east fell under the domination of the Swedish Vikings who traded along the Russian rivers as far as Byzantium, and whose trading stations provided the nucleus of the new Russian state. Gradually, northwards colonization began, Russians mingling with the Finns who occupied these vast forest regions.

The Franks, under a series of strong kings, held their own, and under Charlemagne expanded Frankish power in all directions. A buffer state with Barcelona as its capital was created to keep any further Moslem expansion in check. The pagan Saxons were conquered and forcibly converted to Christianity. Charlemagne defeated the Lombards and proclaimed himself their king. He then set up the East Mark, later to become known as Austria, to protect his eastern flank from plundering raids by eastern nomads. Charlemagne had created a new empire, and was an emperor in all but name, and this title a grateful pope conferred on him, on Christmas Day 800, in Rome. But Charlemagne's empire was short lived. It was divided among his grandchildren, France and the Spanish March going to one, Germany to another, and a middle kingdom to the eldest, Lothar (hence Lotharingia, Lorraine) who also inherited the title of emperor. It was not long before the brothers were fighting among themselves, weakening their defences at the very moment when the Vikings, Magyars and Saracens were erupting out of their homelands.

The Viking successes were spectacular. Fierce warriors, they possessed shallow-draughted longships, which could both sail across oceans and penetrate deep into the continent, following the rivers. Their piratical raids started towards the end of the eighth century. In just over 100 years they made themselves masters of half of England, established footholds in Ireland, Scotland and the Isles, occupied what was to become Normandy (after Northmen, the name given to these Vikings from the north) in France, set up a string of trading stations along the Russian rivers, and gave Russia her first political unity, (as well as their name *Rus* – the name given to the Vikings by the Finnish inhabitants of the region), and made a thorough nuisance of themselves in the Mediterranean. Some of them even seem to have gained a brief foothold in America, five hundred years before Columbus 'discovered' it. As Normans (Northmen), they invaded England in 1066, and shared out the land among themselves, and created a group of principalities in southern Italy and Sicily, which blended all that was best of Roman, Greek and Moslem civilization to produce a brilliant new culture.

The Magyars were dreaded and ruthless nomadic horsemen who had migrated from the region between the Volga and the Urals. In 955, they launched an invasion, which threatened to engulf all Germany. However, Otto the Great succeeded in crushing his foes, and was hailed as the saviour of Europe. The Magyars eventually settled quietly in Hungary.

At the same time new Moslem invasions threatened Europe. The Saracens carried out piratical raids from North Africa on Sicily, Sardinia and southern Italy. Soon, they swept all non-Moslem trade from the Mediterranean and severed the commercial ties which had linked Europe with other areas since classical times.

The eastern half of the old Roman Empire succeeded in holding the Germanic invaders at bay, and, under Justinian, even won back parts of the western empire. But his successes were short-lived, and gradually and relentlessly the Byzantine Empire shrank. The Moslems began a wholesale conquest of the eastern and southern provinces of the Empire, while Bulgars and Slavs were settling the Balkans. A ring of hostile peoples was tightening the knot around Constantinople.

By the year 1000, the basic shape of ethnic Europe had taken place. True, Spain remained to be won back by the Christians, and the Moslem Turks still had to conquer the Balkans, but, generally speaking, the peoples who inhabit the regions they live in today were settled in those lands by one thousand years ago. There were to take place smaller movements, frontiersmen and colonizers, but the days of mass tribal movements were over. Of course, since then there have been endless

3. Round dance by thirteen soldiers. Athens, 8th century B.C.

wars; rarely has there been a span of one generation when war was not raging in some part of Europe, and the political map of Europe has been drawn and redrawn many times, not always taking racial considerations into account. Thus today, many countries contain ethnic minorities who have found themselves on the 'wrong' side of the border. But only rarely (in 1923 and 1945 for example) has there been a major resettlement of peoples. This does not take account of those peoples who wars and economic hardship have uprooted in their millions, and who, in countless numbers, have left their homelands to emigrate to the far corners of the world.

Perhaps here is a good place to give a warning: it should not be imagined that when historians write about mass movements of peoples, that every member of the tribe joined in. Very rarely has this happened, and in most cases there are those who stay behind to try their fortunes with the newcomers who have moved into their homelands. Nor did those invading peoples necessarily outnumber the population into whose lands they were streaming; they came in their thousands, maybe in their tens of thousands, but certainly not in their hundreds of thousands. Sometimes they imposed their own language and culture on these new lands, but often enough it was they who were the recipients of the language and culture they found.

A second little warning – not always does invasion result in wanton destruction. Admittedly, the Vandals, who gave their name to the English language, appear to have been singularly destructive, whilst the Angles and Saxons who invaded England had little interest in the cities and civilization which the Romans had left behind them, and largely ignored urban life, preferring to carve out clearings in the forest in which to set their homesteads, but most of the German tribes had, through trade, had a foretaste of the good things of the civilized Roman way of life, and, far from wanting to destroy it, wished to share in its benefits. Life in Italy, Spain and southern France did not change drastically, although ownership of land did. Nor were all the Germans pagans when they broke into the Roman Empire. Many had already been converted to Christianity, albeit to the 'wrong' creed, but it only took a very few generations for the newcomers to intermarry and blend with the local population. And it was the Franks under Charlemagne who, in the early years of the ninth century, gave the lead in renewing Christian culture – the Carolingian Renaissance.

Charlemagne's empire collapsed and was replaced by a German one. The early emperors of what came to be known as the Holy Roman Empire looked eastwards for expansion and colonization. Looking eastwards also were the Crusaders, few of whom were inspired by those lofty ideals generally associated with them. No kings participated in the First Crusade to the Holy Land – it was the landless younger brothers of the nobility who had no inheritance to look forward to in the west who went east, in the hope and expectation of grabbing new territories in which to set up their very own kingdoms. And this they did. Within fifty years, the Holy Land had been carved up into 'Latin' domains. They didn't last long, however, and all fell eventually to the Seljuk Turks.

The Byzantine Empire survived. Its capital, Constantinople, at the crossroads of Europe and Asia, was fabulously rich through trade. The emperor himself lived much in the style of an eastern potentate, living in eastern luxury with his harem, and rarely if ever emerging from his palace. Indeed, the Byzantine Empire territorially was as much eastern as western, until the Turks overran the Asian provinces, and Greek music and dance owe more to Asian influence than to western. The beginning of the end of the Byzantine Empire was heralded, in 1204, by the Fourth Crusade. It had been the threat posed by the Moslems and the loss of the Holy Land, which triggered off the Christian counter-attack known as the Crusades. The Empire, in drastically reduced circumstances, was to survive for another 250 years, but never did it truly recover from the infamous act of betrayal which occurred in that year. The Venetians had long been expanding their trading empire, and were naturally jealous of Constantinople. They persuaded the most recent batch of crusaders to redirect their attention from the Holy Land to Holy Constantinople itself. This they did. They attacked the city, went on an orgy of looting which lasted for several days, and in the name of God committed all the atrocities that invading armies perpetrate on their enemies. From this time the Byzantine Empire had a Latin emperor until 1261, when Michael Paleologus regained some territories for the Byzantines.

Constantinople, behind her massive defences, had held off attacks up until this time. The rest of the empire was less successful. Slavs and Avars had succeeded in penetrating into the Peloponnese as far back as the sixth century, but they were peacefully absorbed. However, Arab corsair raids took a toll of lives which left many islands and coastal regions greatly depopulated. For 150 years (810-961) they occupied Crete. Towns contracted in size; even once mighty Athens was reduced to the state of a small provincial town. Now, after the sack of Constantinople, mainland Greece fell an easy prey to the Frankish barons from Flanders, Burgundy and Champagne. Just as the Holy Land had been carved up into Latin kingdoms in the previous century, so in the thirteenth century was the mainland carved up into feudal estates. By the middle of the fourteenth century, the Serbians had extended their empire deep into Greece, and Catalan mercenaries grabbed what small territories they could. The Turks were in control of Macedonia and Thessaly by 1400, and were closing in from all sides for the kill.

Of the Franks, a few ruined castles and churches are all that remain, though undoubtedly they added their blood to the ethnic mix which is Europe's rich heritage. The Greek emperor managed to oust the last of the Franks in 1430, only twenty-three years before Constantinople fell to the Turks. The Venetian influence was greater, at least in the islands of the Aegean and Ionian Seas. They were quick to benefit from the temporary eclipse of their rival, and established themselves in various places, clinging on to some of their possessions even after the Turks had conquered the empire. They were not finally dislodged from Crete until 1669, and they even carried out a successful brief reoccupation of their strongholds in southern Greece from 1690 to 1715.

Let us turn our attention towards Russia for a moment. In 1237, the various Russian principalities were conquered by Mongolian tribes, who had been united by Genghis Khan, and launched like a thunderbolt on a campaign of world conquest. In 1242, the Mongols had penetrated the outskirts of Vienna, and western Europe seemed to be theirs for the taking, but the death of their leader took the wind out of their sails, and, like the Huns of Attila, they retired to their homelands to elect a new ruler. Central Europe was not to be molested by them again, but the Mongols established themselves as a ruling caste in Russia, though allowing the various Russian principalities to govern themselves, so long as they paid tribute to the Golden Horde, as the Tatars in Russia were called. Mongol domination changed the course of Russian history, and created a break between Russia and western European civilization. It was finally brought to an end in the 1490's, when Ivan III initiated a series of attacks, which opened the way for the complete defeat of the Tatars and their assimilation into the Russian state.

In the west the Christians gradually pushed the Moslems back, and by the time the Christians in the east were destroying Constantinople, the Moslems in the Iberian Peninsula had had their territory reduced to an area around Granada. This last stronghold collapsed in 1492, the very year that Columbus 'sailed the ocean blue', and forty years after the Ottoman Turks had overthrown and occupied the Byzantine Empire (1453). The Iberian Peninsula was once again Christian; Greece and the Balkans had been won for Islam.

The eastern Crusades may have been destructive and ultimately unsuccessful, but they did have the effect of stimulating trade. This in turn led to mushrooming growth of towns and the eastward expansion (named by German historians as the *Drang nach Osten*) of German settlers into the Slavonic heartlands. Religious orders grew incredibly wealthy and carved out vast regions for themselves. A military-religious order, which came to be known as the Teutonic Knights, was founded at the time of the Third Crusade, and began the conquest of the pagan Slavs in Prussia. Having conquered the area, the Knights abandoned their religious character, and settled down to found cities, and become a landed nobility. In 1410, they suffered a crushing defeat at Tannenberg at the hands of a united Lithuania and Poland, and whilst they retained an autonomy over East Prussia, West Prussia was handed over to the Poles.

Considerable numbers of other German settlers moved into lands either occupied by Slavonic peoples, or into areas of forest and swamp, and began to clear or drain the land, to create for themselves a place to live and grow their crops or husband their animals. In the towns they came to dominate urban life. Trade and education were virtual German monopolies. Bohemia welcomed German immigrants, and this brought to an entirely agricultural country an influx of artisans and traders, who established themselves in the new towns, where they retained their own law and native language. They became a foreign population in the midst of the Czechs. The Baltic Sea became a German lake. Many towns, to protect themselves and to strengthen their trading links, allied to form the powerful Hanseatic League. Unlike past movements of peoples, however, there was now less mingling of the races, and Germans and Slavs lived their separate lives.

So we can close our history as far as folk dance is concerned. The ethnic map of Europe is now complete with the Christian reconquest of the Iberian Peninsula and the Moslem occupation of the Balkans. Regardless of future political juggling with frontiers, wars, and the inevitable flood of refugees, the ethnic groups have established their basic territorial claims, and any future influences on the folk dance will have more to do with trade, movements of armies, and, most of all, that feature which will more and more raise its international head – fashion.

2

A LITTLE MYTHOLOGY

They say that once upon a time the Labyrinth in mountainous Crete contained a path, twining between walls which barred the view, with a treacherous uncertainty in its thousand ways, so that its baffling plan, which none might master and none retrace, would foil the trail of any guiding clues.

Virgil: The Aenead (30-19 B.C.)

Have you ever played the whispering game? One person whispers a message or short story to the next person, who then passes it on to the next, and so on, until it gets back to the first person again. The message or story usually ends up bearing little resemblance to the original. So how can one expect the elements of folk dance, after 150 generations have passed it down from parents to children, to have much resemblance to what was danced back in those far off times? How do we even know what they danced? Well, of course, we don't, not exactly. But we can hazard some guesses, and not altogether haphazard and random guesses at that.

We can examine the rich store of mythology in detail, and, by analytical study, interpret the stories, and give ourselves a much better idea of what the ancients believed, and how they observed their religious rituals. Nor is the parallel with the whispering game completely valid; the stories of the gods and goddesses, heroes and villains, were told over and over again by the storytellers of each of those 150 generations. By the time a child had grown to adulthood, he or she had heard those stories a hundred times, and knew them as well as did the storytellers, so that they in their turn could pass them on to the next generation, probably hardly changed at all. Neither are we totally reliant on this oral tradition, for the legends were set down in writing at a very early period – over 2,500 years ago. That is, of course, if the Ancients got it right in the first place. There are many instances when they did not, and usually deliberately so.

The Judgement of Paris is a case in point. The legend, as it has come down to us from very early times, is of the hero, Paris, son of King Priam of Troy, being invited to choose between the three goddesses, Hera, Athene, and Aphrodite, as to which of them was the fairest. Paris awarded the golden apple to the Love-goddess, and thereby landed himself in deep water from the two irate and jealous rivals. But it was not Paris who was making the award to one of the three goddesses, but the Great Goddess, in her trinity, who was rewarding Paris (actually it was the young Dionysos), with the apple which conferred immortality. It was the same with Adam. Had he been kicked out of the Garden of Eden merely for pinching an apple, one might have thought the punishment rather severe. But Adam, by accepting the apple, showed that he aspired to immortality, and it was for this presumption that he was

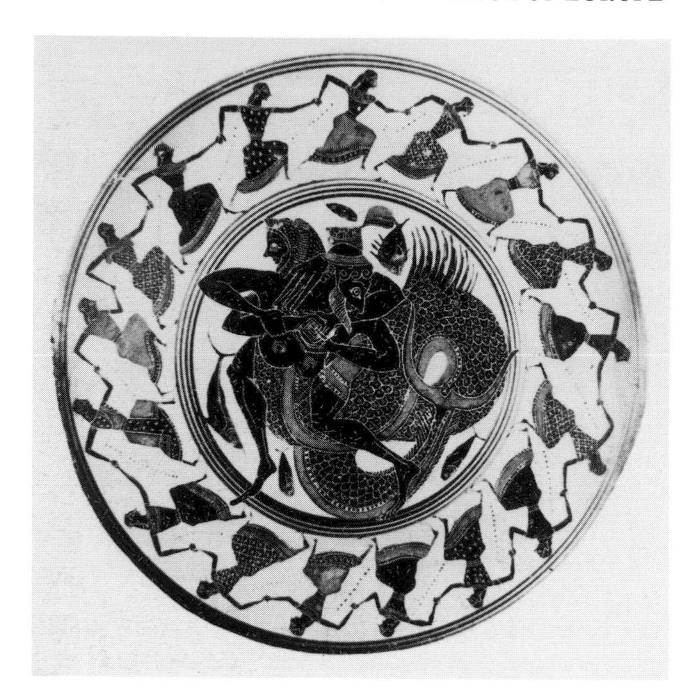

4. Herakles wrestling with Triton, encircled by dancing Nereids. Greek, mid 6th century B.C.

punished. The ancients had other reasons for tampering with their legends. When society changed from being matriarchal to patriarchal, all the stories which explained the origin of things had to be changed as well, in much the same way as a modern totalitarian dictatorship rewrites history to suit its own ends.

Man's most ancient myths conceived creation itself in terms of the dance. According to Greek mythology, Eurynome, the goddess of All Things, before she created the world, danced, setting in motion behind her a wind. This she rubbed between her hands, thus creating the great serpent, Ophion. Eurynome continued to dance in order to warm herself, dancing ever more wildly, until Ophion, grown lustful at the sight of her, coiled around her and coupled with her. Later, taking the form of a dove, Eurynome laid the Universal Egg from which, when it hatched, tumbled all things that exist: the sun, moon, and planets, the earth with its rivers, trees, plants, and all living creatures – so ancient is the dance.

The Latvian sun danced: "The little sun danced on the silver hill, gold shoes on her tiny feet." (As amongst the Germanic peoples, the Latvians regarded the sun as female – the French have *le* soleil and *la* lune, but in German the genders are reversed.) The legend continues: "A bush with white blossom grows on a rock in the middle of the sea, and thence every evening the sun goes to dance." What a pretty idea the sun having its very own maypole dance!

Europe, in the Neolithic period, appears to have had a fairly homogeneous system of religious ideas. Man worshipped the Earth Mother in her various forms; Hestia, goddess of the Hearth, always received the first victim of a Greek sacrifice. Her celestial symbols were the sun as well as the moon, though, in the early Greek myths, it is the moon which has precedence. The moon inspired greater superstitious fear;

5. Head of goddess with round dance of worshippers on her crown. Cyprus, late 6th century B.C.

unlike the sun, its light does not dim as the year wanes, and the moon was believed to bring or deny water for the fields.

The moon has three phases: new, full, and old, and this is reflected in the Earth Goddess's three phases: maiden, nubile woman and old crone. The goddess (as Mother Earth) became identified also with seasonal changes: spring (maiden),

6. Goddess with chain of dancing worshippers. Boetian, Archaic period.
© Photo R.M.N.

summer (woman), and winter (old crone). As yet another triad, she was conceived as the maiden of the upper air (Selene), nymph (nubile woman) of the earth or sea (Aphrodite), and crone of the underworld (Hecate). Here we have three triads or nine goddesses, representing, in various aspects, the supreme Goddess, and hence the sacredness or magical significance of the numbers 3 and 9.

Originally, according to Hittite mythology, the matriarch of a tribe annually chose a lover, a king who would be sacrificed when the year ended. He became a symbol of fertility. His blood would be sprinkled to bring trees, crops and animals to fruitfulness, and his flesh would be torn to pieces and devoured by the queen's priestesses, wearing masks of mares, sows or bitches. Similarly, the Maenads, the womenfolk of the Centaurs, who worshipped Dionysos, and who derived their uncontrolled wild behaviour and remarkable strength from eating (according to Robert Graves) a mushroom, *amanita muscaria*, at their wild autumnal feasts, raged about the countryside, drug-crazed, tearing animals and children to pieces. This same drug may well have been used by the Vikings to send them berserk and to engender increased strength to fight successfully. Today, sadly, some of our athletes also take drugs thinking to improve their performance.

The next development was to put to death the king as soon as the sun, with whom he was identified, began to lose its strength. Another king, his tanist or twin, then became the queen's consort, to be duly sacrificed in his turn at midwinter. Herakles (Hercules) was one such king who was sacrificed at midsummer. He was originally a pastoral sacred king, the rain-maker of his tribe, who carried an oak club – the oak tree was sacred because it attracts lightning, and it provides mast to feed to the animals. His sacred symbols were the acorn, the rock-dove, which nests both in rock clefts and in oaks, the mistletoe, which grows on oak trees, and the serpent

7. Spiral carvings on stone at entrance to chamber and passage, Newgrange, Ireland, prehistoric.

– these are all sexual emblems. Herakles was leader of the orgiastic rites and had twelve companions including his twin (tanist or deputy). Each year he married the Queen of the Woods (compare Maid Marian). He made rain by rattling his oak club in a hollow oak, and stirring a pool with an oak branch – sympathetic magic.

At the end of his half-year reign, at midsummer (after which time the sun began to lose its strength), he was led into the middle of a circle of twelve stones arranged around an oak. He was then ritualistically slain, and his blood sprinkled to make the tribe vigorous and fruitful. His twelve companions then performed a wild dance around the funerary pyre. Six months later, his tanist was in turn sacrificially killed to make way for the New Year Herakles, who is a reincarnation of the murdered king. Mythology has plenty of examples of such sets of twins, Spirits of the Waxing and Waning Year: Osiris and Set, Herakles and Iphikles, Butes and Erechtheus, Hercules and Poeas, Bran and Belin, Baal and Mot, Castor and Polydeuces (better known perhaps as Pollux), Adam and the Serpent, Cain and Abel, Theseus and Perithous, Idas and Lynceus, Romulus and Remus – the list is endless.

Thus kingship developed, though still the sun, the symbol of male fertility, remained under the moon's tutelage, as the king, nominally at least, continued to remain under that of the queen, though he might deputize for her, donning false breasts and wearing her magical robes.

At first time was calculated by the cycles of the moon, and important ceremonies took place at certain phases of the moon. The seventh full moon brought the death of the king as the year turned. The solar year was early calculated to have 364 days with a bit left over, and divided into thirteen cycles of the moon of 28 days each.

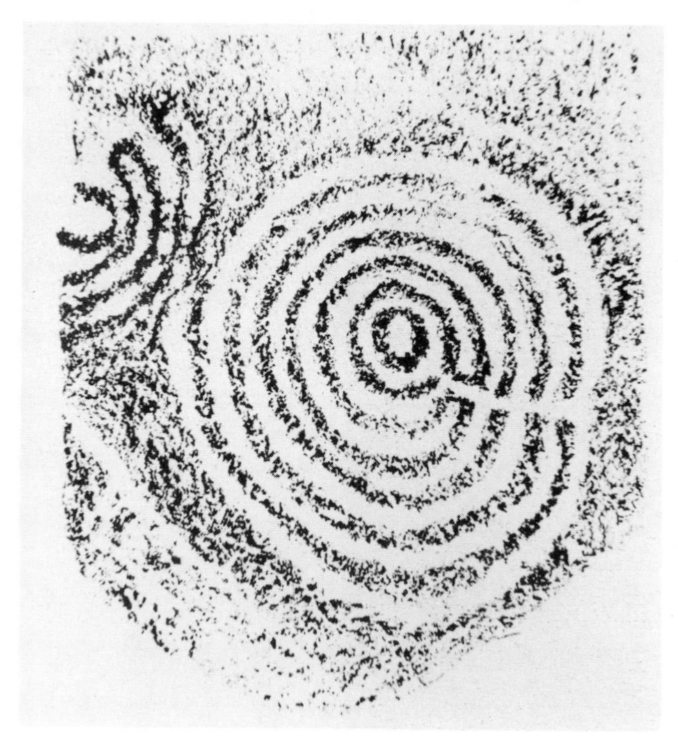

8. Spiral carving from cemetry of Cauldside Burn, Kirkcudbright, Scotland, prehistoric.

(28 was a sacred number. It was the normal period of woman's menstruation, and thus the moon could be worshipped as a woman.) The week divided into seven days, each day being presided over by the sun, moon and the then five known planets: Mars, Mercury, Jupiter, Venus, Saturn). We still name the days of the week after them or their Germanic equivalents; this is also reflected in their French names:

Sunday	Sun	Dimanche (Lord's Day)
Monday	Moon	Lundi (Lune)
Tuesday	Tiw=Mars	Mardi
Wednesday	Woden=Mercury	Mercredi
Thursday	Thor=Jupiter(Jove)	Jeudi
Friday	Freya=Venus	Vendredi
Saturday	Saturn	Samedi

The calendar of popular festivals was geared to these thirteen lunations. The sun passed through the thirteen lunar months, and, with an extra day added, made up 365, to complete the earth's revolution of the sun. This extra day was placed at the end of the thirteenth month, and became the most important day of the year, when the queen chose the new sacred king. The thirteenth month was the sun's death month, and thus the continuing superstition that 13 is an unlucky number.

The Aeolian and Ionian infiltrations of Greece, during the early second millenium B.C., were gradual and less destructive than the Achaean and Dorian ones which followed. The new invaders had a vital impact on the indigenous social structure, as they provided the sacred kings, a male military aristocracy in the service of the female theocracy. The king was the representative of Zeus, or Poseidon, or Apollo.

9. *The Hollywood Stone. Co. Wicklow, Ireland, prehistoric.*

The marrying of these kings to the local moon-priestesses gave rise to the myths of the various seductions of nymphs by the gods.

In course of time, the kings grew tired of being sacrificed after such a short period, and managed to have their reign lengthened to a hundred lunar months. However, the fructification of the fields and crops still needed to take place, and an arrangement was entered into whereby the king annually suffered a mock death, yielding his crown for a day (the intercalated one) to a surrogate boy-king, who was sacrificed at the close, his blood being used to fructify the fields. Invariably the sacrificial boy-king was one of the king's sons, and this gave rise to many legends. It was explained that Herakles killed his children in a fit of madness and quite out of character. Zeus survived due to his mother's cunning. Achilles was also lucky; his elder brothers had all been sacrificed, but when his turn came it was time for his father, Peleus, to die. Achilles' brothers had by their deaths achieved immortality, the usual reward for the sacrificial victims. (Achilles himself had yet to attain this and he was vulnerable in the heel. More about lame gods follows later.) The soul of the sacred king on his death would escape in the form of an eagle (like the soul of Herakles). The sons of the king who were annually sacrificed in his stead and who, after a single day's reign, were burned, were assured immortality by rising like the phoenix from the ashes of their pyres. Such fates awaited Cretan Dionysos, son of Zeus; Icarus, son of Daedalus; Phaëthon, son of Apollo; Gwern, son of Matholwch; Ganymede, son of Tros; and Mermerus and Pheres, sons of Jason.

However, despite this postponement, at the end of his term the king must finally die: he might be torn to pieces by drug-crazed priestesses, killed by a spear or axe, or be wounded in the heel by a poisoned dart, flung over a precipice, burned, drowned, or killed in a chariot crash that had been pre-arranged. Another way in which he might be killed was by being gored by a wild animal whilst out hunting. The Sardinians still have a dance which harks back to these ancient Greek legends. In this dance, the boy who has been dancing in the centre of a circle of dancers is suddenly gored by a wild beast which rushes amongst them. He falls down as if dead, and a mournful song is sung as he lies there, prostrate and motionless. Then a girl appears, carrying a basket of

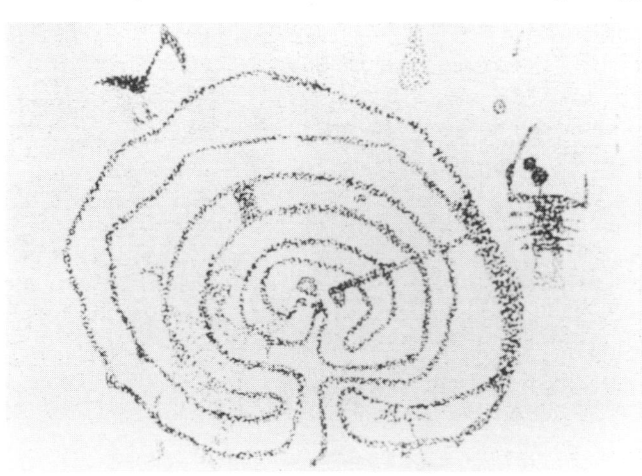

10. Labyrinth carving from the Naquane Rock, Val Camonica, Italy, prehistoric.

flower petals which she strews around him. He jumps up, and the lively and joyful dancing is renewed.

In due course, an unlimited male monarchy superseded female worship. Much of Greek mythology is in fact a veiled account of how these changes came about. Thus the story of how Perseus cut off the head of Pegasus's mother, the Gorgon Medusa, probably relates to the invasion of Greece by the patriarchal Hellenes in the second millenium B.C., and who subsequently challenged the status of the Triple-goddess. Because of its moon-shaped hooves, which featured in rain-making ceremonies and the installation of the sacred king, the winged-horse Pegasus was sacred to the goddess. The cutting off of Medusa's head reflects the overrunning of the goddess's shrines. Similarly, when the Python is killed by Apollo at Delphi, we see recorded the capture by the Achaeans of the Cretan Earth-goddess's shrine. The attempted rape of Daphne, who escaped through the goddess Hera metamorphosing her into a laurel bush, suggests the suppressing of the Maenad colleges by the Hellenes.

The matrilineal tradition was further seriously weakened by the Achaean invasions of the thirteenth century B.C. The king was now allowed to reign for his lifetime, until finally, under the Dorians, patrilineal succession became the established custom.

Greek legends invariably related historical events, enveloping, and elaborating on, the tales of their gods, goddesses, and heroes. Over thousands of years many of these myths have become so garbled as to make it impossible to derive any real sense and meaning from them. Others, however, are open to fairly exact interpretation. The myth of Theseus and the Minotaur is one such, whose story can be used to relate

11. Turf-cut maze. Visby, Gotland. Swedish, prehistoric.

precise historical events, and which also tells us much about the spread and adoption of religious cults. There are many legends concerning Theseus and the Minotaur. Here is the essence of just one of them (the Cretans told quite a different tale):

King Minos of Crete was the son of Zeus and Europa. Zeus had seduced Europa by disguising himself as a bull, and carried her off to Crete. There she bore Zeus three children, Minos, Rhadamanthys and Sarpedon. The three children were adopted by Asterius, the king of Crete, who subsequently became Europa's husband. Minos eventually succeeded to the throne of Crete and married Pasiphaë, who developed a passion for Poseidon's white bull (this is a second bull). With the help of Daedalus she succeeded in coupling with the bull, but produced by this unnatural union the monstrous Minotaur, half man, half bull.

Poseidon's ferocious white bull had been brought by Herakles from Crete and let loose on the plain of Argos, where it rampaged all over the place killing men in their hundreds, among them Minos's own son, Androgeus. In requital for the death of his son, Minos ordered the Athenians to send seven youths and seven maidens every ninth year to Crete, where, in the labyrinth, the Minotaur waited to devour them. The third time the tribute fell due found Theseus in Athens, and he, through pity for those parents whose children were chosen to be sacrificed, offered himself as one of the victims. After many adventures, Theseus and his companions arrived in Crete, and there Theseus fell in love with Minos's daughter, Ariadne.

Before leaving Crete (hurriedly after the Pasiphaë affair), Daedalus gave Ariadne a magic ball of thread, and taught her how to enter and leave the labyrinth. He told her to tie the loose end of the thread to the lintel of the entrance door; the ball would then roll along the passages of its own volition, unravelling as it went, and find its way into the centre, where the Minotaur lived. Ariadne gave this magic ball to Theseus, and instructed him to follow it until it led him to the monster, which he should kill on the spot. Theseus, spattered with the bull's blood, emerged triumphant from his mission, and, taking Ariadne and his companions down to the harbour, they boarded his ship and set sail.

Some days later, they arrived at Naxos, where Theseus abandoned Ariadne (some say because Dionysos demanded her for himself). From Naxos, Theseus sailed to

12. Detail from the Tragliatella Vase. Etruscan, 7th century B.C.

13. The Tragliatella Vase. Etruscan, 7th century B.C.

Delos, there sacrificing to Apollo, and performing athletic games in his honour. This was the occasion, incidentally, when the custom of crowning the victor with palm-leaves was introduced. A horned altar (built by Apollo himself, and one of the Seven Wonders of the World) stood beside the round lake of Delos. Around this altar, Theseus and his companions, according to Plutarch, danced the Crane Dance, which consisted of "labyrinthine movements, trod with measured steps to the accompaniment of harps". The Crane Dance was still performed in his day (1st century A.D.):

> *The Delians still perform this dance, which Theseus introduced from Knossos; Daedalus had built Ariadne a dancing floor there, marked with a maze pattern in white marble relief, copied from the Egyptian Labyrinth. When Theseus and his companions performed the Crane at Knossos, this was the first occasion on which men and women danced together. Old-fashioned people, especially sailors, keep up much the same dance in many different cities of Greece and Asia Minor; so do children in the Italian countryside, and it is the foundation of the Troy Games.*

In Greek, *geranos* means crane, and many scholars have linked the steps to the movements of the bird. However, the name used to describe the dance could also be derived from the root *ger-*, which denotes to wind, as of rivers and snakes. A Geranos is danced still on many Greek islands, but it is not the same type of dance as the ancient Geranos.

The Theseus myth in fact relates how the Athenians revolted against their Cretan overlords, who had introduced a bull-worship cult into the mainland. Theseus's raid on Knossos, while the main fleet was away in Sicily, took place about 1400 B.C. The peace treaty concluded with King Minos of Crete was ratified by the marriage of Theseus, son of the king of Athens, with Ariadne, the Cretan heiress. The Cretans observed a sky-bull cult, and it was in bull-form (ill. 14) that the king would seem to have coupled ritually with the chief-priestess in her capacity as Moon-cow.

It was once thought that the corridors of the palace at Knossos represented the labyrinth of the myth. However, it appears that there was an open space in front of the king's palace, which was occupied by a dance-floor, with a maze pattern, perhaps marked out in mozaic pavement, which guided the dancers as they performed an erotic spring dance in honour of the Moon-goddess. Homer wrote:

Daedalus in Knossos once contrived
A dancing-floor for fair-haired Ariadne.

Another ancient version is one in which the dance was performed by dancers who wore wings (ill. 118), and hobbled, representing the movements of the cock-partridge (a bird sacred to the Moon-goddess). This bird hobbles in his love-dance, holding one heel ready to strike his rivals. We must now tread a labyrinthine path ourselves in order to learn something of the relevance of the 'limping' or 'hobbling' step, before we come back to this spot again.

14. Detail from vase with bull-masked dancers. Greek. Reproduced by Courtesy of the Trustees of the British Museum.

In many religions, the sacred king's strength was believed to reside in his feet, or more specifically in his heels. In Welsh mythology, Math, son of Mathonwy, king of North Wales, was required to keep his foot in the lap of a priestess. This office of royal foot-holder survived in the royal court in Wales until medieval times, but was then assigned to a man (hence footman) rather than a woman servant. The heel was regarded as being the one vulnerable part of sacred kings. Thus we have the heel of Achilles, which was pierced by an arrow loosed from the bow of Paris; Medea's pin mortally wounded Talus; his namesake was wounded in the ankle by a poisoned arrow shot by Poeas; the brother of the Ben Gulban Boar lanced the heel of Diarmuid; that of Harpocrates was stung by a scorpion; Orion suffered a similar misfortune for inadvertently having touched Aphrodite; the heel of Balder was pierced by the god Holder at the instigation of Loki; Egyptian Ra's heel was stung by a snake sent by Isis; so too were Orestes, and Cheiron and Pholus the Centaurs, wounded in the heel; Oedipus also, although here the myth has become muddled and the laming should belong to the end of the story rather than the beginning; that of the Hindu god Krishna was pierced by an arrow shot from the bow of his brother Jara; in the Roman ritual of crucifixion, originally the victim being the annually sacrificed king, the nail was driven into the side of the foot to pin it to the cross; Llew Llaw, the Welsh god (New Year Robin) killed his father (the Wren), alias Bran, when he shot his arrow into his foot.

15. Vase showing bull-masked dancers. Greek. Reproduced by Courtesy of the Trustees of the British Museum.

In British folklore, the Robin Red Breast represented the Spirit of the New Year. On the extra day, which fell outside the thirteen 28-day lunations which made up the Celtic year, the robin set out armed with a birch rod to kill his predecessor, the wren, the Spirit of the Old Year. The robin is said to murder his own father, and this accounts for his red breast. The tanist (wren) had killed the king (robin) at midsummer – remembered in the children's nursery rhyme, though here for the sake of the rhyme it is the unfortunate sparrow who is unfairly blamed:

Who killed Cock Robin?
I said the Sparrow,
With my bow and arrow.
I killed Cock Robin.

A connection with Robin Hood will be made in the chapter on Morris dancing.

Coloured and gilded shoes were a symbol of royalty among Celts, and sacred kings were presented with special buskins at their marriage. Until the reign of King George II, they figured in the English coronation ceremony. When Byzantine emperors were crowned, they wore purple buskins. Theseus was given sandals by his mother; Perseus had special shoes, as did Mercury with his winged sandals (the addition of wings lending sanctity rather than speed). Sacred kings were not allowed to put their heels down on the ground; they had to walk on their toes. The god Dionysos wore the *cothurnus* or high-healed buskin and walked with a limp. Sacred kings adopted this swaggering gait, either because they too had suffered laming, or in imitation of it.

16. Theseus and his companions. The François Vase. Greek.

Tragic actors on the Greek stage did likewise, and wore the *cothurnus* in honour of Dionysos.

Other sacred kings were lamed in other ways. Jacob was lamed during a wrestling match with an angel; his hip was displaced, the injury forcing him to walk with a lurching gait and on his toes. Abraham too had a sacred thigh. We read in I Kings, XVIII, 26, how the priests of Baal danced at his altar and cried out for Baal to light the spring bonfires and burn up the corpse of the old year. The Authorised Version of the Bible has them leaping up and down, but the original Hebrew word, formed from the root PSCH meant 'to dance with a limp'. Pesach, the name of the Passover feast is derived from the same root. The Passover was a Canaanite spring festival which was adapted to commemorate the escape from Egypt. At Carmel, the priests must have danced with a limp to encourage the lame god to appear, armed with his torch. 'Baal' means 'Lord', and the lord in this case was 'Jah Aceb', Jacob – the Heel-god.

Jah Aceb was also worshipped at a place between Jericho and the Jordan called Beth-Hoglah (the 'Shrine of the Hobbler'), which place has been identified as 'the threshing-floor of Atad'. Here the devotees danced in a spiral, making limping movements in honour of the lame king, Jacob. St. Jerome, however, mentions this place in connection with a round dance performed in honour of Talus, whose name means 'sun', and to whom the partridge is sacred. In Greek legend, Talus was thrown down from a great height by Daedalus, but was transformed by the goddess Athene into a partridge while still airborn. The Arabic word for hobble comes from the word for partridge, and so the dance was presumably a hobbling one. Moreover, the dance probably mimicked the courting display of the cock-partridge, which flutters around in circles with a hobbling gait, made so by the fact that it keeps one foot held always in readiness to strike at any encroaching rival. The Roman scholars and poets, Hyginus and Ovid, by identifying the hero Perdix, 'partridge', with Talus, confirm the connection between the hobbling partridge and the lame king.

Partridges were then, and still are in many Mediterranean countries, used as decoys to lure other of these game birds to their deaths. It seems that a bull-cult was superimposed on a partridge-cult, and that the Minotaur, to whom youths and maidens were sacrificed, represented the decoy partridge in the middle of the brushwood maze. The Minotaur was the centre of a ritual performance originally in honour of the Moon-goddess, who in Crete was the mother of Talus. The hobbling dance of the partridge was later transformed into one to honour the Moon-goddess Pasiphaë, the mother of bull-headed Minos. The spirally-danced Troy-game, which in Delos was called the Crane Dance, had the same origin as the bull-cult dance.

Just before we retrace our steps, it should be mentioned that there is a connection between the lame king and the mysteries of smithcraft: Jacob and the cult of the Kenite Smith-god; Talus with the smith Daedalus; Wieland, the Scandinavian Smith-god was lame; the very name of Dionysos may have implied that he was a lame god; Vulcan, the Roman Smith-god, was lame and had to walk with the aid of high-heeled gold shoes, and Hephaestus was lamed when he was thrown down, like Talus, from a great height.

So here we are, back safe and sound at the entrance to the maze again. The dancing floor at Knossos was laid out with its labyrinthine convolutions for the dancers to follow in their ritual partridge dance. It probably followed in design the traditional brushwood maze which had long been used to lure partridges towards a decoy bird, caged in the centre of the maze, and the pattern probably also represented 'Spiral Castle' or 'Troy Town', where the sacred king went after death, and from whence he hoped to return. An Etruscan wine-jar from Tragliatella (ill. 13) depicts two mounted heroes; the first is carrying a shield with a partridge device, the other a duck device. The first has escaped from a maze marked *Truia* (Troy), where the sacred king was due to die like the decoyed partridge in the brushwood maze, to be succeeded by his tanist. A female figure robed like a priestess guides him to safety. These two represent Theseus and Ariadne. Additionally he carries an Easter-egg, the symbol of resurrection. It was at Easter time that Troy Town dances were performed on the turf-cut mazes of Britain. Similar labyrinths existed in Etruria, on Samos, and on Lemnos. According to legend, few heroes ever succeeded in returning alive from this world of the dead; Theseus was one of them. (The others were Herakles, Dionysos, Orpheus – Greeks, the Babylonian Bel and Marduk, Roman (or Trojan) Aeneas, Cuchulain of Irish legend, and the British Arthur, Gwydion and Amathaon.) Theseus's adventure in the Cretan Labyrinth is part of the same myth as his expedition into the Underworld. He entered the Cretan labyrinth of Knossos, where he killed the 'bull-headed monster of the double-axe' – the *labis* from which the word labyrinth is derived. He returns safely thanks to the help given him by the goddess Ariadne. The Greek mythographers combined the story of the hero who defeated Death with the historical sacking of Knossos by raiders from Greece about 1400 B.C., and the defeat of King Minos, the Bull-king.

The spiral (as later the maze) pattern was a symbol of death. This symbol is often found at the entrance to ancient tombs. In front of the entrance to the round barrow of Brugh-na-Boyne (now called 'New Grange') in Ireland, there is a broad slab carved with such spirals (ill. 7), though here they are multiple spirals; the line on reaching the centre doubles back upon itself to bring you out of the maze again, which pattern symbolizes death and rebirth. In passing, it is interesting to note that in 1699, in New Grange, were found two skeletons, stags' antlers, bones, and nothing else. The antlers were probably the king's sacred head-dress, like the horns worn by the Celtic god Cernunnos. Similarly, we may compare the sacred horns of Moses (ill. 49), of Dionysos, and those shown on the coins of Alexander the Great.

Spirals are also to be found at Mycenae in Greece. One can see the development of the spiral pattern into the maze by comparing illustrations 8 and 9. There are other maze patterns cut into rocks in the Val Camonica in northern Italy (ill. 10), at San Jorge de Mogar, near Pontevedra in Galicia, and near Tintagel in Cornwall. The Naquane carving shows, to the upper left of the maze, a bird (a crane?), and on the other side a figure holding a sword. Coins from the third century B.C. have maze patterns on the reverse, and are evidence that the Theseus legend was by then well established, and a Roman graffito dating to the first century A.D., scratched on a wall in Pompeii, demonstrates that the legend had taken root there also; the graffito, additional to the maze pattern, bears the inscription: 'Labyrinthus hic habitat Minotaurus' (In this labyrinth lives the Minotaur). Eighteenth-century sources tell us that the mazes to be found at Pimperne, Burgh and Somerton were nicknamed the 'Walls of Troy', and the patterns sometimes cut by Welsh shepherd boys were described in a book on the antiquities of Wales, in 1815, as the 'City of Troy'.

There may or may not be a connection between those carvings to be found in Ireland and Greece. Irish tradition has it that the Tuatha dé Danaan, a confederacy of tribes, were driven northwards from Greece by peoples invading from Syria. They first settled in Denmark to which they gave their name, 'the Kingdom of the Danaans', and eventually reached Ireland by way of North Britain in 1472 B.C. 200 years later, around the time of the fall of Troy, another invasion took place. This came by people sailing westwards from Thrace, by way of the Mediterranean and Atlantic, arriving in Wexford Bay. They were persuaded to pass on into North Britain, where they became known as the Picts or 'tattooed people'. The Venerable Bede in his Ecclesiastical History writes that the descendants of these people still spoke a non-Celtic language.

Whatever doubts there may be regarding these Irish traditions, it is remarkable how many similarities exist between Irish and Greek mythology, and how one finds such similar patterns cut into the rock in both Ireland, North Britain, Scandinavia, and Greece. Modern dating techniques show that the Irish burial chambers are even older than those in Greece, although the spiral and maze patterns could have been carved on the door posts and lintels at a later date by people taking over existing shrines. Further examples, and recognized today as of even greater antiquity, are those on Malta. Interestingly enough, a Cretan maze pattern has been discovered cut on a rock face near Bosinney in Cornwall. Bosinney is closely associated in legend with King Arthur, another hero who 'harried' Hell. It would appear that a maze dance was brought to Britain sometime during the third millenium B.C., by neolithic agriculturalists from the eastern Mediterranean. Rough stone mazes of similar pattern to the British turf-cut ones have been found in Scandinavia (ill. 11) and Russia. Many cathedrals and churches in south-eastern Europe possess ecclesiastical mazes which were formerly used for penitential purposes.

In England, turf-cut mazes are often referred to as 'Troy Town', in Wales 'Caer-droia'. It is probable that it was the Romans, who so named them after their own Troy Game, which was a dance performed in labyrinthine patterns and in honour of Augustus's ancestor, Aeneas the Trojan. Pliny mentions the same dance being performed by children in the countryside in Italy, and Lucian in his essay 'On the Dance' makes mention of popular dances performed in Crete, which were connected with the story of Ariadne and the labyrinth. As far as we can tell, the Crane Dance of Delos was also adapted to a maze pattern. According to Plutarch the dance which Theseus performed on Delos was a Crane Dance which was danced around a horned altar, and represented the coiling and uncoiling circles of a labyrinth. The crane was both sacred to Athene, as well as being the inspiration for Hermes's invention of letters. Hermes, messenger of the gods, was said to have created the alphabet after watching migrating cranes make different shapes as they flew in formation to their summer breeding grounds; (other versions give Palamedes the credit for inventing the alphabet.) In 1605 Polwart wrote:

The crane must aye
Take nine steps ere shee flie.

This gave rise to one theory that the Crane Dance was imitative of the birds' courtship display (cranes too perform a love dance), and that each phrase consisted of nine steps and a leap. The number nine would prove that the bird was sacred to the Triple Moon Goddess.

The seven youths and seven maidens who were the nine-yearly tribute, probably represented the seven Titans and Titanesses who presided over the sun, moon, and the five known planets. In some maze-dances, the participants held a cord, either to help them gauge the proper distance between each dancer, or maybe to represent the ball of twine carried by Theseus in the labyrinth. At Athens, there existed a rope dance, mentioned by Aristophanes, called the 'Cordax' in which the rope was used for a similar purpose. Ariadne (the name means 'very holy') was the title of the Moon-goddess who was honoured in the dance.

There is a wonderful account of the dance in Homer's Iliad, Book XVIII where he is describing the fashioning of the Shield of Achilles by Hephaestus:

> *Also did the glorious lame god devise a dancing place like unto that which once in wide Knossos Daidalus wrought for Ariadne of the lovely tresses. There were youths dancing and maidens of costly wooing, their hands upon one another's wrists. Fine linen the maidens had on, and the youths well-woven doublets, faintly glistening with oil. Fair wreaths had the maidens, and the youths daggers of gold hanging from silver baldrics. And now would they run round with deft feet exceeding lightly, as when a potter sitting by his wheel that fitteth between his hands maketh trial of it whether it run: and now anon they would run in lines to meet each other. And a great company stood round the lovely dance in joy; (and among them a divine minstrel was making music on his lyre), and through the midst of them, leading the measure, two tumblers whirled.*
> (From the translation by Andrew Lang, Walter Leaf, and Earnest Myers; Globe Library, Macmillan & Co. Ltd. London 1961.)

The original Troy Games are described by Virgil in the Aeneid (written between 30 – 19 B.C.):

> *The riders now moved in gay procession past the whole seated gathering in full view of their kindred. Next, Epytides in a carrying voice shouted a long command to the parade and cracked his whip. They were ready. They first galloped apart in equal detachments, then in half-sections of three broke ranks and deployed their band as in a dance; and then, at another order, they turned about and charged with lances couched. Next they entered upon other figures, with rank facing rank across a space between; and they rode right and left in intertwining circles. And they began a pretence of armed battle, sometimes exposing their backs in flight and sometimes turning their spear-points for attack. Then they made peace again and rode along in an even line. They say that once upon a time the Labyrinth in mountainous Crete contained a path, twining between walls which barred the view, with a treacherous uncertainty in its thousand ways, so that its*

baffling plan, which none might master and none retrace, would foil the trail of any guiding clues. By just such a course the sons of the Trojans knotted their paths, weaving in play their fleeing and their fighting, like dolphins that swim through the salt sea-water, cutting the Carpathian or African straits and playing as they cross the waves. Much later, when he was girding Alba Longa with her walls, Ascanius inaugurated a revival of this Trojan Ride with its mock-battle, and taught the early Latins to celebrate it just as he had celebrated it in his youth with the other Trojan boys. The Albans taught it to their sons. From them, by succession, Rome in her grandeur inherited it and preserved the ancestral rite. And to this day the boys are called 'A Troy' and their regiment 'Trojans'. Here ended the Games held in honour of Aeneas' sainted father.

(From the translation by W.F. Jackson Knight;
Penguin Books, London 1958).

Connected with the British turf cut mazes is the game 'Nine Man's Morris'. Its other names of 'Siege Troy' and 'The Troy Game' suggest that it is of considerable antiquity. It was played on an area which was either cut into the turf, chalked out on the floor, or carved on a wooden surface. Its layout could be described as a simple labyrinth: three concentric squares or oblongs had two lines forming a cross. The two players each had nine counters (which could be stones or sticks), and the object was to try to get three of these counters in a row and positioned on the intersections of the lines, or in the same three corners of the squares. The game was also given the name 'Merrils' after the counters or *morrells* used, which seems to link it with hopscotch, called in French '*Jeu de Merelles*'. Hopscotch too may well have been derived from a maze pattern, and researchers have seen in the progression of the player from one square to another the initiate winding his way through the labyrinth, or the pushing of a stone from square to square as the guiding of the soul towards the exit. In Cornwall they had a spiral form of hopscotch which they called the 'snail creep', which brings to mind the many chain-dances which form a snail figure.

In Germany they had a game of bowls which used nine pins (to be seen in ill. 38 & 39), each of two players having one wooden ball. The game was called 'Kegelschieben' (from *kegeln*, to bowl), and seems to have been closely associated with the Nine Man's Morris. Contests, in which only men could participate, were connected with a dance, the 'Kegelschiebtanz' or 'Kegeltanz', performed after the winner had been chosen *Kegelkönig* (king-bowler). Other related dances, such as 'Kegelquadrille' or 'Königsquadrille', were for four couples in a square, with either a man, a woman, or a couple in the centre. The English 'Ninepins' (four couples plus one man or woman in a square), the Scottish 'Eightsome Reel' (four couples in a square), the Flemish 'Kegelaar' and the German 'Jägerneuner' (both with nine persons – three men and six women in threesomes) are also connected, and may indicate that the Nine Man's Morris, like the Kegelschieben, was both a game and a dance.

We have now seen that myths are not always quite as fanciful as the stories would at first make us believe, and, in fact, often offer a firm historical basis on which to build our dances.

— 3 —

CIRCLES AND CHAINS

Every day, every hour calls forth the dance. During the week as on Sundays one finds in every spot a happy group dancing, most usually in a circle.
Goethe on Alsace.

When one considers the limitations imposed on us of possessing only two legs, it is quite amazing the variety which circle and chain dances have achieved, from the simple steps of the Faeroe islanders to the intricate footwork to be found in the Balkans and, at the other end of Europe, in Brittany.

The circle is magic. It protects whatever is in it from the evil influences without. Sick people or animals can be cured by having prayers or charms recited around them, or a bridal couple ensured of fertility whilst inside this protective ring. Circling a sacred building, tree, fire or other object is common to most religions; Christians walk round the outside of their churches, Islamic pilgrims to Mecca pass seven times round their sacred Black Rock. Today people still dance round their maypoles and bonfires, even though the original sense of the ritual has been lost, and it is now merely done for fun. Every year on August 11th, several towns in Ireland have their Puck Fairs. On this day a goat is decorated and hoisted up onto a platform. Below they dance for three days to the accompaniment of a band. At the end of the celebrations the *Puck* is lifted down and handed back to its owner unharmed. The mountain shepherds of Catalonia also dance round a goat. In France they dance round a cockerel which is later presented to the best couple. Today there is no sacrifice, though undoubtedly these were originally sacrificial rituals.

The winding chain and above all the 'snake' have magical properties also. So too do 'wheel' figures: the Balkan 'kolo' means wheel, as do the Spanish 'ruela' and the Austrian 'Rädl'.

Man's earliest myths spoke of the creation of the world as a vast cosmic dance. His earliest dances, those which took place at the time of the summer and winter solstices, around a tree or fire, or at harvest time, were all circle dances, in harmony with, and reflecting, the powerful forces of nature about him. He danced for a purpose, and not merely as recreation. In the tale 'The Farmers of Kolbeck' by the Brothers Grimm, we learn that: "On Christmas night, in the year 1012, Farmer Albrecht, with fifteen other farmers and three of their wives, danced in a ring in the churchyard to noisy song, while the priest said Mass." Karl Spiess in his 'German Folk Song' relates how: "Twelve youths with their leader, Cervelus, wanted to dance a round. They had Merswind and Wibekin who were twin sisters with them, but they needed a third girl. So they sent for Awa, the daughter of the priest, who at that very moment was in church while her father was celebrating the Mass. As soon as she joined them, they began their round. Holding hands they danced in a circle to loud singing and stamping out the rhythm with their feet." The interest in these two quotations is the requirement to have a third female in the group. The number three was obviously significant and important, and the three females must have had a certain rôle to play in the dance. We may presume that we have here a sung and danced ballad with a definite theme and dialogue. While the rest danced round in a circle, those who were acting, or perhaps miming, the words of the ballad, stood in the middle. The text of one of these ballads dates from the year 1200.

An even earlier example, that of Notker of St. Gall, dating from the year 1000, is the oldest in which the words and music are inseparable. In this the rhythm of the words dictates the rhythm of the steps and movements of the dancers. We learn that they hopped, stopped, and turned, and performed generally according to the structure of the song. It seems that it was the usual form of round to sing and dance in a circle, while some of them acted out in pantomime the story-line of the ballad, standing in the centre of the circle. That these song-dances go back into more ancient times is suggested by the rhythmic structure of the verses, which Albert Czerwinski relates to the ancient Indo-Germanic hymns.

In Germany, the circle dances were accompanied by singing until, in the seventeenth century, instrumental music began to replace song. A text from 1653 mentions bagpipe, hurdy-gurdy, shawm, fiddle, jew's harp and rummelpot. They also used lyre, drums, tambourines, cymbals and pipes.

Another early description (1150) of the circle dance comes from Jring von St. Blasien, who saw the dance on one of the islands off the north coast of Germany during a church fair. He wrote:

> *The leader of the round went into the centre and moved about, stamping his feet and shouting, and threw a stick on which he had hung a glove into the air and caught it again. The rôles of the lead singer and dancer were very*

17. Ring Dance from 'History of the Northern Peoples' by Olaus Magnus. Swedish, 1555.

important. The lead dancer was invariably the strongest youth and often quite bruising fights broke out amongst the young men as to who should have the honour of carrying the wand of office and lead the dance.

The Minnisinger, Göli, mentions the round dance as being performed in courtly circles. In the thirteenth century, there is a reference to the 'Treialtrei' being one of twelve French dances in which various figures are performed, amongst them, a couple dancing round on the spot, threading the circle through an arch, moving in a figure of eight, and making a bridge or doorway. This would rather imply that the circle broke to make a chain and was then reformed. Similar dances are still to be found in somewhat degenerate form as children's dance-games. In these, one child will perform actions in the centre while the rest dance round, then form an arch, move into a chain, and maybe form a double circle.

In the Aargau, they had a circle and chain dance which was performed in springtime. They made dandelion chains, and carried these around in their own chain-circle dance. A second outer circle danced round the inner circle and then they moved into the centre to form a new circle. The dancers now in the outer circle formed arches with their raised arms to allow the dancers in the inner circle to resume their original places and start all over again. This seems to be a truly ancient dance. Of a similar antiquity are those dances which have only one dance motif. In the 'serpent' dance from the Pinzau in Salzburg, the dancers commence in a circle. The leader forms with the person on his right an arch, through which the dancer on his left leads the others. The end dancers then turn under so that the whole circle is back to the centre. The leader and his partner then make a further turn and the circle is reformed to face the centre.

Up to the year 1203, the accompanying songs were simple short refrains:

Sprach der Bertschi mit begir,	*Said the bridegroom with desire,*
so schullen wir ains singen,	*we should sing together,*
zu ring um alle springen.	*and dance round in a circle.*
Der red warent sie vil fro,	*Everyone was full of joy,*
des huob der Bertschi an also.	*and the groom began once more.*

We can picture the dancers singing a snatch of verse while dancing in a circle, or forming a chain to lead through an arch, to form a further circle. As the Minnisingers in Germany and the Troubadours and Trouvères in France developed the song-ballad, so the dance itself developed. For example, compare the extract quoted with this more developed dance rhyme from the fourteenth century:

*Das schaffet alls die minn, die minn,**
das wir leben ane sinn.
Das schaffet alls der wein, der wein,

* die minn = courtly love, hence Minnesinger

das wir müssen fröhlich sein.
Das schaffet alls das gold, das gold,
das niemand ist dem andern hold.
Das schaffet alls das pfant, das pfant,
das man borget so ze hant.
Das schaffet alls das spil, das spil,
das ich nit mag behalten vil.

"It is all through love that we live in sin. It is because of wine that we have to be merry. It is because of gold that each does not trust the other. It is through borrowing that each person gets what he needs. It is all owing to play that I cannot keep anything."

Neidharts von Reuenthal, who died in 1240, left us the earliest example of the more developed ballad. This relates the dualism of the joys of summer and luck in love on the one hand, and the sorrows of winter and unluckiness in love on the other. A story line develops, and this is reflected in the interplay between the couples in the circle or chain. We begin to get the earliest examples of those dances which are still favourites today, with their teasing gestures coming into play: scolding, kissing and so on.

Neidharts also mentions dancing indoors in winter, when they danced round a table instead of a tree, as they would have done outside, and Eckhart, in his 'Monumenta Jutreboc', writes about a dance round an old wheel, symbol of the sun, which the peasants performed in nearly all the regions of northern Germany, at weddings. They would set fire to the wheel and dance around it. That they also danced at weddings around barrels is shown in the prohibition by the city council of Magdeburg, in the year 1544, as smacking too much of paganism. The ban cannot have proved very effective, for as late as 1911, we hear of a dance around a barrel, on which a burning torch had been placed, being performed on the Lüneburg Heath, very close to Magdeburg. We also have a reference from 1224 by Cäsarius von Heisterbach, of a dance round a maypole in Aachen. Another reference from the thirteenth century mentions a violet festival in Vienna, where they danced around the first violet of spring. The violet was fixed to a pole which was set in the ground, and the people danced around it.

The famous Minnesinger, Hans Sachs, has left us a song, 'The May, the May, which brings us so many flowers', in his 'Fastnachtspiel' (Carnival play), 'Der Neydhart mit dem Feyel' (The Jealous Lover and the Violet), from the year 1562, which also describes a 'lead' singer and 'after' singer. We may suppose that the others danced in a circle around the lead singer standing in the centre. The Strasbourg Chronicle from 1349, talks of the company standing in a circle around the best singer who was thus the lead singer, and they began to sing as they danced. At this period they had various dances, generally called 'Springtänze' (springing, not spring, dances). The words of one surviving song from the fifteenth century say: "I am springing in this ring." These dances were also popular amongst the craftsmen.

Other ancient dances were the 'Sünnros', which contained a weaving figure, 'Halbmond' (half Moon), and 'Snidertanz' (Tailors' dance). The windmill provided another dance figure with its star formation, and which appeared in circle, sword

18. Carole from the 'Remède de Fortune' by Guillaume de Marchaut. French, 14th century. © Photo R.M.N.

and hoop dances alike in a variety of forms. So also with the Half Moon and Tailors' dances, which could be danced in a line formation, one dancer following another without holding hands. Obviously in the weaving pattern hands would have to be loosed. A dance might develop from a circle into further patterns and figures, to conclude back in a circle. One can imagine the lead singer-dancer leading his line through an arch formed by the raised arms of two of the dancers, making mill-wheel figures, weaving, turning stars for several people, or a couple turning with one or two hands round. Some of these figures were to be found in the sword and hoop dances. Springing from these broad categories of dances: swords, hoops, rounds, developed all the vast variety of individual dances, some of which have been preserved almost unchanged to the present day.

Evidence of chain dances dating back to the New Stone Age exists in the rock paintings from Norway, and from the Bronze Age in those from Lökerberget in Bohuslän in Sweden, one of which shows six or seven men dancing in a chain. Further examples come from La Cayera, Pena de Mogos, near Pondevedra in northwestern Spain, one of which shows a similar line of eight dancing men, and above them is the pattern of a spiral, suggesting that this is the figure that they are making in their ritual dance. Later evidence comes from the statuettes and vases from Cyprus and Olympia, dating to the second millenium B.C., which show similar chains of dancers. They sang as they danced, and we know from surviving fragments of songs, that the shepherds of ancient Greek Parnassus danced a six-step figure, exactly as it is still danced today in the Faeroe Islands. This figure, known throughout Europe, is one of the earliest branles.

The chronicler Neocorus, about the year 1590 described a 'Long dance' in these words:

> *The lead singer who has also one to help him, has a drinking glass in one hand and begins to sing. When he has sung one verse, he stops and all the rest repeat the first verse of the song. When they have repeated one verse, the lead singer resumes and sings another verse, to be repeated by the rest. When they have sung thus one or two verses, one of them comes in front of the others and dances the first time and then asks the others to join in the dance. Then everyone joins hands in a row, and one dancer can thus lead up to two hundred dancers.*

The example most commonly quoted of a branle which has survived the passage of time in all its primitive simplicity is that of the Faeroe Islands. Here, tightly linked, following the lead dancer who sings the ballads to which their dances are performed, they dance for hours on end, endlessly repeating the same basic step of: step to the left and close, step to the left and close, step to the right and close. This six-beat step cuts across the four-beat music but catches itself up every three bars. The effect that the dance has on the participants is almost hypnotic – it is as if an electric charge is going through the linked hands from one end to the other, and the dancer who does not enter into the spirit of the dance, like the sceptic in a séance session, can ruin the whole thing, and break the current.

The Swedish version, the 'Trimmekendans' is another of the type of sung ballad dance to be found widespread over northern Europe. Both men and women joined in these dances which had fairly basic steps; for example, some may have moved as this one, described in the sixteenth century: "Take three steps forwards and three steps to the side, pause with a balancing movement of the body, and then move three steps backwards." In Sweden the long dance was especially associated with the May festival and with the wintertime dance around the fir tree. In Denmark it played a special rôle at weddings. In the southern Netherlands it was a spring dance, and is preserved in the 'Carillon van Duijnkerke', and in the village of Eijsden the celebrations, a fortnight before Whitsuntide, culminate in the 'Cramignon' which winds its way in and out the houses and inns of the village. Similarly in Austria in the 'Schwabentanz', in the 'Rückelreih' of Mecklenburg, and the 'Reigen' of Allgäu, each preserves something of its own character. So also do the chain dances of Sardinia (Ballo Tondo), and of Bulgaria, Yugoslavia, Romania and Greece, each have their own ethos. The same may be said of the chains of Provence, Normandy, and Brittany.

One does not need to travel half way to the North Pole to find chain dances which have been preserved in ancient form, untarnished by the accretion of centuries. Lying just across the English Channel, Brittany possesses a wealth of chain dances unrivalled and unsurpassed anywhere else in Europe. What these dances lack in the explosive excitement engendered by many of the Balkan chains, Brittany's Gavottes and Ridées make up for in intricacy of steps and precision of performance. Using the eight beats of a typical branle, the Breton dancer, by accenting any one or two of a variety of beats and half-beats, forms a dance which takes immense concentration and observation before it can be copied. The repertoire spans the whole gamut from the most simple to the most complicated, and, unlike similar dances in Provence, has been spared the attentions of the dancing masters.

Having mentioned the name *Ridée*, it may be an opportune moment to comment on the 'Laridé de Pontivy' which has acquired a degree of fame. The delightful story which somehow has attached itself to this dance has, unfortunately, no foundation in fact, and has only served to confuse the meaning and derivation of the word *ridée*.

The story relates how the maidens of Pontivy, a town in the centre of Brittany, were wont to dance around a statue of Venus, said to have been put there by the Romans, in the hope that this would protect them from becoming wrinkled. True, such a statue does exist, but near a village called Baud at some distance from Pontivy. Its origins to say the least are uncertain. Various suggestions have been that it was a Roman idol, or even an Egyptian one. Certainly it became the object of pagan worship, and for that reason was repeatedly thrown into the local river by order of the Church, and each time fished out by the people. The statue was heavily restored in the eighteenth century, and now bears little resemblance to Venus, goddess of beauty, whom it is supposed to represent. *Ride* in French means 'wrinkle'; *rider* means 'to wrinkle', and the past participle in its feminine form, *ridée* means 'wrinkled'. However, all this has nothing to do with the dance in question. In fact, although some dances are referred to as *ridée*, that of Pontivy is never called *ridée* but always *laridé* or *laridenn*. Often, in Brittany, one refers to dancing *à laridé*, and as the dance was

19. 'La Danse devant Amour'. Branle. French, 15th century. © Photo R.M.N.

usually, and until recently always, accompanied by singing, the *laridé* here merely refers to the style or wording of the song and literally means dancing to *tra-la-la*. Many songs contained lines which, if they ever had any meaning, have none now. English equivalents might be: *with a hey nonny no*, or *fol-de-rol-day*. In the Breton language one finds such couplets as:

A laridondènig é a laridondéno
A larilarilala a larilalèno.

There was a special spring dance which the farmers performed at the beginning of spring, progressing through the village and round their fields and woods in a long chain. This kind of dance was adopted to be used in the service of the Church. Thus in Bornhofen in Franconia, Germany, at 'Fastnacht', a procession, which led into forty hours of prayer, adopted a step similar to that used in the Echternach spring-procession, moving forwards, sideways and backwards: they might take five steps forwards, two or three steps backwards; or alternatively, one to the left, one to the right, and one forwards. Sometimes the chain would divide into small links of as few as three dancers to allow them to progress the more easily down the narrow streets of their medieval towns and villages.

The 'Ballo Sardo' or 'Ballo Tondo' is an ancient Sardinian round dance, the dancers encircling the musicians who often sit to play, as the dance sometimes goes on for hours. On the patronal feast of St. Elfisio at Cagliari in early May, the crowd dances in solemn fashion around the principal piazza. There is no bounce or spring about the 'Ballo Sardo'. It is danced close to the ground, though, when the music becomes more lively, the men will kick their feet higher and indulge in some fancy footwork. The women, however, continue to glide along in a most dignified manner. The dance is mentioned by Homer, who states that Ulysses marvelled at the agility of the island's dancers.

The people of Alsace seem to have had a particular passion for the dance. Fischart in his 'Gargantua' (1576) wrote: "Terrible calamities such as the plague, the devastatations of great conflicts, only increased the passion for dancing. There were Danses Macabres, dancing in the graveyards, epidemics of the Danse de Saint-Guy (St. Vitus' Dance)." Jacques de la Grange in 1698 wrote: "One used to see in the province nothing but violins and dancing." The Prince-abbott Martin Gerbert at about the same time observed: "There is scarcely another country where there is so much singing, dancing and music-making as there is in Alsace." Fifty years later, Goethe was writing: "At Strasbourg, every day, every hour calls forth the dance. During the week as on Sundays one finds in every spot a happy group dancing, most usually in a circle." We know the names of several Alsatian medieval dances, thanks to the very preachers who, in the sixteenth century, condemned the impious practice of dancing, and named names: 'Der schwarze Knabe' (the Black Boy), 'Der blau-Storke' (the Blue Stork), 'Der Scharrer' (the Stamper). It is perhaps a good thing that the 'Pissepot' has been consigned to oblivion. In a few cases we still have the airs which accompanied them.

Switzerland has its 'Paarreigen', round dances performed in couples. The *coraules* of Gruyère still preserve their medieval character as well as their tunes. The dances

'Moléson' and 'Mariâdzo' are two examples. These start with the dancers going round with hands joined before breaking up into individual couples. Songs are usually sung for the round dance, though in the case of 'Moléson', only the words "À Moléson, à Moléson" have been retained. Moléson is the name of a mountain, hence *à Moléson* means 'to the mountain'. Another tradition still alive in the Gruyère region is the long open chain or farandole. Phelipe de Remi, in 1270, described one such chain thus:

Tel carole ne fu pas veue:
Près d'une quart dure d'une lieue.

"Such a carole had ne'er been seen: More than a quarter-league long (over one mile)."

Church edicts of the eighth, ninth, and tenth centuries, sought to ban those dances which became too boisterous, and smacked of pagan origins. In the 'Lex Caroli et Ludovici' we read: "Those singing and jumping dances with their shameful and voluptuous songs and devil's plays are, whether performed in a public place, in

20. 'Der Fackeltanz' (Torch dance) by Albrecht Dürer. German, c.1516.

houses, or in any other place, forbidden, for they are left over from the customs of the pagans." In this, of course, they were quite right.

As with the sword and hoop dances, some of the oldest guilds adopted the long dance as their own special dance. An illustration (cover and ill. 41), from the year 1561, shows the Butchers in a Fastnacht procession, the first and last dancers carrying the insignia of their craft.

The development of the chain into two or three people dancing in procession took place in early medieval times, at the very moment when the court dance split from the folk dance and went its own way. Already in 1210, Wolfram von Eschenbach in his Parzival, talked of the new dances coming into the Thüringian court, and Neidhart von Reuenthal, at about the same time, bemoaned the fact thus: "They shouldn't do those funny dances which belong in the servants' quarters." Minnesingers generally were agreed that formerly the dancers had performed with grace and style, and that the peasants' dances with their waving arms and stamping feet were suited to little else than jumping up and down on the grapes to crush them, and that they looked more like cows trying to flick away the flies with their tails. Obviously, the court soon refined these dances and left the peasants to do their dances in their own way.

The Provençal 'Farandole' is something of an enigma. No one knows where the name came from or what it signifies. The earliest reference to it dates only from 1775. Various theories have been postulated, none of them with any great conviction. It has been linked with the Trojan myth and with the dance performed by Theseus and his companions after they had escaped from the Cretan labyrinth. Today, the name *farandole* can be used for almost any chain dance. However, in Provence, this popular dance has been taken up by dance groups which have elaborated upon the steps and honed them to perfection in the classroom, to be used in competitions. Farandole-schools practise little else but trying to outdo rival neighbouring groups in the intricacy and complexity of steps, and in the co-ordination of the dancers. Today, farandole has little to do with folk dance. It is the product of the dancing masters of the army and the marine who, when they were not instructing their soldiers and sailors, could earn extra money by teaching the towns' people and villagers of Provence. It was also brought back by the returning soldiers and sailors. And so the steps of the classical ballet came to be fastened on to the basic dance, until a farandole came to be an extended *enchaînement* of intricate steps: *pas de bourée*, *sisonnes*, *jetés battus*, *échappés*, *entrechats*, *pas piqués*, *pas de ciseaux*, and many more. Most towns and villages of Provence have their *Farandoleurs*. One finds them practising their steps in the classroom, progressing, as in a classical ballet class, from the *barre* to the centre, ever learning new *enchaînements* to be used in the next competition.

Generally, the farandole moves to the left, starting with the left foot. Perversely, it was the famous dancing-master J.B. Duffaut himself who proved the exception to the rule, by insisting that it should travel to the right. But the original peasant farandole undoubtedly moved in a clockwise direction. Sometimes handkerchiefs or cords are used to link the dancers, less in imitation of Ariadne's thread, as to help the dancers to keep a firm grip on each other, when sweating palms would make this less easy to maintain.

If the farandole came from Greece, then it changed its direction in its new country, for in Greece all circles and chains go in a counter-clockwise direction. In Greece there are three basic forms of the chain and three ways of holding. The holds and chains are interchangeable. Most commonly seen is the open circle, holding hands, with elbows bent, so that the left arm of one dancer and the right arm of the next person make the letter 'W'. Then there is the straight line, usually of about five dancers who hold shoulders. Thirdly there is the curved line with the dancers linked with a basket hold, the left arm lying over the right arm of the next dancer. The dance space available usually dictates which form will be used.

During the warm (often too hot) months from May to October, Greece becomes a tourist playground. The sky is blue and the sea is warm, and this is also the time to see folk dancing. Nearly every village has its *panigyri* (feast), and with a well-prepared itinerary one can see as much dancing as ever one could wish. At sometime, somewhere, someone will be dancing. The feast of the local patron saint is eagerly anticipated and is attended by all the villagers and, if possible, by those who have left to settle elsewhere, and buses bring groups from neighbouring villages to join in the fun. They attend Mass in the morning, many having to join in the service outside, because there is not room enough for everyone inside the church. Then, in the afternoon, lambs are roasted on spits, and the people dance, in the church forecourt, village square, or threshing floor, until the early hours of the morning. Or they may celebrate the patronal feast at a nearby monastery, in which case, off they all go with their mules and donkeys loaded up with bedding (for they will stay the night, often sleeping out in the open), food, and goods for sale, and, when they get to their destination, they will sit down to a communal meal, and afterwards sing and dance and talk.The musicians are paid for playing, and often itinerant Gypsies turn up in the hope of earning a few drachmas.

The first dance in the village *panigyri* is for the villagers only. Each person has his set place in the dance, and there is a strict order of precedence which must be observed. Usually, a self-appointed master of ceremonies will ensure that everything is done correctly. Most often, the men come first in the circle in their allotted places according to age or seniority (which usually means the same thing), and then the women, similarly ordered, or sometimes the married taking precedence over the unmarried. In many of the islands, when the circle is formed of groups of kindred, the husband leads, and following on in succession come his wife, their eldest son and his wife, the second son and his wife, and so on. Often the priest himself is invited to lead the first dance.

In former times it was not permissible for men and women to hold hands in the dance (not even if they were married). This was resolved by linking with a handkerchief, or by putting a child or an elderly person in between. The *panigyri* used to be the occasion when the matchmakers would be busy, and the dance provided the only opportunity for the young people to exchange glances. There was no question of a boy inviting a girl to dance. Knives have been drawn for less. Today this oppressive protocol is much more relaxed, though still not as free as in the West, and, as the evening progresses, the boys will show off to the girls in their dances, and the linked chain dances will give way to couple dances.

The 'syrto' and the 'pedekhto' are the two basic categories of Greek dance. In the *syrto* the feet are moved in a dragging or shuffling motion, where as the *pedekhto* has hops, leaps, jumps and springs. Some dances are a combination of the two. The terrain of the land also conditions the way in which the steps are performed. Thus in the mountainous regions we find mainly slow *pedekhto* and a few slow *syrtos*; in the plains, the feet of both categories of dance pound the ground, whilst on the islands and coastal regions, the *syrtos* are more lilting and the *pedekhtos* have lighter and more intricate footwork.

The 'Kalamatiano', as its name implies, originated in Kalamata, and is one of the most popular dances in Greece. It is a modified *syrto*, in which not only the leader performs leaps, turns and embellishments, but the line of dancers are given hops and skips to dance as well. The dance is performed to a 7/8 time signature, the bar being divided thus: $\bar{1}23/\bar{4}5/\bar{6}7$, the steps being long, short, short. It is a lively, carefree dance performed in an open circle. From Byzantine times, Kalamata has been a silk manufacturing region, and the silk handkerchiefs produced were highly prized. It was customary for young men to present their sweethearts with these as a symbol of love. In days gone by it was not the done thing for a boy and a girl to be seen holding hands (it was tantamount to a declaration of intent to marry), and even in the dance it was required that the boy should offer his handkerchief for the girl to hold. The handkerchief still plays a prominent rôle in Greek dance.

The Albanians divide their folk dance into three categories: the lyric, the epic, and a combination of the two. (Lyric dances are the more numerous.) The style of the lyric dance is simple, usually very slow and smooth, with a subtlety of movement and elegance which creates a mood of warmth and calm. It is poetic and full of delicacy. Lyric dances divide into: work, ritual, wedding, erotic, humorous and mimic. The epic dance, as the name implies, echoes the great events of Albanian history and the long struggle against foreign oppression. These dances show the strength, bravery, and fighting qualities of these mountain people. Epic dances divide into those which display a fighting element and those which show aspects of their daring. Naturally, these dances are stronger, more rhythmic, and faster than the lyric dances. It is not

21. Kolo by Caroly Pop de Szatmmary. Serbian, 1868.

unusual for the two styles to be blended. All Albanian circles and chains move counter-clockwise.

Head, body, and hand movements play an important part in Albanian folk dance. Both men and women hold themselves very elegantly, one might say nobly. The women hold their heads still, and lower their gaze, while the head movements of the men, particularly in the epic dances, are in character with the dance.

There are various hand-holds. One is with the arms held straight diagonally down forming a 'V' with the next dancer. It is used by men, but more so by women, and usually in a closed-circle formation. A second way is with the arms bent and hands held at shoulder level, thus forming a 'W' shape with the next dancer. This is the hold most usually employed by women, and mixed men and women, but less so by the men on their own, and is found more in open than closed circles. Another way is with arms bent and hands clasped a little above head height, and is used mainly in the north of the country, by men more than by women. These hand-holds are varied by linking with index fingers or handkerchiefs instead of the whole hand. In northern Albania, the men also use the shoulder-link hold whilst, in the south, they often link closer by taking the arm round the back of the neck of the next dancer. Sometimes the men in the centre of the line adopt this hold whilst the outer dancers link with the 'W' hold. Yet another way is to cross the arms behind the next dancer. This hold is found in dances from the region of Skoder, in mixed dances, and in women's dances from Mokra in Pogradeci.

The use of the handkerchief often lends an additional touch of elegance and refinement to a performance by the lead dancer in the chain, but above all by the solo performer. It is said in Albania that the more accomplished the dancer, the more he will use the handkerchief in his dance. The handkerchief-hold also enables the lead dancer to perform movements such as turns, acrobatic leaps, back bends and twists, which would be inhibited by a hand-hold, and is a particular feature of the men's dances of Çamërie. In both men's and women's solo dances the handkerchief almost takes on the character of a partner, being flicked in the air, to the side or down, the women sometimes furling and unfurling it as they hold it by the diagonal corners.

There are three basic formations in Albanian dance: closed circles, semi-circles, and dances in two parallel lines. The closed circles were used to dance around some sacred ritual object. In the semi-circle the end dancers often curl the line in and then move out again. In wedding dances of southern Albania it is the bride who leads the chain with quiet dignity. There could hardly be a greater stylistic difference between her gentle demeanour and the dynamic, grand performance of the leading male dancer in the Çamërie dances, bending right back until his head touches the ground, whilst the other dancers pass over him, or even dance on his body. The dances in two parallel lines may be either one line facing the other, or one behind the other, in semi-circular or straight lines, or on a semi-circular line divided in half, or the two leading dancers breaking away to perform their 'solo' whilst the line continues its steps behind them.

Albanian dances can be further divided into those which have one part and those which have two. In the first, the dances remain the same from beginning to end. These are for the most part the lyric slow dances, such as 'She walks like a bee'. Or the dance may begin slowly and expressively and become more lively: 'Kercim burrash katundarçe', 'Vallja në sini', 'Nusja e fajës'. The other dance form starts off in the same slow and tranquil manner, speeds up, and then develops choreographically with all its repertoire of leaps, turns, and bends.

Sources for Russian dance go back to the eleventh-century chronicles. The development of Russian folk dance followed three main lines: the 'Khorovod' (choral dance), the 'Plyaska' of improvised nature, and dances with defined and established figures. The choral dances, 'Khorovody', are extremely varied. Their main feature is the combination of the movement of a huge mass of participants with songs, often with the acting out of the content of the songs. These may reflect various aspects of the work of the peasants such as ploughing, tilling, sowing millet, scutching the flax or other field labours. Some use the theme of choosing a husband or bride, or relations between boy and girl, their quarrels and reconciliations, or the separation of sweethearts. Others may ridicule idlers who shirk work, dressy wives, drunken husbands, or lily-handed young ladies incapable of work.

Normally the *khorovod* is performed in a circle in which the dancers hold hands, or the ends of handkerchiefs, but sometimes their arms hang free. The main performers, playing the persons in the songs, usually go into the centre of the circle, where they sing the words and act out the part of the person they are playing. The others move round in the circle, usually clockwise, and sing the narrative part of the song. Thus, for example, in a *khorovod* performed to a song about sowing flax, three or four girls go into the middle: one plays the rôle of the mother who shows how flax must be sown, weeded, pulled and soaked; the others represent the daughters who imitate the movements of their mother. Another widely known way of performing these choral dances is for the leader to begin the couplet, the others singing the words

22. Kolo by Carl Goebel. Serbian, 1881.

of the characters and illustrating the words of the song with movements. Not all choral dances are performed in a circle. Sometimes the song may be in the form of a dialogue, consisting of questions and answers, and for these the dancers stand in a longways set. Each line performs a couplet in turn moving forwards to do so, and moving back to their original positions when they have finished. Besides the choral dances which contain elements of pantomime, there are those accompanied by singing but without actions. From the simple circle they might develop into more complex figures with snakes, figures-of-eight, crossing and interweaving. Sometimes the dancers begin in couples in a slow stately procession in a circle before breaking off into pairs, dancing around the moving column, before finally rejoining the circle.

The old Russian choral dances performed on important feast days would include the whole population. In some places they had special 'gathering' songs, when the girls would go through the village inviting everyone to the *khorovod* which started the festivities. At the close there were special 'dispersal' songs to bid farewell. Choral dances have been preserved all over the Soviet Union, each region having its own particular character. In the north, in the region of Archangel, they have an inherent staidness, even stiffness of movement. The girl glides 'like a peahen', and may only look at the boy at the end of the dance. There are few mime actions here. In the regions of Moscow, Kalinin, Ryazan and Voronezh, the choral dances are much livelier and display a greater freedom and variety of movement. A 'Plyaska' may be performed in the middle of the ring, those moving in the circle jumping and turning to their neighbours as if in conversation. In the south-western regions, Kursk, Bryansk, Orel, there are the so-called ' Karakhody' which are clearly a sort of mass *plyaska*. The accompaniment for a *karakhod* is not singing but instrumental, the musicians standing in the middle of the circle. The dancers don't hold hands in the circle, but stand in twos or threes and move clockwise. In the couple, the girl usually moves backwards in the circle, whilst the boy shows off his skill and agility facing her. If a boy is dancing with two girls, then the girls dance facing each other or circling one another. From time to time, one of the dancers may sing or shout a *chastushka*, a short refrain.

The *khorovody* are usually only danced to song accompaniment. The patterns of the dances vary. They may move in a circle (always clockwise); in *stena na stenu* or wall-to-wall, that is in a longways set; *ulitsa* (street) in which the dancers move in pairs along the 'street' and cast off to right and left to return to their original places, or in a chain snaking its way through a 'gate' or 'hurdle' and so on. Sometimes the movements of the chain had a representational character, reproducing the plaiting and unplaiting of wattle ('Zapletisya pleten'), hop picking ('Kakza rechen'koi yar-khmel'), pricking out cabbages ('Veisya , veisya, kapustka'). In olden times amongst the eastern Slavs, *khorovod* songs formed part of the song-cycle of the agricultural calendar, being a variety of spring song. In many Ukrainian and Byelorussian localities, *khorovod* games (so-called *tanki* and *haivki*) have preserved their link with the spring season up to the present day. Stately measured movements in 5/4, 6/4, 7/4 predominate in the melodies of the slow *khorovod* songs.

The most typical Bulgarian chain dance is the 'Vodeno Horo' or 'led' horo. In this, the first and last dancers, waving a handkerchief or carrying an insignia of office, wind the chain into a spiral at both ends and out again, usually at breathtaking

23. 'Slåtteröl på Svartsjö' by Pehr Hilleström. Swedish, 1785.

tempo. *Horos* are met with under numerous names, some showing a foreign origin, such as Serbian, Wallachian, or Greek *horos*; others take the names of animals: sheep, hare or geese. One is called 'Lentils', another, 'Paidushka', is also called the 'Cripple' because of its limping step. The 'Rachenitsa' is a lively dance which gives the dancers freedom to improvise. Often a competitive element is introduced into the dance, each dancer attempting to outdance the next. It is a favourite at weddings and is danced by both sexes. There are other *horos* just for men or just for women. Often traders adopted a *horo* as their own, so that now we get Masons', Potters', Butchers' and Shepherds' *horos*. Sometimes these reflect work actions.

4

SWORDS, HOOPS, GARLANDS AND STICKS

In the beginning, they say, Rhea, charmed with the art, ordered dances to be performed not only in Phrygia by the Corybantes but in Crete by the Curetes, from whose skill she derived uncommon benefit, since they saved Zeus for her by dancing about him; Zeus, therefore, might well admit that he owes them a thank-offering, since it was through their dancing that he escaped his father's teeth. They danced under arms, clashing their swords upon their shields as they did so and leaping in a frantic warlike manner. Thereafter, all the doughtiest of the Cretans practised it energetically and became excellent dancers.

Lucian: On the Dance (2nd Century A.D.)

Greek mythology and literature abound in references to the dance which held an important place in the lives, education and especially religion of the people, and we should look to Greek legends to find the origins of at least one form of sword dance. In the early days of this world, we read, before Man inhabited the earth, Rhea, the Earth goddess, wife of Cronos, taught the art of the dance to the Curetes, sons of the Earth, who lived on the island of Crete. Now Cronos had the nasty habit of devouring his children, so Rhea, in order to save her youngest son, Zeus, hid him in a cave on Crete, and substituted a stone wrapped in swaddling clothes for the infant. Cronos swallowed the stone and, believing it to be his son, was satisfied. Zeus was placed in the care of the Curetes who, to drown the cries of the baby so that Cronos would not discover the deception, danced around him, shouting and leaping, and clattering their swords against their shields. They were successful, and, thereafter, when Zeus had overthrown and replaced his father, the Curetes became his priests, and continued their dances as cult rituals.

So we see that the clashing of swords on shields does not necessarily make this a *war* dance. Leaping, shouting and stamping, clanging of bells and clashing swords, in short, anything to make a noise, had a twofold purpose: by sympathetic magic to quicken the growth of nature, inducing fertility by strenuous activity and encouraging crops to grow tall by high leaping; and secondly to frighten away evil spirits with the deafening noise. Metal objects like swords and shields would make the most noise when clashed together, and it is as well to bear this in mind in any discussion on sword dancing, thought by many originally to have been *pyrrhic* or *war* dancing.

The meaning of the word *pyrrhic* may also have come from a misinterpretation of the Greek word. There are references in Greek literature to a Cretan funeral dance, the *prylis*, which was performed by men wearing armour, dancing or processing

24. Sword dance from Anglo-Saxon manuscript.

around the corpse, burial mound or funeral pyre. The Mycenaean Greeks had a similar dance, and Pyrrhus, son of Achilles, was credited with its invention. But the true etymology of the word *pyrrhic* may come from the Greek word *pyr* meaning a fire. We will see later that in many European countries, people leap through the smoke of bonfires, or drive their animals between fires, to purify them and protect them from evil spirits. The *pyrrhic* dance later turned into a combat dance and was performed at the funerals of warriors. Still later it came to form part of the training of boys in Sparta, and persisted there until well into the Christian era. In Athens, boys were trained in the dance to prepare them for military service. Plato described the Spartan version as containing postures and movements for attacking an enemy with bow and arrow, javelin, blows of various kinds, and of "bending aside, ducking, leaping, crouching to elude blows and missiles". Athenian youth seems, however, to have been taught a more graceful form of dance. In time, the *pyrrhic* dance took on Dionysiac characteristics, and dancers are portrayed carrying *thyrsi*, wands tipped with ivy or pine cones, and torches instead of spears. But however the Athenians and Spartans applied the *pyrrhic* dance to their own ends, the original dance was for ritual purposes and not as a method of training warriors.

Lucian, the second-century historian, wrote his 'On the Dance' in the form of a dialogue between Lycinus and Crato. Crato had condemned the Dance, accusing the men of being effeminate (nothing changes). Lycinus, in defending the art, brings the gods' and goddesses' love of dance to his defence:

> *In the beginning, they say, Rhea, charmed with the art, ordered dances to be performed not only in Phrygia by the Corybantes but in Crete by the*

Curetes, from whose skill she derived uncommon benefit, since they saved Zeus for her by dancing about him; Zeus, therefore, might well admit that he owes them a thank-offering, since it was through their dancing that he escaped his father's teeth. They danced under arms, clashing their swords upon their shields as they did so and leaping in a frantic warlike manner. Thereafter, all the doughtiest of the Cretans practised it energetically and became excellent dancers.

Neopolemus (also called Pyrrhus, son of Achilles) is credited with the invention of the *pyrrhic* dance which he originated when he danced for joy over killing Eurypylus. Lucian also credits his skill in the dance as being responsible for the fall of Troy. He tells us also that:

The Spartans, who are considered the bravest of the Greeks, learned to do the Caryatic, *another variety of dance exhibited at Caryae in Lacedaemon. Even now you may see their young men studying dancing quite as much as fighting under arms. When they have stopped sparring and exchanging blow for blow with each other, their contest ends in dancing, and a flute player sits in the middle, playing them a tune and marking time with his foot, while they, following one another in line, perform figures of all sorts in rhythmic step, now those of war and presently those of the choral dance, that are dear to Dionysos and Aphrodite.*

Lucian describes another dance, the String of Beads, so called because girls and boys alternate:

The boy precedes, doing the steps and postures of young manhood, and those which later he will use in war, while the maiden follows, showing how to do the women's dance with propriety; hence the string is beaded with modesty and with manliness.

He refers to other dances, and goes on to point out that:

Not a single ancient mystery cult can be found that is without dancing, since they were established, of course, by Orpheus and Musaeus, the best dancers of that time, who included it in their prescriptions as something exceptionally beautiful to be imitated with rhythm and dancing . . . At Delos, indeed, even the sacrifices were not without dancing, but were performed with that and with music. Choirs of boys came together, and while they moved and sang to the accompaniment of flute and lyre, those who had been selected from among them as the best performed an interpretative dance.

Lucian goes on to talk of the Ethiopians who terrified the enemy by their war dances, the Roman dance called 'Salii' which was performed in honour of the war-god Ares – "a dance which is at once very majestic and very sacred" – and how Ares was taught to dance before he was allowed to learn to fence.

So, like morris dancing, sword dancing too has ancient roots, much more ancient than the dances plotted on the map of northern England by those who believed that the English long and short swords came respectively from Norway and Denmark with the ninth-century Vikings, never bothering to enquire if there was a tradition of sword dancing in those countries for the Vikings to bring with them in the first place. The answer to their theory is that there is no tradition of hilt-and-point sword dancing in Scandinavia and that, in any case, the English sword dance is much older than the Viking age.

The English sword dance has to do with the ritual killing (in this case decapitation) of the god-king, to ensure the renewal of fertility, by sprinkling the blood of the sacrificed victim on the ground, in the belief that this will fertilize the earth and bring forth a good crop. In the English sword dance (as also in many other countries), the participants are linked by holding each others' swords (lengths of iron or wood, or, in the case of the rapper-swords, flexible steel). They move quickly, turning under or stepping over the swords, making endless 'cat's cradles' with their blades, turning again to reform their circle and, again, twisting in and out, to reach the climax of their performance as the swords are interlocked around the neck of their leader. The swords are suddenly withdrawn and the leader falls down 'dead'. In some cases, the decapitation is symbolized by the knocking-off of the leader's headgear. Again like the morris dances, these sword dances were enacting an ancient ritual. The dancers often disguised themselves by blacking their faces (ill. 27), not because they thought they were Moors (or worse, as the author read in one festival leaflet, because the dancing was performed by miners who had just emerged from the pit with faces blackened by coal dust).

Again, as with morris dancing, some sword-dance teams are accompanied by a retinue of characters: the hobby-horse, a man-woman (sometimes called Besom Betty or Dirty Bet), a king and queen, or lord and lady, and of course the doctor, who is there to revive the slain leader. Unlike the morris dance which is performed mainly in springtime, however, the sword dance belonged to midwinter, the time when the god-king's powers were finished, and he had to be replaced by a strong new leader, who could guarantee fruitfulness in crops and animals.

In England, two distinct forms of sword dance exist, and each has its own area of distribution, and are exclusive to the north. Yorkshire and South Durham have 'long-swords', which are rigid and longer than those of Northumberland and elsewhere in Durham, where shorter and flexible 'rapper-swords' are used. The rapper-sword has two handles, the hilt having a swivel to enable the blade to twist as the dancers make their figures. This allows for the most intricate patterns to be made, and somersaults and jumps to be performed. Interspersed between the figures, the dancers perform steps and shuffles. The rapper-sword dance must be of later provenance, as sprung steel could not be used until 1740 when a process for fashioning it was invented. It has been argued that rapper-sword dancing cannot be described as sword dancing, and that, indeed, some rapper dancers do not claim to be such. The rapper itself is something like a scraping tool once used by miners. Nevertheless, there seems no logical reason to believe that the rapper-sword dance did not evolve out of an existing ancient form of sword dancing. The figures made include sunwise-circling, weaving over and under the linked swords, somersaults by one or sometimes two of the performers, and then the interlinking of the five rappers to produce the 'lock' or 'rose'. All the elements are there: the performance at midwinter, the leaping (somersaulting), the lock symbolising the killing, the raising of the rose to symbolize rebirth, are the traditional ingredients.

The long-swords, with their rigid blades do not permit the intricate style of performance associated with the rapper-swords. Long-sword dancing is an ancient ritual. It is not *pyrrhic* dancing; in other words it is not dancing to train men to fight, (which again one unfortunately reads in festival brochures, written sometimes even by the performers themselves). This shows a lack of understanding of the original purpose of the performance. The dancers are, after all, actors in the usual drama of death and resurrection. Once more, we see the swords interlaced into the 'lock', 'knot', 'nut', 'star' or 'rose' (according to local terminology), around the neck of the leader, who is then decapitated and brought back to life again. The rapper-teams consist of an odd number of dancers (five), while the long-sword dances have an even number: six or eight.

The dancers are introduced by a leader in song, and as each is named, he steps forward with his sword over his shoulder, and follows the leader round in a circle. On the conclusion of the song, each dancer grasps the tip of the sword in front of him, swords are lowered from shoulders and an open ring is formed. Or the leader may sing a purely introductory song for the team as a whole:

Oh, good people give ear to my story,
I've arrived here quite by chance,
And I brought these lads blythe and bonny,
Intending here for you to dance.

It's not for your gold or your silver,
Nor yet for the greed of your beer,
But we've taken this day for a pleasure,
To welcome the good people here.

In the place of their own habitation,
In the land where they're all born and bred,
There are no finer lads in the nation,
Nor are more gallantly led.

Now my boys are ready for action,
With a spirit and courage so bold,
They were born of noble extraction,
Their fathers were heroes of old.

Now if they be as good as their fathers,
Then their fathers deserve just rewards,
For it's all our company desires,
Is for you to see how we handles our swords.

Of the English longsword-dance teams, Grenoside and Handsworth (South Yorkshire) can boast an unbroken tradition. The six dancers of Grenoside, performing on Boxing Day, carry 'swords' a metre long, and, linking together, weave intricate figures. The climax of their performance comes in the 'decapitation' of their captain, the seventh member of the side, who wears a rabbit-skin hat. The dancers' swords lock around his head, knocking off his cap as they are withdrawn. The captain falls down dead, but as the dancing is renewed he comes back to life again. The Grenoside dancers dress in red decorated jackets, white trousers with a red stripe, and black caps. Handsworth also dance on Boxing Day, linking their sword-dance with a mumming play, 't'Owd Tup' or Derby Ram. Their dress is a military jacket with silver decoration, burgundy caps, white trousers, and black gaiters.

In Loftus, Cleveland, too, the sword-dancers continue to dance in the tradition of linked swords. In 1927, Mr. J. Winspear of the North Skelton sword dance team, reminiscing about an old Plough Stotting from Loftus where he had started off dancing thirty-eight years previously, wrote:

> *They used to dance on the village greens, going from one place to another, especially after the crops had been harvested and Christmas time, and I was told that there was a lot of good old-fashioned beer consumed when they turned up at the public-houses; the man with the jug was always busy . . . There are seven figures to complete the dance and there are eight dancers. I will explain why we only had six. It often happened when we were out of work we would go out street-dancing and collecting, and when we shared the proceeds it meant more for each man. There are eight dancers because it takes the form of the old-fashioned ball-room*

25. Sword dance to bagpipes. English, 14th century.

dancing in what is called 'sets' which means four on one side and four on the other.

In continuing an old tradition, the dancers were at the same time able to pick up a little extra money, which in turn stimulated the desire to keep old customs alive.

At Flamborough in Humberside, there is a fishermen's longsword dance team. The fact that they carry wooden laths, which they hold in the left hand, suggests that these represent tools employed in the repairing of the fishing nets, and the weaving and threading of the figures represent this occupation. Another traditional team is the Royal Earsdon Sword Dancers from Tyne and Wear, 'royal' after they performed before King Edward VII, and who claim to be the last traditional rapper-sword team still active in an area where once every coal-mining village had its team. This team sports white shirts, waistcoats with rosettes, and red breeches. Competition amongst the rapper-sword villages brought about an almost professional approach to training and the elaboration of ever more complex figures. Now the various rapper-sword teams bring great amusement to the onlookers by their mock agony of trapped fingers, though genuine injuries do occur, and more than once the author has seen blood trickling down the face of a performer unfortunately sliced by a blade.

The complexity of the dance varies from the simplest type, to be seen in Andalusia in Spain, which has only two figures, the chain and the passing under the swords which are held above their heads in a 'bridge', to elaborate and intricate dances possessing a dozen figures and more.

The origins of the sword dance are unknown, but, as Violet Alford observed, its connection with regions rich in metals and possessing mines dating back into prehistory is so strong, that a convincing case can be made out for it being created by mining communities. Of course, there are exceptions to this observation; there are many mining areas which do not possess a tradition of sword-dancing, and there are places which do possess this tradition which are far away from any mining site. However, the argument is very persuasive, and, if correct, would make good mythological sense.

Caves, any sort of hole in the ground, or subterranean passages, were regarded by early Man as being places of magical significance. These were entrances to the womb of Mother Earth herself. Stone Age man did not paint on his cave walls merely because it seemed a convenient surface to cover with his scenes of hunting, ritual dancing, and so on, but because the place itself enhanced the magic of the scenes he depicted. Caves were his temples before temples were invented. Holy too were grottoes – many are the grottoes today dedicated to the Virgin Mary, and wells still retain for some the belief that throwing coins into them will grant their wishes.

It was not merely the holes in the earth that carried a magical connotation but the people who worked them, extracted the flints, and later the ores and precious metals. According to Strabo, the Curetes and Corybantes "discovered and forged iron and many other things which were useful for the purposes of life". The swords forged from the ores were often regarded as possessing magical qualities – how many legends do you know which contain references to a magical sword, a sword often embedded in a rock, and only able to be removed by the young man destined to be king, or given by some goddess, or magical personage such as the 'Lady of the Lake'?

And what more powerful magic could you possibly have than a dance performed by miners linked by magic swords?

This seems to be corroborated by the fact that it was not only in metal producing mining areas that the sword dance appears to have originated, but also non-metalliferous mines such as salt in the Austrian Salzkammergut, the Spanish gypsum, lead, and lime workings of Aragon, and the coal and ochre sites of England.

There is a very strong and consistent folk tradition of dwarfs or magicians mining and guarding underground metals, and this belief at an early date became extended to other materials extracted from the earth. These miners had long made votive offerings to an earth goddess. It was natural that they would evolve a religious ritual making use of metals available. One way to drive away evil spirits was to make as much noise as possible, and the loudest din that could be made was the striking of swords against shields, powerful magic which was used by the Curetes, as already seen, in guarding the infant Zeus. Ever since then, priestly dancing brotherhoods have performed their rituals, to protect and preserve their magic powers, and to fulfil a secondary function, of 'magicing' in the spring. Again, the clashing of weapons and the clanging of bells provided the noise which could drive away the evil spirits of winter, while the stamping of the dancers and the striking of the ground with sticks or swords would wake up Mother Earth, and their leaping would show the corn, flax or whatever, how high it should grow. The Curetes are said to have "leapt for full jars", for "thick fleeces on their flocks", as well as for the growth of the harvest.

The priesthood was charged with the protection of the mining, smelting and forging of metals. Smiths in most mythologies were magicians. They alone possessed the magic necessary to produce the weapons and agricultural implements on which Man depended for survival. Is it any wonder that, according to legend, they were deliberately lamed to stop them running away to offer their services to other masters? Many of the swords they fashioned possessed magic qualities, and were even given names: King Arthur's 'Excalibur'; St. George's 'Oscalon'; and 'Birting', handed up to the Dane from his father's burial mound. The sword gave its possessor greater power both physically and magically to subdue his enemies. Imagine what the possession of a fine metal sword meant, when one's enemies only had flint and bone weapons, or the far greater efficiency provided by metal tools and implements.

Sword dancers did not always employ swords in their dances, but might use other implements, often tools of their trade. The English Flamborough swords are wooden staves, nearly one metre long, which may represent the implements once used for making nets or ships' mats. The Coopers of Nürnberg used iron hoops like the ones they put round their barrels, and the Glovers of Perth used their skin 'scutcher', a tool used in beating the leather to soften it. Sticks rather than swords have long been used by sides, who still claim to be sword dancers. The Roman Salii, who although they wore a sword strapped to their waists, still used a stave to strike their shields. The rapper sword may also be likened to the scraper used by miners in their work, which too had a handle at both ends. The sword-dancers of Oviedo, in the mining region of the Asturias, which was on the pilgrim route to Santiago de Compostela, have adopted pilgrims' staves instead of swords into their dance. At Hio, near Vigo in Galicia, they still perform a pilgrims' dance with sword-dance figures, but carry pilgrims' staves instead of swords. Their dance consists of heys, figure-of-eight, star, St. Andrew's cross, and a 'clash' above the captain's head. An old account describes the captain, his back to the *châsse*, dancing rapidly, whilst making the four sword points touch his forehead, eyebrows, ears, cheeks, mouth and breast, and seems to indicate a dedication of an ordained ritual victim. At Redondela they also have discarded the swords, but here they use long sticks, which they carry by a thong attached to the thick end of the stick. Danced by a fishermen's confraternity, this dance used to be called the 'Danza Marinera'.

The Salii of Rome were, ritualistically speaking, the direct decendants of the Curetes of Greek legend. They were twelve in number, who came out on March Ist, the old Roman new year's day, and on nine other days, and danced in the new year. The celebration of March 14th was known as the 'Mamuralia'. The dancers carried an *ancile*. This was a small oval shield, curved inwards on either side, which was said to have fallen from heaven in the reign of Numa. There being a prophesy that the stability of Rome was bound up with it, Numa had eleven others made exactly like it, by the skilled craftsman, Mamurius Veturius, so that the real one

26. Entry by the Vice-regent João de Castro into Goa. Tapestry made in Brussels, 16th Century.

should not be stolen. The safekeeping of these shields, which were sacred to Mars, was entrusted to the Salii, who had to carry them through the city once a year with special ceremonies. On March 14th they held a feast in honour of Mamurius, in which they made sacrifices to him, while beating on their shields with staves. It seems likely that the name Mamurius concealed that of the god Mars (Mamers) himself. The Salii of Rome were divided into two colleges: the 'Salii Palatini' consisted of twelve life members of the patrician class. At their head was a *magister* (master or leader), a *praesul* (leader of the dance), and a *vates* (leader of the song). The cult of the Salii Palatini originally had to do with the worship of Mars. A second, and later, college, the 'Salii Agonales' or 'Colini', had to do with Quirinus, the Sabine name for Mars.

However, as always happens, the original festival was adapted and transformed into a popular spring holiday. The Mamuralia became a 'scapegoat' ceremony, in which a man, dressed up in animal skins, and representing the Old Year, was led through the city, beaten with white rods, and driven out. The feast of Anna Perenna was another occasion at this time for feasting and carousing. Anna Perenna was an ancient Italian goddess, probably the moon-goddess of the revolving year, who, renewing her youth every month, was regarded as a goddess, and who bestowed long life and all that contributed to it. About full moon on the Ides (15th) of March, the Romans feasted together in the open air, in a grove of fruit trees, at the first milestone on the Flaminium Way, outside the city. They wished each other as many years of life as they drank cups of wine.

The Salii thus attended the spring festivities, and saw to the driving out of winter and the bringing in of spring. They were still dancing in 382 AD, when there is a record of their altars being repaired, and in only slightly modified guise are they dancing still today, as sword dancers or morris dancers spread across Europe.

There is only one reference to sword dancing in Ireland, and this is from the seventeeth century, but this does not necessarily imply that sword dancing did not once exist there generally, and silence of its existence in Brittany likewise does not mean that it is unknown in the rest of the Celtic world, as is claimed by those who seek a Germanic origin to sword dancing. It used to exist in Wales, the Highlands and Islands of Scotland, and is very much alive in Galicia in the far north-west of Spain, whose inhabitants regard themselves first as Celts, and only second as Spanish. Dance historians of the last two centuries have claimed a German paternity for the sword dance, and maps have been drawn pin-pointing the spots where sword dances were and are to be found, and from that claimed its origins in Germany, or in those regions in eastern Europe colonized by Germans in the Middle Ages. Yet their arguments are not completely convincing, and there are so many places never colonized by Germanic tribes but which were formerly colonized by Celts, that a Celtic origin seems more probable than a German one. Having said that, however, it is still more likely that sword dancing pre-dates both the coming of Celtic and Germanic peoples to these lands which today boast the possession of sword dances. It really must be stressed again that folk dancing is far older than people give it credit for, and just as morris dancing pre-dates the invasion of the Moors, so sword dancing is older than the coming of the Vikings, and before them the Germans, and before them the Celts.

Meanwhile, back in Galicia, the dances are for the most part performed by fishermen and sailors, and, hardly surprising in the region which possesses Europe's foremost centre of pilgrimage, Santiago de Compostela, it is on St. James's Day, July 25th, when the greatest celebrations occur. The 'Gremio' or local confraternity of fishermen, marching in three files of five dancers, arrive at their local church, linked not only by swords but also by red cords, on which are hung metal rings, through which the men place their left arm. Only the leading three men carry swords, the remainder clack castanets in their right hands. Four fishermen carry out the statuette of St. James, mounted on his white charger, and the company drops on one knee, the captain placing the three swords in front of him on the ground. He then steps over them, followed by the other dancers, who cast off and return to their places. Then the three front dancers pick up their swords, the points of which the captain grasps, and he leads them off on a snaking procession, every now and again breaking into a figure, which passes underneath the *châsse* which bears the saint, and which is held aloft on poles, borne by the four fishermen. Now the three men carrying the swords suggest a sort of beheading, sticking the sword points into the back of their captain. But he does not die, and the procession continues. The red cords seem to have replaced the swords, which must once have been held by the rest of the dancers, just as the beheading appears to have given way to a symbolic prodding of the captain's neck and collar bone. There is no lock to be found in any of the Galician dances. One can only presume that these things existed, but now have long been forgotten

The dancers of the Perth Glovers' Company in Scotland carried scraping implements rather than swords. The dance is delightfully described by one of their number, following a performance given in 1633, on a raft, in honour of King Charles I.

> *His Majestie's chair being set up upon the wall next the Tay, whereupon was a flat stage of timber, clad about with birks, upon the which for his Majestie's welcome and entry thirteen of our brethren of this our calling of Glovers, with green caps, strings, red ribbons, white shoes, with bells about their legs, shering rapers in their hands, and all other abulzement, danced our sword-dance with many difficult knots and allafallajessa, five being under and five above their shoulders, three of them dancing through their feet, drinking of wine, and breaking of glasses about them, which (God be praised) was acted without hurt or skaith to any, which drew in to great charges and expenses to the sum of three hundred and fifty merks (yet not to be remembered), because we were graciously accepted by our sovereign and both estates, to our honour and great commendation.*

Further on, the account describes the mounting by one ring of dancers on the shoulders of another ring, to be seen also in Greek and Balkan dances.

A reference from 1590 talks of a sword dance and a 'Hieland' dance being shown to Anne of Denmark, wife of James VI of Scotland, in Edinburgh, when twelve men, bedecked in "hats of flouris" performed. In 1623, 'gwysseris' (guisers) of Elgin were fined forty shillings for having "past in ane sword dance in Paul Dunbar's closs and in the kirkyard". As this took place on January 7th, and the dancers were masked, they were probably celebrating Hogmanay according to the old calendar.

Sir Walter Scott noted down a Shetland dance, when he visited the islands in 1814. Helped by these notes, the islanders of Papa Stour have revived this dance, now called the 'Seven Champions of Christendom'. The performance takes the form of a monologue by St. George, with dance steps interspersed, and then the sword dance follows. In turn the seven champions make their entrances: St. George is followed by St. James of Spain, St. Denis of France, St. David of Wales, St. Patrick of Ireland, St. Anthony of Italy, and St. Andrew of Scotland. The introductions by St. George having been made, they dance a single under, and then a bridge, developing into a tunnel of swords, as each pair step under the raised swords in front. They form a lock (here called a shield) with their seven swords, and this is handed from one dancer to the next, each holder going into the centre, while the rest dance in a ring round him. The last dancer throws the shield down onto the floor and joins the ring, and St. George closes the proceedings. Their swords now of strip steel were formerly of straightened herring-barrel hoops. The back shuffle step which is generally now used would have been, when danced by more experienced dancers, the more spectacular 'treepling' step.

A Scottish dance, which seems to have combined Highland sword and hilt-and-point sword dancing, was described in a letter written in 1924. It concerns an eight-man sword dance, performed fifty years prior to the date of the letter, in which two dancers placed their swords on the ground, with the other six dancers forming a ring round them, and pointing their swords inwards towards them. The letter continues:

> *The dance began slowly to pipe music and grew faster and faster, the two dancers avoiding both the ring of swords and the two weapons laid on the ground. When one of the performers grew exhausted he danced into the place of one of the six swordsmen who took his place. So the dance continued until all eight had taken part, when the two swords were swiftly taken up and seven formed a ring round the eighth man with their swords pointing at his throat.*

This pointing may be the unwoven lock. It is to be found in Spain, as we have seen, where the swords prod the captain's neck, and in the French Baccubert, in which the swords are placed on the leader's shoulders, but not woven into a lock.

The reference to a sword dance in Ireland comes from an account of 1600 by Fynes Moryson, secretary to Lord Mountjoy:

> *The Irish delight much in dancing, using no arts of slow measures or lofty galliards, but only country dances, whereof they have some pleasant to behold, as Balrudery, and the Whip of Dunboyne, and they dance about a fire commonly in the midst of a room holding withes in their hands, and by certain strains drawing one another into the fire; and also the matachine dance, with naked swords, which they make to meet in divers comely postures. And this I have seen them often dance before the Lord Deputy in the houses of Irish lords; and it seemed to me a dangerous sport to see so many naked swords so near the Lord Deputy and chief*

commanders of the army in the hands of the Irish Kerne, who had either lately been or were not unlike to prove rebels.

Czechoslovakia has a sword dance, the 'Pod Šable' (literally Under the Sword), preserved in its purest form at Kopaniče in the foothills of the White Carpathians, though performed elsewhere, especially by woodcutters up in the hills. It is danced at the end of Fasching when the boys are rewarded for their singing and dancing by the houswives, who put a joint of bacon onto the point of the leader's sword. The dance is performed by five boys carrying wooden swords which are painted red and inlaid with *hrkóvky*, brass rings which are used to decorate horse's harness. They are led by a *Gazdou* who carries a real metal sword but does not take part in the dance proper. Originally accompanied by a bagpiper, now they may have the luxury of bagpipes, violins, or a cimbalon combination, that is, cimbalon, clarinet, string bass and violin. The dance starts with a promenade round singing 'Horenka Hora', going counter-clockwise with the left hip to the centre, making one step with each beat, using the sword almost like a walking stick. Then they start to dance, linking up hilt-and-point fashion, using the same jumping step throughout, getting faster and faster as they progress through their various figures, with swords over right shoulder, in a circle with swords aloft pointing towards each other, stepping over swords into the middle, turning, and forming the knot.

'Paličkovy Tanec' is a Slovenian hilt-and-point sword dance using batons rather than swords. In this the number of participants is not restricted. This dance also

27. Sword dance in Zürich in 1578.

travels counter-clockwise. It is rightly pointed out by those who believe that Germany sired the sword dance that Czechoslovakia, especially the towns and mining regions, was colonized by Germans in the Middle Ages, but they do not take account of the fact that these dances come from areas beyond the pale of Germanic colonization.

The 'Bal del Saber' belongs chiefly to Vicoforte but has spread to the Piedmont village of Fenestrelle and to other villages in the gold-bearing region of Dora Riparia in Italy. Here they perform a hilt-and-point sword dance led by a Harlequin. There is also a local traditional figure, Brighella, who found her way into the Commedia dell' Arte, cuirassiers and a Turk. In this dance, Harlequin has the swords stacked on his shoulders in an unwoven lock, and later is hoisted on the swords in a standing position, to fall to his feet when the swords are suddenly withdrawn. Today, a play accompanies the dance rather than the dance being an interlude in the play. Two Moors appear in the dance-play at Vicoforte, whose job it is to carry off the dead body of Harlequin after he has been tried, condemned, and hoisted on the lock of swords from where he makes his will. Brighella clad in white, Moors, a Senator, and several other characters, act out this dance-drama. A maypole figure is also performed. Whilst Turks and Moors put in an appearance at many of these village festivities, the term 'Morisca' has never attached itself to the dances (see chapter on morris dancing).

There is no 'death' in the sword dance performed at Pont de Cervières, near Briançon in the Dauphiné, France, though an unwoven lock is formed by the swords being placed on the shoulders of one of the dancers. It is interesting to learn that the three places where the dancers perform are marked out by young fir trees 'stolen' from the communal forest. This stealing for ritual purposes is common throughout Europe, and examples may be quoted from Catalonia, where the *Diablots* of the 'Danse des Gitanes' steel cabbages, in Engand where the Padstow *Mayers* steel flowers, and in Greece where the mummers help themselves to chickens. In Provence and Spain the stolen goods may include musical instruments, plants or animals, but the theft was essential if the magic towards which they were to be put was to be effective. According to local tradition, their dance came from the Romans, and the song accompaniment is supposedly of ancient Greek origin. Song is perhaps the wrong term; mouth-music is probably nearer the mark, for the singers race through their tune without words, using a 'tra-la-la'. 'Le Bakubèr', as this dance is called, is performed on the day on which they celebrate the patronal feast of Saint-Roch, on August 16th. The young people come together in the square outside the church, in the main square, and near the bridge, and perform a ceremonial sword dance, which, in this out of the way place, has been handed down since time immemorial from father to son. As expected, the number of participants has to be odd. In former times, the dancers wore warrior equipment and gilded helmets. Today they are dressed simply in white shirts and trousers, with a wide red *taiole* or cummerbund around the waist. They walk forwards in a single file behind a standard-bearer and form a circle. A group of women intone a chant without words to accompany them, which adds further to the impression of great antiquity.

The first part of their dance consists of nineteen figures. The dancers, facing the middle of the circle, put their swords on the ground in front of them in the form of a star, salute each other, and take up their swords again to form a chain, each taking the point of the next dancer's sword in his left hand. Starting with the left foot, they move in a clockwise direction, making a small circle next to the first one which it replaces. The leading dancer then passes under the swords of the other dancers, moves into the middle of the circle which joins up around him, each having the left elbow bent under the right arm of his neighbour, finishing up with their swords crossed in a star around their leader's neck. In this position they move carefully forwards on the left foot, drawing it back next to the right, throwing the right leg back and lowering the right knee until it almost touches the ground, all the while turning very slowly to the left. This first *enchaînement* is called 'la lève' (the lift), and probably indicates the lifting of the corpse, which 'le Bakubèr' has subsequently lost. The second part of the dance, as its name of the 'Figures' suggests, is a series of geometric patterns, circles, squares, triangles, the swords forming a star and then a square, a chain, and the salute with which they commenced terminates the dance.

The 'Bakubèr' is a fine example of a traditional rite taking root in an isolated village, and which has been preserved almost intact with the original belief which gave it motivation. Still today, the villagers superstitiously worry lest, by any mischance, the observance of this traditional rite cannot go ahead at its appointed time in the calendar, and they guard their dance jealously from neighbouring villages, refusing to allow outsiders to learn their dance. There is even today a deeply rooted feeling that the efficacious nature of the ritual would be destroyed if the magic became known to strangers. The origin and significance of the name 'Bakubèr' is hotly disputed, but one explanation links it nicely to a further symbolic significance, that is, that the name derives from *bal cubert* or covered dance. On the eve of the festival, the dancers had to take themselves off into the forest to 'steal' the fir trees

28. 'Kermesse de la Saint-Georges' (Sint-Joris Kermis) by H. Cock after Pieter Brueghel. Flemish, 1601.

which would be used to mark out the three areas reserved for the observance of their rite. At the same time these young men, accompanied by the girls of the village, picked wild flowers, herbs, and branches of greenery, to construct their 'May', symbol of the solar disc which, fastened by garlands attached to the four trees set up in each corner of the dancing area, would figure above their heads during their dance. Thus their dance was covered, or performed under a lattice of greenery, with the solar disc held at the centre.

Provence, in the south of France, can boast numerous sword, baton, arch, and garland dances. One of the jewels of such dances, and one which best preserves the essence of the fertility ceremonial, is 'les Olivettes' (Olive-groves). It became incorporated into the celebrations which terminated the olive harvest, when, at one time, one saw the men, armed with swords, chasing the women, who defended themselves by hurling handfuls of olives at them. Its eternal theme, the struggle between summer and winter, became, in Roman times, attached to the celebrated rivalry between Julius Caesar and Pompey, which had a profound effect on the region. So the young people dressed up in the ancient costume of Roman gladiators, carrying, anachronistically and randomly, swords or toy pistols. In two columns, they ranged the streets, following their leader, called variously according to region: Prince, Marshal, Consul or Emperor. A herald whirling a stick, and a Harlequin haranguing the crowd, preceded the cortège. They danced to a lively tune, performing various steps and figures. Then, on arrival at some suitable place, the music would break into a march tempo, they would commence a mock fight with shouts and clashing sword blades, and then they would surround Harlequin and place their swords round his neck and simulate his decapitation. Next, they would place their swords on the ground and interlace them to form a lock on which Harlequin was hoisted aloft. From this vantage point, Harlequin would harangue the crowd, comment on any grumbles, scandals or local events, and woe betide the miser whose offering to the dancers was insufficient. Here is one example:

A la Basso Carrièro,
I'aviè un bèu moussu,
Quand lou vesien passa,
Li disien 'Lou Tartu',
En aquèu gros richard
Qué li a oufert cinq francs,
Li jouine an respoundu:
'Garda-vœu per de pan'.

"In Lower Street lives a fine fellow. When we would see him pass, we would call out 'the Mule' to the great rich man who gave but a measly five francs. The young people told him: 'Keep it to buy your bread'." A fast galop round using their swords as hobby-horses, pawing the ground in imitation of the movements of a prancing horse (symbol of fecundity), and a salute finish the dance.

Here in 'les Olivettes' we have all the ingredients which go to make up a fertility ritual: jumps, beaten steps, prancing horses, the fight between the spirits of good and evil, shouts, clatter of sword-blades, and the resurrection of the spirit of vegetation in the symbolic figure of Harlequin. Writers in the past have seen this dance as the fight between the indigenous inhabitants and the Moors, in the same way that the 'Bal du Sabre' of Fenestrelle, in Italy, has been seen as the battle with the Saracens, who had come to snatch their womenfolk as they danced 'les Cordelles'. But just as the Morris in England pre-dates the coming of the Moors to Spain, so does 'les Olivettes' find its origins far back into prehistory.

'Les Olivettes', in forms often unrecognizable from the original but still tenaciously retaining the name, is to be found scattered about Europe. Taken by itinerants or soldiers, the dance appears in places which have never known the olive – the Ardennes for example. In some places it has degenerated into a children's game in which two children form an arch with their raised arms while the rest pass in file underneath, and, just as in 'Oranges and Lemons', a child is trapped by the abrupt lowering of the arch (the *degullada*) made by the two leaders, and a question has to be answered or the trapped child takes over as one of the arch makers. In the Ardennes, in the small village of Hargnies, 'les Olivettes' concludes the fun and games which take place on the feast of the local patron saint on October 1st. To represent the olive trees around which it is supposed to be danced, three chairs are substituted, their legs carefully balanced on dried peas, nuts or corks. Then everyone dances in a circle round the chairs, and anyone who dislodges one has to pay a forfeit. The tune used is still the old air, though the words are changed:

Lan, lan, la,
Laissez les passer,
Les enfants de la Lorraine,
Laissez les passer,
Ils auront du mal assez.

La, la, la,
Let them pass,
The children from Lorraine,
Let them pass,
They'll have trouble enough.

In the east of Belgium, the battle between two groups has degenerated into a fight using brooms. In Le Blaisois, the name of the dance has been corrupted to 'Jolivettes'. At Wielsam in Luxembourg, they use thirty chairs, and sing:

Ah, laissez-les passer,
Ils sont passés par la Lorraine,
Nous allons les manger,
Les Olivettes après souper.

Oh, let them pass,
They've come by way of Lorraine,
We are going to eat them,
The Olives after supper.

The Walloons sing:

Rou, la, la, les jolies passées,
Des Français dans la Lorraine,
Rou, la, la, les jolies passées,
Les Olivettes après souper.

Tra-la-la, these nice travellers,
The French in Lorraine,
Tra-la-la, these nice travellers,
The Olives after supper.

At Malmédy they dance to the name of les Olivettes, 'les Cordelles', which accompanies it in Provence. Following even more tenuous threads, we find in Burgundy (Danse des Noix) and in the Basque Country (Kadera Dantza) dances, or rather now games, in which the person having to pay a forfeit has his face blackened by a woman armed with a frying-pan, and in which chairs precariously balanced feature.

When one thinks of dancing in Andalusia, it is Flamenco which first springs to mind, but here too sword dances are to be found. In the Pueblo de Guzman in the province of Huelva, over towards the Portuguese border, the sword dancers go from house to house, performing their hilt-and-point figures, and receiving sweets and drinks at the doors of the houses they visit. This dance comes from a mining area, the Rio Tinto mines, which were being worked as long ago as 2000 B.C., to provide silver for Solomon's temple. They dance simple figures before the statue of the Virgin, and then carry the statue up the mountain, on top of which the Virgin was said to have appeared. If they met a procession from another village with its own Virgin, both sides would set their statues down, hurl insults at each other's Lady, and start fighting, before attending all together a festal Mass on top of the rock.

Toledo, world-famous for its steel industry, could hardly be without its sword dancers. They too incorporate into their dance the *degollada* or beheading, placing their swords around the neck of the leader who, however, manages to escape. Castile is rich in men's ritual dances. In Burgos they dance with swords and tiny metal shields, clashing these together as they execute steps similar to the English Morris. They then lay down their shields and link up in hilt-and-point fashion around their leader, and perform the usual figures of over and under the swords, moving in a counter-clockwise direction, before making the lock on which their leader is hoisted, and from where he shouts "viva Espagna". He is then lowered and the knot raised aloft. All now break off to dance round individually before reforming around their leader, dancing under raised swords, moving round with swords over left shouders and lastly making a final salute.

When Don Quixotte attended the wedding of the wealthy Camacho near the bride's Castilian village, he was informed that there would be "dangerous dances with swords and little bells". At Obeja in the Sierra Morena, the dancers come out on the day of San Benito, and again on March 21st and 22nd. They go in procession up the bare slopes to the hermitage of their patron saint. It is a religious occasion and they sing:

Water, Eternal Father,
Water, oh my Father,
Do not let the clouds pass
Without dropping rain.

In such an arid region, this fertility rite is readily understandable. They repeat the dance, which consists of simple movements called *tiempos* over and over again. Linked in hilt-and-point formation, they make a *puente* or bridge of their swords, and all pass underneath. The leader stops, and the swords are woven round his neck. The lock, as at Burgos, is called *la horca*, the gallows. He sinks down, *la deguëllo*, and then the *cadena* or chain sets off once more.

It is the nationalistically-minded Spanish Basques who do not recognize any difference between the regions on either side of the Spanish-French border, and who have introduced their 'Viscaya', Biscay sword dance into the French Basque Country, so that today this dance is often performed in place of their own very different traditional dances. Now some French Basque dancers have adopted a dance, costumes and music which are alien to their culture, and perform the dance mistakenly as their own. For all that, the Viscaya is impressive. It came originally from the Biscay iron-mining and steel-producing region. The figure in which each dancer clashes swords with his partner and the man behind or in front is called *ezpata jokoa*, sword-play, and another figure is performed to a 5/8 rhythm, the *zortziko*. Only the last figure, the *txonkorinka* is a hilt-and-point figure, and now the captain is raised aloft by his shoulders and ankles, and, above the heads of his companions, he lies rigid, stretched out horizontally, while the rest point their swords towards his dead body. At Arexinaga, the captain stands on the lock, and when the dancers' swords are withdrawn he falls to his feet.

One reference to the Basque sword dance comes from Vitoria in Alava, in 1486, when it was prohibited "on account of the scandalous behaviour and shedding of blood occasioned by them". In the province of Guipúzkoa, the 'Espata Dantza' (sword dance) was often performed in church in front of the high altar. The Durango men fight with little shields instead of swords. They perform the Biscaya figures, *banakoa* (one by one), and *binakoan* (two by two), where the swords are laid on the ground and sent spinning out singly or in twos, and they raise the captain on their shields. The company-like formations of the Basque dancers are peculiar to this region, and the Basques themselves consider their dances to be 'war' dances. It has been written of them that they "were not taught nor did they learn any arts

29. Sword dance from a Nürnberg manuscript. German, c.1561.

but those of war". The Basques are content to believe this, for if they admitted that their dances were of pagan origin, they could hardly expect to be given a place of honour in ecclesiastical processions and admitted into the churches to dance. They do not trouble to explain away the raising of their captain and, as at Arexanaga, the unmistakable death and resurrection being enacted.

In the village of Zumárraga in Navarre, Spain, four files, in hilt-and-point formation, the captain holding the points of the first line of swords, progress to a pilgrim chapel above the village, and there the captain kneels, still holding the sword points, and then with two companions, he enters the chapel to dance before the altar. The village of Ibio in northern Spain, on the seaward side of the forbidding mountain range, the 'Picos de Europa', has kept its dance untainted by Moorish influence. Here, wooden batons instead of swords are used, and the lock is formed by piling them up like spillikins, not woven together, and on this perilous platform the captain is raised. They dance to the sound of a drum and conch shell. They also have a man-woman character, 'Zorromoco', and all come out at the turn of the year. It was not the mountains that protected this dance from Moorish influence however. In the same village they had a morisca, which was a cavalcade of young men, some with their faces blackened to represent Moors, the others white to represent Christians, and they came out at Carnival time on Shrove Tuesday. It seems that, having one morisca, the villagers of Ibio were content not to meddle with their sword dance, which has thus retained its original character. This district also has several stick dances, 'Palillos', and a garland dance, 'Arcos'. This last has a figure called *horca* (the gallows), in which the leader stands to salute the audience, with the garlands draped around his neck.

Korčula on the Yugoslav Adriatic has its sword dance, the 'Kumpanija' or the 'Ples od Boja', quite independent of the well-known 'Moreška', which is performed on the same island. The dancers come from several different mountain villages to Blato, where they perform on the feast day of St. Vincent, April 28th. A flag-waver, mace-bearer, spearman, and a character dressed in Napoleonic costume, accompany the dancers, who dance their way through some twenty figures: reviewing of troops, a progressive hey, circles, snails, and the usual sword-dance figures of under the swords, hilt-and-point circle, over your own head, and arches formed by stepping over one sword and passing under the next. The cutting-off of the captain's head is merely hinted at, the swords being held over his head. There is a mock combat, which is interrupted by the man in Napoleonic dress, and the combatants are reconciled. The Church has drastically changed the performance from the days when the captain used to behead a live ox and carry its head around. The villagers relate how sentinels used to stand on the hilltop, searching the horizon for the pirates who periodically raided the islands. When a pirate vessel was spotted, a drum sounded the alarm, and the women and children fled into the hills, leaving the menfolk to fight off the pirate bands. The 'Kumpanija' supposedly served as a lively and picturesque reminder of those times. The performance ends with the 'Starinski Tanac', an old folk dance of Korčula.

In 1866, the authorities on the island of Lastova (Lagosta), forced the dancers to carry wooden swords instead of the real ones, following a fight. The 'Pokladari' (Carnival dance) is performed after Epiphany (January 6th) and during Carnival, and has a close connection with the expelling of winter on Shrove Tuesday. At dawn on this day, a rope is fixed on the cliff top above the town, and the other end tied to a stake at the bottom. After the Carnival banquet at midday, the dancers go out to meet their 'scapegoat', a straw-stuffed figure seated on the back of a donkey, and accompanied by a man dressed as a bear, who plays the part of the fool. The guy is attached to the rope, and run up and down like a flag three times, the speed of its descent predicting the quality of the harvest to come. The sword dance which is performed afterwards, in front of the church, is danced around the figure, which has to suffer the indignity of being struck by the swords and afterwards burned, the silence of the crowd contrasting eerily with the noise and shouting which accompanied the running of the guy down the rope.

The Maltese dance 'la Parata' seems to be an ancient pagan rite, which has now become overlaid by, and confused with, Malta's historic association with the Knights of St. John. A ring of 'Christians', equipped with wooden sticks and shields, circles clockwise around a ring of 'Turks'. The dancers clash their swords, and perform a hey and progressive cross-overs. A 'bride', today a little girl, is hoisted on the shoulders of the leader, who is dressed in the cloak of the Grandmaster of the Order of St. John.

On the island of Ischia, lying in the Bay of Naples, is the 'N'drezzata', formerly danced by men, as shown in old photographs, half of them dressed as females, but now danced by mixed couples. The dancers carry wooden swords in their left hands, and short clubs in their right hands. Traditionally they danced at Easter or Midsummer, but now there is no fixed date. The dance is divided into two parts, each made up of seven scenes, and there is much clashing and crossing of swords and clubs, these violent and frenetic blows being accompanied by rhythmic stamping of feet. At the end of the dance they lay down their instruments and form a lock onto which the corporal (leader) steps, to be hoisted into the air, from where he addresses the onlookers. Flute and drum and little bells accompany the dance, and the dancers themselves make a murmuring, resembling the sound of a spinning wheel.

The Netherlands no longer possesses a sword dance, but that once sword dancing was widely performed is attested by archive documents and the frequent prohibitions imposed by the towns' authorities. Indeed, the 'Wapenreier' (weapon-chain-dancers) actually competed against each other in the province of Zeeland. Belgium is much richer in living folk traditions. In Bruges, we have records of sword dances dating back to 1389. An even older reference, from 1224, does not specifically mention dancing, though, at this Whitsuntide procession at Huy, the rest of the traditional ingredients are there:

> *Old and young of the masculine sex at the College of Huy, assuming the dress of women with beards shaven, remind one of the ancient ludi . . . They have the Emperor, the King, the Leader, the Knight and the Abbot. Certain of them are armed with shining breastplates and helmets carrying naked swords in their hands . . . and all others as well as they could dressed up like women, who during the Pentecostal feasts, none remaining at home, went in procession, two by two by lanes and squares singing.*

Throughout the Low Countries (present-day Netherlands, Belgium and Luxembourg), many town councils paid the dancers to perform at Carnival time, and frequently the guilds furnished the dancers. At Arnhem, the Duchess of Gelderland and the burgomasters provided sword dancers and musicians for the Carnival Eve celebrations. The fourteenth-century Archers' Guild of Tongres seem to have formed the two societies of 'war' dancers of St. Michael and of Gulpen, who feature regularly in records of the succeeding centuries, until they disbanded towards the end of the nineteenth century. In Liège in the Walloon country, the sword dancers appear with the hobby-horse. Records of their existence go back to the sixteenth century. In the next century we read of the sword dancers appearing in the procession celebrating the entry into the city of Ferdinand of Bavaria, Prince-Bishop of Liège. The sword dancers on this occasion performed 'la Danse Macabrée', nothing to do with the 'Danse Macabre', but named after the seven brothers 'Machabées'. (We come across a Judas Maccabeus in a sword-dance play at Lübeck. Namur also possessed this dance.) The dancers are also called by the name of 'Matachins', a name applied to the sword dance which has the traditional beheading of the leader.

A painting executed by Pieter Brueghel the Elder (ill. 28), depicts dancers performing a hilt-and-point sword dance. Once common throughout the Low Countries, today there are only a few examples remaining. The Traweitel or Trawanteldans of Westerlo is justly famous; to the intricacies of the sword-dance

30. Sword dance of the Nürnberg knifesmiths. German, 1600.

figures have been added the complicated manœuvrings of a hoop, through which the dancers manage to negotiate their bodies, passing the hoop one to another without letting go their sticks. Once performed by various guilds, today it is but infrequently to be seen, when it is danced by the Guild of Marksmen of Kempen or by the Boerke naas Westerlo. We may presume that originally the dance was performed using swords, but that at some time the performers were forced to adopt sticks instead; Flemish archives are littered with prohibitions on the use of swords. As long ago as 1548, there is a reference to the sword dancers of Eeklo carrying wooden sticks, and receiving for their performance the sum of 24 Paris shillings. A description by Edgard Wauters of the Trawanteldans as performed by the Guild of St. Sebastian of Westerlo, reveals various interesting elements: the formation of a star, the dramatic pause in the drumming which accompanied the dance, as if the moment of execution had arrived, followed by the five beats of the clashing swords, and the riding of the sticks in hobby-horse fashion:

> *There were six dancers led by a captain who stood on the outside of the circle. These six dancers each held in their hands a stick of about 80 cms. in length. The captain held a hoop of one metre in diameter*. Drums were beaten during the whole dance; when they performed the* bridge *the beat accelerated. The dancers came on in line behind the first dancer, each holding his stick over his right shoulder forming an open circle. Then the captain threw down the hoop into the middle of the circle. The sticks were then pointed to the centre of the circle while the men walked round clockwise holding the stick of the person in front. The first dancer took the hoop on his stick and crawled through, the others following his example, all this while the circle kept on moving. The last man threw the hoop back to the captain who caught it on his stick. Now two dancers formed a* bridge *by holding the stick horizontally while the others walked underneath in pairs. Then the sticks were intertwined into a star, while the circle advanced with small shuffling steps. The circle was closed while the second* bridge *was formed. During the performance of this figure the captain threw the hoop back into the middle of the circle. The first dancer, placing himself in the middle of the hoop held it up with both hands while crawling through while the circle kept on moving. The hoop then rested on two sticks, being shaken. Two other dancers crawled through until at the end the hoop rested on the six sticks.*
>
> *The next figure started like the previous one with this difference: now first the feet were put through the hoop,* so vice versa. *Then all the dancers turned underneath their sticks and stood with their backs against each other. The sticks, crossed like a star, were beaten in time one against the other. The drum beat stopped for a second; the drummer gave one loud*

* One metre in diameter is an inaccurate gauge – the hoop is in fact quite small, and only just large enough for the dancers to pass through.

bang, and five other beats followed with the sticks one against the other. The dancers turned round, unweaving the star, then the circle was closed again, followed by the lining up of all the dancers, riding horse on their sticks and leaving the dancing area.

The first mention of sword dancing in Germany is by the Roman historian Tacitus, in the 1st century A.D. In his 'Germania', he describes naked youths passing the eve of battle in shouting and dancing with unsheathed swords and uplifted spears, performing warlike movements. He relates that it was done all over Germany as a sort of display for pleasure and amusement. Tacitus says also that it developed skill in weapon training as well as grace and agility. He continues that they did not dance as professionals, but simply to bring enjoyment to the onlookers. But surely, in these northern climes, this nudity could only have been of a sacerdotal nature. This is the only written reference to sword dancing in Germany until we come right down to the fourteenth century. This reference explains that sword and hoop dances had the same kind of form as the peasants' chain dances.

Commencing in the twelfth century, urban life began to develop. At first many of the town dwellers led a double life as artisans in the town, while at the same time working their fields outside the town walls. They were peasants who had come to live in the towns, and they brought with them their country traditions and pastimes. Thus they introduced their dances into an urban environment. In course of time, these artisans, in order to regulate their trade and protect their interests, formed guild organizations, and not unnaturally, these came to adopt many of the country traditions into their formalized ceremonials, in particular, the initiation ceremonies, when apprentices were admitted to the guilds. Thus the traditions of the peasants were taken up by the guilds. Up to that time, the sword and hoop dances had played an integral part in village life, where they were danced by the young men in accordance with the time of year when these dances should be performed. It is because, in the age before the formation of the guilds, when it was only the peasants who performed these dances, that very little written reference was made to sword and hoop dancing. However, with the advent of the guilds, came the sources upon which researchers rely: account books itemizing the amounts paid to such-and-such a group for performing the sword dance on such-and-such an occasion. A literate middle class began to emerge with the ability to document these ancient dances. With the adoption by the guilds of these dances, after the middle of the fifteenth century, the references become legion.

The first of these is from the the year 1446, from Braunschweg. In the 'Shigt Bok der Stadt Brunswyk', it is noted that, on February 28th, 1446, on 'Fastnacht' (Shrove Tuesday), the assistants of the Blacksmiths came together to dance with swords. It seems natural and obvious that the guild of Blacksmiths should adopt the sword dance as a part of their ceremonial, just as it was for the Coopers, who put metal rings on their barrels, to take the hoop dance as their particular dance. The book goes on to mention that the mayor of the town was not too keen on them performing the sword dance, in case inter-guild rivalries led to fighting and bloodshed. A reference two years later, from the town of Eger, related to the payment of twenty groschen to strolling players for dancing the sword dance on Fastnacht. Later documents from

1549 to 1551 mention the performance of the sword dance by the sons of the upper class burghers. From 1488 to 1524 there is an annual account of the dance being performed by the guild of Furriers. In 1551, in the town of Hall, it was a group of acrobats who performed dances with swords. The transition from dancing for pleasure or tradition to the paid entertainer had been made.

Henceforth, in the urban environment, the sword dance is the prerogative of the guilds and the professionals, though, undoubtedly, out in the countryside the age-old traditions would be preserved, and the traditional dances would have been performed at the requisite times of the year. A notice from February 19th, 1487, in Cologne, sets out that the Blacksmiths' apprentices might be allowed to dress up and perform their mummings, but that it was too dangerous for them to perform the sword dance.

The first of very many references in the Nürnberg archives to sword dancing is from the year 1490, in which mention is made to the performing of the sword dance during the 'Schembartlaufen' of 1462. Here it was the Knifesmiths and the Furriers who danced it. An account in 1701 relates how in 1349, after a revolt by the Knifesmiths against the authorities of Nürnberg, they nonetheless danced with their swords unsheathed. References to sword dances by the guilds were regular right through the following centuries. So we learn that in Strasbourg, in 1794, the Shoemakers, Furriers, and Bakers also performed the sword dance. By then, the

31. Hoop dance from a Nürnberg Schembart manuscript. German, c.1561.

Butchers and several of the other guilds had got into the act, and all were adopting sword or hoop dances as a part of their guild ceremonials, and both the sword and the hoop dance might be performed at the same time. Several engravings from the fifteenth and sixteenth centuries (ill. 114-116) show processions, with musicians leading different groups of sword and hoop dancers.

Often these dances were accompanied by songs. Here is one of thirteen verses used to accompany one of the Knifesmiths' sword dances:

Danntzen wir den Messerer Tanntz Zu dieser Fassenacht.
Wir haben geferdte Röcklein ann,
Sind gar zierlich gemacht.
Die Klingen lassen wir schallenn
Wir springen dapferr dreinn,
Der Tanz (tut) uns gefallen,
Wir tanntzen ihn gemainn.

"We are dancing the Knifesmiths' dance, on this Shrove Tuesday. We have handsome costumes, which are very well fashioned. We let the sword blades ring out; we jump bravely about; we do like the dance; we dance it together."

In Germany, the earliest record we have of the 'Schembart-' or 'Schönbartlaufen' is 1350, but this Carnival celebration dates back to ancient times. Guilds and town councils had come into conflict during the fourteenth century, and there were insurrections and bloodshed. The Butchers' and Cutlers' guilds, when trouble flared up in 1348-9, remained loyal to the city council, and were rewarded with the prerogative of dancing during the Carnival celebrations, and they have performed a hilt-and-point sword dance periodically since that time. That the dance belongs to a pre-Christian ritual is shown by the season at which it is performed, the 'turn of the year', when spirits from the underworld return, and the dancers, wearing bells, and disguised to represent both the returned souls and those who drive them away, when it is time for them to return from whence they came. The Butchers' privilege was to dress their gang as *Schemen*, or spirits, and these seem to have adopted something of the rôle of bodyguards to the Butchers, and were not allowed to 'run' with the Coopers' guild. Dating from the middle of the sixteenth century there are various prints (ill. 29 & 30) showing two locks formed by two sides of sword dancers, and the two men mounted on their swords are fighting. The Swiss Guards of Louis XIII of France also used to perform this mock combat.

Through the writings of Ambrosius Oesterreicher in 1561 and Hans Weber in 1600, we learn that on Sunday, February 16th, 1561, and on the following Monday, the Knifemakers were permitted to show their dance. They were nicely dressed in white tunics, caps on their heads and swords in their hands. Horseriders were on hand to keep back the crowd of onlookers. They danced in front of the houses of the city dignitaries, showing their various figures: "A frisking figure, a dance in three time, the Bridge, the Making of the Rose, the Parade to follow the Battle", as well as the scene of decapitation, and fights with other weapons and sticks. The second day saw a repeat performance for the general public in the market place, and the whole thing was rounded off by a 'Dance of the Virgins'.

In 1604, in order to overcome a ban on performing the sword dance, the Blacksmiths of Hildesheim gave as their excuse the beneficial nature of dancing it in promoting fitness and agility amongst the farm labourers.

As the guilds lost ground economically at the beginning of the seventeenth century, when also trade in Germany declined and the whole situation became aggravated by the devastation of the Thirty Years' War (1618-1648), the members of the guilds were no longer permitted to carry swords. The sword dances were now carried on by those who were allowed to carry weapons, that is, the soldiers. But after the devastations of the Thirty Years' War, weapon-carrying soldiers were unwelcome visitors to the towns and villages. The heyday of the guilds with their elaborate processions was all but over. However, it soon occured to the young people that they could earn a few pennies by dancing in public. They based their dances on the old sword dances, and used lances, sticks, axes or clubs instead.

Hoops were often substituted for swords, but the same figures were performed and the lock made, and they were performed at the same time of year, during Fastnacht. In fact, on some occasions, the dancers used hoops in the afternoon, and in the evening danced the same dances but carrying swords instead. Such a Coopers' guild hoop dance, the 'Schäfflertanz' is performed every seven years in Munich. That it started life as a sword dance is attested by a reference in 1788 to the hoop dance alternating with the sword dance, and presumably the Coopers thought it more appropriate to use their cask hoops instead of swords.

A Coopers' dance in Hungary started out as a sword dance. In the wine-growing region of Erdőbénye, the guild members danced the 'Bodnártánc. It is unique in Hungary, and it has been presumed that it was introduced by German settlers. A linked-sword dance, it was used in the initiation rites of admission into the guild for new members. Swords were later replaced by other instruments according to the craft dancing it: for example, sticks, hoops, kerchiefs.

Fastnacht is actually only one day, Shrove Tuesday, but the term has been extended to encompass the whole of Carnival. Indeed, in Cologne, Fastnacht begins on November 11th and is celebrated right up to Shrove Tuesday itself. Also in common with the sword dance was the adoption of hoop dances by the various guilds. Almost every guild had its own sword or hoop dances. Especially prominent in city archives were the guilds of Swordsmiths, Knifesmiths, Barrel-makers, Furriers and Tailors. Less prominent, it is somewhat surprising to find the dances performed even by the guild of Book-binders.

The earliest reference we have to hoop dancing, unlike the sword dances mentioned by Tacitus, dates only from 1411, when, in Bautzen, it was danced as a guild dance. According to the Starkschen Chronicle of the city of Nürnberg, it was performed as part of the Schembartlaufen of 1462. In 1487 sword and hoop dancing was forbidden by the town council of Cologne. Tobias Schmidt wrote in his 'Zwickauer Chronicle', in the year 1518: "Twenty-six men danced during the night in the courtyard of the castle a hoop dance. Each dancer had a burning light on his head." In 1538, the Tailors of Strasbourg danced a hoop dance wearing Moorish costume. The chronicler goes on: ". . . and they were all blackened like the Moors, with black knitted caps and white veils, with white shirts, and bells tied round their knees, and large hoops decorated with ivy. They also danced this dance throughout the town." In 1541, the Tailors obtained permission to dance the hoop dance at the same time that the Shoemakers were allowed to perform the sword dance. In 1550, the Butchers, in white shirts, danced in Esslingen, during the night, with hoops and lights, accompanied by drums and pipes. In 1551, in Ulm, eight dancers, dressed up as farmers, danced during the day the sword dance and at night the hoop dance.

Among Man's earliest beliefs was the idea that the sky was the seat of all natural forces: wind, rain, thunder, lightning. The vault of the heavens he saw as a vast arch, and represented this in his ritual dances by a half-hoop, an arc. This would serve also to represent the arch of the rainbow which joined the sky to the earth. The rainbow was linked quite obviously with rain, and its colours were reflected in those used in the multi-coloured ribbons which decorated the arches and the costumes. To stimulate Nature to be bountiful, Man would also decorate his arches with fruits or vegetables of the greatest size and perfection which he could manage to collect.

Arch dances are almost numberless, and are (or were) to be found scattered far and wide across Europe. Today they exist in profusion in France and Spain, and to a lesser degree elsewhere. The chronicle of Buëhler mentions, for example, that in 1536 during Carnival, the Tailors ran through the streets, their faces, hands and feet blackened. They were dressed in white shirts and breeches tied above the knees by ribbons with bells tied to them. They held large hoops wreathed with ivy, and were preceded by a leader and a fool who amused the onlookers.

As with the sword dance, we have a description from 1555 by Olaus Magnus of a sort of hoop dance using bows:

> *Another practice of the young men is that they dance according to certain rules a bow or hoop dance. They go round in a circle singing quietly about the deeds of ancient heroes, and then to flutes and drums perform some very noisy music. With slackened bows they go for a certain time quicker and weave, as normally with the swords, a 'Rose' in the shape of a hexagon. They jump in like manner to fish through the hoops, and in order to make it nicer and louder, they wear brass bells and jingles. Following the leader (named the King) they copy him in their movements and singing.*

The hoop dance, like the sword dance, was adopted by the guilds, but it was based on a more ancient traditional peasant dance. There is a poem of 1602 by Jakob Frischlin, which tells us that: "In between their work the peasants danced in a circle in rustic fashion, holding a special bow, and Hansel kissed Gretel, and they threw themselves around in the dance, with great laughter to the accompaniment of bagpipe and shawm and country song." The poem goes on to describe the peasants performing various other dances including a 'guild' dance, which is further evidence of the rustic origins of the hoop dance.

The hoop dances were, among the peasants, often linked with poems of a certain dramatic nature (compare the link between sword dances and mummers' plays). In parts of Austria, they were still being performed up to the Second World War. The salt-miners took over the sword and hoop dances and continued the tradition of reciting the poems which accompanied the dances, but gradually, in the hands of the guilds and salt-miners, the spectacle of the grand processions gained ground at the expense of the poems, which were gradually discarded and forgotten. Interestingly, in the hoop dance of the Hüttenbergers and the Gastein miners' dance, the mine workers gave to their dance figures the names of the various features from their mines, such as: 'vaults', 'tunnels', 'bridges', 'galleries', and 'pit shafts'.

Here is a verse which was used to introduce a hoop dance from Bavaria:

Ich tritt herein wohl also fest,
grüss den Hausherrn, die Hausfrau und alle andern Gäst.
Grüssen wir uns einander nit,
die Leute möchten moan,
wir warn koane rechten Spieler oder Roaftänzer nit.
Rechte Spieler und Roaftänzer sind wir genannt,
wir ziehen durch Königs- und Kaiserland.
Wir reisen ein Gasen aus, die andere ein,
dabei können wir noch brav lustige Spieler und Roaftänzer sein.
Unsere Eltern habn gmeint, wire warn schon lang gstorbn und verdorbn.
Jetzt sein wir wieder lustige Spieler und Roaftänzer wordn.
Hiaz bin i do unter dem grean Ring,
werd schaun, dass ich mich kann drauss schwing.
Jetzt bin ich do unter den gran Kranz,
Spielleut machts mir auf's lustigen Roaftanz."

32. Fastnacht hoop dance of the Nürnberg craftsmen. German, c.1561.

"In comes I, so fit and strong. I greet the host, hostess and all the other guests. We do not greet each other (in case) the people may complain (that) we are not true players and dancers. (But) we are well-known as players and dancers. We travel through kingdoms and empires; we go from street to street, where we can be good and merry players and dancers. Our parents think that we are long dead and gone, (but) now we have become merry players and dancers. Here am I under the green ring. I will see if I can swing outwards. Now I am under the green wreath. Musicians, let me have a lively dance!"

Similar verses are to be found accompanying many garland dances from the sixteenth and seventeenth centuries. Other verses tell of the leader's prodigious appetite, which explains his great size, or they may become dialogues between the various characters to amuse the audience. Thus one dancer tells that he is a great eater, another gambles with the devil, a third is like a witch cooking broth with rats and mice, making medecines and potions out of strange ingredients. A fourth is a noble hunter of deer and mountain goats, though he has not actually succeeded in bagging any. A fifth steals wood from the forest to sell in the market, in order to get money to spend on getting drunk at the inn. One might ask a companion to shave him because he cannot shave himself, or extract a tooth which is aching. They also played the rôles of travelling quacks and barbers in the plays which they performed along with their dances. And so, with a great deal of slapstick, noise and 'business', a 'customer' would be seized and shaved, or have a tooth pulled (ill. 32 & 46), upon which he fell to the ground as if dead. With much further ado he was revived. These plays are still to be seen today in certain country areas in Germany at Fastnacht.

The time of year of the performance of these plays and dances is indicative of the nature of the themes, whilst a further indication of their ritual nature is in the names given to the characters in the dances by the peasants. So we get: 'Green in the Wood', 'Smell of the Beetroot', 'Jump in the Clover'. Perhaps also the number of the participants is significant. The twelve dancers may have something to do with the twelve months of the year. A series of illustrations by Hans Sebald Beham (ill. 57) relates characters to the times and seasons of the year: 'Philip May', 'John Fallowman', 'Egidius Autumnman', 'Simon Wineman', 'Martin Winterman', and so on. Twelve was the usual number to perform sword and hoop dances in Germany, unlike the Celts whose 'magic' number was thirteen, in relation to the thirteen lunar months of the year.

Basle and Bern in Switzerland also possessed Coopers' hoop dances. The leader carried a small hoop with three glasses filled with wine. The other dancers carried larger hoops and were linked in a chain, jumping over and passing under them, before forming a basket-like lock, into which the leader stepped and was hoisted three times, and then the hoops were raised to form an arbour, under which the leader stood. He had to swing the wine-filled glasses over and under his legs, round his head, and to drink the health of his patrons from the middle glass. Amongst their number, the troupe had a bride and groom who usually ended up in the fountain, thus keeping alive the tradition of the fertility figures of the bridal pair and the water magic for the crops.

Illustrations of the sixteenth century show scenes of Carnival in Zürich (ill. 27), with people in animal disguise, fools and clowns, the sword dancers with bells on their legs, wearing decorated caps and their faces blackened. An eighteenth-century painting of the Basle Coopers' dance shows the dancers in procession, followed by a leaf-bedecked Bacchus sitting astride an enormous cask, drinking wine, with Harlequin in attendance. It is not surprising to find this connection between the Coopers and Bacchus, for both, for different reasons, had an interest in wine. In the Fêtes des Vignerons in Switzerland, France, or wherever the grape is grown, out come the Coopers with their hoops and wine glasses to celebrate the vine. Even in strictly Calvinist Geneva, the Coopers danced their hoop dance.

A further connection between the hoop dance and the sword dance is the sword-dance plays, which occasionally accompany the hoop dance. There is also the fascinating woodcut by Olaus Magnus (ill. 34) of a Swedish sword dance taking place in a courtyard. On the right-hand side of the picture six men, with swords held erect in their right hands, are dancing in twos. Behind them six more men are dancing with hoops. They are accompanied by a piper, a drummer, and two horn players. This comes from his 'Historiae de gentibus Septentrionalibus', published in Rome in 1555. Here is his excellent description of the dance:

> *This dance takes place in accordance with artistic rules and with song with a Leader at their head, is learned during their adolescence under the guidance of skilled men. They produce this play publicly in Lent. It is called by the Italian word 'Masquerade'. Before Lent young men in great numbers practise this dance for eight days. It is done like this: first they make three turns with swords raised but sheathed. Then they unsheathe and raise the swords. They then stretch out their arms and while the dancing slows down they each seize the other's sword so that one holds the point and the other the hilt and at the same time they change order so as to form a hexagon which is called the Rose. This they dissolve suddenly by drawing out the swords and again raising them whereby a Rose is formed over each man's head. Finally they strike the flats of their swords violently against each other, dance slowly and solemnly then quicker and eventually at a breathless pace. Those who have not seen this with their own eyes can hardly imagine what a beautiful and delightful sight it is when a numerous and armed company at the short commands of one man quickly and with agility get into formation for this act. The clergy are allowed to join in as it is performed in a courteous and respectful manner.*

The Swedes also danced a hoop dance and a play, in which the verses (in Swedish, Latin and German) were sung. In Finland, in the predominantly Swedish-speaking town of Porvoo (Borgå), a hoop dance was once performed. Denmark too must have had a sword dance, for the Smiths' Guild of Copenhagen, in 1554, set out fines for dancers who were clumsy, let go the hilt of the sword, or tripped over the sword, and in 1431, dancers in Ålborg who failed to appear without a valid reason were also fined. In both Copenhagen and Ålborg, the sword dance was performed at Carnival time, but it is significant that the dances belonged to the towns, and there is no record of them having been performed in the countryside. These Scandinavian examples were in all probability imported from Germany, to be used as guild dances, in imitation of those of the various cities of the Hanseatic League, which had such strong trade links with Scandinavia.

In some places, the swords are gone completely, leaving only hoop or garland dances. In the Spanish-Basque province of Guipuzkoa, the dancers actually put down their swords and pick up hoops, and continue to dance the same figures as before, now linked by arches instead.

In Valencia in Spain, they have an ancient dance which they call 'Danza de Polonesas', in which four girls carry arches completely unadorned (the arches not the girls). The image of the celestial arch serves also as the bow of the hunter or warrior. In the 'Ball dels Arets' and the 'Savoiana', young shepherds carry bells on their chests, and hold arches decorated with multicoloured ribbons and little bells. At Saint Isle de Vallaltat, a devil who heads the 'Dance of the Gypsies' is placed under an arch, and wears multicoloured ribbons at his wrists, elbows and knees.

A similar representation is to be found in 'Los Arcos' of Burgos, in which twelve girls arrive in two parallel lines, cast out, and then form a circle, performing *chassés-croisés* which they repeat four times. They then interlace the arches to make a cage in which they enclose a child, symbol of growth. The cage is then formed into a spiral which divides into two columns, eventually finishing in four lines. At Belorado the arches are made of willow wands and are decorated with

33. Coopers' dance in Münich. German, c.1830.

flowers. The dancers wear white clothes hung with garlands, coloured ribbons and scarves. Again the dancers perform *chassés-croisés* and pass a child underneath the arches. At Betanzos on May 2nd, children hold an arch over a three year-old whose eyes are blindfolded. They sing that winter is about to finish, and then, uncovering the infant's eyes, they herald the coming of spring. The infant symbolizes the new god, spring incarnate. This ritual has degenerated almost into a children's game, and in Majorca at Alcora, it is the children who dance the 'Cercollets' in which they form a spiral, again a pattern full of symbolism.

The dance of the 'Pastores' at Castellon de la Plana, Villaréal, has shepherdesses wearing white skirts decorated with coloured bands, flowered hats, and carrying arches garlanded with greenery and flowers. The shepherdess who leads the two lines of dancers holds her apron out in front of her, appealing thus for an abundant harvest. San Sebastian's arch dance is for the men only, and the dancers are chosen for their tall stature. They carry especially large arches covered in foliage and flowers, and form up in two lines, their leader going ahead of them.

The 'Cercollets' of Villafranca del Penedès is again typical. The dancers in white tunics and floral hats advance carrying arches, in two lines of four dancers preceded by a leader. After the ritual promenade in serpentine form in and out of the lines, they all face each other, swaying their arches. The leader, moving off to his left, walks in a zig-zag path, snaking his way between the dancers, and then repeats this to the right. Each dancer holds out one end of his arch to his neighbour, and they then make a spiral, bringing together the tops of the arches to form an umbrella. They then set a child on top, and a man climbs onto this platform and hoists the child high above his head. Setting the child down again, the man then turns himself upside down, grasping on to an arch, and in this curious position he makes his *parlement* or speech. This inverted position has been interpreted as a rain charm.

Sometimes this arch dance, its mimed drama evoking the renewal of Nature, is woven into the 'Moxiganga'. This name which derives from the Arabic *Magxiguachah* implies the idea of the hidden face, that is, the dancers must be masked or at least have their faces blackened to prevent recognition. This dance finishes in some of the dancers climbing on the others' shoulders to make an 'altar', a high tower, again interpreted as a sign for Nature to provide abundant crops of just such a height. This human tower is also used to complete the dance 'Els Arcs' of the region of Burgos, in which the dancers sway their flower and bell-decked arches from side to side. Another 'Moxiganga' commences with the dance, the 'Cercollets', and then the dancers take hold of shields made of wood, which they strike with sticks or swords. They raise in the air their captain, who says his piece, whilst another dancer is hoisted onto the shoulders of his companions and unfurls a banner. The rest of the company point towards the sky with their index fingers. It is a rain-charm, in this case linked to the prosperity of the grape harvest. In the Christianized version, the pointed fingers are replaced by lighted candles. At Llofrin, for the 'Ball dels Cercols' the dancers dress in white tunics, their bodies garlanded with flowers, bells on their legs, and wearing pointed hats topped by multicoloured ribbons and bells. They carry floral arches. The pointed 'dunces' hats are rain-charm headgear, though such hats were also worn by magicians, perhaps for similar ends.

Cantabria in northern Spain, virtually cut off from the south by a dramatic and almost impassable mountain range, retains many ancient rites, little changed over the centuries. As expected, the dancers wear white clothes with bells attached, red neckerchiefs, and red scarves wrapped several times around their waists. We find here again the castle or human tower, with the most agile member of the group climbing to the top to give his speech. The dancers are usually accompanied by a fool variously called: 'Rabanero', 'Zorroloco', or 'Zoromoco', according to the region. He sets about the dancers and the onlookers lashing out with a stick to which is attached a horse's tail or plait of hair, or a club with studs on it. He wears the pointed hat of the 'masters of the rain', a huge bell suspended from his neck and smaller bells covering his chest. He marks out the rhythm of the dance on castanets. For the dance, the 'Arcos', the dancers make a figure named the 'triumphal arch' in which six of the group line up with one knee on the ground behind their captain. The 'Zoromoco' stands behind them flanked by two supporters. These three then climb upon the shoulders of the others, and lift their arches, while the leader makes a salute. Next they form two parallel lines and make a vault with their arches, passing underneath the arch formed by the leader and the next dancer, and then repeat this over the inverted arch. A circle is formed after various figures have been performed, and the arches are set about the neck of the leader to symbolize his death. He soon revives, however, to dance a lively solo. Similar dances, but with a multiplicity of variations, are to be found in village after village in this wild region. Always the dances are of a solemn and sacred nature.

In France too arch dances are legion: the 'Cerceaux' dance of Quercy; the 'Ramadet' of Gascony; the 'Treilles' of the Languedoc, the 'Cieuclé' and the 'Jardinières' of Provence are the most popular.

The 'Treilles' of the Languedoc is specially adapted to a vine-growing region: the arches are decorated with leafy vine branches and grapes. The dancers, again dressed in white, with red *taioles* or scarves wrapped about their waists, make serpentine figures over the ground. They then form two parallel lines moving outwards and inwards to form a double circle or figure-of-eight before ending up again in two lines. The dancers seem to imitate the movements of the ancient grape gatherers, but actually they are performing the limping step which is to be found all over Europe, and serves to honour the lame god of wine, Dionysos, in an effort to promote fruitfulness. At a given command, they move forwards inverting their arches – an appeal for rain. In the procession in Béziers on Ascension Day, the guild of Bakers follows the cortège of the 'Treilles', their heads crowned with foliage and a round loaf of bread in their hands, as if to associate a rite to protect the vine with one similarly to serve the corn, these two elements, wine and bread, being considered, in the Mediterranean basin, as essential to the well-being of Man. The 'Treilles' was danced "very well and in great triumph", in 1503, before Archduke Philip, son-in-law of Ferdinand of Aragon, and again, in 1564, before Charles IX.

The 'Jardinières' of Provence, based on the magic encircling of one's territory, is reminiscent of the cortèges which the Etruscans and the Romans used to make around their fields to purify them and to make them prosper. Christianized, they became part of the Rogation processions instituted for similar ends, in 471, by St. Mamert, bishop of Vienne. They took place after the three days of abstinence and prayers which preceded Ascension. Originally they were performed by women, which implies that they were a rain charm. With the old reasons for the rituals gradually losing their purpose, the dance came to be performed by both sexes. Today it is usually performed by a line of men holding floral arches, and girls with aprons folded at the waist and carrying baskets of flowers, fruit or vegetables. Each man holds one end of the arch out to the girl opposite, thus forming a vault, under which the couples pass in turn, and they then perform the same figure passing over the arches which have been inverted. The arches are next crossed, a figure-of-eight is formed, followed by a large circle, in which the girl to the left of each man is 'sheltered' by his arch. Then a serpentine figure is danced by the girls moving in front of and behind the men until they return to their places. The dancers reform their lines, and a young 'god' appears, carrying on his shoulder an urn from which water trickles, yet another symbol of rain. Sometimes the urn is carried on the end of a pole. One end of each dancer's arch is placed against the urn so that the men form a circle, the girls standing on the inside of this circular tunnel. The dancers perform gestures suggestive of pouring out libations and hand movements indicative of plant growth. Leaps into the air to stimulate Nature terminate the dance. The urn is supposed to be broken at the end of each dance as, indeed, they still do in Spain in the 'Morratxes'. Usually, in France, the urn is dispensed with altogether, the dancers in the centre content merely to hold the end of each arch.

In the 'Jardinières', the dancers usually have a leader who calls out the figures. He has replaced the fool, an indispensable character in vegetation rites, who by his gestures and contortions has to attract the mirth and laughter of the onlookers, which is in itself a rain charm. The dancers again use the *ped-cauquet* or limping step. The crosses made by crossed arches are called in French *casse-diables* (devil-breakers), and were certainly a pre-Christian exorcism. Bells on the arches frightened away evil spirits, whilst serpentine, spiral, and figure-of-eight figures were also significant. Originally, the ceremony was a part of the encircling of one's fields and farms to bring protection and prosperity, but over the centuries it degenerated into a mere spectacle, and was used to welcome guests of honour.

There are sword-dance plays in Germany, but rarely as developed as those found in England or Greece. Usually they take the form of a few verses spoken by the leader from his perch on top of the lock made by the swords of the dancers. But Unterwesen stages a performance in which a sword dance, a bow dance and a hoop dance are followed by a 'Ship-on-Wheels', manned by pirates, which is attacked by a king and guisers mounted on horseback. Thuringia has a plough bearing reminiscent of the English one, and Lübeck's Bakers' guild performed a play with King Arthur, Charlemagne, Geoffrey of Bouillon (a Crusader hero), Caesar, Alexander and Hector, Joshua, David and Judas Maccabeus – a wonderful jumble. There is the inevitable fight and symbolic death. At Überlingen on Lake Constance, the Vintners' Guild dancers come out on Shrove Tuesday. In the morning they go to church, all except the fool who is not allowed in. Neither must he speak, but only crack his long horse-whip as he guides the dancers to their place of performance and goes about collecting money. Interspersed with hilt-and-point circles, the dancers perform five figures, which include arches and a snail, before they each grab an onlooker and dance a waltz to finish.

In Austria, we find hoop and garland dances in which, instead of forming a lock, the arched garlands are used to make an arbour. In Oberwölz in Styria, and Hüttenberg in Carinthia, we again meet the tooth-extraction and shaving mime (ill. 32 & 46). Hüttenberg also has a bride, though now she is no longer the man-woman figure, but the local beauty queen. She is called the Bergmann's Bride, and dances a ceremonial dance with the Bergcommissioner. The Palental has fools dressed in clothes covered in little tabs of cloth, and they bring luck and fertility to the fields and farms. Their name of *Mehlweiben* (Mealwives) suggests that once they were man-woman figures. Pulling a tab from their clothing and putting it under a hen will encourage it to lay.

The Salzkammergut is a mining area *par excellence*. Its mines, which date back far into prehistoric times, produce, or have produced, gold, silver, lead, tin, coal and, above all, salt which gives its name to the region. And here lies a whole conglomeration of sword-dance villages, many of which have preserved their dances up to the present day. The dancers of Dürrenberg near Hallein perform a mimed dance which depicts their salt-mining work. Twenty men, dressed in miners' working clothes, a sergeant and a flag-bearer, perform this ceremony. Nowadays carrying wooden swords, to the accompaniment of fife and drum, they perform various figures, the sergeant speaking a verse for each one. They perform a circle in hilt-and-point formation around the flag-bearer, and make a bridge with crossed swords over which the sergeant steps, before making a 'mine gallery' through which they all go, and a ladder of swords from the top of which the sergeant recites another of his verses before sliding down. They then mime bucket-lifting, and following this they make the lock on which the sergeant is lifted. A few trick or display items conclude the performance. Other dances are still to be seen in Aussee, Ebensee and Mondsee, as well as in Halstatt, the village which gave its name to the first Iron Age period.

Czechoslovakia can still boast a handful of sword dances, which are currently performed. The village of Podámcok possesses one in which six dancers, bedecked

34. Sword and hoop dance from 'History of the Northern Peoples' by Olaus Magnus. Swedish, 1555.

in hats with ribbons, feathers, and sprays of flowers, carry pliable metal rods. In Stráni, Moravia, their swords are flat and broad, and are strung on one side with small brass rings that jingle like bells at every movement. The name of their dance is 'Fasancare', a Slavic corruption of the German Fasching, Carnival. They take to the houses they visit good luck and prosperity, perform their dance and enact a fragment of a play. Moravia is yet another mining region which has its sword- and hoop-dance villages. More lie in the Carpathians and in the Tatra Mountains near to Hungary. Here in Bystrice, four men form the lock of swords, while a fifth carries a basket of gifts to be handed to the householders who share in the luck of their visit. They dance to the accompaniment of a strange song, which seems to infer a ritual killing, which is no longer a part of the dance. Kaplitz in Bohemia has a Carnival sword dance, which has a special figure called the 'gate' through which the dancers pass. Another village has a straw man; the height he manages to reach as he jumps over the swords, indicates the height to which the hemp will grow. At each house visited by the dancers, the mistress must dance with the straw man. In two German-speaking areas, Oberhai and Ruckendorf, there are folk plays attached to the dances. Transylvania, with its racial mix of Hungarian, Romanian, and German, is another mining region where sword dances are to be found, some belonging to Shoemakers' and Coopers' guilds.

A garland dance is often performed at weddings by boys and girls together. 'Arquillas' (Little Circles) is to be found in the Basque Country and right the way across to Galicia. In the Basque Country today, on both sides of the Pyrenees, one can find a dance performed with arches, danced by girls alone, but this is the invention of the National Youth Societies of Biscay, and is not traditional. The Franco régime did much to destroy the traditional ways, and encouraged such inventions.

If the 'lock' was a symbol of ritual death, it was also used to symbolize the elevation of a king or leader, so that he could be hailed by his people. Witigis, who was chosen to succeed Theodoric, king of the Ostrogoths, gives a striking account of his own elevation:

> *Our kinsmen the Goths amid a fence of circling swords raising us in ancestral fashion upon a shield by divine guidance bestowed on us the Kingly dignity . . . For know that not in the corner of a presence chamber but in wide spreading plains I have been chosen King.*

Pelayo, successor to the last Visigothic king was in turn raised on the shields of his adherents, and in the Asturias and neighbouring New Castile, the sword-dance lock is called the *escudo* or shield. Gregory of Tours described how the Franks also raised Clovis and again his grandson, Sigibert, on their shields. Similarly, according to Hungarian folk mythology, Arád, the conqueror and first prince of Hungary, when he was chosen leader by the seven tribes he led in battle, was raised up on the shields of the seven tribal chiefs. In England, there are a few sword dance teams who similarly hoist their leader aloft, and one German side hedges its bets by first decapitating the fool before raising their captain on their intertwined swords.

Besides dances with swords or hoops, there is a whole variety of dances from almost every country of Europe using every imaginable type of instrument or tool.

Among the oldest must be those using spears or lances. Illustrations of these go back to the Ice Age. There is a Bronze Age plate from Torslunda in Sweden and a bronze knife from Lycke in Denmark which show spear dances. The spear dancer in the Torslunda illustration is accompanied by a figure wearing a wolf mask.

In Lungau, Austria, there is a dance called 'Russentanz', using spears and sabres. In Spain, the 'Dantza de Romeros' also uses spears. As in other countries, the agricultural labourers and shepherds danced the ancient weapon dances, with intricate steps and figures, using whatever instruments came to hand. The Carnival *Perchten* dancers used to jump high over their shepherds' sticks. In the Basque Country we find them using axes (Jorrai Dantza), as they do in the mountain regions of the Carpathians and Tatras. In the Asturias in northern Spain, there is a 'Danza Prima', and again in the Basque Country the 'Pordoidantza' which use spears. All over Spain we can find stick dances. In Naples and Ischia they decorate their sticks with flowers. Variations of stick dances are found in Hungary, where the stick is passed from hand to hand under the legs. In Czechoslovakia the sticks are embedded in the ground and danced round. Shepherds in the Tyrol also have a stick dance. In Ost Friesland, Pomerania, there are diverse dances using brooms, or those huge spoons used for ladling corn.

The Hungarian 'Hajdú' (Heyducks) use a variety of instruments: swords, sticks, axes, whatever comes to hand. The 'Hajdú' were originally herdsmen who needed to, and well knew how to, defend themselves. They had an important part to play in both the economic and the military life of Hungary during the sixteenth and seventeenth centuries. The 'Hajdú' dance is often used in a wider sense to denote the dance style of those people inhabiting the Carpathian Basin. It is also used to describe men's and couple dances performed without the use of instruments. There have even been references to "women skilled in the Hajdú Dance". Great warriors were not ashamed to display their prowess in this dance, though it has lost something of its popularity since, in certain places, it degenerated into a herdsmen's dance and lost its warlike character. Bagpipe, shawm, fiddle and drum were used to accompany the dances. One tune, or rather rhythm, which became the most characteristic of music was given the name 'Swineherd's' rhythm. In its heyday, the dance was used to display virtuosity at victory feasts, wakes, or court entertainments, and we even hear of 'Hajdú' dances being performed in the heat of battle.

The 'Hajdú' dance could be performed either by a man on his own or in a group, in a linked circle, and, occasionally, dancing in mixed couples. The dance was characterized by the skilful handling of the sword or battle-axe, was mainly improvised, and contained warlike or fighting actions, with crouching and leaping movements. Edward Brown, in 1673, wrote in his 'Brief Account of Some Travels in Hungaria, Servia, Bulgaria etc.':

> *Before I came into Hungaria I observed no shadow or shew of the old Pyrrhical Saltation, or Warlike way of dancing, which the Heyducks practise in this Country. They dance with their naked Swords in their hands, advancing, brandishing and clashing the same; turning, winding, elevating and depressing their bodies with strong and active motions: singing withal their measures after the manner of the Greeks.*

The herdsmen's dances of the Carpathians have preserved many elements of the 'Hajdú' dance, whether it be Hungarians, Gypsies, Slovaks, Ukrainians or Romanians who are performing them. Called variously: 'Hajduch', 'Odzemok', 'Zbójnicki' and 'Haidóu', the remnants of these ancient dances fall into two groups: the 'Botoló' (cudgel) and the Swineherd's dance. The 'Botoló' is perhaps the most ancient and unspoilt herdsmen's stick dance to be found anywhere in eastern Europe. It belongs to the herdsmen and Gypsies of the northeastern fringe of the Great Hungarian Plain. A 'duelling' version of the 'Botoló', with various blows, cuts, thrusts, and warding-off movements is performed using cudgels, swineherds' axes, staffs, shepherds' crooks, whatever instrument comes to hand. The dance is made up of slow steps of attack, dodging and retreating, forwards and backwards, thrusts and withdrawals, with leaps, turns, crouches, kneeling, and even sudden freezing of the actions.

There is also a mixed 'Botoló' in which the man shows off, he carrying a staff or other instrument, she being unarmed. Playfully he attacks her, and displays his skill at keeping his staff turning in close proximity to her body despite her efforts to stop him. The solo version of the 'Botoló' is purely a display of virtuosity in handling the staff, passing it under each leg in turn, round the back of the body, holding it in both hands and jumping over it, or crossing two sticks on the ground and dancing around them in Scottish sword-dance fashion.

The Swineherds' dance was usually danced by two lines of men facing each other, passing their axes back and forth as fast as they could manage, twirling them, and jumping over them, or placing them on the ground and circling round them. Weapons are often replaced by sticks, various batons, even musical instruments, ribbons, hats, whips and bottles. The dances display the brilliance of the dancers in passing the objects used from one to the other, or dancing over them without touching them, kicking them away, or damaging them. Dances of this type were known in most parts of Europe from earliest times. In Hungary, they experienced a veritable renaissance owing to the Turkish wars, and have been preserved in great wealth up to the present day by the herdsmen.

In mountainous Montenegro, a tribe of shepherds who settled there in the early eighteenth century have their own special sword dance, the 'Borbena Rugovska Igra'. Two dancers, wielding curved swords vie with each other for the favours of a girl. The dance ends when the vanquished rival acknowledges defeat. Another dance, now rarely performed, is the 'Kalač', a dance with five figures in which the dancers hold crossed scarves, which probably are substituted for the original swords.

A dirk dance is still performed on the Isle of Man by a descendant of the Kermode family, who were honoured with the title 'King's Dancers'. The 'Reeaghyn dy vannin' Sword Dance of the Kings of Man, is reputed to have been a part of the ancient Celtic Tanist ceremony, in which the heir to the Manx crown took arms, and received the acclamation of the people. The story goes that the Norse, who became rulers of the island, were warriors but not dancers, and so, instead of the heir apparent performing the ceremonial dance himself, a Celtic chieftain was delegated to dance in his stead. The clan so honoured were designated King's Dancers, and this dance has been performed by one of the descendants of the original chieftain since Norse times. In the dance, the dirk is both brandished in the air and laid on the ground to be danced round and over.

Another Manx dance, 'Mylecharanes March' or 'Cutting off the Fiddler's Head' was performed at New Year, and the fiddler was ceremoniously killed when the *laare vane* was carried around. The fiddler was then restored to life, blindfolded and led towards the *laare vane*. He knelt down with his head resting in her lap and answered questions put to him by the company, his answers supposed to be oracular. Questions often related to courtship or marriages, prospects for the new season's crops, catch and weather. In the dance, six men each carry two stout sticks, and strike their own and their companions' sticks during the various figures and whilst performing the *sand step*. This involves making three quick kicks round and outwards without the sole of the foot completely losing contact with the ground, and then bringing it across behind the other foot, transferring the weight simultaneously, at the same time hopping on the supporting leg. The fiddler who accompanies the dance is for his pains ceremoniously killed in the last figure. The dancers circle the fiddler, holding their neighbours' sticks as well as their own, and dance clockwise, making the circle ever smaller. When the fiddler is so hemmed in that he can no longer play, each man draws his sticks out and upwards, completely hiding the fiddler, who drops to the ground, and clash their sticks together above him with a wild shout. The dance is interesting in that it combines some of the elements of both morris and hilt-and-point sword dancing, though the time of year when it is performed (New Year) must set it in the latter category.

'Bwoaill baccagh', also from the Isle of Man, is a dance for six men each carrying a short fisherman's knife tucked into his belt. The dancers enter and form two lines, before each man in turn throws his knife into the ground. Then they squat and perform a cobbler's step, another figure, and repeat the cobbler's step, thrusting their legs out to the sides. Then they take up their knives and perform a figure, tapping each other's knives as they pass. To end the dance, they spring into a line, thrusting their knives above their heads, and shout "hogh!".

'Lheim Braddan (the Salmon Leap) is for thirteen men and also comes from the Isle of Man. Two dancers named *Cummaltaght* and *Eiyreydeyr* are followed by ten *guillyn* in pairs and by *Braddan*. All wear long white tunics and headcloths apart from Braddan, who is bare-headed and wears only a shirt and kilt or trews. Cummaltaght carries a short sword, Eiyreydeyr has a wide criss, while each guillyn carries an osier rod which he holds in his right hand. The guillyn form two lines facing each other, while Cummaltaght and Eiyreydeyr stand at the top facing down the set. The guillyn then dance across and back, and then a hey, whilst Braddan dances jig steps in front of each of them. As he honours each of them before passing on to the next, the guillyn strikes him with his osier rod, before holding it out to be grasped by the neighbour on his left. At the final stroke, Braddan lies down on his back to face Cummaltaght. The guillyn dance round him, and then Braddan leaps over the rods to kneel before Cummaltaght. The guillyn raise their rods with a flourish and shout, and Cummaltaght gives Braddan the sword, and lifts him up to face down the dance, while Eiyreydeyr places the criss round his waist. Then Braddan springs up and is lifted onto their shoulders. They carry him off holding the sword upright, and the guillyn follow carrying their rods held high. In days of old, they called this dance 'Hero-feat'. It is very much in keeping with those dances one sees in France and Spain in which the sacrificial leader is born aloft. It is believed that the dance was formerly done by the fishermen, though it is also known to have been danced by the crofters.

The swords of Irish dances have been replaced by brooms, sticks, garden implements, or merely chalk lines. In Clare, where it is still performed, it is called 'An Gabhairín Buí. In the Stick dance, the dancer passes the stick under his legs, his arms and around his body in time to the music.

The Lithuanians have an axe dance (Kirvio Šokis) in which the boys encircle a girl, who holds an axe and sings. At a certain moment she flings the axe in the air, and whoever catches it is entitled to a kiss. 'Mikita' is a lively men's stick dance.

The Highland Scottish sword dances have been left to last because they do not easily fit in with any other category, except perhaps those dances performed over crossed sticks, ribbons, pieces of straw, tobacco pipes or even chalked lines, which are to be found in most countries of Europe. Little is known of the origins of the Scottish solo dances such as the sword dance Ghillie (sometimes Ghille or Gille) Callum or the other Highland favourite (not itself a sword dance) Seann Trubhais. Concerning this latter dance, one story relates that the dance was indicative of the disaffected Highlanders who, forced to abandon their beloved kilts in place of trews, kicked off this hated garment. If the kilt and the tartan were banned after the rebellion of 1745, nevertheless the trews were a garment commonly worn by Highlanders long before the Jacobite uprisings. Scann Trubhais was probably inspired by an ancient pantomimic and amusing dance which, in the hands of the dancing masters, changed completely into the graceful dance it has now become, and made suitable for girls to perform in the ballroom. Similarly, Ghillie Callum has its own legends, and with its crossed swords has naturally been seen as originating in a dance performed before a battle or to celebrate victory. The dance seems to have been brought down to the Lowlands by Highland cattle drovers who, when their trading was completed, competed with each other (and probably with Lowlanders too) in feats of strength, in piping and in dancing. From this grew the Lowland 'Highland Games' with their piping and dancing competitions.

Founded towards the end of the eighteenth century, the Scottish regiments played a significant part in the propagation of dancing, regularly holding inter-regimental Highland games with their dancing, Foursome Reels, the Highland Fling and Ghillie Callum being the principal dances performed. Just as in Hungary, country lads were lured into the army by the dance; Scottish recruiting sergeants, regularly to be found at country fairs and markets, kitted out in their resplendent dress-uniforms, could hardly fail to attract a crowd of admirers and to impress the girls who in turn would be equally impressed by their suitors accepting the King's shilling, and thus suddenly finding themselves signed up for service.

If Ghillie Callum is a solo dance, the Lochaber and Argyll Broadsword dances are for four dancers, dancing around four swords placed tip to tip in a cross formation. Eventually, the sword-dance steps passed into the dancing masters' repertoires and, considerably adapted, found their way interpolated, quite out of context, into 'ballroom' dances.

— 5 —

MORRIS, CHRISTIANS AND MOORS, AND OTHER BATTLES

I can dance, I can play,
I can do the Shepherd's Hey.
I can dance, I can sing,
I can do most anything.
Song to accompany Shepherd's Hey.

When a bearded, turbaned, Afghan warrior approaches an English morris dancer at a folk festival in Chester and accuses him of 'stealing' his dances (the steps and figures of their respective dances were apparently so similar), where does one begin?

The prehistory of Europe is a subject for endless argument and controversy between scholars, and the origins of European culture still provide cause for much conflict between researchers. Peoples have been moving north, south, east, and west, for many thousands of years. If the Indo-European languages (to which family of languages most European languages belong) came to Europe from the Indian sub-continent, need we be quite so surprised to find dances of striking similarity on the way? Many of the activities engaged in today: folk dancing, mumming, children's games, are far older than they are often given credit for. Some may even date right back to the Stone Age. It would be helpful, then, if we could trace these lines connecting our culture with its roots. However, there is no simple line to trace, or single root from which this rich folk culture has grown. Indo-European languages may have spread across Europe from the east, but where did the builders of the megaliths and monuments, like those at Carnac in Brittany and Stonehenge in England, get their inspiration from? From Crete and the eastern Mediterranean, we were led to believe. But more recent scholarship suggests that these western edifices are even older than those found in the Minoan world, and were probably brought north from Africa.

The peoples who inhabit Europe today are as varied as their languages. Whole groups of tribes have crisscrossed Europe. Some entered Europe from the east, traversed the continent, and passed on into Africa by way of Spain (the Vandals). Others moved northwards from Africa across the straits into the Iberian Peninsula (Iberians). Some settled down, retaining their distinct identity, culture and language (the Magyars and the Basques). Others, over a period of time, intermarried with the indigenous population and produced a new race (Romanians), while some indigenous populations, particularly those living in inaccessible regions of mountains (Albanians), forest (Slavs), or swampland (Karelians), retained their character little affected by outside influences. In fact the peoples of Europe sit on the map of Europe

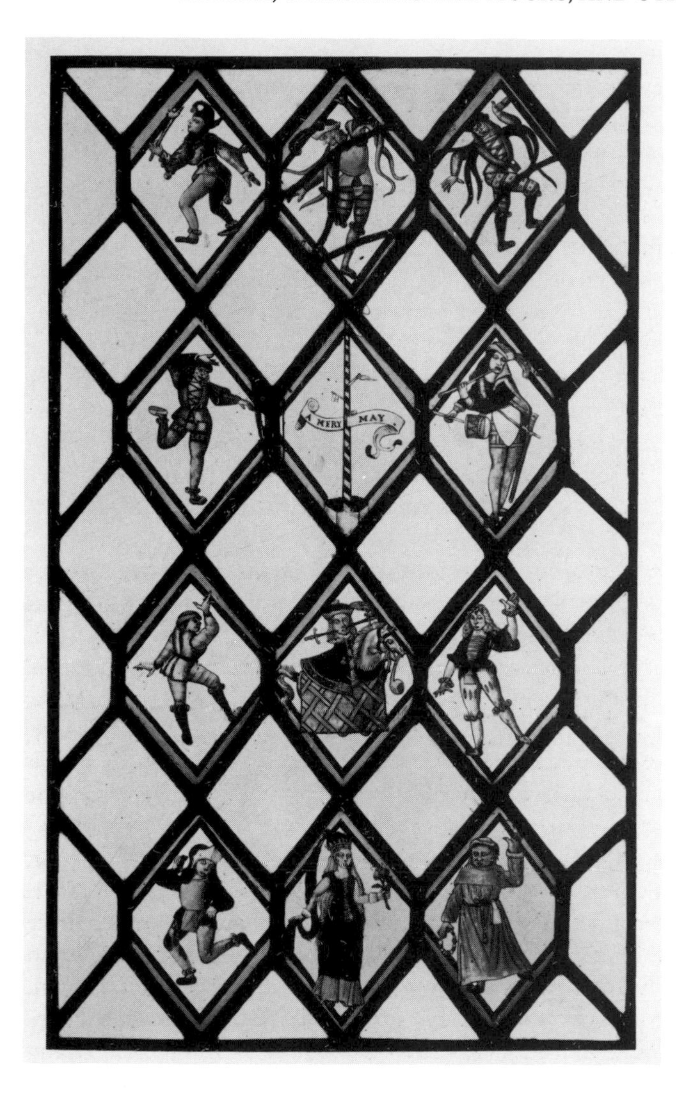

35. The Betley Window. English, c.1510. By courtesy of the Board of Trustees of the Victoria and Albert Museum.

like the colours in a rich Persian carpet. They are individual, unique, possess their own distinct languages and dialects, and sing and dance their own distinct songs and dances.

This is not to say, as has unfortunately been said, that any race of peoples is of 'pure' blood, or superior or inferior in any way to any other. Every people in Europe is a mix of races, and how they have come to be who they are, to live where they are, and to sing and dance the way they do, is the fascinating background to folk culture today.

If we cannot know for certain where morris dancing came from, neither can we be sure from whence it derived its name. The generally accepted theory is that the name comes from the Moors who invaded Spain in the eighth century. But does it?

In medieval England, people used to utter the oath, 'Marry!' or 'Marry Gyp!'. They were swearing an oath in honour of Mary Gypsy, or St. Mary of Egypt. Robin Hood swore by her. This Mary supposedly sailed to the Holy Land, where she settled as an anchorite. She is, in fact, a personification of an ancient sea-goddess named Marian. This sea-goddess, or 'merry-maid' as mermaid used to be written, is the love-goddess who rose from the sea, Aphrodite, one of whose sacred attributes was the scallop-shell (see Botticelli's 'Birth of Venus'; Venus risen from a scallop-shell and standing in a myrtle grove – the myrtle was also sacred to her; compare the offering of myrrh and frankincense, a similar resin-based perfume and an ingredient of incense, to the Virgin Mary at Bethlehem). Mary Gypsy's worship was abolished by the Roman emperor, Constantine – please note, this was 400 years before the Moors came to Spain, and 1000 years before we get the first mention and representations of 'morris' dancing.

Returning crusaders brought the cult of Mary Gypsy back to their home countries, with scallop-shells stitched to their caps, as did the pilgrims who trecked across to St. James's shrine at Santiago de Compostela in north-western Spain. Their songs provided the corps of the repertoire of the troubadours with their tales of courtly love. King Richard I of England introduced these ideas of good manners and courtesy to England – and the country, so engrossed in Mary worship, became 'Merry England'. A brief mention in a sixteenth-century account is enigmatic: "The May Marrians were men in women's clothes contrary to Deut. xxii. 5". Does this refer to May morrismen (Mary's men), or to Mawd-Marian who begins to appear in references to morris company at about this time?

In time, Mary Gypsy became identified with the Saxon 'May Bride', who was paired with the Celtic Merddin (Merlin), now in England named as Robin Hood. 'Rof Brecht Woden' was the Saxon name given to Merddin.

Now Robin Hood features in many morris sides. The name Robin seems to come from an ancient word meaning a ram or a devil. The French *robinet* is so named because in fountains it was shaped like the head of a ram. Once upon a time, witches in Somerset called their god Robin, as did the fourteenth-century witch of Kilkenny, Dame Alice Kyteler call her god, 'Robin son of Art'. The devil was often portrayed as a ram with cloven hooves. Interestingly, the Sanscrit for ram is *huda*. Robin (Latin – rubens) means red-breast. In British folklore the robin red breast symbolised the Spirit of the New Year.

The background to Robin Hood has become complicated by the fact, as so often happens, that a mythical figure has been confused with an historical character. In this case, Robert, son of Adam Hood of Wakefield in Yorkshire, was outlawed in the reign of Edward II, and spent several years as a bandit in Sherwood Forest. Either he, or his later admirers, identified him as Robin, a spirit of the greenwood, who renamed his wife, Matilda 'Maid Marian'. The outlaws formed themselves into a coven of thirteen, and Maid Marian joined in the ritual orgies as Robin's bride.

The May Games, of course, were of much more ancient origin than the legend of Robin Hood. These May Games were the 'Feast of Fools' and the play of the 'King and Queen'. Robin became incorporated into the plays, and new plays were written. Before the end of the fifteenth century, Robin was already one of the leading figures in the springtide festivals. Traditional participants in the morris dance, before the advent of Robin Hood, had been the 'Queen of the May' and the 'Friar'. They were, and remained for some time, quite independent of the Robin Hood legend, and their rôle in the morris dance was separate and unlinked to Robin. The association of Robin Hood and Maid Marian in the spring and summer festivals, grew out of a French pastoral play, 'Robin et Marion', composed in 1283 by Adam de la Halle, and formed part of the May Games in France. This tale is of a shepherdess who resists the advances of a knight, and remains loyal to her lover. An English poet in c.1376 had Robin and Marian participating in rustic festivals, and thus at this early date, we have our two main protagonists linked with the more ancient festivals. Marian became the Queen of the May, and Robin became the King, and together, beginning in the sixteenth century, they presided over the May games.

Lythe and listen, gentilmen,
That be of frebore blode.
I shale you tel of a gode yeman,
His name was Robyn Hode.
(A Gest of Robyn Hode, c.1500)

Hood has the same meaning as 'hod', or the log cut from the sacred oak, which was burned on the yule-fire at midwinter, and in which the robin was believed to reside: the wood-louse which ran from the yule-log as it began to burn was called 'Robin Hood's Steed'. Robin himself, in popular belief, escaped up the chimney in the form of a robin. When yule-tide ended, Robin went out to kill his rival or tanist, Bran, who had enjoyed himself as the 'Lord of Misrule'. Bran disguised himself as a goldcrest wren, but was always caught and killed by Robin.

In Welsh mythology, Llew Llaw was symbolised by a stag which was sacrificially killed and flayed by his twin Gronw, and the pieces distributed among his followers. Perhaps Robin Hood was similarly worshipped as a stag. He is there in the Abbots Bromley Horn Dance. Stag's-horn moss is sometimes called 'Robin Hood's Hatband'. In May the stag's coat turns red. In Greek mythology Actaeon was turned into a stag and was torn to pieces by his own hunting dogs. Perhaps the Abbots Bromley dance belonged to a stag cult.

'Merry' is a corruption of Mary. Days celebrated in her honour were 'merry' days. The most special day was May Day, when people danced around maypoles, ate special cakes, drank special ale, indulged in archery contests, played on *merrytotters* (see-saws), and drank *merribowks* (vats of milk-punch), but most especially of all, and this brought down on them the wrath of the Church, they indulged in 'mad-merry marriages', when lovers went off into the greenwood and did what they were only supposed to do during wedlock. Some of these 'marriages' were blessed by a renegade friar called Friar Tuck. The *merrybegots*, who resulted nine months later, often bore the name of their father: Robinson, Hudson, or more commonly after the name of Robin's deputy, Little John (or Jenkin): Johnson, Jackson, Jenkinson. Morrises and Morrisons may also derive their patronymics from such amorous escapades. And now it should be noted that the word 'morris' was formerly written 'maris', which is to say that 'morrismen' were not Moorish men but Mary's men.

The Christmas merry-night plays, so important a part of English yule-tide festivities, are preserved to this day in the mummers' plays still to be seen on festive occasions in many parts of England. The principal theme is the death and restoration to life of one of the characters, the Christmas King or Christmas Fool. The theme is as old as Methuselah. In ancient Crete the god Dionysos was killed, boiled in a cauldron, and then eaten by the Titans, later to be brought back to life. The Cretans acted out this drama, as later did the 'wild women' during the Lenaean festival at Athens. We can see a representation of this ancient Lenaean religious practice in a Stone Age Aurignacian cave painting at Cogul in north-eastern Spain.

Morris dancing is to be found in many European countries, especially in places made almost inaccessible by mountains, forests, or hostile terrain. The Pauliteiros in the Tràs-os-Montes in Portugal, the Basques, Burgos in northern Spain, all share many common elements: white beribboned clothing, flowered hats, bells. Scattered all over the Balkans, Hungary, Austria and Czechoslovakia, one finds dance troupes similarly attired, and dancing similar steps and figures, waving handkerchiefs or clashing sticks.

Morris dancing evolved out of ancient primitive spring rituals. It pre-dates the coming of the Moors to Spain by thousands of years, and this form of dancing was practised by peoples who never had contact with the Moors. Morris dancing today is the vestiges of pagan religious ritual, where the dancers enacted the eternal drama of death and resurrection, the conflict between light and dark, summer and winter, good and evil.

One custom which took place at Whitsuntide saw the hunting and killing of a stag in the forest of Wychwood. The flesh would be sacrificially eaten by the morrismen. In similar spring rites, the leader or 'squire' of the morris exercised supreme authority. Other characters came to include a hobby-horse or similar animal-man, a fool, and a man-woman or dame, sometimes called a 'Betsy'. In some countries they became Columbuses, Pantaloons or Harlequins. In many Basque masquerades the young men double up and enact subsidiary rôles, often disguising themselves as women. In Portugal, the Pauliteiros are dressed as men-women, with white skirts added to costumes which otherwise are similar to the English morrismen. In Romania, the Călușari are medecine-men. Similarly dressed in white, with flowered hats and ribbons, and carrying sticks, they will dance to cure the sick. Their name denotes them as being 'little horses' – animal-men. In Djev-Djali in Macedonia, we find the 'Rusalii' dancers, sweeping away the evil spirits of winter with their scimitars.

The Morris is generally thought to derive from the Spanish 'Morisca'. Here we have a stylised combat between two sides, black representing darkness and winter, and white (or sometimes red) representing light and sun, and indeed this conflict is often portrayed in terms of Christians fighting Moors, but to claim that this is the origin of morris dancing is to misunderstand the meaning behind the rituals. The very essence of this primeval combat between winter and summer, darkness and light, denotes a far more ancient lineage.

There are morris sides in England who do blacken their faces: the Britannia Coconut Dancers of Bacup in Lancashire; and some sides in the Cotswolds and near to the Welsh border, for example, and in former times probably every side did so, and this has led many to see in this the portraying of Moors, and their

Kemps nine daies vvonder.

Performed in a daunce from London to Norwich.

Containing the pleaſure, paines and kinde entertainment of *William Kemp* betweene *London* and that Citty in his late Morrice.

Wherein is ſomewhat ſet downe worth note; to reprooue the ſlaunders ſpred of him: many things merry, nothing hurtfull.

Written by himſelfe to ſatisfie his friends.

LONDON

Printed by *E. A.* for *Nicholas Ling*, and are to be ſolde at his ſhop at the weſt doore of Saint Paules Church. 1600.

36. 'Kemps Nine Daies Wonder'. English, 1600.

rituals as a conflict between Christians and Moors. This belief seems to receive confirmation in some of the stylised conflicts encountered in Spain between these champions of Christianity and Islam, and in Yugoslavia between Christians and Turks. But morris men did not blacken their faces to make them look like Moors; they blackened their faces to disguise themselves. To be recognised destroyed the magic. Mummers for the same reason blacken their faces, and when even St. George with blackened face announces, "In comes I", it can hardly be claimed that he is trying to represent a Moor.

In Elizabethan times, a black man was called a Blackamoor or Morisco. Hence, a disguised or black-faced Whitsuntide dancer would be described by a Shakespearean character as "leaping like a wild Morisco".

Again, the idea that morris dancing was brought back from Spain and Aquitaine by returning soldiers in the service of John of Gaunt in the fourteenth century is untenable; morris dancing existed long, long before this time in England, and let us remind ourselves that dances portraying the same eternal theme of the conflict between life and death, light and dark, exist right the way from India, through Europe, to the westernmost point – remember our Afghan warrior!

In England, traditional Morris nearly died out, but not quite. Of the 250 or so sides active around the year 1800 only 14 had survived by the time Cecil Sharp came along. So while much of present-day Morris is a revival, there are still a few teams who can claim an unbroken tradition. These include: Bampton, Headington, and Abingdon in Oxfordshire, and Chipping Campden in Gloucestershire – these are all 'Cotswold' morris sides.

The Cotswold Morris is danced by six men dressed in white, with coloured sashes and ribbons, and wearing spring flowers and ribbons in their hats which may be toppers, bowlers, boaters, and so forth. They wear bells and ribbons on their legs, and carry white handkerchiefs or decorated sticks. In attendance there are a variety of characters: a fool who may be dressed as a clown, a country-bumpkin or a man-woman who usually carries a stick, to which is attached an inflated pig's bladder, with which he hits the dancers and anyone among the onlookers who gets in his way. There may also be a cake-bearer who carries the good-luck-bringing cake impaled on a sword. The set dances are composed of two sets of three dancers who perform 'challenges', mock fighting, clashing of sticks, energetic leaping and stamping. Some of the figures have been 'borrowed' from country dances.

The Processional Morris can be seen today, preceding and following one of the rushcart processions which, at the end of summer, annually wind their way from church to church, and pub to pub, around the villages of Yorkshire, Lancashire and Cheshire. Proceeding in two lines (the number of dancers is not limited), they twirl brightly-coloured, decorated sticks. The dancers are dressed in flower-decked hats, white shirts decorated with coloured ribbons (usually red for the sun, blue for the summer sky, green for the spring corn, and yellow for the ripened corn). They wear breeches rather than trousers, and iron-soled wooden or leather clogs.

The Britannia Coconut Dancers, traditional processional morris-dancers, are the most striking of all morris teams: dancing along the streets of Britannia and Bacup on Easter Saturday, they have blackened faces, wear red and white skirts, black breeches, and clogs. The eight dancers have a 'whipper-in' to clear enough space for them to dance, though originally his purpose was to drive away evil spirits. The dancers' 'coconuts' are in fact cotton-bobbins, and these are clattered together in one of their set dances; garlands are employed in another dance. The accompanying tunes may be derived from popular songs of the nineteenth century but their dances are traditional.

The best-known of English processional dances is the Flora or Furry Dance, performed each May-time at Helston in Cornwall. The dance commemorates the thwarting of the devil who, in the form of a dragon, was threatening to destroy the town, but who, when he saw the inhabitants all dancing like a serpent through the streets, was so overcome that he fell into Love Pool and was drowned in a cloud of steam. Today, on May 8th, the town's people come together to dance. In the morning, the children, dressed in white, and wearing flowers of different kinds to identify which schools they attend, dance. They are followed by the procession in which a strictly-controlled number of adults take part, the men dressed in formal morning attire with toppers, and a lily-of-the-valley, their town emblem, in their button-holes, their ladies dressed in their Sunday best. The town band heads the parade, playing the tune which has now become world-famous, having reached number 1 in the pop charts. The procession dances its way through the streets, though no longer into all the shops and houses as of yore. Once upon a time, these *mayers* carried may-blossom and greenery with which they dusted the walls and furniture, driving out any lurking evil spirits remaining from the winter, and bringing spring-cleaning good fortune to one and all. It may well have been these branches of may-blossom which have given way to the sticks and handkerchiefs carried by morris dancers today.

37. Perchten from a lithograph by J. Rattensperger. Austrian, 1807-1866.

It is not certain whether the Welsh 'Cadi Ha' was a processional morris dance or peripatetic, like the Abbots Bromley Horn Dance, where the dance moves from one location to another. It was not apparently a continuous procession like the Helston Furry. The dancers hiked quite long distances, and only danced on, performed their dance, and danced off at chosen sites. They wore disguise and blackened their faces, which gave rise to the belief in some quarters that the dancers were miners from Flint. We have seen how a similar erroneous idea caused some people to think that morris dancing was introduced to Lancashire by coal miners. The *Cadi Ha* had the usual fool and man-woman figure. A Branch-bearer formerly carried a birch branch which was decorated with flowers. Here is an account of the dance from Flintshire in the May of 1900:

> *The dancers who were mostly miners employed in the neighbourhood had started from Bagillt early that morning dancing along the road. There were twelve men in the party: eight dancers dressed in baggy white trousers, white shirts and straw hats and wearing knots of blue or pink ribbon to denote their side of man or maid; then there was* Bili *the clown, with a tail coat, white waistcoat, and silk hat and* Cadi *his wife who was dressed in a black skirt, red shawl and gaudy hat with a white veil and carried a white parasol. As regards the other two men, one played the concertina while the other carried a huge piece of goose which was to represent Summer. All except the youth who carried the goose had blackened their faces.*

Another description was written in 1914 by two students from Bangor University:

> *The dancers stand in two lines of four men on one side and four 'maids' on the other facing. The Master stands at the end of the men's line, while Bili and Cadi stand apart, Bili at the end nearest the Master and Cadi at the other end. The men do a sort of patter step in their place while Bili and Cadi advance between the two lines of dancers, hold right hands and turn in the centre then retire to their original places. The men and maids then cross over, back to back waving their handkerchiefs as the Master calls a 'whoop' right shoulder backing to places, left shoulder backing to places. Bili and Cadi again advance up the middle, then Bili leads Cadi back to her end followed by the master and his partner, who cross over and change places continually whilst dancing after them and followed in turn by the other couples, two by two, this procession dances along for some distance, and when Bili and Cadi turn and face the others, the two lines are again formed and the first two figures danced in place.*

The Rev. Peter Roberts, wrote in the 'Cambrian Popular Antiquities' published in 1815:

> *To this festival (Whitsuntide) the only appropriated amusement that I know of is that of morrice-dancers. According to Shakespeare it should*

> *seem that the number of persons who represented this dance was nine**. *The dancers are all men: their dress is ornamented with ribbands and small bells are attached to the knees. The dance itself is somewhat like that of 'Country Bumpkins', and, in the course of it, someone of the more active exhibits a kind of somerset, with the aid of two others. They are attended by a Jack and Gill, or as they are called in Wales, the Fool and Megan. The fool is the same as the clown of the old comedy; the megan, a man dressed in women's clothes and with the face smutted to represent a hag. Both entertain the mob by ridiculous tricks; and the megan generally solicits contributions from the spectators, and keeps off the crowd by the dread of blows of her ladle.*

'Y gaseg eira', a Morris dance for eight men, may have been introduced by the Staffordshire men who worked in the Nantgarw potteries. It is similar to a Lichfield morris dance, as is the solo jig 'Dawns y marchog'. In this, according to Margretta Thomas, the dancer performed his steps in apparent imitation of the trotting, cantering and capering of a horse to four points, ending with three leaps.

Spain was not occupied by the Arabs with any degree of uniformity either in regard to space, degree or time. Indeed, the northern provinces of Galicia, the Asturias, and the nucleus of the Basque Country successfully resisted concerted efforts to conquer their lands, and supplied the spring-boards for the Christian reconquest. This was already well underway even before the end of the eighth century, only a few years after the Arabs had crossed into Spain from North Africa (711). The whole of the Iberian Peninsula north of a wavy line drawn from Oporto in the west, through Pamplona, to Barcelona in the east, was back in Christian hands by the beginning of the tenth century. Therefore, when considering Arab influence on Spain, it should always be borne in mind the very uneven impact from north to south. The extreme north was never subdued and occupied, and, by the year 1250, only a small province around Granada was left under Moslem control, which lasted until 1492 (the year in which Christopher Columbus sailed the ocean blue), by which time even this small province was back in Christian hands. The music and dance of Spain, so very different from the rest of Europe, may owe more to the Visigoths who occupied Spain and western France before the Arab conquest, than to the Arabs themselves. The Visigoths came out of the border lands between Europe and Asia, north of the Black Sea, and having wandered through Greece and the Italian peninsula, finally, in the middle of the fifth century, reached the west where they settled and where their vibrant culture flourished.

Lérida in Aragon has a Morisca, which is of particular interest to anyone wishing to get to the bottom of the problem of the Morisca, and the part it plays in the morris, sword dance, and in mummers' plays. We first hear of a morisca in 1149, when, at the betrothal of Petronilla, queen of Aragon, and Ramon of Barcelona, as one of the

* Rev. Roberts is confusing the dance with the game 'Nine Man's Morris' which is mentioned by Shakespeare - see page 33.

court entertainments, appeared "amongst the minstrels and many dancers, Moors and Christians who gave a feigned combat". The Moors had been driven from Lérida only the previous year. Here in Aragon we can observe how the morisca came to be superimposed on a much more ancient dance form, a dance which had long been performed in the service of seasonal ritual. Sword-dance villages abound in Aragon, and they quickly adopted the new 'invention' of Lérida's morisca, in the wake of the retreating Moors. With the advance of the 'Reconquista' spread the companies of 'Moros y Cristianos' along the coastline of Valencia into Castile. The triumphant Christians were now not averse to copying Moorish fashions, many of them adopting Moorish modes of dress, and soon their dramas, dances, ballades, romances, and songs had their blackamoors, romantic queens, and tragic young princesses. They copied Moorish architecture for their houses, which they furnished with Moorish fountains and courtyards, aped Moorish manners, dressed in Moorish clothes with Moorish embroidery patterns, and listened to Moorish music.

Into the Corpus Christi processions in Spain, and later in Flanders, came the dark-faced Moors, and the black-faced Moor was adopted into the Carnival celebrations in Germany and Switzerland. And just as the Anglo-Saxons imagined that the walls built by the Romans had been erected by giants, so dolmens in Portugal were seen as 'caves of Moors', and the Roman walls in the French Pyrenees were 'built by the Moors'. The Moor entered the masque, and the masque swept the courts of Europe. By the time Louis XIV was sitting enraptured, watching a 'Carrousel' in 1662, Moors, Turks and Saracens had become synonymous and interchangeable. When Granada fell to the Christians in 1492, the Moors lost their final foothold in Europe. But now Saracen pirates infested the Mediterranean, and the Turks, having conquered Constantinople in 1453, were spreading their power and control insidiously northwards.

The silver and salt mines of the Aragonese country, at the foot of the Pyrenees, were being exploited long before the Romans came. Since that time, zinc, manganese, cobalt, lead, and coal have been mined. There can be little doubt but that the sword dances which proliferated in this region are of ancient origin, and were danced hundreds of years before the coming of the Moorish invaders.

In Sena, near Huesca, on October 2nd, the villagers celebrate the feast of their Guardian Angel. On the previous evening, they light a bonfire before the church, and sing the 'Romance del Angel' late into the night. The next morning, they parade round the village and finish up in the church, where the bells ring out to proclaim the fiesta. Afterwards they perform their dance. Divided into Christians and Turks, with bell-pads on their legs, and carrying sticks (later changing to swords), they dance before their *Angel Custodias*, before performing their hilt-and-point sword dance, 'the Wheel', first in the church at festal Mass, and then in the village square. The performance is called variously, 'El Dance', the 'Auto Sacramental', or the 'Pastorada'. During all this, the Christian and Turkish generals harangue each other, before the Turks are finally converted to Christianity. A fool, dressed as a devil, rushes about, fireworks exploding from his tail, and the dance ends with a little boy-angel being hoisted onto the shoulders of four bigger boys, dressed as girls, who themselves are standing on the shoulders of the men. It is then the turn of the mayor; holding a wand topped with a bunch of basil (a plant used for midsummer divination), he speaks his *dichos*, improvised satirical verses on any matter he chooses. The fiesta gives him licence to air any grievances, comment on the peccadillos of anyone in the community, and expose any scandals he wishes, before turning his attention to the weather. All then go to their festal dinners. While morisca elements have strongly tainted this dance, and the Church has taken it under its wing, nevertheless, all the ancient sword-dance elements are there, including an attached weather ceremony. In this region of sheep farmers, where the climate can be particularly harsh, and the shepherds are dependent on their animals for food, clothing and merchandise, their concern with the weather is understandable.

In the dance celebrating the feast of St. James, at Torres del Obispo, there is no morisco taint, but the other elements found at Sena are there, with stick and sword dance, the sprigs of pagan basil and bunches of grapes, and the speech by the 'Rapálan', who represents the head shepherd. In other villages strung out along those foothills, one can find similar celebrations, sometimes the dialogue between Christians and Turks playing a greater part than the dancing. When Huesca, the provincial capital, celebrates the feast of St. Lorenzo, the dancers each carry a stick and a sword, which they tap together as they go in procession behind the bagpiper. In their dance they perform a snail round the captain, forming a lock with their swords as they wind up around him. The fiesta is enlivened by the appearance of dancers from neighbouring villages, bringing with them their maypole, hobby-horse, or Carnival-type giants. At Ainsa in Sobrabe, this mingling of the morisca with

38. 'Peasant Dance' by N. Meldeman. German, 16th century.

ancient pagan rites is even more apparent, for here, additional to the conflict between Christians and Moors, we get something of the death and resurrection theme, though in this case the resurrection is the conversion of the Moors to Christianity, after they have been cut down in battle. The conversion which follows the battle scene, is a long piece in the style of hero-combat and mummers plays in England, with the characters shouting their lines in a monotone.

On the French side of the Pyrenees, in the provinces of Bigorre and Béarn, men dressed in white, wearing ribbons and bells, and carrying sticks, dance during the spring Carnival, going the rounds of the villages and outlying farms bringing luck. In return, they are given the food which they have silently indicated they wish to receive. They are not called the 'Mauresque' but 'les Balladins', the dancers. In the French Basque Country, they do precisely the same thing, and although they are but a stone's throw from the birthplace of the Morisca in Spain, they are never called by the name of Mauresque. Back in Spain, there are countless towns and villages whose dancers' dress is almost identical to the English morris, yet none of them are called morisco.

In Portugal we have the Pauliteiros dancers in white shirts, with white, three-tiered skirts edged with *broderie anglaise*, broad-brimmed black felt hats banded with red ribbon with tails hanging down the back and decorated with small bunches of brightly-coloured flowers sticking upright from the headband, sleeveless hip-length waistcoats, brightly-coloured fringed shawls as worn by the women for headscarves, striped socks and ankle boots, each dancer carrying two short sticks. Eight dancers form a longways set, constantly moving to change the direction of the set, hitting sticks against the other dancers' sticks as well as their own as they change position, the sticks occasionally being carried under the arms to allow the dancers to play castanets. They perform a rather heavy running step with feet picked up but not with much *balon*, and occasionally a step akin to the English morris step but again without the spring. The dancers of St. Brancaï de Manosco in Provence also wear white shirts, bolero and wide sash, and a three-tiered, knee-length skirt over white trousers, and floral hats. In the 'Danse des Quenouilles' of Toulouse, the dancers are dressed in white, with short white skirts over white trousers, and white floppy wide-brimmed hats. The dancers of Burgos in Spain wear similar apparel and yet the term 'mauresque' is never applied to any of these dancers.

We do know more or less when and how the name came to England (if indeed our morris is derived from *morisca* – see p.94). The English were for centuries involved in the Spanish Reconquista. In the days when half of France belonged to the king of England, and the wine trade with Gascony involved much to-ing and fro-ing by merchants and sailors, when English archers and infantrymen, either through treaty or as mercenaries, were constantly fighting for rival claimants to the thrones of Aragon and Castile, they certainly had plenty of opportunity to learn about the morisca. They brought back ballads and romances, and probably dances based on the theme of Christians versus Moors. In Belgium and Germany, it was the Crusaders, coming back from the Holy Land who brought back the theme of Christians against Saracens. This had nothing to do with the Spanish morisca, though the name attached itself to these performances. In Germany it is called the 'Moriskentanz', but is in fact a mere collection of local folk dances. The Alsatians also have a 'Moreskentanz' which, at the beginning of the sixteenth century, was danced in Strasbourg by the guild of Tailors, using the same figures as for a hilt-and-point sword dance. A French explanation for the term 'Maure' (Morris) is that the 'Danse des Morts' (Dance of Death) has been confused with a hypothetical 'Danse des Maures'.

The 'Moreška' is to be found along the Adriatic coast and on the Dalmatian islands. What opinions have been expressed regarding the origins of the moreška conflict. Some believe that it was originally danced by the Arabs (Moors); others say that it originated in Spain, and portrays that country's struggle against their conquerors. We are told that the moreška spread to other Mediterranean countries, to Italy, Corsica, France, and thence to Flanders, Germany and England. It flourished in the fifteenth and sixteenth centuries, and survived into the seventeenth and eighteenth centuries. It took root on the island of Corsica where, in one moresca, Muslims and Christians fight for the town of Aleria, while in another they fight

39. 'Peasant Kermis' by Hans Sebald Beham. German, 1535.

for the town of Mariana. Eighty fighters on each side are each armed with two swords, and the dance has twelve figures. A solo violin accompanies the whole conflict. Interestingly, one of the figures is called 'espagnolette'.

On Korčula, this same figure is called 'spanjoleta'. In the Korčula dance and play depicting a Christian victory over the Moors, the White King fights the Black King for the hand of a beautiful captive girl, who loves the Chrisian king, and refuses to respond to her Moorish captor. The armies of the two kings enter with banners and swords. The kings hurl insults at each other, and then start to fight, the two armies clashing swords with their opposite numbers. The kings dance in a circle, threatening each other with their swords, and this is followed by various dances in which the armies join in, fighting in pairs with alternating sword thrusts and parries. The Black soldiers are eventually surrounded and fall down wounded, dying and defeated. The Black King surrenders, the girl is released and receives a kiss from the White King.

The moresca was known in the nineteenth century on Elba, in one place being performed as an equestrian dance. In Genoa, Naples, southern Italy and Sicily, Christians and Moors have fought each other through the centuries in the morisca. A type of morisca was known on Malta, while in seventeenth- and eighteenth-century Venice, it was known as 'Saracinesca'. Earlier, in the fifteenth and sixteenth centuries, we find it performed in Ferrara. Swords, torches, even spades and hoes (ill. 38 & 39) might be used as fighting weapons. In one of the dances a soldier protects a damsel in distress against a dragon, which displays unmistakable signs of wishing to satisfy its appetite for its favourite food.

At Souto das Neves, near Barcelos in northern Portugal, the battle is between Charlemagne and the Moors under Admiral Balao. But the battle is not always between Christians and Moors. In some of the Basque *pastorales*, medieval outdoor plays, we can find the opposing forces representing Israelites and Canaanites, Medes and Persians, French and German. In the *pastorale* of Joan of Arc, it is the English who become the Turks. In other battles, the opposing forces are Moors and 'Buffoons', or Spaniards and Portuguese. The fight between the Cross and the Crescent is not essential to the ceremonial battle.

If in certain cities the moresca was adopted as a court entertainment, in others, Siena for example, it was developed in the sixteenth century as a less aristocratic drama, the main protagonists being peasants, hermits, and those people who had deserted the countryside for the town. Their fights among themselves, which they named morisca, were usually to gain the favour of some lovely damsel. The moresca was also introduced into Sienese pastoral plays. Catalonia has a charming couple dance called 'la Morisca' in which the Moorish prince agrees to free his beautiful captive if she can outspring him in the dance. Thus they dance together leaping from time to time.

On the Isle of Man, the people used to elect not only a Queen of the May (or of Summer), but a Queen of Winter also. Each was attended by her ladies-in-waiting, and by twelve male retainers. Those of the Queen of the May wore red cockades, those of the Queen of Winter wore winter clothing and sprigs of evergreen. A mock battle ensued, and after several setbacks, the Queen of Summer put her adversary to flight. In Austria too battles between summer and winter are known.

The theme of Christians versus Moors may well have been grafted onto the much older theme of summer versus winter, and where we have two opposing forces, the names Moorish, morisca, may be accounted for. This could be stretched to apply to English morris dances which feature 'challenges', or the Abbots Bromley Horn Dance, in which the three white stags menace the three black stags, but the real theme of the English morris is the age-old one of driving out the evil spirits of winter and bringing in the spring. Cecil Sharp long ago concluded that "the faces were not blackened because the dancers represented Moors, but rather the dancers were thought to represent Moors because their faces were blackened". The blacking of faces was to preserve anonymity. Those taking part must not be recognized, otherwise the magic is broken.

In the Iberian Peninsula, the term Moorish was often used as a synonym for 'pagan', and the name Moorish has become quite wrongly and misleadingly attached to something which existed long before the Moslems overran Europe.

One of the strangest survivals is the 'Mouriscada', performed annually at Sobrado near Valongo in Portugal. The performance begins at midday, when the 'Mouriscos' (Moors) and 'Bugios' (Buffoons), led by their kings, march into the village. Next follows one of the *bugios*, seated back to front on a horse, and miming the sowing of flax. The ground he has sown is then harrowed and ploughed with two donkeys, whose yoke has been harnessed upside down. The plough must then fall to pieces, so that everything has been done in inverse order. Next, the *Mouriscos* dance with drawn swords. They line up in two ranks, and their king dances down the middle. The top couple cast off and, followed by the others, meet at the bottom, and come up the centre in pairs. The king then leads them in a snail for which they form a single file, unravel themselves, and divide into two files before quitting the dancing area. It is then the turn of the *bugios* to perform, all except the king wearing masks. Battle ensues, and the king of the *bugios* is overcome and mourned as dead by his followers. But all is not over yet. The *bugios*, dragging a huge *bicha*, a dragon made of sacking over a wooden frame, come charging in putting the *Mouriscos* to flight and rescuing their king. The final 'dança do santo' gives a Christian finish to the ceremony, danced in honour of St. John, in front of the church.

In Provence, they danced the 'Moresque' with great gusto right up to the end of the nineteenth century. This 'armed' dance was referred to by fifteenth-century chronicles as a dance of the court and the theatre, and as being performed to the accompaniment of flutes and trumpets by richly costumed dancers, with little bells at their ankles and wrists. It was to be seen performed during court ballets and mystery plays. Thoinot Arbeau wrote:

> *In my youth I saw in goodly company, after the supper, a young boy, blackened with soot, his forehead bound by a piece of white or yellow taffeta and with bells on his garters dance the Moresque, moving the length of the hall, tracing a sort of path before going back to where he had started, before setting off similarly on a different course, and this several times. The Moresque dancers moved to a binary rhythm. They started by stamping the feet and then those dancers who found this too painful substituted heel beats, their toes gripped tightly. Some wanted to dance using both*

foot stamps and heel beats. The doing of all three sorts, especially the foot stamping, engendered (for the dancers) podagra and gout.

Apparently they danced barefooted.

The Moresque was danced during the last days of Carnival and on special feast days. At Trets, on the eve of Epiphany as dusk was falling, the young people went out of the town carrying baskets of dried fruits to meet the Three Maji. The Maji were greeted with the gifts and a speech of welcome, they in turn presenting the speaker with a purse filled with coins. The speaker, pretending to refuse to share with his friends, fled back to town, hotly pursued by the others, and when they finally caught up with him in the square, they danced a Moresque around him. In the Var region, at Grimaud, Fréjus, and elsewhere, the dancers wore short white tunics decorated with ribbons, and their faces blackened with soot, their 'pagan rites' illuminated by the light of pine-resin torches. At Caillan they carried burning pine cones on top of sticks. Two lines of men, one line dressed as women, ranged about the village running and jumping one behind the other, performing *chassés-croisés* and *entrechats*. In the Comté de Nice, the Master of the patronal feast carried a halberd, which conferred on him the right to lead the Moresque. As the young folk didn't have the money to organize the ball, this honour was put up for auction. At Istres, the Moresque formed a part of a veritable ballet where 'shepherdesses' revolved carrying distaffs, rakes, sickles and flails, and were followed by Turks dancing a slow and solemn farandole. Then came the Moresque dancers, wearing white tunics, little bells around their wrists and calves, a sword in their right hands and an orange in the left. Each one placed himself between two flower-decked ladies, then fought a mock combat, striking sword blades with another cavalier, and finally presenting the orange to his lady. The orange is a sun-symbol.

The Moresque was danced at many great ceremonials: in 1447, Queen Jeanne de Laval, the wife of King René, was welcomed to Toulon by a 'genta moresca'. It was danced again in 1498 when Caesar Borgia was entertained in Avignon. In 1564 at Marseilles, it was performed before Charles IX by Spanish soldiers. In several provincial towns the Moresque was followed by a sword dance, danced to a military march. Two lines of men and 'women' (men in travesty), wearing a costume supposedly worn by savages, faced each other, barring access to the street. One line tried to force a way through with their swords, the others holding them back, their sword blades clashing. They leapt into the air, changing direction and partner, and ran from one side of the street to the other. Thoinot Arbeau described it under the name of 'Danse des Bouffons et de Matachins', and traced its lineage to the sacred dance of the Salian priests of Rome. It was undoubtedly even older than that.

A dance with its counterpart to be found in Bacup, Lancashire, where it is danced by the Britannia Coconut Dancers, is still danced in several places in Provence. It is the 'Danse des Coco'. An odd number of dancers, their faces and hands blackened, are accompanied by a fool whose head is crowned in feathers, his chest loaded with amulets, and brandishing a sabre. He leads on two lines of dancers, one line wearing white trousers and black shirts, with pointed crowns on their heads, the other line dressed in women's white skirts and black blouses, and wearing similar headgear. All the dancers have half-coconut shells strapped to their elbows, knees, and chests, which they strike in time together. When they reach their dancing place, they form a circle round the fool who, whilst the coconut dancers perform their frenetic gyrations, waves his sabre in windmill sail-like movements, and emits piercing cries. A similar type of dance, the 'Moratons' is to be found on Majorca. Here the dancers wear, fixed to various parts of their bodies, semicircular pieces of wood about the size of coconut shells. They dance, clattering the hand-held pieces of wood against themselves and other dancers.

These dances contain between them various aspects of ritual dance: the pointed hats used in rain rituals, the dressing up in travesty, the use of black and white garments, and the presence of a fool who is almost indispensable in a ritual concerning Nature and the regeneration of vegetation, and of course the inevitable blacking up of faces to preserve the *incognito* of the performers.

6

GUISERS, HOBBY-ANIMALS AND MUMMERS

Behold the days come, behold the kalends come, and the whole devlish public procession goes forth. The new year is consecrated with old blasphemies. Whatever deformities are lacking in nature, which creation does not know, art labours to fashion. Besides, people are dressed as cattle, and men are turned into women,

Severian in 400 A.D.

The Roman Kalendae, the twelve days of their New Year festival, were celebrated by the wearing of disguises and the participation in wild orgies, which included human sacrifice. Men dressing up as animals, and also behaving like wild beasts, may be seen to represent those demons which, at that time of the year, were allowed out of the underworld. They are known as *kallikantzaroi.* These kallikantzaroi were anciently believed to be groteque creatures, black, deformed, with the ears and legs of goats or asses, who spent the year in the underworld, attempting to destroy the great tree which supported the world. The tree was able to recover itself during those twelve days when the creatures emerged on Middle Earth, to destroy any person or living thing which they came upon.

Carnival, which occurs a little later in the calendar, approximates to the Greek Anthesteria, the spring festival which took place between mid-February and mid-March, and was a wine festival in honour of Dionysos, who was both God of Wine (or fruitfulness) and Lord of Souls. Thus, the Anthesteria was at the same time a festival of All Souls, when the ancestral spirits visited their former abodes, to be ritually entertained and then expelled and sent back from whence they came, namely the underworld. It was a festival of purification, of spring cleaning, of renewal.

The etymology of the name Carnival is disputed. The Oxford English Dictionary defines it as coming from *carnem levare*, the putting away of flesh (as food). However, a more likely derivation comes from the *carrus* or *char navalis*, a ship on wheels which was used to carry the dance leader and chorus into the performing area where, in ancient Greece, they enacted the life, death and resurrection of Dionysos. In 540 B.C., Thespis, the famous dancer and singer who has given his name to actors (thespians), likewise arrived on stage in a *char navalis* when he performed the *goat song* – the *tragodia*, which gives us our word tragedy. Thespis came from Icaria, which was the chief seat of the cult of Dionysos.

The ship on wheels was described by Tacitus in c.98 A.D. It represented the ship or waggon of Nerthus, a Germanic Earth Mother, and contained a mysterious object, which was thought to be the symbol of the goddess. The ship was brought out each spring and paraded round the village and outlying farms to renew the fertility of the earth. The custom was still observed in 1133 in the Rhineland where a monk of St. Trond near Tongres described it:

> *Wherever the ship halted there was shouting and dancing far into the night . . . When this execrable dance was broken off the people ran hither and thither making a noise as though they were drunk.*

40. *'Zamalzaïn – le Cavalier Cheval' by Robert Lépine. French-Basque.*

They probably were, for this was the time when the usual codes of behaviour were relaxed, and everyone let their hair down. Sometime later the burghers of Nürnberg incorporated the ship into their Carnival celebrations. Their play, the Schönbart or Schembartlaufen was performed each year. Nerthus became Berta or Perchta. Her followers, the Perchten, are the masked figures who appear as witches and devils at Carnival time in many countries. The ship appears again in Tarascon, France, during the procession when onlookers are drenched in water by the 'crew'.

The Greek Anthesteria, the Roman Feralia (Februum), and the Celtic Festival of the New Year, were all identical in purpose. All Souls 'christianized' these festivals. The ghosts of the underworld were believed to be malevolent to humankind, and, to render them harmless, they must be allowed to visit the world of the living, so that they could be placated by sacrifice, food and gifts, before being sent on their way. During the feast of Lupercalia, which formed part of the Roman Feralia, two youths donned the hides of the goats and dogs which had been sacrificed, and ran amongst the women, flicking them with strips of the hide of the animals, in order to purify and ensure fertility. The animals were sacrificed in order to placate the ghosts and evil spirits of the underworld which impaired fertility, and the act of purification was essential to ensure its preservation.

The period from All Souls' Eve (Hollontide) to Shrove Tuesday (Carnival) took in the coming of dead souls to visit their homes and a time for festivity. In seventeeth-century England, the festival was known as Revels, and was marked by the giving of gifts and the visiting, by disguised persons, of the houses, to bring good luck. The timing of the appearance of dead souls varied in different parts of Europe. In the Celtic world, New Year occured in November, and consequently Hallowe'en took place on October 31st. The Greek and Roman New Year came in January, while in northern Europe it comes at midwinter. Much of the European continent celebrates Carnival, like the Greek Anthesteria and the Roman Feralia, as a season of purification, now called Lent.

The Norse name for it was *Jól*. Jól was a sacrificial feast for the purpose of promoting the fertility of the land and of man. It has somehow got mixed up with a feast in honour of the dead, though in an agricultural society, which is tied to the yearly cycle of the four seasons, and birth, reproduction and death, it was natural to link together fertility and death. In these northern climes, the ancient customs concerned themselves with sacrifice to the gods and to the dead, and food and drink were a concomitant element in these rites.

The Norse god, Odin, like Dionysos, seems to have been honoured both as the god of the dead, and as god of intoxicating drink and ecstacy, and, again like the Greek Dionysos, may have been feasted in both these capacities. Intoxication and ecstasy were generally believed to promote communication with the gods. Yule beer was used in northern Europe as a sacrifice, the dedication of the contents of a drinking horn to each of the gods being made and thus 'sacrificed', the rest being consumed in the gods' honour by the partakers of the feast. The 'toast' was for "a good harvest and for peace". The old Norse *til árs ok til friđar* has a wider connotation. Besides its meaning of a good harvest, the word *ár* also means a harvest of the sea, that is, an abundance of fish; and *fridar* has a sexual connotation which encompasses fertility in both man and animals.

Failure to observe the requisite sacrifices could bring down calamity on the whole community, and it was every individual farmer's duty to ensure that the rituals were correctly observed in his house. The dead were believed to haunt the living around the time of the winter solstice, and it was the custom to leave food and drink on the table for the yule ghosts. People believed that what they did not give voluntarily would be taken from them by force. The dead must be placated. These dead souls, *julereien*, were believed to arrive, riding through the air on horseback with Odin himself at their head. At this time of year, the farmer had to ensure that everything was kept tidy around the farm – things left carelessly lying about were liable to disappear.

The tradition of scattering straw on the floor on an important occasion is of ancient origin, and continued long after the introduction of wooden floors. Sleeping on straw during this period of the winter solstice was also an old custom. It has been seen as an ancient fertility rite. In some northern countries, beds were vacated to make room for the visiting ghosts at All Souls. The straw used during Yule was believed to have magic qualities. From the grains that fell from the straw could be predicted whether the next harvest would be good, or whether one should prepare for a bad harvest. According to which sorts of grain fell to the floor, so such crops should be sown. After the holidays, the yule straw was gathered up to be used for various kinds of magic: some was made into crosses which were fastened above doors for protection; or used to cure sick animals; or saved until the spring and then scattered on the fields to ensure a good harvest. Another custom connected with the pagan *jól*, and seen as part of a harvest rite, was the making of straw figures, both human and animal. People believed that the spirits of the grain lived in the field, and, as the corn was cut, this spirit retreated until finally it was caught in the last sheaf. The spirit might be in the shape of a human, a hare, or a goat. In some places, this last sheaf was saved to be fed to the farm animals at *jól* to ensure their health and fertility in the coming year. Elsewhere, these figures, fashioned from the last sheaf to be cut, were believed to represent the spirit of the grain and to have magical powers, and were set up in the place of honour at Yule. Today, in Sweden and Denmark, straw goats are sold at Christmas time.

Special cakes or loaves in the shape of, or symbolizing, animals, particularly goats, pigs, and chickens, were baked at yule tide, and the crumbs from these had magic properties: healing power, and the ability to promote growth and fertility. In Sweden, a special cake was baked from the grain which fell from the straws picked up in the fields at the end of the harvest. The cake must be saved until the spring, when the crumbs were scattered in the fields during the ploughing. In Norway, yule cakes should be baked from such grain. The last straws left by the harvesters were gleaned by the children. Each bunch was called a *bruse*, an Old Norse word meaning goat

The going about in processions wearing animal masks and heads has its roots in ancient times. Greek literature often makes reference to bird dances. We read that bird catchers used to dance to hypnotize owls so that they could capture them. On the island of Rhodes the children would disguise themselves as birds and, carrying a replica of a swallow, would go from house to house, dancing and singing, demanding gifts of food which they would steal if it was not given to them voluntarily.

There was a connection between the goat of the pagan pageant and the spirit of the corn, and between these pageants and the night-ride of the dead. These maskers or guisers had the task of ensuring that the correct observance of the festivals was carried out, that the various taboos on certain activities were faithfully observed. The hideous and frightening masks of the guisers mirrored what people believed these ghosts looked like. The yule goat was made to look the most scarey of them all. The guisers went from house to house, often performing the sort of mischief which the yule demons were believed to inflict as punishment on those who offended against the taboos. To go 'yule goat' is still a popular tradition in parts of Norway where nowadays it is the children who dress up. When yule was driven out at the end of the holidays, windows and doors were opened, the whole house swept clean, while people beat the walls with sticks and shouted: "Out goes the yule!", and with it the ghosts and demons that had been their feared guests over the past days.

Since time immemorial, on these occasions people have disguised themselves as spirits or ghosts, animals and demons, to summon the spirits of the underworld, malevolent to humankind, to appear, in order that they might be placated and rendered harmless by the ritual giving of food and gifts. Over the centuries, as the original religious significance has been lost, the seriousness of the rituals degenerated into buffoonery.

The acting out of plays, accompanied the disguisings. The characters usually included an old woman nursing a child, a hero or bridegroom (who was the child grown to manhood), a maiden or bride, an antagonist who attempts to molest her, and in the ensuing fight kills the hero, a doctor who revives him, and on the fringe

41. Fastnacht chain dance of the Nürnberg butchers' guild from a Schembart manuscript. German, c.1561.

of the activities of the main protagonists are gypsies or smiths, who go through the actions of forging a plough-share and indulge in an obscene pantomime. The hobby-horse was another aspect of this play-acting. He usually falls down dead and is revived, or is gelded by the gypsies or smiths.

On Candlemas Day (February 2nd) at Arles-sur-Tech in Rousillon, they perform a 'marriage' followed by a ritual death. Hunters set out in the morning, accompanied by a Catalan cobla-band playing a special 'bear' tune, and eventually capture their bear (a man in disguise). As they all dance back into the town, the bear frequently breaks away from his captors and runs off in pursuit of the lady, Rosetta (a man-woman), whom he seizes and hugs. Several times he is beaten off, but eventually, as tradition decrees, he leads the lady, his spring bride, into his cave, where he regales her on cake and wine. Then the bear goes on the rampage, attacking various strange characters who have casks for heads, garlic leaves for hair, and often faces painted both front and back like Januses. The bear is again captured, shaved, and, as he again breaks away from his tormentors, is shot. He is carried away to the accompaniment of the singing of the traditional dirge. The traditional death has followed the traditional marriage. If this originally symbolised the marriage of the god to the wife of the king, once common to other countries and religions, then it is the only surviving instance in Europe. (Greek mythology is full of examples of a god, usually Zeus, lying with the wife of the king, the outcome being twins, one the son of the god, the other the son of the king, hence the large incidence of twins.)

There are other bears in Roussillon. In St. Laurent de Cerdagne, Plà, and Prats de Moolo, there are two, dressed up in sheepskin headdresses, and sacking for clothes. They roam around the village, and anyone caught by them is rolled on the ground, and gets sooty or oily paw-marks over them. They have even been known to go into bedrooms and roll on the beds, leaving their black marks behind them. They have two 'barbers' in female attire, who are in fact brides, and who shave the bears and dance with them.

Church leaders inveighed against all this disguising, though in Spain they were cleverly turned into parish amusements or devotional duties. Pacianus, bishop of Barcelona in 370, provides us with an early reference to animal disguising. The poor bishop was tormented by the belief that he himself was responsible for the propagation of this pagan practice. In condemning it, he had described so accurately the stag-disguise and the performance that went with it, that he had inadvertently, so he believed, popularized it. He laments: "Oh, what have I committed? I think they would not have known how to act the stag play if I had not shown them by criticizing them."

St. Augustine (387-430), a few years later, wrote the often quoted sermon: "If you ever hear of anyone carrying on that most filthy practice of dressing up like a horse or a stag, punish him most severely!" And Caesarius of Arles (470-542) preached against the dressing up in animal heads and putting on women's clothing: "Do not allow a stag or a calf or any monster to come in front of your house!"

In 636, St. Isidor of Seville refers to the country people as having been wont to dress up "in the shape of beasts, cattle and bull-calves, on the Kalends of January, and to run about hither and thither". Another seventh-century reference is by St. Aldhelm, abbot of Malmesbury in Wiltshire, who castigated similar 'runnings' amongst the Saxons in his Wessex: "Long ago, horses and stags were worshipped in temples, in crude stupidity among the impious."

These animals may long ago have vacated the temples, and even ceased to be worshipped, but they remained long afterwards, an essential part of the popular festivals of the 'pagans'.

In passing, it may be of interest to point out that the Romans referred to people living in the countryside (*pagi*) as 'pagani', hence our word 'pagan'. Pagan has come to be synonymous with 'heathen', but this is not the Latin meaning of the word. Thus when the clerics, writing in Latin, refer to pagans, they mean no more than 'country-dwellers'.

In 915, Regino of Prüm warned the Germans of his diocese of "going about in the guise of a stag or a calf. May you repent!" Obviously they didn't heed his warning, for still today they celebrate their 'Fasching' with the wearing of masks. Another tenth-century churchman, the Frankish Pseudo-Theodore of Canterbury, decreed: "If anyone on January Ist goes about dressed as a stag or a calf, identifying himself with the nature of beasts, dressing up in the hides of animals, those who in such a way change themselves into animal forms shall do three years' penance, for such things are devilish." St. Eligius of Rouen

42. Mummers from the 'Romance of Alexander'. French, 14th century.

added to the "absurd things: calves, stags and games, the preparation of tables overnight, the giving of presents, and excessive drinking". Burchard of Worms, in c.1024, threatened his flock with a thirty-day penance if they continued to put on animal disguises. At the Synod of Worcester in 1240, it was the clergy themselves who were forbidden to take part in the "disreputable games or dances", and in the May game "King and Queen play", and lastly not to "raise up rams on high".

Of course, no one ever listened to these admonitions, but they did not always get away with it unpunished. One young man in the Langue d'Oc committed the impious act of dressing up in a calf skin one Carnival, and the skin stuck to him as punishment. Prayers had to be recited over him before he was able to take the skin off. Another youth rode his wooden horse into church. His punishment was for him and his horse to be consumed in the flames from the fire that broke out at his feet.

Pictorial evidence of the long history of animal guising is abundant. The Romance of Alexander (ill. 42), a fourteenth-century Flemish manuscript, given as a wedding present to Elizabeth Woodville, consort of Edward IV of England, shows men wearing masks of donkey, monkey, goat, bull, and eagle. Another illustration is of a boy enacting a stag while dancing to the accompaniment of pipe and tabor. There is an engraving from 1561 (cover and ill. 41) which depicts the Nürnberg Butchers' guild performing a farandole in which the dancers are accompanied by various hobby-animals. The Betley Window (ill. 35) shows, along with various morris dancers, Maid Marian, Friar Tuck, a decorated maypole, and a hobby-horse, the 'rider' strangely shown with a sword through his cheeks. Vases, over 2000 years old, in the Numantia Museum in Soria, Spain, show warriors carrying spears, and wearing what can only be described as a hobby-horse frame around their waists. One vase has a man, his arms stuffed into bulls horns, performing a ritual act. Today, in this very region, the hobby-bull still makes its appearance at the appropriate festival.

References in plays of various periods show the popularity of the morris and its accompanying characters. Thus, in William Sampson's 'The Vowbreaker', (1636), one character grumbles: "How like an everlasting morris dance it looks, nothing but hobby horse and Maid Marrian." A poem of the time records the scene in London's Fleet Street:

Good Lord! I heard a tabor playe
For God save me! a morrys daunce.
Oh there was sport alone for mee
To see the hobby horse how he did prance
Among the gingling company.

Churchwardens' accounts are also revealing, and introduce the enigmatic figure of Robin Hood. Whilst the morris and hobby-horses were paid for out of parish funds, Robin Hood went around 'gaderyng' money to help. Thus, one entry of 1515 read: "Rd at Whetsontyde of Roben Hodes gaderyng . . . 139–5d". In Tavistock in 1464, the "Mayers child fro daewnsing with the hobye hors" was paid twopence, whilst it cost three shillings in 1541 for "paynting of the hoby horse clothes". In a madrigal written by Thomas Morley, the lyrics go:

Ho! who comes here with bagpiping and drumming?
O, 'tis the morris dance I see a coming.

And then the crowd was warned:

Stand out awhile! You come too far in, I say in
There, give the hobby horse more room to play in!

The famous morris, danced in 1598, from London to Norwich, by William Kemp, was celebrated in Thomas Weelkes's lines:

Since Robin Hood, Maid Marian,
And Little John are gone a,
The hobby horse is quite forgot
When Kemp did dance alone-a.

It has been claimed that Robin Hood is indentifiable with the hobby-horse. The hobby-horse has been given various names, among which are: Hobby, Hobyn, Robin, Robbie, and we have the various 'Hooden' horses, especially in Kent. Robin Hood has been seen as a supernatural being, and as a sex symbol, and there is no denying the sex-symbolism of most hobby-horses, particularly those which cover unwary girls with their skirt.

Robin Hood is one of the characters to be found in the Abbots Bromley Horn Dance, though there is some doubt as to the legitimacy of his presence there; it has been claimed that Robin Hood and Maid Marian may be nineteenth-century introductions. The dance was referred to by Dr. Robert Plot, seventeenth-century Historiographer Royal, as the Hobby Horse Dance. He describes the horse as carrying the bow and arrow, and makes no mention of a man-woman or a fool. The dance was apparently performed at midwinter, not as now in September. Late in the nineteenth century the costumes of the guisers were replaced (they have since been replaced once more), and it has been argued that these costumes were inspired by the Betley Window, formerly in Betley Hall, Staffordshire, and at the same time, Robin Hood, a fool and a female figure known as Maid Marian joined the merry band. The hobby-horse, in this instance, we are told, originated in a display organized at Straford-upon-Avon in 1886, in which the characters followed as closely as possible the characters and costumes of the Betley Window. This window is over one hundred years older than was once thought, and seems to belong to the time of Henry VIII, that is to the early sixteenth century. If Robin Hood and company are a later accretion to the dance, at least it makes good mythical sense, and lends some meaning to what must be an ancient fertility rite.

The Padstow 'Old Hoss' or ''Oss 'Oss' comes out on May 1st to the accompaniment of:

Rise up, Mrs. Johnson, we wish you well and fine,
For Summer is a-come unto day.
The horse is in his stable and is waiting for a ride,
In the merry morning of May.

Rise up, Mr. Rosevear, we wish you well and fine,
For Summer is a-come unto day.
You've a shilling in your pocket and I wish it was in mine,
In the merry morning of May.

The Padstow horse is a very strange beast. He is circular, some five feet in diameter and as black as the devil. His covering reaches the ground, hiding his legs and any unwary girl who happens to be caught up inside it. From the rim protrudes a tiny horse's head, and from the back a cow's tail. The man inside wears a hood which sticks up through the centre of the disc, and is topped with a horse-tail plume, has two glaring eyes, and a broad red tongue hanging from its mouth. This is not 'animal and rider' so often found, but pure, savage, pagan animal, belonging to a dark prehistoric age. It had been terrifying folk long before it put the fear of God into a French raiding party back in the eighteenth century, and set them scrambling back to the beach.

As already stated, May Day sees the Padstow horse terrorising the girl bystanders and dragging them under his skirts to jig around before being released. This ensured that the victim would be married within the year. The ceremony really starts at midnight on April 30th, when the townsfolk are summoned by the 'Mayers', who

43. 'The Storming of Hell' showing the ship-on-wheels, from a Nürnberg Schembart manuscript. German, c.1561.

then go out into the woods to cut fresh may branches to decorate the streets:

For we are to fetch home the Summer and the May O,
For Summer is i-come O
And Win-i-ter is agone O!

The Padstow Old Hoss (or Oss Oss as some prefer to call him) used to have his hands besmerched with black lead, which left its mark on any girl caught beneath the cloak. This blacking was another sign of ancient fertility rite. Then they all went off to the Treator Pool where Hoss had a drink and sprinkled the bystanders, sympathetic magic to make Nature feed the soil with her rain. Amusingly enough, a second horse has been introduced into the Padstow ceremony. The Temperance Horse, as the rival is called, was brought in because the traditional horse and his *Mayers* acquired a certain notoriety by their drunkenness and disorder, not that the Temperance horse and his handlers have a much better record.

At some point during the festivities Oss Oss falls down dead, before leaping up and renewing his antics. Two songs accompany the dancing and actions:

Unite and unite, and let us all unite,
For summer is a-come in today.
Whither we are going we all will unite
In the merry morning of May.

The young men of Padstow they might if they would,
For summer is a-come in today.
They might have built a ship and gilded it with gold
In the merry morning of May.

The young maids of Padstow, they might if they would,
For summer is a-come in today.
They might have made a garland of the white rose and the red
In the merry morning of May.

Then there is the dirge for the dying Hobby-horse:

Oh, where is St. George? Oh where is he, oh?
He's out in his long boat, all on the salt sea, oh.
Up flies the kite, down falls the lark-oh.
Aunt Ursula Berwood, she had an old ewe,
But it died in her own park, oh.

With the revival of Oss, Oss, the singers renew the first song.

In Minehead, Somerset, two hobby-horses prowl the streets from April 30th to May 3rd. One used to be owned by the fishermen living along the quay, and has thus become known as the Sailors' Horse or Quay Horse. The Town Horse is called by the district where his current owner is living, and may thus be known as Alcombe Horse

44. Mummers from the 'Roman de Fauvel'. French, 14th century.

or wherever. Both horses are accompanied by a musician and a drummer, while the Town Horse enjoys the additional company of four 'Gullivers' or 'mummies' dressed in hessian and brightly coloured material, and they are masked. In the same way that the Padstow horse seizes girls from the crowd, so too are they waylayed by the Gullivers, who hold the victim in a horizontal position, to be 'booted' ten times by the horse. On the last night, the girl will dance with the horse, hidden beneath his skirt.

In the Abbots Bromley Horn Dance, six dancers dressed in pseudo-Tudor costume carry reindeer horns mounted on wooden deer heads. They start in the early morning at the church, and wend their way through the streets of the village, visiting outlying farms and the stately home of Lord and Lady Bagot (who provided the current costumes). They are accompanied by a jester, a boy carrying a crossbow (Robin Hood), a man-woman (Maid Marian), a hobby-horse, and two musicians, one playing a diatonic harmonica, the other a triangle. Additional sounds are made by Robin clattering his bow-string. Maid Marian carries in one hand a wooden ladle and in the other a short stick, both blatant sex symbols. The horn dancers carry three white-painted and three black-painted sets of antlers, and they dance a 'challenge', representing the conflict between the forces of good and the forces of evil.

References to hobbies on the continent are legion. In the south of France there is a positive bevy of them. The 'Chevalet' of Ste. Lumine de Contais dances round an oak tree on Whit Sunday, attended by two swordsmen. 'Poulain' of Pezenas needs several men to carry him, while the Basque 'Zamalzaïn' performs *entrechats huit*, stepping onto a wine-filled tumbler and leaping off again.

Here in the upland regions of the Basque Country we find the 'Mascarades', complex performances governed by strict tradition. The players are divided into two groups, the 'Reds' or 'Beautiful Ones' and the 'Blacks'. The Reds have five principal characters: the 'Kantiniersa', dressed to suggest a *cantinière* or cutler of the French army, but wearing a woman's skirt and apron; the 'Cherrero', literally Pig-man, who has sheep-bells tied around his waist, and carries a stick topped by a horse's tail with which he sweeps the ground at the head of the procession; the 'Gatuzain' or Cat-man who carries a spring-trellis, which has been interpreted as a symbol for lightning; and an 'Ensenaria', a standard-bearer. A hobby-horse accompanies them, the man smartly dressed in military scarlet tunic and gleaming breastplate, and a high crown decorated with flowers, ribbons and mirrors, the horse being an oblong frame with a white lace saddle-cloth. There are also in attendance: gelders and blacksmiths, a lord and lady, and a peasant and his wife. The 'Blacks' are raggedly dressed in battered hats and muddy boots. Sometimes they have their own 'black' hobby-horse and standard-bearer, and are accompanied by tinkers, knife-grinders and gypsies.

Various dances take place: a gavotte, a winding farandole, and climaxing in the 'Godalet Dantza' (Wineglass Dance) (ill. 40), in which the various characters dance around a tumbler of wine, taking it in turns to step onto the glass and spring off again, without spilling a drop. The most skilfully executed step is done by the hobby-horse, for he cannot see his feet because of the skirt he is wearing, and must feel carefully with his feet for the tumbler. The hobby-horse's reward for this skilful display is to be set upon by the blacksmiths and gelders, who mime shoeing, and gelding (this usually demonstrated by tossing two corks into the crowd), and then he falls down exhausted, but suddenly revives, and leaps high into the air above the heads of all around him. In these Basque masquerades, all the elements come together: processional, country, chain, spectacular, and ritual dance. The principal figures have the character of morrismen, their attendants carrying sticks. Here too is the opposition of two forces, two different groups of dancers. The horse's exhaustion through gelding, and subsequent recovery, approximate to the resurrection. At one time, there used to be a barber who cut the master knife-grinder's throat, a doctor who revived him, the tinker's wife gave birth to a baby, and a bear who figures in many European mumming plays.

Tarascon has its Tarasque (ill. 47), a dragon needing several men to carry it. La Tarasque makes two appearances: on July 29th the docile creature is led to church by a small girl representing St. Martha, who sprinkles it with holy water whenever it threatens the crowd. This commemorates the saving by St. Martha of Tarascon from a man-eating dragon. On Whit Monday, a less docile Tarasque rushes through the streets accompanied by dancers. Another fiery dragon resides in Barcelona. Mons in Belgium also has a dragon. Escorted by devils, leaf-clad wild men, clowns and hobby-horses, it parades through the streets. Onlookers try to snatch ribbons from it for good luck while it is 'attacking' them. Eventually it is slain by St. George or a local hero, Gilles de Chin.

In the Catalan Pyrenees, hobby-horses fight the Moors, and the 'Mulafera' has a neck long enough to put its head on balconies and into windows, and belch fire and smoke, enabled to do so by having its mouth stocked with squibs. Here too there is an eagle wearing a royal crown, and dancing elegantly with pointed feet.

Romanian hobby-horses are connected with All Souls' Day and with midwinter feasts. Like the Călușari, they compose a brotherhood, each member undergoing an initiation ceremony before he may take part. They meet at crossroads or where nine boundaries meet, and there their leader ties bells on their legs, and sprinkles water over them nine times. They carry a decorated pole which, after their nine days' dancing they throw in the river. The number of dancers must be uneven. A fool accompanies them, and another man disguised as a goat. During the proceedings one of them dies, loudly lamented, and of course comes to life again.

One of the handsomest horses to be found anywhere in Europe comes from Cracow in Poland. The 'Lajkonik', as this beautifully caparisoned horse and rider is called, represents the Polish cavalier who, sometime during the twelfth or thirteenth centuries, captured the horse and accutrements of a Tatar horseman. Thus dressed and mounted, he returned to Cracow and scared everyone silly until he revealed himself as Polish. The ensuing celebrations are supposed to have given birth to the 'Krakowiak'.

Athens has a hobby-horse festooned all over with paper streamers. Many hobby-animals and mummers are thus adorned so that people may snatch tabs from the costume in order to bring themselves good luck.

'Little horses' performed at a feast given in honour of Don Alfonso of Castile at Valencia in 1269. Musicians 'with wild horses' entertained at the coronation of Alfonso IV of Aragon in 1327. There are references to the fifteeth-century guilds in Spain paying for the hobby-horses, and in Portugal the 'cavalhinos' took part in the Corpus Christi processions and the midsummer and parish feasts.

Not all hobby-animals are of the 'ridden' type. There are the 'head-on-pole' sort, the carrier often concealed beneath a sheet. To this category belong the Welsh 'Mari Lwyd', the Antrobus horse, the Wild Horse-skull hobby of Higher Whitley, Cheshire, and the sheep's skull (*Y Fari*) occasionally used in Glamorganshire. Czechoslovakia has its maskers wearing, rather than carrying, the head, and in Poland they have a skull of a goat or other animal with real teeth, fixed on a long pole.

The midwinter outings of the Mari Lwyd have become inextricably mixed up and confused with another custom of guising or wassailing. And so one finds, in Wales, a singing contest between the Mari Lwyd party and the people of the house, who are apparently trying to keep out those who are supposedly bringing them good luck. This custom seems to have arisen out of an older practice when *gwasseilwyr* (guisers) with blackened faces, and carrying a wassail bowl competed in song with the householders. If the inmates failed to respond with their own verses, the wassailers had to be admitted. To add to the complicated picture, the guisers were sometimes accompanied by a *Punch* and *Judy*. It is small wonder that householders sought to keep them out, when we learn that they carried staves with which they beat each other – and presumably everyone else, but whilst they were well padded under their own garments to cushion the blows, other were less well prepared. And an unruly crowd they could be. Margretta Thomas related how on one occasion Punch raked out the fire with his poker and Judy swept the hearth, and then set about brushing the walls with her dirty broom. On occasion, Mari Lwyd's leader would perform a step dance with Punch and Judy, when they would end by gripping each other's waists and whirling round "with such velocity that they would end up quite dazed". This sort of bad behaviour made the Mari Lwyd party unwelcome. 107 year-old John Evans recalled that they were a rowdy and drunken lot, and that his mother packed him indoors and shut the door and curtains.

A vivid description comes from a letter published in the 'Gentleman's Magazine' for March 1819:

> *Without troubling you or your readers with many impertinent observations upon the subject of the Morris Dance in all its various forms and which has been illustrated by many abler hands than mine, allow me to give you a plain statement of such modifications of that ancient dance as are still exhibited in this part of the country, not during the 'Merry Month of May' but like that recorded by Dr. Plot, at Christmas and mingled with the usual exhibitions of that festive season.*
>
> *The most conspicuous feature is the* Aderyn bee y llwyd, *Bird with the grey beak: this is formed by the skeleton bones of a horse's head furnished with artificial eyes and ears, and highly decorated with ribbons and coloured paper; it is borne by a man whose person is concealed beneath a long cloth; his part is to imitate the amblings, curvetings, startings and kickings of the horse; he is attended by a groom, whose business it is to sooth his affected angers and fears and keep him within proper bounds; three or four partners in the profits of the exhibition who are by turns horse, groom or attendants accompany him from house to house and after a due exhibition of the horse's various antics a hat is put into his mouth, and a collection levied upon the spectators.*
>
> *Another exhibition is called, correctly, 'The Merry Dancers'. There are usually three persons dressed in short jackets which, as well as their hats, are decorated with a profusion of paper ornaments: they proceed from house to house dancing in each a sort of reel chiefly, I believe, peculiar to Wales; after dancing the heys and setting, two of the dancers, by turns, take strong hold of each other's wrists and continue turning round for a much longer time than would be sufficient to make an ordinary head completely giddy.*
>
> *The Welsh are generally very good dancers, and very fond of it, and on these occasions, particularly, they keep time with the musick in a most energetic shuffle upon the floor, somewhat similar to a particular step in the old hornpipe, which is also occasionally danced by one of the 'Merry Dancers' if any of the party happen to be particularly expert.*

The musick is generally the harp, which I am sorry to observe is daily declining and the detestable fiddle is superseding the native instrument.

A frequent but not universal accompaniment of this merry dance are the conspicuous and grotesque figures of Punch and Judy. The gentleman is dressed according to the taste and ability of the wearer – generally in a cap, a mishmash of some animal's skin with the hair on, and the jacket is either much decorated or entirely composed of the same materials. A fox's brush (if it can be got) or some other hairy ornament is pendant behind, and a concealed bell tinkles about his hinder parts. His right hand wields a rod with which he plentifully belabours his wife Judy, who is personated by the tallest man the party are able to procure. He is habited in female attire, the face blackened, and an enormous broad brimmed, slouched beaver hat upon the head.

The two dance a pas de deux *to give occasional rest to the other performers. The step of this dance is a sort of shuffling run, in very short steps, somewhat resembling what in fashionable assemblies twenty years ago was known by the name of the 'partridge step'. The jingle of Punch's bell is the only music, and the frequent application of his rod to Judy's back the most* striking *part of the performance. The merry dancers are*

45. 'Schemenlaufen from Imst' by Karl von Lutterotti. Austrian, c.1820.

not always accompanied by these figures, but each occasionally form a separate exhibition. Old Christmas day is that upon which these, as well as 'Aderyn bee a llwyd', make their appearance.

On the Isle of Man, the 'Laare Vane', a white mare, appears with 'Mylecharane's March', a sword dance. The Laare Vane used to appear on Twelfth Night, when it went round snapping at the diners until it was finally chased out. The custom used to be that each unmarried young man was assigned to look after one of the unmarried girls of the village, to give her presents, and take her to dances. She became his "valentine . . . for the year and for longer if they be agreeable. Praise and joy, peace and plenty to them".

In Ireland, the white mare is called the 'Láir Bhan', and comes out on the night of St. Stephen's Day, when it is carried round by the Wren Boys. The wren-hunting is a ritual luck-bringing visit in which a live wren is carried round from house to house enclosed in a box. The white mare appeared too at one Irish St. John's Eve fire:

When the fire burned for some hours, and got low, an indispensable part of the ceremony commenced. Every one present of the peasantry passed through it, and several children were thrown across the sparkling embers; while a wooden frame of some 8 feet long, with a horse's head fixed to one end, and a large white sheet thrown over it, concealed the wood and the man on whose head it was carried, made its appearance. This was greeted with loud shouts as the 'white horse', and having been safely carried by the skill of its bearer several times through the fire with a bold leap, it pursued the people, who ran screaming and laughing in every direction. I asked what the horse was meant for, and was told it represented all cattle.

At San Feliu de Pallerols in Spain we find a mixture of 'ridden' hobby-horse and sword dancing. The riders are helmeted and they carry swords, the hilts of which are draped with lace handkerchiefs, and they perform a mock joust. At some time in the past there must have been a 'beheading', for the joust is called the *degollada.* Hobby-horses, dancers, and the devil himself, appear in the pilgrimage to the miracle-working cave at Zorita, Spain. Here, the Virgin causes every ill to vanish. The women who attend the pilgrimage are called *Caspolinas,* meaning they come from the region of Caspe, but, as Caspe was the original name of Gibraltar, it might imply a very ancient origin to the pilgrimage. This is led by the bishop of Zaragoza in person. Fireworks, 'lightning', and 'thunder', help to drive away any unwelcome spirits that might be in attendance on the devil, who is there to harangue the onlookers.

Sweden has bear-guisers, who often appear at weddings. In the provinces of West Gothland and Halling, several bears arrive and dance around, waving handkerchiefs. Then, in a circle, with heads to the centre, they go down on all fours, their legs stretched out behind them, and bounce up and down, moving first to the right and then back to the left.

The 'Hestleikur' dance in Iceland has a horse accompanied by two 'skjaldmeyjar' (shield-maidens), and has been processing from door to door, dancing and bringing good luck, at least since the twelfth century, when an Icelandic bishop accused them of singing "shameful, dishonouring songs, improper to listen to". These guisers would enter a house, dance with the horse until it limped, lift the affected hoof, spit on it, beat it, turn the horse on its head, and throw it up to the beams of the roof, all the time singing *vikivakar* (wanton songs) about the horse and the shield-maidens. The 'Hjartaleikur', also from Iceland, had a stag with lighted candles attached to his horns. He and any girls present sang love-songs and played a hind-dance game. The hind-mother would divide the players into harts and hinds. The harts were then blindfolded, and each would choose a hind to whom they were 'married' by the hind mother.

Carnival 'runners' exist all over Switzerland. Hobby-horses and hobby-goats of the head-on-pole type, accompanied by guisers, run through the village, knocking on windows, and making as much din as possible. Sometimes they appear in wedding groups of guisers: bride and groom, grandfather, grandmother, and a black-faced devil are privileged to seize any eatables from the house they visit, while the remaining members dance. On New Year's Day at Laufen, masked men in skins and with enormous cow-bells around their waists, and long sticks in their hands, rush wildly about, though they neither act out a play nor dance. The Nüssler of Schwyz perform a drum dance. They dress in *Blätzlichleid*, leafy clothing, masks, a strap of bells over their shoulders, and each carries a 'magic' broom. They assemble in *Rotts*, troops accompanied by drummers, and dance from one inn to another from dawn till dusk, executing brief leaping movements as they go and making their bells jingle all the while.

Mummers, called *Butzen* or *Kläuse*, go about on New Year's Eve (St. Sylvester's Day), wearing fantastic costumes and richly-decorated head-dresses, and carry enormous bells which they clang noisily as they leap about. At Shrovetide, the *Rölleibutzen* of Altstätten in the canton of St. Gall, come out in their elaborate head-dresses and masks. They too have a strap of bells (*Rölleli*) over one shoulder. They carry small squirters (ill. 45) with which they sprinkle the onlookers, especially unmarried girls. They are led by their *Butzenköni* (king of the maskers) and his mounted officers.

In Austria one comes across guisers wearing a variety of masks: bears, goats, straw-men, and horses, wearing huge cow-bells round their waists, and jumping as high in the air as the weight of the bells allows them, again to create a deafening ringing. In some regions, the runners set out early in the morning of the last day of Carnival, to visit the outlying farms. They usually have to trudge through deep snow, for this is the depth of winter in this snowy land. The farmers leave outside a tray of corn and eggs to show the Fasching or Carnival runners that they are expected. The leader, dressed all over in red, precedes them, whiffling away the spirits of winter, and clearing a path for spring. When they reach their destination, the leader lifts his broom aloft, and the others form the 'Radl', and perform the wheel-dance round him, before entering the house. Often in attendance is the hobby-horse which, as in Cheshire, is offered for sale, is shod by the smith, and then drops down dead at the feet of his new owner. He is resuscitated by a doctor, and is led away. Also to be found is the old woman carrying a baby, following the plough as it is paraded by the runners. A bear is hunted in Upper Styria. It is shot by a poacher, the police arrive on the scene, and a mock trial is held in the farmhouse. The maskers burst into the house and steal the food.

The Carnival runners to be found in the provinces of Salzburg, Styria and Tyrol, are divided into two groups: the 'schöne' (beautiful), and the 'schieche (ugly) Perchten'. The beautiful ones are well-behaved and smartly dressed, with bells, ribbons, and tall crowns adorned with mirrors. The ugly ones are unruly, and clad in rags, wear grotesque masks, and are hung about with mice and rats, chains, and cow-bells. They all carry sticks, the beautiful having ribbons on theirs, the ugly having devils' heads.

The 'Schemenlaufen' (Carnival-running) of Imst near Innsbrück is fascinating. Again, the *Schemen* are divided into two groups, called 'Scheller' and 'Roller', male and female, though both are played by men. They get their name from the bells they wear fastened to their belts; huge cow-bells for the Scheller, and little sleigh-bells for the Roller. Additionally, there are 'Spritzer' (ill. 45) who squirt water on the onlookers, 'Kübele Maien', who wet them with damp cloths, and 'Hexen' (witches) in grotesque masks. They do a round dance with much leaping in the air, to encourage the crops to grow. The festivities are not an annual event, and they say at Imst that the year when the Schemenlaufen is held, there is always fruitfulness and plenty.

In Czechoslovakia, weddings are sometimes attended by guisers dressed up as a bear and a ram, who walk before the bridal pair. They appear again at Carnival

46. Hoop dance of the Nürnberg craftsmen. German, 16th century.

time. In Bohemia, a wedding is acted out with the bridal pair in company with a father-in-law, a bear and its trainer, a Jew, a sweep, a shepherd, a fool, and a ghost. At Carnival, they perform a special dance, the 'Ruchadlo' (the Coulter), in which the movements of the plough are mimed.

Poland, as elsewhere, celebrates Carnival with the putting on of disguises. Between January Ist and 6th – the real Kalends, 'Colendas' (wassailers), accompanied by a goat, wolf or bear, indulge in the usual practice of roaming the villages, cracking whips and rattling cans, and chasing the girls. In some districts, a goat's head with a movable jaw is carried around on the end of a pole. In the region of Brzesc, an old man with horns on his hat, and carrying a sword with barley straw attached to it, announces that the Jew's mare (himself) is dead. The son begs money to bury him, and is given some by a nobleman. The old man comes back to life, and dances with his son. Now the son wishes to marry, and dancing and the giving of presents follow. Special round breads in the shape of animals are baked. These are the 'Nowe Latka' (New Year's) and bring prosperity to the household.

Hungary has the usual masked characters: the old woman carrying a broom, a shoeing-smith, a wedding group of bride and groom, and a chimney sweep. The play, with the selling of the hobby-animal (it is not always a horse), the collapsing and dying of the beast, and its revival, are all there. Hungary also has the 'regölés', who now no longer wear masks, but still bear the names of animals, bull, cat, pig, and others. They have the task of wishing girls or newly-weds fertility for themselves, their land and animals.

Romania has all the usual animal disguises with the addition of one wearing a stork's head, and with bells on its legs.

Bulgaria has a 'camel' which makes its appearance at threshing time, and goes about at night dancing. This is, in fact, an immense hobby-horse type creature with an animal head. Its leader brings good fortune and fertility, and receives wheat from the farmer for his good offices. In the celebrations marking New Year, guisers called 'Kukeri', wearing huge headdresses which have wings, feathers, animal heads above, face masks below, cow-bells around their waists, armed with swords and clubs, go from house to house, leaping and making a din, to bring good luck and fertility. Accompanying the animal-men go the spring-bride with the new-year baby in her arms, and a black-faced Arab who is the rival of the bridegroom for her favours. After choosing a king, they undertake the ritual ploughing and sowing. In the Strandja region, they dance on stilts, which may denote the imitation of ancient gods or cult heroes – giants.

'Koledouvane' is the name they give to the Christmas carol-singing rounds, bringing health and fertility to the homes and farms they visit: "May there be as much health in this house as there are many stars in the sky." The young men elect their leader, *Stanenik*, who in turn chooses a *Blagoslovnik*, who utters the good wishes and blessings. The *Stanenik* carries, wrapped in a white towel, a ring-shaped bread decorated with sprigs of basil, strings of popcorn, maize and raisins as a sign of fertility. The *Koledari* carry nosegays of ivy and boxwood, strings of popcorn hanging around their fur hats or, in the Dobroudja region, wreaths made of dried prunes and lumps of sugar, and trimmed with red thread. They also carry specially baked ring-shaped buns, one on top of the other on their shepherds' crooks.

On *Sourvaki*, St. Basil's Day (January Ist), groups of *Sourvakari* (boys) go from house to house bringing New Year's best wishes. They carry *sourvaknitsa*, which are decorated cornel twigs, and tap everyone on the back for good luck, reciting:

Beat, beat the year,
A joyful year,
Big ears of corn in the fields,
Red apples in the orchards,
Yellow corn on the cobs,
Large bunches of grapes on the vines,
A house full of children,
A purse full of money,
May we live happily until next year,
Until next year, Amen!

The *sourvaknitsas* are made by decorating twigs of cornel with wool, beans, popcorn, dried fruit, dried chilli peppers, garlic, small bread rings and coins, threaded on red string. Sometimes they also put apples and ears of wheat onto their branches.

Greece has its New Year (here the feast of St. Basil) play. The usual bride and groom, Arab and doctor, make their appearance. The bridegroom wears a fustanella and fez, carries a sword, and wears bells. The Arab has a mask made of sheep or goat skin. He attempts to seduce the bride, and in the ensuing fray the bridegroom is killed. A doctor revives him, and up he jumps to dance with the other characters. Similar plays are also to be found in Macedonia, Albania and Bulgaria. In some villages they have the 'kalogheroi', the Venerable Ones, wearing headdresses made from goat skins, blackened hands, and wearing bells, accompanied by the bride (sometimes two brides), the old woman carrying a basket containing a baby, gypsy-smiths, and other characters carrying swords and whips. In one pantomime they forge a ploughshare. The baby grows too big for the basket and demands food, drink, and a bride. The baby now grows to manhood, goes through a marriage ceremony, is shot by one of the *kalogheroi*, is lamented by the bride, but is returned to life. The ploughshare is then trundled about, one of the characters following behind scattering seed from a basket, while they all shout: "May wheat be ten piestres a bushel . . . that the poor folk may be fed!"

On the island of Skyros, a Carnival dance is performed. The three principal characters are: an old man, a maid, and a Frank. The maid is a man-woman in bridal attire. The Frank has a sheep-bell tied to his waist, and a conch shell to blow. The old man wears a shepherd's cloak inside out, a mask of animal fur, and a great number of sheep-bells fastened round his waist. Together with the other bell-laden dancers, they leap about making a deafening noise. In the Thracian village of Aghios Georghios, on Carnival Monday, they perform a play with a kind of sword dance. The players are two *kalogheroi*, who wear head-dress masks made of animal skin, blackened hands, and bells round their waists. One carries a crossbow, the other a phallus. There are two brides played by men, an old woman, who carries a basket containing a doll, which is referred to as a bastard, gypsies and policemen. During the drama a ploughshare is forged, and a plough driven round in an anti-clockwise direction. The *kalogheros* who carries the phallus somehow becomes identified with the bastard, is married to one of the brides, is shot, mourned by his wife, and then comes back to life again. In similar mumming plays in Thessaly and Macedonia, there is a doctor on hand to revive him.

In some places bonfires are lit and they dance round them, either the usual dances which they here perform with exaggerated and grotesque movements, or special songs with lewd words and gestures, such as 'Pos to trívoun to piperi' (How they grind the pepper). In this dance, which is also a favourite at weddings, the dancers rub against the ground with different parts of their bodies. 'Aghía Sotíra is another favourite in which the dancers link hands between their legs.

The Adriatic island of Lastovo has a Carnival pageant. The islanders tell their own story to explain something which is of much more ancient origin. A swarthy-faced effigy (*Poklad*), representing a Turkish pirate, is burned at the stake, after a storm had dispersed the raiders' ships. The Carnival procession makes its way through the town, stopping at certain places to enact the different scenes of the play. The characters are familiar: a mother, a doctor with his assistants, a vetinary, a Turkish envoy, an admiral, a standard-bearer, all accompanied by musicians and the *pokladari* who are the various other participants in the festivities. In the play, the envoy who has been sent by the pirates to demand the surrender of the town, and has been captured, is tried and burned, as the townspeople sing and the church bells ring. Similar plays are to be found on neighbouring islands as well as on the mainland, both on the coast and inland.

47. *La Tarasque. Provençal.* Photo M. Lacanaud.

In Serbia the *Koledari* come out between January 2nd and 6th. Two men dress up as monsters, with humped backs and masks with horns representing sheep's heads. They are accompanied by four singers and the *snaska*, a man dressed as a woman, and carrying a distaff. The masked dancers go through the village, stopping in front of each house in turn. Before going inside they play at balancing on a seesaw, and then, brandishing swords and ringing bells, they enter to sing their songs.

Slovenia has preserved the ancient custom of the *Kurenti* or *Koranti*. In various villages, between Twelfth Night and Shrove Tuesday, groups of masked figures make their way from house to house. They wrap themselves in sheepskins pulled well over their heads, their grotesque masks having a long nose and tongue, teeth made from white beans, horns and feathers. Cowbells hang from their waists. Each masquerader carries a long stick called a *ješevka* to which the skin of a hedgehog is attached. They lead a devil who carries a pitchfork, and who is ensnared in a fishing net. They are accompanied by *orači*, ploughmen, who also wear masks. Into each farmyard they drag a small wooden plough, and make as if they are ploughing a furrow. Sand, supposed to represent sugar-beet, is poured into the furrow. For bringing good luck to each household they are given presents.

The Manx had their 'Hop tu naa', a processional dance which was performed on the night of October 30th by couples dancing through the streets with lighted turnip lanterns. Dressed as witches, they went from house to house, frightening away evil spirits and being rewarded in some way for their services. It was a very simple dance, with alternate couples changing place by the second couple moving forwards under the arch made by the first couple, the second couple then repeating this either by forming the arch, or by casting out back to their own places. The whole dance was done to reel or running steps.

The 'Helg yn dreean', a progressive dance, was supposedly performed by the Wren Boys when, by the light of torches, they buried the wren on St. Stephen's Night. Half the boys were dressed as women. Additionally there was an old woman, the *Ben-treoghe yn Dreean*, the Widow of the Wren, whose part it was to wander in and out amongst the dancers, finally spinning round and round with the *bush*. The dance formerly was performed around the bush, which was honoured by the dancers, first by the men and then by the 'women'. The dance degenerated into a children's game for boys and girls, in which, at each progression, the odd girl tried to capture a partner, the one left without a partner having to dance with the bush.

The Manx also have a mummers' play which features St. Denis of France, St. George of England, and St. Patrick of Ireland. The usual fights take place in which St. George is mortally wounded by St. Denis, who is in turn run through by St. Patrick's trusty sword. Both are revived by the doctor. At the end of the play, the 'White Boys' Dance' is performed. Six men dance a hilt-and-point sword-dance around the doctor. A rose is formed from the interwoven swords, onto which the doctor is hoisted, to be carried off, supporting himself on the shoulders of the first two dancers. St. George has his own solo dance, 'Daunse noo George', during the play, when he performs a 'Highland' sword dance over two crossed swords.

The seasonal round of life in England, as elsewhere, was once marked by ceremonials performed exclusively by men wearing a disguise. As time passed, ceremony dwindled, until only the appearance at the correct time and the disguise remained to mark the ritual, which became difficult to understand in the more sophisticated times of recent history.

One of the most persistent rituals is that of the mummers' play, still surviving in scattered places in the British Isles. The performances usually occur during the Christmas period, though they are a feature of the winter months from All Souls to Easter. They take place in the streets at Marshfield in Gloucestershire on Boxing Day, and at Midgley in Yorkshire at Easter. Performances are also given in public houses, dance halls, halls of large houses, as at Uttoxeter in Staffordshire, and Antrobus in Cheshire, or the performers make the rounds of outlying farms as they still do in Ireland.

Here is a description of mummers' performances from the early years of the twentieth century:

> *A group of men stand silently in a semi-circle to the rear of where they are to perform. They are disguised either by a poor attempt at dressing in character, or by strips of paper or ribbon sewn to their everyday clothes, and hanging from their hats over their faces. They remain silent and immobile until, when it is their turn to speak, they step forward, declaim their lines in a loud voice, devoid of any inflexions, and stand back at the conclusion of their speech. The performance only shows lively action when two of the performers fight each other with swords, and even this may be formalised into rhythmic clashing, until one is killed and brought to life again by a wonder-working doctor.*

Performances today are usually much livelier and more entertaining than these sound to have been, possibly because the ritualistic background has now been replaced by the purely entertainment aspect, and so the performers are free to *ad lib* as the fancy takes them.

'Mummers' is the common name for the play, but it is also applied to the black-faced children who, until very recently, swept the hearths of houses in West Yorkshire and south-east Lancashire on New Year's Eve, making a humming sound all the time. In Derbyshire and Staffordshire, the performers in the play were known as 'guisers'; so were the men and women in Cornwall, who changed clothes, blacked their faces, and danced in the streets. Sometimes the latter also performed a play independently.

Two of England's best known mummers' plays are those of Ampleforth and Revesby. The Ampleforth play falls into five sections. In the first, the king tells his father, who is the clown, that he wishes to get married. He is introduced to the queen, pays her court, but then decides that he would prefer to remain single, and they quarrel. The clown and the king begin to fight, but they are interrupted by the queen, who states that in any case she prefers the clown. Now the clown announces that he wishes to see the king dance, but the king in his turn asks the clown instead to sing a song. The clown sings the 'Love Song about Murder', which doesn't please the king, who then sings the song himself. It is now the turn of the dancers, who are introduced one by one in two calling-on songs sung by the clown. After they have danced, a 'stranger', dressed in ordinary clothes, comes into their circle. The dancers form the 'lock' with their swords around his neck, and as they withdraw them, the stranger falls down dead. Promptly, the dancers run off leaving the clown alone with the corpse. The king returns, and accuses the clown of the murder. To exonerate himself, the clown calls the dancers back, but they all deny the murder, and the last, no.6, accuses the king, who accepts the blame for killing the 'old man', whereupon the clown denies that the dead man is old, because he is in fact his son, and he himself is quite young. All kneel round the corpse and sing a mock psalm, and the clown reads out the dead man's will. A doctor is called for, and he comes in riding on the back of another man. He enumerates the places he has travelled to and the ills he can cure, though he fails in reviving the corpse. The play ends with the clown himself bringing the dead man back to life again, by drawing his sword from the throat down to the groin of the stranger, who then springs to life.

In the Revesby version, the play begins with the fool introducing his five sons, and then he fights the hobby-horse. With their swords the dancers form the 'lock', which here is called the 'glass', and the fool looks at himself in it before throwing it on the ground and jumping on it. One of the sons announces that they have decided to cut off his head, at which the fool kneels, and, with the swords about his neck, he makes his will. He falls dead, and the dancers announce that they have killed "our father like ye evening sun". The fool revives, and the dance is performed, after which all leave except the fool and Cicely (the 'bride'), whom the fool now begins to woo. The sons also

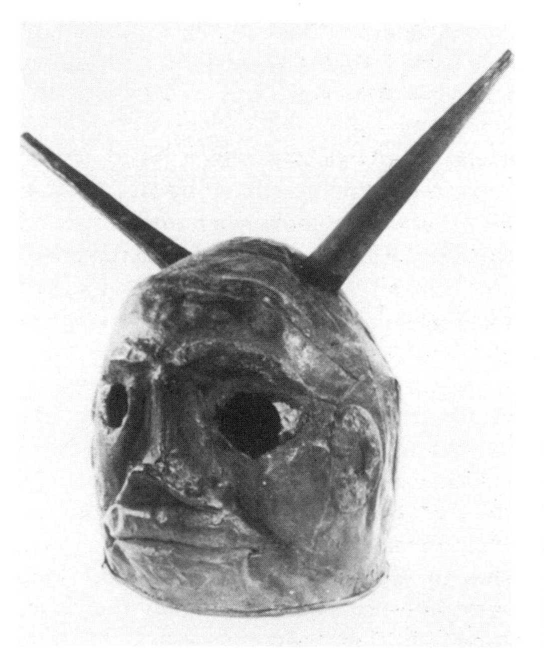

48/49. Devil's mask (Left) and Mask of Moses (Right) from the Jeux de la Fête-Dieu. Provençal. Photos M. Lacanaud.

try to woo her, but Cicely chooses the fool, who grows younger as the sons grow older.

These plays contain the essential formulae of making the will before being killed, the making of the lock of swords to bring about the death, the denial of guilt by the murderers, and the cure by a doctor or other character (the doctor probably being a late introduction to the play).

Here is a complete play from Yorkshire where it is still performed:

(Enter the Jester)

JESTER   A room, brave fellows, pray give us room to sport!
Unto this room we now wish to resort
And to make our merry rhyme.
Good sirs, 'tis Pace-egging time,
The time for goose pies doth appear.
So we have come to bring you good cheer,
To the sound of a trumpet and the beat of a drum.
Make room, make room, and let our actors come!
We are the jolly actors who travel the street,
We are the jolly actors who fight for our meat,
We are the jolly actors who show a pleasant play.
So, step in, St. George, and clear the way!

(Enter St. George)

ST. GEORGE   In comes I, St. George, from old England I did spring.
My famous name throughout the world doth ring.
Many a goodly sight and kingdom have I known,
And made false tyrants tremble on their throne.
Once I followed a maiden to the dragon's gate,
Where, confined in dungeon deep, she did await her fate.
Then I resolved with true knight errantry
To break down the door and set the maiden free,
When lo, a giant nearly struck me dead,
So with my sword I cut off his head.
I travelled this world all round and round,
But a man to equal me I ne'er have found.

(Enter Bold Slasher)

BOLD SLASHER   I am a valiant soldier, Bold Slasher is my name.
With sword and buckler at my side I hope to win more fame,
And for to fight with me I see thou art not able,
And with my trusty broadsword I soon shall thee dismemble.

ST. GEORGE   Dismemble? Dismemble? Thou hast not the power,
For with my broadsword I soon shall thee devour.
So stand, Bold Slasher, let no more be said!
For if I use my sword I soon shall break thy head.

BOLD SLASHER How canst thou break my head if it's made of iron, and my body lined with steel?
My hands and feet are knuckle bone, and I challenge thee to feel.

(Music – they fight; Bold Slasher is run through and falls)
JESTER Alas, alas, Bold Slasher is slain.
Oh, what must I do to raise him up again?
Here he lies in the presence of you all,
I lovingly for a doctor call.
A doctor, a doctor, ten pounds for a doctor!

(Enter doctor)
DOCTOR In comes I, the doctor, and now you'll plainly see,
I owe my art to cleverness, and my activity.

JESTER That's all very well, doctor, but tell me, how much is thy fee?

DOCTOR Ten pounds is my fee, but since thou art an honest man, five I'll take from thee.

JESTER Tha'll be wondrous cunning to get any. But tell me, doctor, how far have you travelled in your doctoring?

DOCTOR From Italy, Titaly, and Germany, France and Spain,
And am returned to cure the diseased in England once again.

JESTER And what diseases canst thou cure?

DOCTOR Absolutely all sorts: the itch, the pitch, the palsy and the gout.
Why, if a man's got nineteen devils in his skull, I'll cast twenty out.
I have in my pocket crutches for lame ducks, spectacles for blind bumble bees,
Pack saddles for grasshoppers and plasters for broken-backed mice.
Why, I once cured Sir Harry of a nagtail fifty-five yards long.

ALL How long?

DOCTOR Sixty-five yards long. Surely I can cure this poor man.
Here, Slasher, take a little from this bottle,
And let it slither down thy throttle!
And if thou be not quite slain,
Slasher, rise and fight again!

(Slasher revives)
SLASHER Oh, my back! My head is wounded,
And my heart's confounded.

To be struck out of seven senses into fourscore,
The like was ne'er seen in England before.

(Exit Slasher – enter St. George)
ST. GEORGE In comes I again, St. George, the famous champion bold,
And with my trusty broadsword I won ten thousand pounds in gold.
'Twas I who fought the fiery dragon, and brought him to great slaughter,
And, by these wondrous deeds I won the King of Egypt's fairest daughter.

(Enter Prince of Paradine)
PRINCE OF PARADINE I am the Prince of Paradine, born of high renown,
And soon I will fetch St. George's lofty courage down.

ST. GEORGE Stand fast, thou black Morocco dog, or by my sword thou shalt die!
I will pierce thy body full of holes and make thy buttons fly.

PRINCE OF PARADINE Draw forth thy sword and slay,
Pull out thy purse and pay!
For I will have a recompense before I go away.

ST. GEORGE Ah, noble Prince of Paradine, where hast thou been,
And what goodly sights hast thou seen?
Dost thou think no-one of the age,
Dare such an one as thee engage?
Put up your sword, throw down your spear!
I'll fight you without dread or fear.

(Music – they fight and the Prince of Paradine is slain)
ST. GEORGE See, the Prince of Paradine is dead,
And all his joys entirely fled.
Take him, cast him to the flies,
That ne'er again he come before mine eyes!

JESTER Why did I ever call thee friend?
Thou proud and saucy coxcomb, be gone!

ST. GEORGE Coxcomb? I defy that name.
And with my sword, thou shalt be stabbed for the same.

JESTER Stabbing is the least I fear.
Put up your sword, thy end is near!

(They fight, but are suddenly interrupted by Beelzebub)
BEELZEBUB In comes I, old Beelzebub,
And on my shoulder I carry my club,

And in my hand a dripping pan.
Don't you think I'm a jolly old man?
Give me money, and have no doubt,
If you don't, I'll sweep you all out.
A drop of your big vat would make us merry and sing,
To have shillings in our pockets would be a very fine thing.
If you don't believe these words I say,
Step in, Ghostly Stallion, and lead the way!

(Enter Dick and his Master)
MASTER In comes Dick, and I, his Man,
We've come to see you once again.
This horse was alive, but now he's dead.
He's nothing but a poor old horse's head.
Stand up, Dick!
This horse has travelled high, he's travelled low,
And he's travelled both through frost and snow.
This horse has travelled where the roofs were thatched with pancakes,
Where walls were built with penny loaves,
Where the streets were paved with dumplings,
And black puddings growing on apple trees.
Stand up, Dick!
This horse has an eye like a hawk and a neck like a swan,
And a tongue like a lady's pocket-book, now read that if you can.
He's a very fine horse; he's of a very fine mould.
We've got to keep him clothed to save him from the cold.
Stand up, Dick!
Going down yon hill last night, poor old Dick fell down, And he broke both shafts off.
So, ladies and gentlemen, see what you can give to buy Dick a new cart,
Not for him to pull, but for me to ride in.
Stand up, Dick!
This horse has but one leg, and so he's obliged to beg.
But what he begs it is but small,
For he's obliged to feed us all.
Stand up, Dick!

BEELZEBUB "Hold, fearless donkey!", I hear the morris men cry,
For the lads go shouting, "bravo", when I go riding by.
I never use the whip, 'cos he trots along so fast,
And though his age is ninety-nine, he makes it to the last.

ALL Stand up, Dick!
(Singing) And now we've arrived at the end of our play,
And we hope you've enjoyed it this fine festive day,

For we're valiant young men, and we've told you our tale,
And now our delight will be in drinking your ale.

A variation of the so-called 'St. George's Play' peculiar to Cheshire and its borders is the 'Soulers' Play'. Performed on or near All Souls Day (November 1st), the characters include the Black King of Morocco and a Black Prince Palatine, who may originate from the Black Prince, son of Edward III, and who was the first Earl of Chester. The play has somehow attached itself to the custom of 'soul-caking' or 'soul-appling', whilst the White Horse, which is both comic and terrifying, has joined the cast, although it performs no integral part in the play.

The 'Plough Play' is yet another version of the death and resurrection theme, and is most prevalent in Lincolnshire and the adjoining regions, Cornwall, and in a line between the two counties. It is performed on Plough Monday, which is the first Monday after January 6th or old New Year's Day, which is the end of the agricultural holidays. The play in the Midlands is performed by guisers, who are variously called 'Plough Stots', 'Plough Bullocks', 'Plough Jags'. A sword dance is an integral part of the play. The hero or intended bridegroom is sometimes called the 'Ribboner', whose adversary is the Recruiting Sergeant, and the attendant company are the Tall Hat Men. Some of the performers may once have worn animal disguises, hence Plough Bullocks. The play also alludes to the annual sacred marriage, death and revival, and to the child who grows to manhood in time to become the bridegroom for the next cycle of birth, marriage and death. The plough itself is a universal symbol of virility, and sometimes forms part of the construction of the hobby-horse.

In France, 'Carementran' (*Carême entrant* or Lent coming) was a grotesque effigy, sometimes of a person known to the onlookers. 'Sa Majesté Carnaval', as it was called, was tossed up and down in a sheet, carried on a wheeled stretcher, or hoisted up on a waggon, and filled the rôle of scapegoat. It was held responsible for all the ills that had been inflicted upon the people in the previous year. It was put on trial, found guilty, and condemned to death, either by drowning in the sea, being thrown into the river, being hanged from the Pont-de-Chamet, or set on fire while everyone danced around.

Associated with Carnival in Provence are four dances in particular. 'La Danse des Boufet' (*Soufflets* – fire-bellows) is performed on Ash Wednesday. On coming out of church after the Mass, wearing women's chemises or white trousers, cotton bonnets tied with coloured ribbons, a scarf tied round the neck, with bells on their arms, the dancers proceed to the square in two lines. Their cheeks floured, their foreheads sprinkled with ashes, they walk with a hobbling step, hopping from one leg to the other, performing jumps, *entrechats*, and pigeon's-wings, before continuing their limping walk and singing bawdy couplets. After each couplet they put the nozzle of the bellows, decorated with ribbons and bells which each carries, against the posterior of the dancer he follows. They thrust spectators aside by showering them with the flour and ash with which the bellows are filled. In the squares, at crossroads, in front of the houses of notables, they reel off their couplets while forming themselves into a spiral or circle, manœuvring their instruments in suitably obscene manner. They are usually liberally regaled with wine wherever they halt, and this obviously helps them complete their itinerary. When the dance is performed at night, alternate dancers will carry a burning torch, and in the squares, for further illumination, they will set up a large paper moon with candles inside. The moon symbol is mirrored in the spiral figure which features in the dance, just as the god of vegetation is honoured by the limping step. White clothes and bells again suggest that here we have the relic of some ancient fertility rite.

The second dance is the 'Danse des Fielouso' (*Fileuses* – Spinners' Dance). The idea of a thread crops up in a number of myths dating back to prehistoric times. The magic linkage is found in sorcery and folk medecine, in religion where angels and devils link up with the dead to carry them back to their respective worlds. Does not the Earth Mother have as one of her attributes a spindle? This symbolism is also attached to the Moon-goddess and to the Fates who controlled Man's destiny through their spinning. In this dance, boys, dressed in female garb, carry in the right hand a huge spindle topped by bells, and transformed by the use of multi-coloured paper and a candle into a lantern. In the other hand they carry a shuttle round which coils the thread from the distaff. A masked Harlequin goes in front followed by a couple holding a spinning-wheel and a spool. Two dancers, one carrying a lantern to symbolize the moon, the other a lantern to represent the sun, and the *fileuses*, when they reach their dancing place, move into two concentric circles around the others. After some quick steps (*chassés croisés*), one circle is formed, from which each 'spinner' in turn steps out to sing a couplet of a satirical nature, with a final verse by Harlequin, who delivers such scathing lines that the most thick-skinned social offender must cringe when he hears his sins exposed to public ridicule. The presence of spindle, distaff and lanterns indicates quite clearly the fertility nature of the dance.

Early Man was fascinated by the moon which he watched wax, wane, but regenerate herself again and again. He believed that she controlled the action of the waters, the tides, all nature, and growth as well as death. The moon was also the great enchantress. Ancient legends have had the moon appear, as it were, a spider weaving its web, the cosmic veil, linking all beings and all things by its invisible threads. Many countries have dances which illustrate this concept. Spain in particular preserves a great number of rites little changed over the millenia. In Barcelona, in the 'Ball dels Barils', the participants are linked by cords held across the street, and suddenly lowered to entangle unwary onlookers. This rite has degenerated almost into a children's game, but is a relic of those customs in which the progress of some procession presumed beneficient is held up in order to increase its efficacy: thus in the 'Estacada' of Breil and among the Bravadeurs of St. Tropez, and at Barjols where the procession carrying the saint is held up by the discharging of blunderbusses at the feet of the porters of the saint's statue.

In the 'Danse des Fileuse' of Var we have a coming together of two separate ideas, for in this the dancers are linked by ribbons to a man in the centre, who has the ends of the ribbons attached to his waistband, and around whom the dancers perform. He is thus the 'maypole-man', representing as he does the cosmic tree. Here in Provence, the 'fileuses', wearing little bells round their wrists and on the distaffs which they carry, dance round a 'hunter' tying him up inextricably in their ribbons, until he disperses them by blasting off his blunderbuss. Couplets of the song used to accompany this dance refer to the supposed laziness of the moon, who preferred to dance rather than to spin.

50. *Jeux de la Fête-Dieu with the ship-on-wheels. Provençal.* Photo M. Lacanaud.

In the village of Ribagorca in Spain, so strong is the belief in the power of the cord to drive out evil spirits, that during the whole year, the peasants keep bits of thread to make, come the feast day, a cord which stretches for several kilometres, and which is drawn by a donkey through the streets, until the square is reached where the ritual will take place. A devil, a 'majoral', and a master shepherd pass their comments on the happenings of the year, the weather, the harvest, and as usual find some personage whose pecadilloes they can castigate. Here in Spain, the 'Filadora Paressosa' or 'Maria Paressosa' again refers to the lazy nature of the moon.

In Provence, in 'la Lano', the dancers perform various work actions to do with wool: shearing, carding, spinning and weaving, corresponding to the Basque 'Cançon de Lino'. At San Feliu de Codines in Spain, the 'Ball de la Filade' has men and women facing each other miming spinning, and dancing little 'mills'. In Cerdagne, there is a ritual during which the children are otherwise distracted at a given moment, when originally the chief priest and chief priestess would perform their ritual coupling, but now instead the distaffs are set on the ground and the dancers must dance nimbly over them without touching. Finally, picking up the distaffs, they make a circle and dance round anti-clockwise in honour of the moon. The Provençal 'Farandole del Varlet' is led by a woman spinning, followed by a bull, a labourer armed with a goad, and a farandole of women moving to the right to form a circle round the bull. In Ibiza the 'Baile de Filera' is usually performed at marriages. The groom and his friends dance round the bride who mimes spinning, and the dance finishes amidst noise and shouting to drive away any lurking evil spirits. At Bulgarian weddings too one sees a woman carrying a distaff and spinning as she dances.

'La Fricassée' is another dance which preserves merely the vestiges of its ancient significance and is now little more than a children's game. In this dance a couple tease and scold each other, kicking, smacking, pulling hair, nose and ears, before making up, and finally embracing. We find similar dances all over Europe. Let us look again briefly at the 'Godalet Dantza', the Basque wine-glass dance. In it the knife grinders sharpen the sword of the seigneur. One of them has his throat cut, but is revived by a doctor. The gelders start a fight, kicking and lashing out and pulling each other's noses as in the 'Fricassée'. Then they catch the hobby-horse and geld and shoe it. The poor old horse appears to be on its last legs, totters for a few painful steps supported by its attendant grooms, but then shows signs of revival, starts to jump and dance nimbly about, before making its prodigious leap, and then is held high above the heads of the onlookers, just as Harlequin is raised on the lattice of swords in the 'Danse des Olivettes'. There is good reason to believe that originally the 'Fricasée' also was one of those rites which had to do with death being succeeded by the regeneration of nature.

Fighting dances in various forms are to be found in nearly all countries. In Sweden, as part of the May festivities, two troops of horsemen confront each other. The chief of one side, dressed in furs to represent winter, throws snowballs at his adversary, who is dressed in greenery and spring flowers. Summer naturally triumphs. In some parts of the German world, Winter is dressed in straw, Summer in ivy. These fighting games, above all between the sexes, of which 'Fricassée' is an example, were done to stimulate the forces of vegetation to renew themselves.

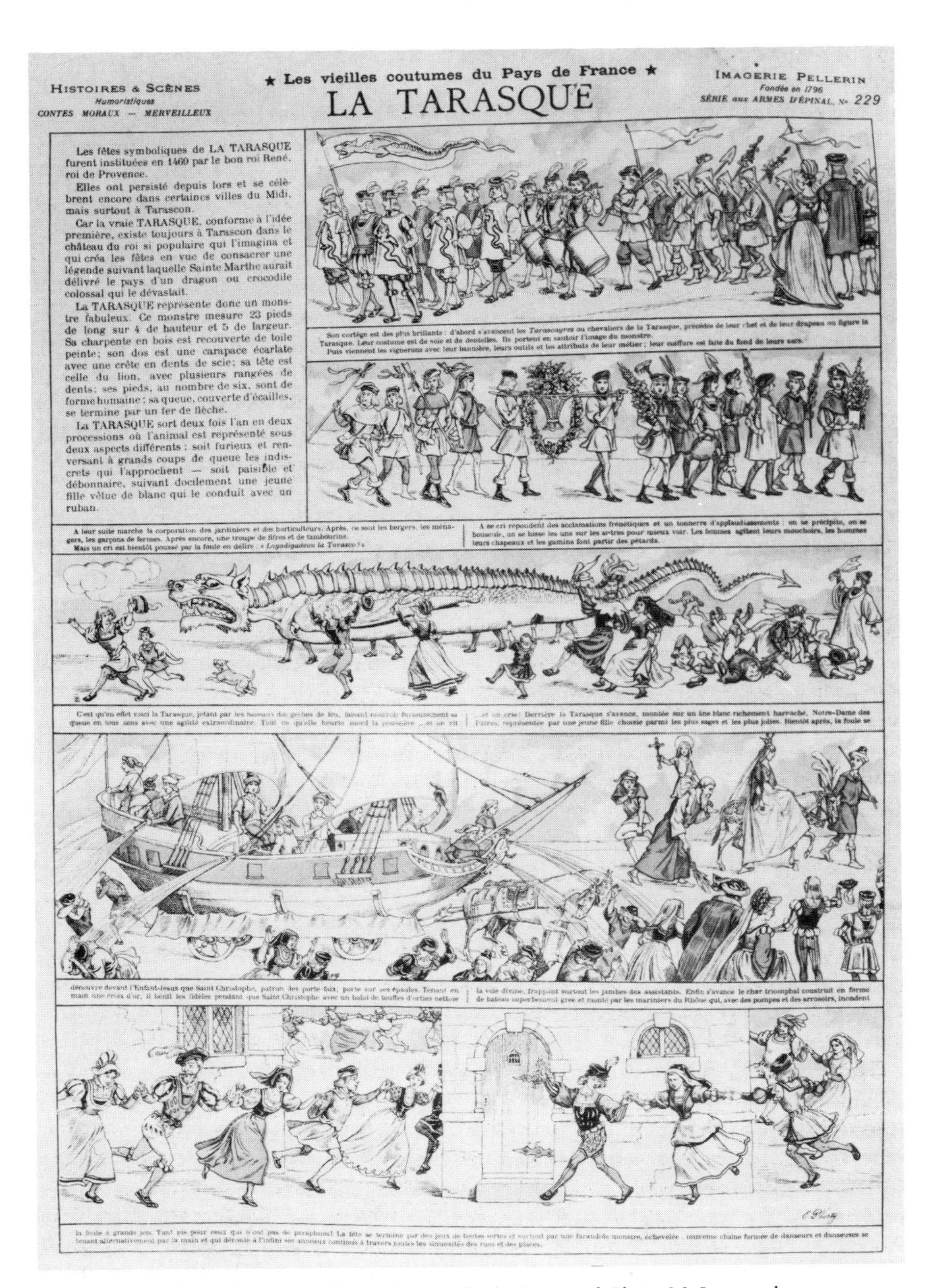

51. *Procession of the Tarasque with the ship-on-wheels. Provençal.* Photo M. Lacanaud.

The theme of the 'Fricassée' is mentioned in 'La Basse Danse' (1521) by Antonius Arena. Later it was a favourite of the soldiers of the First Empire who spread it far and wide, where it degenerated into the children's game we know today. In the region of Tours at the end of the nineteenth century, we read that boys and girls stood facing each other in lines, giving each other kicks with their clogs, clapping hands together, the boys leering at the girls, chasing them manacingly, before finally meekly kneeling down in front of them. They called this dance 'l'Arlésienne' which points to its Provençal origin. It is a further example of the transformation of ritual dance to courtship dance. The death of winter theme appears in 'la Fougnarello' (Boudeuse), in the French 'la Fâchée', and in the Greek 'Angrismeno'. The man shows his love for a young girl. Seeing himself rejected, he makes to strangle himself with his neckerchief, but she rushes to him, unties the bond, revives him and shows her disapproval. Then they display their affection for each other, and finally the man kneels in front of his loved one.

'Li Foulié Espagnolo' (the Follies of Spain) is another dance of similar type. By the side of the Etang de Berre in Provence, following on from the Moresque and the sword dance, they perform this Carnival dance to a popular tune in quick tempo. This mimed dance is believed to have originated in Portugal, and became stylised into a courtship dance on its passage through Spain. In the centre of a circle of noisy dancers, half of whom were dressed in travesty and all of whom were armed with swords, a young 'Spaniard' mimed his declaration of love to the young beauty, who proudly rejected his advances. In desperation he stabbed her and she fell to the ground. As the dance continued she gradually revived and pardoned her lover.

The same theme often saw the substitution of a Turk for the Spaniard, and the replacement of clattering swords by chattering castanets. The fact that this dance is special to Carnival indicates its original rôle as part of the theme annually played out of the death of Nature and her glorious renewal in spring. Corrubia described it in his 'Tesoro de la lengua castellane' (1611), and Pedro I, king of Portugal, it is said, liked it so much that he danced it the whole night through with his family and his court. The ritual dance, rapidly transformed into a courtship dance, passed through Spain into France which, at the end of the sixteenth century, was very receptive to Spanish tastes and fashions. Feuillet, in 1713, described it as a dance of the theatre, whose theme much pleased the ballet masters. From there it gained access to the ballrooms of high society. Madame de Sévigné, writing about the son of the Maréchal de Rennes, described how "he dances these lovely chacones, the Folies d'Espagne but above all the passepieds with his wife in a way so perfect and agreeably embellished that it defies description".

The Provençals delighted in these ballets also. At the first sound of the *tambourin* heralding the Moresque, sword dance or 'Folies d'Espagne', the inhabitants went rushing to their doors and windows to enjoy watching the celebrations. Such was the desire to dance without hindrance at Carnival that the young people of La Garde-Freinet, so that they should not suffer from the interdictions of the clergy, started, on the first day of the year, to keep the curé liberally supplied with game: thrushes, young partridges, woodcock and the like, convincing themselves that, by this act of benevolence, they bought themselves the right to dance at Carnival.

The origin of the annual destruction of the 'Carementran', the personification of Carnival, lay in the human sacrifices which were made to ensure the renewal of life, and which were eventually replaced by the substitution of an effigy. Darius Milhaud in his description of the Carnival at Aix-en-Provence summed up admirably the spirit behind the Carnival celebrations:

> *Aix and Nice gave, in modern form, a reverberating impression of this ancient tradition: the spectacular Procession of His Majesty Carnival* (Corso de Sa Majesté Carnaval) *gives the opportunity yearly to a given theme for the artistic realization of the Carnival makers who excel in putting on subjects full of spirit and good humour by means of expressive heads. Modern resources were used to make the illuminations more expressive, the fireworks more sumptuous. These carefully worked creations have robbed the Carnival of its spontaneity, have hidden from sight the primitive sense of magic effecting the prosperity of the countryside. Only the feeling of the approach of the good season shows through in the buffoonery of the people, and remains as the ultimate impulse of the instinctive dance.*
>
> *The degeneration of the rite can be gauged by the measure in which elaborate disguises have been reduced to faces made-up or half-masked. This last expression of the primitive need of Man to upturn the normal order and to change character is far from reproducing, as was done formerly, the mystic union of the sexes for the purpose of fertility, and the inviting of the souls of the dead to manifest themselves during these days in disguise, before being escorted outside the city, to disappear with the 'Carementran'.*
>
> *However, after the debauchery of dance and joyful buffoonery, when in the evening of Mardi Gras, suddenly resounds the decree condemning Sa Majesté Carnaval to a violent death, nothing can stop oneself shuddering in the face of his ephemeral fate, which is also that of Man. And instinctively the spirit carries one forwards towards the optimistic cult of our ancestors born of the prehistoric agrarian mysticism which foreshadowed the regeneration of the soul, in imitation of the seed hidden in the ground. In the starlit night this hope accompanies the notes of the melancholy song of farewell:*
>
> *Adièu paure Carnaval,*
> *Tu t'en vas e iéu m'en tourni . . .*

"Farewell poor Carnival. You are going and I am turning round."

7

COUPLE DANCES AND THREESOMES

The young man jumps up, and towards him moves the girl.
He is like a falcon, and she glides like a swallow.
No sooner are they near to each other than they are already parted.
He tries to grasp her lovingly, but she flies away,
And no-one who watches this couple is able,
In dance, springing and gestures, to better it.

Ruodlieb, 1023.

When did men and women first begin to dance in couples? It is a question which is impossible to answer with any degree of certainty. The earliest written reference to couple dancing dates from about the year 1000 A.D., but undoubtedly people had been dancing in pairs long before that date. One must really look back into prehistoric times, to primitive ritual, in order to discover the earliest evolution of the couple dance.

The first object of prehistoric man's worship was the Mother Earth, the provider of all things to helpless man. In return for her care and protection, Mother Earth had to be worshipped, and, through acts of sympathetic magic, to be encouraged to be fruitful. Man's well-being, indeed his mere survival, depended on Mother Earth annually renewing herself and being bountiful with her crops, fruit trees, vines and so on. Early man believed that he could encourage her to provide for him by ritually performing the sexual act actually in the orchard, in the furrow of the ploughed field, or in the vineyard. At certain times of the year, therefore, couples went off and performed their sympathetic magic in the open air.

Undoubtedly, before they went off thus, the community would participate in some ritual together. One may imagine that, to put the couples in the right mood for the performance of the sexual act, the general dancing would have become blatantly suggestive and erotic, just as it was at weddings until very recent times. In this latter situation, it was not so much a case of religious ritual, as the need for couples to be fruitful and to produce a steady flow of offspring: up to relatively modern times infant mortality was such, that only one child in ten succeeded in living beyond the first year of its life. Many are the dances still performed today which yet contain vestiges of these suggestive actions. Two thousand years of condemnation by the Church has generally stripped them of their most erotic movements, but, in watered down form, they are still to be seen today. As Christianity, and to a greater degree Islam, spread through Europe, pagan worship and ritual declined, leaving behind those remnants of the original ritual devoid of their former reason and purpose. People gradually came to dance merely to amuse themselves, continuing to perform those ancient dances but in a form without meaning.

This is reflected today in the children's game, 'Oats and Beans and Barley Grow', accounts of which, in identical form, are found in Sweden, Italy, France, Spain, and even America, whence it travelled with the immigrants. Mentioned in Froissant and Rabelais it mimes: sowing, mowing, binding, threshing and winnowing.

Oats and beans and barley grow!
Oats and beans and barley grow!
Do you or I or anyone know
How oats and beans and barley grow?
First the farmer sows his seed,
Then he stands and takes his ease,
Stamps his feet and claps his hands,
And turns around to view his land.

Waiting for a partner,
Waiting for a partner.
Open the ring and take one in!
Now you are married and must obey,
You must be true to all you say,
You must be kind, you must be good,
And help your wife to chop the wood."

In the first verse one boy stands in the centre while the others circle around him, singing and miming. In the second verse he chooses a girl who joins him in the centre and they kiss, while the others continue to circle and sing. He then joins the circle, leaving her in the centre, and the game is repeated until everyone has been chosen.

Another question, equally difficult to answer is: When did people begin to dance just for fun? Even before the coming of Christianity and Islam, people had used dance as a social pleasure, to be indulged in just for the fun of it, though, and here we must be careful, it was the higher ranks of society and not the lower and peasant ranks, who hired dancing masters to teach them the social graces, and employed professional dancing girls to amuse them. Early Christian writers, and before them Roman historians, made mention of various forms of dance, such as those with swords round sacred trees or other sacred objects, and dances with the participants wearing masks, but these dances were performed for ritual purposes. It was only as one part of Europe after another adopted the new religions, and the purpose behind the old dances was lost, that the country folk began to dance just for the fun of it, though, as the new world religions did not reach all parts at the same time, pagan practices

52. Peasant dance. German, 15th century.

survived until late in history in some of the more out of the way and inaccessible regions.

The German poet Ruodlieb, in the year 1023, provides us with our earliest reference to the couple dance:

> *The young man jumps up, and towards him moves the girl.*
> *He is like a falcon, and she glides like a swallow.*
> *No sooner are they near to each other than they are already parted.*
> *He tries to grasp her lovingly, but she flies away,*
> *And no-one who watches this couple is able,*
> *In dance, springing and gestures, to better it.*

The interplay between the two forms an important part of the oldest couple dances, and here already we find the basic motifs of the boy's wooing and the girl's repulsing his advances, which are seen in many later couple dances, such as the German and Austrian Ländler and the Italian Tarantella.

Couple dances originated, we may suppose, out of the circle dance. They might be danced in duple or triple time, this depending on the rhythm of the melodies used to accompany the dancing. The lyrics to the songs used were invariably an interplay between boy and girl (still very much the mainstay of the accompaniment to Portuguese couple dances), and the couple reflected in their actions the words of the song. Thus we have the boy chasing the girl and trying to catch her while she

53. 'Couple Dance' by Albrecht Dürer. German, 1514.

eludes his grasp; he tries again to attract her attention but she averts her eyes, he moves in front of her, however, and begs her love until, finally, she relents, and offers him her hand or cheek to kiss; then, full of joy, they dance in each other's arms, although it is seemly that the girl still makes a pretence of trying to break free. Thus, to a sung accompaniment, the couple dance continued well into the seventeenth century, and in some countries continues still, and almost without exception these songs were in the nature of a dialogue between boy and girl.

In different dances, in various regions, a great variety of movements developed: stamping the heels of the boots, hand clapping, parting and coming together of the couple, turning, and finishing perhaps with the boy throwing the girl in the air in triumph. The dance described by Ruodlieb, so long ago, is not very different from many a Ländler danced on St. Bartholemew's Day, in some of the more remote mountain areas of Germany today.

54. 'Peasant Couple Dancing' by Hans Sebald Beham. German, 1522.

55. 'Danse de Paysans' (Peasants' Dance) by Théodore de Bry. French, 1528-1598.

56. 'Danse de Seigneurs et Dames' (Dance of Lords and Ladies) by Théodore de Bry. French, 1528-1598.

57. 'Dancing Peasants' by Hans Sebald Beham. German, 1546.

In Germany, the Minnesingers used existing peasant songs, but embellished and adapted them to suit the more refined circles of court and upper society. A gulf between the classes was already apparent as early as the year 1235. We hear how, at a tournament of the Knights of Magdeburg, the ordinary peasants mocked the aristocratic manners, as:

58. 'Peasant Dance' by Pieter Brueghel. Flemish, 16th century.

> *they danced with sliding step with dainty holding of hands, the ladies in their long trains, with their fluttering eye-lashes and hovering smiles on their lips.*

All this was too much for the rough farmers who much preferred their lusty, jolly 'Hoppeldei' dances.

The boisterous nature of this form of dance is apparent from the ban imposed on it in the year 1404, in Ulm, which forced the couples to dance in single file to

59. 'Slängpolska'. Gripsholm Castle. Swedish, 17th century.

stop them coming into quite such intimate contact. Johannes Gailer von Kaiserberg railed against the kissing and unseemly behaviour indulged in by peasants in their dances. He named one dance as the 'Heigerleiss', and this seems to be related to a dance which the Minnesingers called 'Heierlei'. It may have got its name from the joyful cry of "heia hei!" often shouted as they danced.

A 'Hoop Hei' dance has a long and remarkable history. It combines the progression round in a circle using a step-change step with the Seven Springs to which they shouted "hopp hei!" It was danced to an ancient Seven Springs' tune, and on the seventh jump the couple kissed each other. In Ahlstadt near Rodach, the dancers, during the Seven Springs, threw themselves onto their stomachs or backs. In Kusterdingen in Tübingen, it was a dance for one or at most two couples, and the dance was repeated seven times. Until very recently, it was danced at weddings and church festivals. Sometimes the jumps were replaced by somersaults by the boys, while the girls turned on the spot. In the islands off the north coast of Germany, the boys danced the stamps, knees, elbows, of the Seven Springs.

Von Fischart, in the year 1575, mentions a dance called 'Allemant d'Amour' being introduced into France as a 'German Dance' or 'Allemande', and finding its way back into Germany under a French nomenclature. Vieilleville noted in 1552, that the Allemande was included in the programme danced in honour of the Lutheran envoy, and he commented that the Germans did not dare join in the dance, because

60. 'Peasant Dance' by Franz Placidus Altmuther. Austrian, 1746-1817.

61. Couple dance from a drinking horn. Norwegian, 1731.

the French danced it so perfectly. Thoinot Arbeau describes the Allemande in his Orchésographie (1589) thus:

> *The Allemande is a simple, somewhat sedate dance, known to the Germans, and, I believe, among our oldest, since we are descended from them. It is to be seen that in company, when you have joined hands with a lady, many others may fall into line behind you, each one with his partner. And you shall all dance at once in duple time, moving forwards, or if you prefer backwards, three steps and one* grève, *or* pied en l'air *without* saut; *and at certain times by one step and one* grève *or* pied en l'air. *On reaching the end of the hall you may dance turning around the while without letting go your lady, and the dancers who follow you shall do the same. When the musicians terminate this first part, each dancer shall stop and engage in light conversation with his lady, and then begin the whole again for the second part. When you arrive at the third part through you shall dance to a quicker, livelier duple time using the same steps, but introducing small springs as in the coranto.*

The earliest version of a similar dance dates from 1392. Elsewhere the Allemande came to be variously known as: Alemando, Almagne, Deutscher, Tedesco, d'r Ditsch, Alliwander, Salamander, Schwedischer (for *Schwäbischer* – from German Swabia).

Beginning in the eleventh century, market towns began to spring up along the important trade routes, and as trade grew so did the towns expand. Trade brought

62. 'Old Norwegian Springdans from Hardanger' by R.T. Pritchett. 1879.

wealth, and to those most able to benefit from this came control of the towns. A patrician class emerged who soon grew to rival in wealth and power the nobility. They formed an affluent minority. Below them were those who had migrated to the towns from the countryside, artisans and labourers, many of whom, for some time to come, supplemented their wages by working plots of land outside the town walls. By the twelfth century, control of the towns' affairs lay firmly in the patrician class, the wealthier trades people. At the end of the thirteenth century, and particularly during the fourteenth century, as the guilds grew stronger, they came to participate in the ordering of the towns' affairs. They also evolved their own individual culture. At this time, the nobles and the wealthy patricians, when they danced, moved only in couples in procession in a slow and dignified manner in a circle. The farmers and the lower orders of society, on the other hand, danced turning in a lively, springing fashion. But as a burgher middle-class came into being and began to assert itself, taking into its ranks members from the classes above and below, a new form of dance developed which united the courtly processional dance and the rustic turning dance.

We find for the first time a middle-class type of dance, in which the processional dance came as a 'fore-dance' and the turning as an 'after-dance'.

We still have the texts of the songs which were used to accompany their dances (for remember, it was not until some time later that purely instrumental music was used), and from these we can learn something of the structure of this new form of couple dance. An early text from Salzburg describes a dance called the 'Cow's Horn'. In the fore-dance it says: "Midday sleep is very good in summer, the boy rests and pets playfully his girl friend in the straw, in the cool shade he makes her happy." And for the after-dance we have the girl saying: "I have to go home, the cows have to be milked." This type of dance, in the High Middle Ages, became very popular amongst both burgher and patrician classes, and was generally called 'German Dance' (Deutscher Tanz). The dance, through the trade links which the upper classes had with foreign countries, travelled to England and France where it became known as Allemande. In similar ways were English and French dances introduced into Germany.

Hans von Schweinichen, writing in the second half of the sixteenth century, described a patrician wedding in Augsburg, in which two dignitaries led the fore-dance, and as soon as they began to turn, then those who followed were allowed to join in, and the boys were able to flirt with the girls. An account from 1549, amusingly entitled 'A God-fearing Tract on Un-godly Dancing', relates how:

The typically German dance commences with the most noble man in the company choosing a partner who most pleases him from amongst the

63. 'Couple Dance' by Johannes Plintae. Norwegian.

ladies and girls present. They perform a most serious fore-dance – there is nothing of the lively springing and turning movements here, which belong to the after-dance, but they are better able in this slow section to indulge in conversation. When the music changes to the after-dance, the dancers resort to a less disciplined dance, with nudging, romping about, secretive hand touching, shouts, other improper things, and things about which I dare not speak. At the end of the dance, the gentleman leads his lady back to her seat, and, after bowing to her, leaves her, or, if during the dance he has succeeded in making a favourable impression with her, he may stay to talk to her, sitting on her lap.

How times have changed! It is hardly surprising that we find a series of prohibitions on participating in this sort of dancing. In 1555, 1562, 1572, and in the years following up to 1709, the Church railed against this courting, throwing the lady up, and intimately holding in this after-dance. An ordinance of March 12th, 1755 forbade a whole series of dances: Rummel- (Fair), Hafer- (Oats), Mahder- (Reaping), Schiess- (Shooting), Laufer- (Running), and Kegelschieb- (see page 33) dances.

At the beginning of the seventeenth century, certain folk dances started to develop into 'national' dances, and became associated with specific regions. The

64. 'Friardans på Flodabron' by J.W. Wallander. Swedish, 1821-1888.

most well-known of these were the 'Dreher' (Turning Dance), and the 'Ländler' which could lay claim to the appellation German national dance as, by Mozart's day, in southern Germany, it was known simply as 'German Dance' (Deutscher), and influenced the dances both in northern Germany and abroad. As earlier, it travelled to France and returned to Germany with its new appellation 'Allemande mit Touren' (Allemande with turns), but this type of Ländler had nothing to do with the Allemande which we met earlier. It was also danced in French courtly circles (we have a melody from 1680 used to accompany this dance), and was introduced into the royal court at Versailles at the time when Alsace was incorporated into the French kingdom. A teachers' instruction book from Paris, dated 1768, (ill. 134) illustrates the various figures with their hand-holds from this Allemande, and which are to be found today in the 'Wickler' and many similar Ländler. We learn that this Allemande could be danced in couples, one pair behind the other, or by two men each with a lady on either side. The step was taken to a slow triple time, and consisted of three *pas marchés* very simply performed either forwards or backwards. It was regarded as one of the most pleasant dances at court, though the hand-holds had to be skilfully performed if the grace of the whole were not to be destroyed.

The only thing which this dance has in common with the sixteenth-century Allemande is the name. The Allemande with turns is a completely different dance.

65. 'Der Kirchtag' (Church Fair) by Josef Weger. Austrian, c.1820.

66. *'Dansande Vingåkerspar' by J.G. Sandberg. Swedish, 1782-1854.*

The older form had its roots in the dance which had two parts: the processional fore-dance in duple time, and the after-dance in triple time. The later Allemande with turns evolved from the Ländler with its flirting motifs. A ban on this dance in 1748 for the first time uses the term 'waltz', *waltzen* merely signifying to 'turn' or 'roll'. In 1760 another ban talks of 'German waltzing dances', and prohibits people dancing them in the streets. This ban even had to be read from the pulpit, and the musicians were threatened with hefty fines for playing for them. That these prohibitions were ineffectual is evidenced by fiddle-players' music books of the early 1800's which contain 'waltz' melodies. The term *waltzen* could be applied to any dance which turned, and apparently here referred to the Ländler, the 'Teutsch walzenden Tänze'

(German turning dances). One of the oldest 'waltz' songs was 'O du lieber Augustin' from the year 1670. At this time all the Ländler and waltzes were accompanied by singing. Only later did they begin to leave out the words. Even in 1820, we hear of them singing to accompany the Ländler.

In Swabia, we find besides the 'Schliefer' (Sliding) and the Ländler, a 'Dreischritt-waltzer' (Three-step Waltz) and the German Dance. Here they made a distinction between 'straight' dance and 'open' dance. To the 'straight' category belonged the Ländler in triple time, but notably also in duple time, while in the 'open' category was the German Dance. In Swabia this was a kind of waltz, the precursor of the 'Viennese Waltz'. It was a couple dance, but without the couples touching, each being single and free. The man performed various figures round his lady, who with modest demeanour turned on their own axis. Only very occasionally did their hands touch, and only at the end of the dance did they hold as in the real waltz.

An account from about 1900 tells of a Styrian wedding dance, in which the couple walked side by side up the room, this being followed by the girl turning under the joined fingers of their raised hands. The boy then released the hand-hold, and whilst the girl moved backwards he performed a variety of movements displaying his prowess, shouting, clapping his hands, slapping his thighs and feet, cartwheeling, and generally showing off to the girl. Similar descriptions come from Swabia and Bavaria, where also the Ländler incorporated many of these display elements with hand slapping, and where it was called the 'Schuhplattler':

> *It is a Ländler for one couple only, in which the girl with modestly downcast eyes, turns gently around, whilst the boy dances round her showing in various pantomimic gestures his joy and love. He stamps his feet, marks the beat of the music by slapping his thighs, knees or heels, turns somersaults or cartwheels, jumps over the girl, turns her under his arms, but touching only seldom, until finally, to show he has still enough strength left, he grasps her tightly, hoists her high in the air above his head, and lets her down gently.*

From the old Ländler have sprung today's 'Steirer', 'Schuhplattler', 'Rudenlandla' and 'Altlandla'. The Ländler was a couple dance which originated in the province of Landl in the Austrian heartlands. It had no set figures, and the figures of the dances which followed, as with the waltz and the polka, were purely arbitrary. One did what one liked. From the free 'mixed-up' dances evolved, probably influenced by the Allemande, the numerous new strictly regulated dances. The Landla, Steirer, and Schuhplattler, each developed in its own different way from the 'stem'-Ländler. The Landla emphasized especially the accompanying songs; the Steirer the courtship motifs; the Schuhplattler the clapping and stamping. So, eventually, the Landla lost the courtship motifs, the Schuhplattler the song, and the Steirer the variety of steps.

Having said that, however, it is not quite such a clear-cut differentiation. In the border regions between Upper and Lower Austria, the people know the Ländler by the name Steirer; in a part of Obersteiermark, they understand by the name Ländler a quick Steirer; whilst in Salzburg they call it a waltz, that is, a quickly-played Ländler in the form of a Schuhplattler. In the southern part of Lower Austria they regard a Steirer and a Ländler as the same, and musicians' notebooks use the two terms indiscriminately, the same tune in one being called Ländler, and in another Steirer. A comparison between the old waltz and the Ländler shows the Six-step Waltz as being the same as the Ländler, except that with the quicker tempo comes a quicker turn, but again the picture is complicated by the fact that the Ländler is played in different regions at different speeds.

In the Salzkammergut, the 'Steirischen' became a fixed step and sequence dance, in which all the couples did the same thing at the same time; the singing and the clapping were done in concert. In other regions, a second form of the dance was the 'Steirischer Figure Dance', in which courtship actions are mimed. The idea of community dancing is forgotten and each couple perform their own freely improvised figures. In this there is no singing or clapping. The Schuhplattler as it developed in Bavaria was similar in form to the Salzkammergut Steirischer.

Here is a description of how the Steirer was performed in the Steiermark in 1893:

> *At first they dance arm in arm quite slowly around, then she lays her head on his chest, he puts his arm round her neck, and with his other hand he lifts her hand as high as it will go, and then they turn one after the other under the arch thus made by their arms. Then with her arm still raised she turns several times quickly and nimbly around her partner, and then finally they wind or squeeze themselves with mischievous charm under their arms once more. Then the man lets go his hand, and they clap hands and stamp their feet in time with the music. Lastly one of them yodels the last refrain whilst the other finishes off the dance with a loud shout.*

A well-known variation of the Styrian dance is the 'Dreisteirer', a dance for one boy and two girls. In most of the descriptions, the dance begins with the three dancers swinging their arms while standing still, sometimes singing a verse of the accompanying song. Then they perform a series of figures: moving in a circle, turning inwards and outwards, making a star, 'windows', 'doors', somersaults, and various other turns. Dances for three people have been widespread throughout Germany. Sometimes the dancers were joined by handkerchiefs. In East Prussia, a dance for four sets of three dancers was known as the 'Natanger Fisher Dance'. That dances for two girls and one boy, or two boys and one girl, are very old, we know from illustrations dating back to the thirteenth-century Manessischen manuscript, from the description in a song by Neidhart von Reuenthal, and also from a poem written in 1250 by Wernher dem Gartenaere entitled 'Meier Helmbrecht' (Steward Helmbrecht).

Of similar significance as the Ländler in the development of German folk dance is the 'Dreher' (Turner), which belongs to the oldest known couple dances. Mentioned in the year 1406 in the Schleswig Chronicle, this 'Drehtanz' (Turning Dance) is a forerunner of the later Dreher. This old turning dance, which in earlier times was known as a hopped Drehtanz, remained, over the centuries, the base from which new forms were evolved. Variations include the 'Zweischrittdreher' (Two-step Turner), 'Halbdreher' (Half Turner), 'Dreischrittdreher' (Three-step Turner), and the 'Doppeltrittdreher', (Double-step Turner). The Dreher was a quick and energetic turning dance for couples. In these variations the dancers performed four walking steps and eight full turns, or the boy might perform his clapping and stamping as the girl made small running steps. To perform the three-step turn the girl would step an eighth-note behind the boy, which allowed them better to fit the steps to the turning, and enabled them to turn in a tighter space. In the walking passage, the boy held the girl by his right hand, she either at his side or being led along behind him, or they would dance unlinked, whilst for the turning figure they would be closely linked by both arms.

New variations added to the older dances: change-of-step, hops, galops, and these became new dances in their own right. One of these, danced particularly to Scottish melodies, became known as the 'Schottisch'. The Schottisch came in around 1830, though one of the first Schottisch melodies belongs to the end of the eighteenth century. This dance belonged to a group of new dances which quickly lost their improvised character, and came to have strictly regulated steps and forms.

The 'Polka' emerged about 1840, at first also possessing a variety of figures, but soon developed into a purely turning dance. Some northern regions of Germany kept the original forms under the name of 'Old Polka', and included 'Patsch-Polka' (Slap-Polka), 'Finger-Polka', and 'Kreuz-Polka' (Cross-Polka).

The waltz too had numerous ways in which it could be done, and was purely improvisational. In one version, the couple held one hand only, and danced side by side, before joining in a ballroom-hold to dance turning.

During the second half of the nineteenth century, a flood of new dances swept across Europe: the 'Galopp' (a faster polka), the 'Rheinländer' which combined the Schottisch and Dreher, the 'Polka-Mazurka' which was popularly known as the 'Flea Shaker', and a version of this, the 'Varsovienne' (the Spinning-Polka). As the music used to accompany the dances became ever quicker and thus the dances themselves did likewise, so many of the older figures were dropped, and the dances became purely turning dances. The Rheinländer retained some of its old courtship elements and figures. Some dances kept their jumping steps: jumping one leg forwards, one backwards, and then changing over, or split jumping to the rhythm of the music, clapping, stamping, beckoning with the forefinger, or fist-shaking, and bowing (usually known as 'Grandfather' dances), all elements which undoubtedly date back to ancient times.

The Allemande (Allemander, Allewander in Central Switzerland, Allemanda in the Engadine) concludes with the *Kehraus* (sweep-out). In Appenzell it becomes the 'Schwöbli', after the nickname given to the Germans living there. The initial circle with hand holding is followed by the girls winding their way round between the boys, first of all curtseying or shaking hands, and then the couples twirl round together, finishing off with the *Kehraus*, galloping round the circle.

The 'Hierig' (*hier* = local) of Appenzell and the 'Gäuerler (*gau* = provincial) of Schwyz are courting dances. They belong to the group of Alpine Ländler and Schuhplattler so popular in Upper Bavaria, the Tyrol and Styria. The Hierig is for a single couple with the usual motifs of quarrelling and reconciliation. The Gäuerler possesses those elements of the Schuhplattler which demand a degree of acrobatic ability to perform all the stamping, shoe and thigh slapping, cartwheels and somersaults. Whilst the boys indulge in all this, the girls gyrate gracefully around their partners.

Another old couple-dance which is to be found all over northern Europe is known variously as 'Manchester' or 'Lott is Dead'. It is a dance in two parts: the couples dance four steps forwards and eight runs or *chassés* back; then, to quicker music, they perform eight galops or polka-steps turning.

German version:

Stöck, Stöck, Stöck, Stöck,	*Stick, stick, stick, stick,*
Macht mein Vater, Macht mein, Vater	*My father makes, my father makes,*
Macht mein Vater Stöck.	*My father makes a stick.*
Lott ist todt, Lott ist todt,	*Lott is dead, Lott is dead,*
Jule liegt im sterben.	*Yule lies dying.*
Das ist recht, das ist recht,	*That is good, that is good,*
Krieg mer was zu erben.	*There'll be more to get.*

A variation of this is:

Lott ist todt, Lott ist todt,	*Lott is dead, Lott is dead,*
Julchen liegt im sterben,	*Yule lies dying,*
Röschen kommt, Röschen kommt,	*Roses come, roses come,*
Die will alles erben.	*There'll be more to get.*

In Berlin they sang:

Eins, zwei, drei, vier,	*One, two, three four,*
Mariechen, sollst mal runter komm',	*Mariechen, you should come down,*
der Weihnachtsman ist hier.	*Father Christmas is here.*

In Bavaria we find:

Oans, zwoa, drei und oans ist vier,	*One, two, three and one is four,*
s'Dianderl hebt das kiderl auf	*Dianderl lifts up her skirt*
und zoagt mar ihre knia.	*And shows me her knees.*

The version found in Alsace is called 'Danse des Quatre Pas', and suggests going even further than a mere glance at the knees.

Eins, zwei, drei oder vier!
Maidel, wenn dü danze witt,
So komm un danz mit mir.
Nit eso, nit eso, wie's die Wiwer mache!

Wenn sie g'nüe gsiffelt han,
gehn se heim un lache.

Finf, sechs, siewe oder acht!,
Maidel, loss din Fenschter uf un halt mich uver Nacht.
Nit eso etc.

(Which invites the girl to leave her bedroom window open so that he can spend the night with her.) In this version the dancers, holding as for a waltz, make four *assemblés en avant*, then back with seven *pas chassés*, dancing a polka for the refrain.

Danish version:

Lotte gik, Lotte gik,	*Lotte went, Lotte went,*
Op og ned ad gaden,	*Up and down the street,*
For at se, for at se,	*For to see, for to see,*
Hele vagt paraden.	*The guards on parade.*

Sometimes Lotte is a little girl, but in one Danish version she is a horse, which, on the way to see the parade, eats too many oats and dies.

Norwegian version: Lottistå – also Poor Peter

Poor Peter standing outside my door,
Yes, Mr. Brant, I see you,
Come and kiss me on my ear.

Another version is:

Skakkers Per, Skakkers Per,	*Poor Peter, poor Peter,*
Vil du byta Kniva (Kjerring),	*Will you change knives (wives),*
Vil no du, så vil no eg,	*Will you now, so will I,*
Og kom så du med dina.	*And so come here with yours.*
Sjå dei to, sjå dei to,	*See those two, see those two,*
Sjå dei to forlibte,	*See those two in love,*
Gjev dei var, gjev dei var,	*Give they were, give they were,*
Gjev dei alt var gifte.	*Give they were already married.*

In central Switzerland the dance is called 'Manchester. In Berne it is called 'Languus' or 'Langmuus', indicating that it finshes with a *Langaus*, like the *Kehraus* or 'sweep-out', which sometimes indicates a fast galop to end the dance. Here they sing:

Eis, zwei, drü, vier,
Meitschi, wenn d'hürate witt, so nimm ken Offizier!
Füüf, sächs, siben, acht,
Meitschi, wenn d'hürate witt, so nimm di wohl in acht!

One, two, three, four, if you want to marry lassie, don't take an officer! Five, six, seven, eight, if you want to marry lassie, so take him all in eight!

In the Valais, the dance is known as 'la Gracieuse' (the Graceful One), and ends in a mazurka-waltz. The Emmental 'Languus' has the couples progressing towards the centre, bowing and curtseying to one another, and then changing over to the other side.

The forwards and backwards movements have suggested to some authorities the movement of the Pilgrims' step.

In Hungary, certain old couple dances, predating by a long way the nineteenth-century csárdás fashion, live on today. The couple dance, even if it did not already exist in Hungary, had, by the sixteenth century, certainly become all the rage, and, despite the strongly-worded objections of the Puritan Protestant preachers, the fashionable western European dances, over the following two centuries, took Hungary by storm. Hungarian musical records of the seventeeth and eighteenth centuries list the popular couple dances such as the French 'gaillarde', 'courante' and 'sarabande', the Polish 'mazurka' and 'polonaise', and the German Ländler and Steirisch. These dances were characterized by a different mode of holding and turning, so that the close holds and turns which typify the csárdás had already been anticipated. These dances will have been transformed in, and on their way to, Hungary. Some adopted the musical structure, tempo and rhythm of

67. 'Le Tambourin Basque' by G. Engelmann in the French Basque Country. (The tambourin refers to the musical instrument – see appendix C.)

existing dances such as the 'Leaping Dances', whilst others introduced new musical features with them.

The 'Lassú' or 'Cigánytánc', that is the 'Slow' or 'Gypsy' Dance, was popular in central Transylvania. A slow dance in 5/8 time, it usually followed the men's solo in the evening's dance programme. In certain districts, the dance was started by the dancers standing in a semi-circle in front of the musicians and singing. The couples would then start to move with a slow rocking motion and using a limping step, adopting the characteristic close hold. The tune might quicken, with the dancers using a dragging-limping step in the turning figure. The newer slow csárdás has already replaced this dance in most places. The 'Lassú Magyaros' (Slow Hungarian), in some places danced instead of the slow csárdás, has very simple figures, but a most complex rhythmic structure, alternating 9/16, 7/8, 10/16 times. The 'Kettős' or Dual uses the Swineherds' dance music with a syncopated rhythm. The dance starts with the couples lined up in two columns, holding hands, and then they start the *Jártatós* or walking section. The column formation is broken as the dancers move into the faster *Sirülős* or turning section, and hold in the closed csárdás fashion. The dance is popular in the eastern and southern Carpathians and amongst the Romanian population of Moldavia and Wallachia.

Further couple dances are the 'Marosszéki Forgatős' (Turning Dance of Marosszék), and 'Korcsós', 'Vetéllős' or 'Gyorsforgatós', fast turning dances. One of this type usually features in the middle of the dance programme, following the slow csárdás. In these dances the girl is led from one side of her partner to the other, turning under his raised arm, before releasing their hand-hold so that both partners are free to turn individually. Fast turning dances usually close the evening's programme. The fact that they use tunes of the Swineherds' Dance-type indicates that they are older than the nineteenth-century fast dances. The 'Sebes Magyaros' (Quick Hungarian), 'Sürű Cigánytánc' (Fast Gypsy Dance), 'Összerázás' (Shaking Together), and the 'Szökős' (Jumping Dance), are all popular in different areas of Hungary. Turning one's partner, stamping, and releasing one's partner, characterize these dances.

During the course of the last two centuries, newer couple dances have evolved. Attempts were made in the nineteenth century to stamp a national character on the dance, with the result that the newly-created dances tend to be much more uniform than the earlier ones. Ethnic and regional differences are much smaller, and in consequence they lack the wealth of forms of earlier dances. These dances brought with them fashionable tunes to accompany them. The dancers were introduced to modern tempos and rhythms, usually less complex and more regular, though syncopated and 'dotted' rhythms gained widespread popularity. The new style came from central-western Europe, evolving out of the fashionable dances of the period. Married to the indigenous style, these dances soon took on a highly individual character, seen *par excellence* in the csárdás.

The csárdás is undoubtedly the most popular and important of the Hungarian dance repertoire, and came to influence the couple dances of neighbouring regions: the 'čardáš' and 'friška' of Slovakia, the 'ceardaș', 'Mațegana' and 'Țiganeasca' of Romania, and the 'Mad'arac', 'Ranče', and 'Drmeš' of Yugoslavia. It is the catalyst of all the other dances both new and old. Come together and blended in the csárdás are all the varied ways of holding one's partner;

the complex, refined and cunning changes of posture; using the *félfordulős* (half-turn), *lippentős* (slight crouching), and *átvetős* (taking-over) figures; the ways in which the couples turn whilst holding closely; turning the girl under one's arm; lifting her in a jump and throwing her away. Perhaps we may see in the raising movement an element of growth-magic, already to be found in such Renaissance dances as the 'Volta'. In the fast csárdás, a flirting element, taken from much older couple dances, is present, and opens up scope for the man's solo display, which in turn has been borrowed from the Recruiting Dance.

Arthur Patterson in his 'The Magyars: Their Country and Institutions', published in 1869, wrote the following vivid account:

> *As far as I have seen, the genuine Magyar peasant never dances anything else than the* Csárdás, *but the style of its execution varies in different districts, and it contains so much variety that it never produces a sensation of sameness. Its name is the adjective form from* Csárda, *which designates a solitary public-house . . . The music of the* Csárdás *is at first slow, solemn, I may say melancholy. After a few bars it becomes livelier, which character it then keeps up, occasionally becoming very fast indeed, and at last ends in a delicious whirl of confusion. The movements, of course, correspond. The dance opens with a stately promenade; then as the music quickens, each couple takes a twirl or two, and breaking away brusquely from one another, continue a series of pantomimic movements, now approaching coquettishly, like parted lovers desiring reconciliation then, as if the lady thought that she had given sufficient encouragement, she retreats with rapid but measured steps, while her partner pursues, and gradually gaining on her, seizes her waist; they whirl swiftly round, two or three times, and then, breaking away, recommence the pantomime as before. What makes the* Csárdás *unrivalled as a spectacle is its variety. One seldom sees two couples performing exactly the same figure at the same time. While two separated partners are doing their step with their backs turned on one another, another couple between them are spinning round in the ecstasies of reunion.*

The csárdás is made up of two, occasionally three parts. Each section may be taken as a separate dance; the *csendes* is a quiet section, the *ugrős* a leaping one.

The 'ballos' belongs to the Greek islands. It was the Venetians who brought the name with them although it is derived from an ancient Greek verb *ballizo* which meant to dance or jump about. There are several forms of the 'ballo'. One starts with a double circle, men on the inside, girls on the outside, couples holding with regular hand-hold, or facing each other, or holding left hands in promenade position facing line of direction, the girl moving with opposite footwork to the boy. Another starts in an open circle with 'W' hand-hold. An uneven number of dancers dance a 'syrto' before breaking up into couples to dance the ballo, leaving an odd man out. A third variation has one couple at a time breaking off from the circle to dance in the centre whilst the rest dance round them. The ballos is danced to a 2/4 rhythm and

68. 'Le Fandango sous les murs de l'Alhambra à Grenade' by G. Engelmann in Spain, 1788-1839.

has a lilting movement which is said to represent the graceful gliding of the caïques throught he water. A love motif imitates mating birds, with the boy stretching out his arms as if herding the girl from one place to another, and strutting before her in a showing-off display, before she eventually surrenders herself to him.

'Karsilamas' (the name means face to face) is a dance of supposed 'Pyrrhic' origins, but today it is a couple dance with a love motif, and is danced to a 9/8 time signature divided into quick, quick, quick, slow steps: (i.e. $\bar{1}2/\bar{3}4/\bar{5}6/\bar{7}89$). The girls used to hold a handkerchief across their faces as if they were wearing a veil, like their Moslem neighbours. Now the girl teases her partner by moving the kerchief from side to side, and furling and unfurling it until the boy snatches it from her. The couple face each other and perform the same steps, moving in opposite directions, that is to say, not mirroring each other, but both going to their right, left, etc. The dance is especially popular on the islands off Turkey's west coast and on Cyprus. In the Balkans it is performed at weddings. The Karsilamas without the love motif can also be danced by two men or two girls, in which case they do not link up, but hold their arms out to the side at shoulder level, and face each other roughly a meter apart. Then the music is played fast, and the footwork is energetic and exhilarating. This has given rise to the Greek scolding threat of: "I'll make you dance the Karsilamas."

69. 'Danse Fandango' from 'Delineations of the Most Remarkable Costumes of the Different Provinces of Spain'.

Another dance which is believed to have its origins in an ancient 'war' dance and which retains vestiges of a pyrrhic nature is the 'Sousta'. Today it is essentially a courtship dance. The name *sousta* means spring, and the dancers bounce up and down on the balls of their feet, performing very light steps. This has come a long way from the time when the ancient pyrrhic dancer was supposed to have performed the dance in full armour. On Crete the dance starts in a circle or longways set formation, and then breaks up into couples, eventually linking up again to finish.

The name of the 'Tsifte Telli' means two strings, and refers to the special way the stringed instrument, used to accompany the dance, is tuned and played. There are several types of Tsifte Telli, which may be performed in couples or singly. One has heavy, even beats, another more melodious and sounding almost rhumba-like. The origins of the dance go back to the ancient worship of the Earth Mother and the Moon-goddess. Originally each dance was identified by specific movements, but when the rôles of the goddesses became confused, then so too did the dances, and resulted in a sort of *potpourri* of different dance movements. The undulating movements of arms and body in this dance are supposed to reflect the movements of

70. 'Danse Bolèro', as illustration 69.

the snake Ophion (of the creation myth), or of the water which was associated with the Moon-goddess. The undulating or rolling abdominal movements represented the laying of the World Egg. The dance was performed at fertility rites, and until recently was danced before engaged or newly-married couples to instruct them in the movements appropriate to the love act. Originally the dance was performed by the temple priestesses, but sometimes they were joined by men in the worship of the goddess.

The dance in its various forms became popular, not just as a folk dance but also as an 'art' or professional dance, throughout the eastern Mediterranean. When it lost its religious significance, one form of the dance became a 'Kelekos horos', a charm dance in every sense of the word, from fascination to seduction. The Turkish conquerors had their Christian slave girls perform it in the harem, and its popularity spread to the bazaars and cafés, and, through ambitious and skilled professionals, to the court of the sultan or wealthy noblemen. It became Salome's dance, and the belly-dance, at the same time and in a different form, remaining a folk dance of the peasants. In this, a couple dance opposite each other. The girl's movements are gentle and refined, the boy's more vigorous. She flirts with him, and he succumbs to her charms, and the dance culminates in his whipping out his handkerchief and putting it around her. In a different form again it can be performed by two men or two girls. The dance is performed to a 2/4 or a 4/4 time, and the steps are quick, quick, slow.

Serbia has a lively courtship dance, the 'Katanka'. The couples perform various figures including separating, challenging, turning, and for the man squatting. The girl, whilst she pirouettes, hides her face behind a handkerchief which she holds by the opposite corners. Another lively dance is the 'Lilka' which is accompanied by a song, telling of the rude behaviour of a Turk towards a Serbian girl, as she washed clothes in the river.

There are many courtship dances to be found in Italy: 'dello Specchio' (Mirror), 'della Sospiro' (Sigh), 'della Seggiola' (Chair). The girl might repulse the boy's advances, but usually in the end submits. If not he can be more persistent and carry off his prize. The 'Romagna Stick Dance' and the 'Dance of the Four Corners' (dei Quattro Cantoni) originally were more than polite courtship dances, and represented the rape of the unfortunate girl.

The 'Monferrina' is a charming courtship dance which originated in the Monferrato district, but is now to be found all over Lombardy and Friuli. It is usually accompanied by singing, and has pantomimic actions showing teasing and coaxing. The dance starts with the couple promenading round in a circle, then as the music changes they take hands and perform a cross-step with bent legs.

71. 'La Tarantella' from 'Scènes de la Vie Napolitaine'. Italy.

72. 'Un Bal de Bohémiens' from 'Espagna Artistica y Monumental'. Spain.

There are two variants of the 'Furlana', the 'Furlana Ziguzaine' in 3/4 time which originated in Friuli, and one erroneously called Furlana in 6/8 time which is probably of Venetian origin. The Furlana Ziguzaine, once an erotic dance, still possesses motifs of flirtation, courting, quarrelling and reconciliation. It may be danced by one or several couples.

The 'Saltarello' is another courting dance, particularly associated with central Italy, the Romagna, the Marche, and the Abruzzi, but with endless variations in its different locations. It has no fixed steps or figures, though the mimed scenes of pursuit and rejection, but ultimate submission, are usually to be found. The dance gets its name from the Latin *saltatio* which indicates a jumping or leaping dance, and which was originally associated with spring festivities. However, the Saltarello as it appears in Ciociaria is a *bassa danza*, and does not contain high leaps.

The 'Tarantella' is danced all over the southern provinces of Italy, Sicily and Sardinia. Under different names it is danced in Apulia as the 'Tarandla', and in Calabria, where a variant is called the 'Pecorara' or 'Pasturara', a shepherds' dance. For the story of the supposed connection between the dance and the spider, see page 284. However, when you see old prints of the tarantella (ill. 71) with the dancers clacking castanets, their arms raised as in the 'Jota' (ill. 72), the Spanish roots of the dance seem obvious. Yet there was, until recent decades, in southern Italy, a disease something akin to St. Vitus' Dance, which engendered epileptic fits and trances in the people as they performed a slow whirling movement, rather like the Dervishes of Turkey, and who afterwards had to be kept moving to restore them to normality again. Perhaps this has become linked in people's minds with the story of the person bitten by the spider. It makes a good tale if nothing else.

There is a delightful story which describes the origin of the Sorrento tarantella. Legend has it that the mermaids who had tried to lure Ulysses by their seductive songs, were piqued when he did not respond. Ulysses had been forewarned and plugged his ears with wax so as not to hear them. So they asked the Graces to teach them something to reach him in other ways. The Graces created the 'Sorrentina', a charming dance that no-one would be able to ignore. Unfortunately this did not help the mermaids who, being half fish, could not dance. It was left to the girls of Sorrento and Capri to seduce their audience through their graceful dance.

The name tarantella has only been used in the last four or five centuries. Before that, the dance went under a variety of names, such as 'Lucia', 'Sfessania' and 'Villanella'. The dance is variously interpreted from region to region. In Apulia, the girl dances with great modesty, her eyes lowered and her head bent forward. The boy dances round her, singing, and clicking his castanets, inviting her to dance. She responds, but is careful to avoid bodily contact. He unfurls a handkerchief and waves it, and eventually the girl indicates her submission by catching hold of the other end. In some places, a couple dance in the middle of a circle of dancers, and as each partner tires they are replaced by someone from the circle. In Calabria, the girl may take the handkerchief and wear it on her head or around her neck. At Sicilian weddings the guests dance the tarantella in honour of the newly weds. The various figures show

73. 'Russian Dance' by Armand-Gustave Houbigant, from 'Moeurs et Costumes des Russes', 1789-1862.

in mime the usual actions of greeting, discord, flight, forgiveness, and the final kiss. Throughout the southern-most provinces, the girl maintains a very modest demeanour, but in Naples and Sorrento, however, the girl dances with much greater abandon, her head held high, and flashing her sparkling eyes at her admirers.

Before we leave the tarantella there is one more tale concerning the origins of the dance. Some have linked the dance with the invasions of southern Italy and Sicily by the Moors and Spaniards. Writing of a certain dance called the 'Sfessania', a favourite with the Neapolitans, a visitor described how: "by the sea, on the beach of Posillipo, whenever a Turkish raid was not in the offing, youths and maidens, afire with pleasure, came together in that dance soon afterwards called the Tarantella."

Spain has a wealth of couple dances. 'Seguidillas' is a lively dance containing a series of *copla* (couplets), each in three parts, separated by an *estribillo* or chorus. There are Seguidillas Sevillanas, Malaguenas, Rondenas, and so on, depending on which town or region the dance comes from. Steps, rhythm, and music vary from place to place, but are usually characterised by graceful and continuous arm movements, arched back, legs never quite straight, the head turned towards the shoulder of the arm held lower, and looking at one's partner. The dance patterns generally have the dancers changing places, and thus occupying little dancing space. 'Muiñeira' (Miller's Wife) is another lively dance from the mountainous region of Galicia, in which the feet are lifted high in all the skipping steps, but the most popular of all couple dances is the 'Jota', which possibly originated in Aragon, but has now become the 'national' dance of Spain.

74. 'Fair and Village Dance in Summer' by Karl Kollmann in Russia, 1788-1846.

'Hyndaa yn bwoailley' is a Manx courtship dance in which the boy has his face slapped by the girl, but is later recompensed by being allowed to kiss her. At the end of the dance, the girl kneels down, and the boy swings his leg over her, giving a shout of triumph as he does so.

'Plyaski' of an improvised nature are widespread throughout Russia. They have no established sequences of figures or movements. Depending on the number of participants the plyaska may be individual, couple, or mass. When performed in a couple, the dance reflects the characteristic features of the men's and women's plyaski. The boy's movements are marked by their vigour, dexterity and zest, as he tries to display his skill by the accuracy and intricacy of his stamping, slapping and squatting. The girl at times moves modestly with a gliding step, gracefully waving a handkerchief, or competes with the boy in the complexity of 'tricks'. The most characteristic form of Russian plyaska is the 'Pereplyas'. As its name suggests (the prefix *pere-* implies repetition and excess), pereplyas is a competition in virtuosity of movement, endurance, and inventiveness, and inherent in the dance is youthful exuberance, and sometimes humour. In the old days, only boys participated, taking turns to demonstrate their skill to one another, but today girls also take part, competing with one another or with the boys. The 'winner' is the one who has not only repeated his rival's most complicated trick but performed another, still more intricate and unchallenged.

75. 'Scene in a Village' by Leonel Pereira. Portuguese, 1828-1892.

Polska

Did the Swedish polska come from Poland? Let us examine the connection between Sweden and Poland.

The formal merging of the crowns of Poland and Lithuania, in 1569, made it the largest kingdom in Europe. Poland now stretched from the Baltic Sea almost to the Black Sea, and for nearly a thousand miles from far beyond the Dnieper in the east as far as the Oder in the west. In 1572, the ruling Jagiello dynasty died out and, after a convulsive period of fifteen years, Sigismund Vasa, son and heir of the king of Sweden, was elected to the throne of Poland. On his father's death in 1592, Sigismund became king of Sweden. However, he was unable to unite the two countries and, when he invaded Sweden in 1598, his army was defeated, and in 1600 he was deprived of his Swedish crown. This now went to Duke Charles who, after a period as regent, snatched the crown, and in 1604 became Charles IX. Interestingly enough, it was he who made one of the earliest references we possess to the polska. In a letter to an underling he wrote: "If you do not let this poor widow receive justice, my stick will dance a polska on your back." Sigismund was still overlord of Estonia, though the Swedes were in military occupation, and nominal overlord of Eastern (Ducal) Prussia, while Western (Royal) Prussia was attached more firmly to the Polish state. Over the next ten years there was much intercourse between Sweden and Poland, and when Sweden became embroiled in the Thirty Years' War

76. 'Kołomyjka' by Teodor Axentowicz. Polish, 1859-1905.

77. 'Kuiawiak' by Zofia Stryjeńska. Polish, 1956.

(1618-1648) Swedish armies passed back and forth across Polish lands.

However, even before Sigismund Vasa linked the two countries, 'Polish' melodies were coming into Sweden. Hans Newsidler is the first to mention the name 'Polnisch Tanz' in a book published in 1544. He was born in Bratislava, although he lived all his adult life in Nürnberg. Thus he came from a town where Slav, Hungarian and German came together. Jan of Lublin, who was organist in Krasnik outside Lublin, has left us several dances dating from the years 1537-48 which can be connected with Poland, though none of the after-dances has, at this early date, any typical Polish features. A late sixteenth-century Bohemian version of a dance entitled 'Ein Pollnischer Dantz/Pator – der Nachtanz' bore the title 'Batory Tantz'. One interpretation of its name is that it refers to Stefan Báthory, king of Poland, 1576-86. Another explanation is that 'Pator' is a Latin word for 'opening', and that as early as the late sixteenth century, the Polish dance was used, like the pavan, and in later times the polonaise, as a dignified processional dance to open a court ball or a farmer's wedding.

Jacob de Kerle's 'Selection of Sacred Songs', published in Nürnberg, contained 'Tantz Diomedes'. The name seems to refer to Diomedes Cato, who was born in Venice around the year 1570. After 1590, he was active as a lutenist in Poland, part of the time as court musician to King Sigismund III of the Swedish Vasa family. The four dances in the collection are all labelled with the normal German word 'Tantz', except in the bass part, where one of them is called 'Tanietz', a German form of the Polish word 'Taniec'. The use of the Polish word for dance, the earliest in the sources, and a reference to Diomedes, suggest a Polish origin to the tunes. The part-books are from the collection of the German Church in Stockholm. It is not known how they came there, but it is possible that it was as early as 1593-94. King Sigismund of Poland was crowned king of Sweden in

78. 'Krakowiak' by Zofia Stryjeńska. Polish.

Uppsala in 1594, and it is known that he took with him his Polish court *capella* (choir and musicians) for the celebrations. Diomedes was a member of that *capella*, and there were close connections between the German Church in Stockholm and the Swedish court *capella*. If the part-books did come to Sweden at that time, that would mean that these were the earliest Polish dances preserved in Sweden. Diomedes was not the only Italian who may have brought renaissance ideas from Italy to Polish music. Giovanni Antonio Terzi da Bergamo also wrote dances in the Polish style.

August Nörmiger of Dresden (c.1560-1613) wrote some Polish dance tunes using the three-bar phrases so typical of Polish folk music today. Paulus and Bartholomeus Hessen published their 'Etlicher Gutter Teutscher und Polnischer Tentz' in Breslau (Wrocław) in 1555. Their collection contains the music for 155 dances, all with after-dances in the German style. No distinction is made between Polish and German dances.

We should not imagine that the polska was of one single type. Indeed, the dance existed in a great number of variants, often so divergent that it is difficult to recognize them as the same dance. We have already met, in the context of the development of the German couple dance, the two-part dance, the first part in 2/4 and the second part in 3/4 time. In Sweden the fore-dance or 'walking' part is called *gånglåt*, the after-dance is called the *hupfauf* or *springdans* (jumping dance). In the sixteenth century, the after-dance was developed in a special way in those regions inhabited by German and Polish communities living in close proximity. Remember, since early medieval times, German immigrants had colonised great stretches of eastern Europe, and town life was at this time almost a German monopoly. From these areas the after-dance spread throughout Europe, to northern and southern Germany, Slovakia, Bohemia, Austria, Scandinavia and elsewhere. It started a fashion, and in

79. 'Oberek' by Zofia Stryjeńska. Polish.

some areas, such as Sweden, it became so popular that today it is the characteristic dance of the country.

What was so special about this Polish after-dance can be seen from the rich variety of source material in the form of surviving music. Generally the after-dance music was of the 'Old-time Waltz' type, while the Polish was, for want of a better description, 'polska-like'. One has but to listen to Swedish polska music today to recognize the Polish influence with its distinctive rhythm. Nevertheless, the polska-rhythm seems to have been a fusion of Polish and German elements. Throughout the sixteenth century, it is not possible to distinguish between Polish and German dances, since the publisher mentions them in the same breath. Valentin Haussman, who collected tunes in Poland and Prussia during the 1590's, explained that the after-dances could be performed in either of two different ways: the 'normal' (German) way or the Polish way. He regarded the Polish manner as 'learned' and as belonging to the upper classes, while he calls the German manner 'plebeian'. German culture had dominated the Baltic countries since the Middle Ages, and it would be fair to say that Polish dance as it developed, was heavily influenced by German culture and renaissance ideas. As time went on, the fore-dance gradually fell out of use, and we are left with an independent polska in triple time.

The Nordic polska developed under influences also emanating from Poland: the polonaise and the mazurka. In the eighteenth century the polonaise and the minuet came to influence the 'Sextondelspolskor' (Semiquaver polska), which we find in Sweden and Finland. Polonaises and minuets constitute the corpus of dance-music collections. Often in Swedish fiddle players' books the semiquaver polska is entitled 'polonese' or 'polonessa'. There are however, other types of polska: the 'quaver polska' and the 'triplet polska'. Of these, the triplet polska is believed to pre-date the semiquaver polska, and was already being danced when the polonaise first

80. 'Góralski' by Zofia Stryjeńska. Polish.

appeared in connection with the Swedish King Charles XII's war with Poland. The mazurka appeared first in Poland during the fist half of the nineteenth century and quickly spread to the rest of Europe. In the eighteenth century, the dancers used the promenade, twirl under an arm, a free figure, and the swingaround, and, during the nineteenth century, it was danced both 'on the spot' and whilst progressing round the floor.

In Norway, 'springar' and 'pols' only differ in name according to geographical location, otherwise they are basically the same dance. Springar, in various dialectal forms, is found to the west and south of Norway, pols to the north and east. Any differences in style from one region to another do not follow the nomenclature. For example, the pols of northern Møre displays characteristics of style which are typical of the springar.

In the case of the music which accompanies these dances, the Norwegians tend to talk of either the 'hardingfelespringar' (Hardanger-fiddle springar) or the fiddle springar or pols. The Hardanger-fiddle springar is built up of short themes often only two bars long, and repeated and varied, usually in a very free manner. The fiddle springar or pols is usually of themes of eight bars duration, and these are repeated according to certain given principles. Of course, there are always exceptions to the rule, and there is no difficulty in finding tunes which belong to the 'wrong' category.

Norwegian traditional dances, springar and gangar, have their roots in the dances of the European Renaissance. Older sources indicate that there was originally a first part in duple time and a second part in triple time, and in certain regions of Norway it was danced thus well into the nineteenth century. Of the pols and springar tunes are those where the beats are even (metrical symmetry) and those in which the beats are of different lengths (asymmetrical beats). It may well be that, before outside

ſto. diſſoluto. & corrotto eſſer proſumptu
oſi & temerari oltra il douere. et queſti
ſon quegli che di arte dignissima la fano
ritornar uile & diſhoneſta. magiormente
non eſſendo bene doctrinati & acoſtuma
ti & honeſti nel parlare & ſobrij nellor
mangiar & bere perche la diſſolutio
ne & ebrieta ſonno deſtruttrici dogni
uirtu. Pero dato che haueſſero tutte le
degne parti preditte & non obſeruaſſe
ro queſto nuouo precepto nongli uarre
bono nulla. Et coſi facendo ſerano ama
ti honorati & reueriti in ogni parte.
Et queſto baſti. Segue adoncha la
praticha.

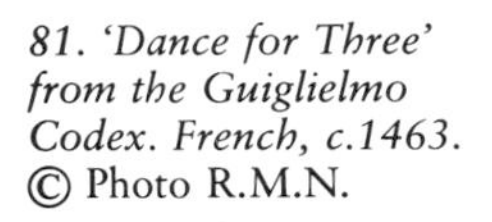

81. 'Dance for Three' from the Guiglielmo Codex. French, c.1463.
© Photo R.M.N.

influences modified the musical accompaniment to the dances, a non-accentuated even measure was used. Some of the tunes may have been polonaises (i.e. Polish), but equally well they may have been minuets, and the influences reaching Norway were generally central European rather than specifically Polish. Indeed, the minuet was absorbed into Norwegian tradition to a much greater extent than the polonaise, of which few traces exist. Undoubtedly, the new fashionable tunes would be used to accompany existing (and much older) dances.

The Danish 'Sønderhoning', 'Fannikedans', 'Jysk på næsen' (Jutland polonaise) and 'Flyvgal' show the surviving tradition of the polsk. We know of the existence of polska-type dances from the late sixteenth century through a number of warnings on the dangers existing to couples twirling around too violently. 'An honour-wreath for all virtuous young ladies' of c.1580 tells us that "it is decent to move forwards without unbecoming turning round", whilst guild rules from 1600 set out penalties for swinging the girls too much. It is said that it even led to deaths amongst the noble ladies of the court.

The Danish King Christian IV (1588-1648) employed several Polish court musicians. One of these, Petrus Fabricius, whilst he was a student in Rostock (1606-8) notated several polsk dance tunes. These are in duple time, two also having a *proportio* in triple time. The peasantry also seem to have danced polskas as early as the seventeenth century. Certainly by the eighteenth century they were popular amongst peasants and nobles alike, though amongst the latter the minuet gained in popularity at the expense of the polska. At a wedding in Randers around the year 1730, the priest referred to the polsk as having three parts: simple beat in which the participants walked, then 'springdans', and finally the *tilgift* or addition, also known as 'Ost og brød' (cheese and bread).

The 'polsk dans' is mentioned in the plays of Ludvig Holberg in the first half of the eighteenth century. In 'Uden Hovede og Hale' (1725), witches dance the polska with the devil. Holberg wrote in a letter about the fashionable dances of his time that "the complicated dances such as the Rigadon and Folies d'Espagne have gone out of use, and now people only like minuets, English and Polish dances, because they are more comfortable than the former". These dances would certainly have been introduced into Denmark directly from Germany.

Up to 1780 the dance was mainly in two parts: 'promenademarch' in duple time and 'springdans' in triple, but there were also polskas in three parts, in which the *fordans* and *efterdans* or *dans-proportion* are concluded with a swingaround or *tilgift*. 'English' dances were popular at the end of the eighteenth century, and thus we find an 'Engelsk Polsk'.

In Denmark, we can distinguish between four kinds of polsk dance: the two-part polsk with march plus turning, known as *springdans* on Lolland-Falster and Zealand, and 'Sønderhoning' on the island of Fanø. Sønderhoning tunes are normally in 2/4 time, but the turning movement has three steps, as the couples progress round the floor. A second category, mostly from Jutland, has the two- or three-part types which end with a swingaround, with the tunes usually in 2/4. The dances are known as *polsk*, *rundtenom*, and possibly *ost og brød*, but are influenced by the 'Engelskdans' with circles and chains. Thirdly we have dances which turn continuously as the couples progress round the floor, and these are known everywhere except on Bornholm and Zealand. Tunes are in 3/4 and are known as 'Jysk på næsen', 'polonæse', 'Flyval', 'Jomfru Lisken', 'Vims', 'Jægermarch' (Hunters' March), and 'Stivben' (Stiff Leg). Lastly there are the dances with more than one part which include a turning step progressing round the floor: 'Fannikedans', 'Vesterbopols', 'Østerbopols', 'Trekant'. All these are from Jutland and Fanø and all are in 2/4 time, though the Trekant may conclude with a Jysk på næsen in 3/4 time.

Many eighteenth- and nineteenth-century songs exist which were originally used to accompany the dancing, and there are many reports of song and mouth-music accompanying the polsk. H.F. Feilberg, priest and folklorist, in 1860, mentioned how the dancers stepped forth and recited a verse or rhyme – a kind of text for the dance – some of them "extremely comical, but also rather crude".

The oldest music in Finland has its roots in the Polish dances which spread to the Nordic countries during the seventeenth century, at the same time as the fiddle became popular in Finland. That polskas in both 2/4 and 3/4 time have been found in old Finnish fiddlers' manuscript books is explained by the fact that polska was the term generally used to denote any dance tune, and these may have boasted a multitude of steps and patterns, and not necessarily couple dances at that, but also circles and chains and *purppuri* (pot-pourris). The first written reference to the polska in Finland is from the mid-eighteenth century, and the oldest polska music is from around 1800.

There is absolutely no connection between the polska and the polka, not even the nationality. The polka started life off in about the year 1830 as the půlka. It was not a folk dance, but was a social dance based on the Schottisch or Polish Krakowiak. Its name may have come from its characteristic 2/4 beat (1/2 = půlka, hence polka). The story goes that one Sunday afternoon, a serving girl, Anna Chadimova by name, was dancing in the courtyard of the house in the town of Kostelec where she worked, improvising a little dance for her own pleasure and singing a well-known tune. Everyone who was watching liked the dance, and the town's teacher, Josef Neruda, wrote it down. The tune was known as Nimra or Madera. The following Sunday the new little dance was all the rage at the village hop. In 1835, the dance was brought to Prague where it entered the salons under the name of polka, and quickly became popular. Soon it was adopted into the music repertoire of the well-known Prague band by its conductor Perera, who took it to Vienna. In 1840, it was danced by the famous teacher of Prague, Raab, who introduced it to Parisian society, who ensured its immediate success. Since then the dance has never looked back, sweeping all before it across Europe and beyond.

Before closing this chapter on the couple dance, it might be an idea to look briefly at some of the Polish dances. In Cuiavia, the 'Chodzony' (walking dance), a peasant prototype of the polonaise (processional dance), leads into the 'kujawiak'. At weddings, the bride is often led round the room by the best man as they perform a ritual chodzony. It is as if she is being shown off to the assembled guests. She turns under her partner's raised arms without releasing their hold, until suddenly the music changes into the kujawiak, and he catches her into the whirling rhythm of the dance.

The kujawiak, when danced as a fertility ritual dance on Shrove Tuesday, was called the 'Podkoziolek' (Goat Dance). It was also danced during the wedding ceremony when, after the bride had been given her cap, she had to dance ritually with her companions and then later with all the other female guests one by one.

The dancers in the kujawiak, oberek and mazurek (it is only called *mazurka* outside Poland) were expected to be able to turn in either direction. The change of direction in Cuiavia was announced by the dancer of the leading couple. Interestingly, the old calls were used which served to change the direction of the animals during ploughing: 'na odsib' (to the right), or 'na iseb' (to the left). In these three dances, as performed in Cuiavia, the accents are placed differently: in the mazurek it is most usually placed on the third beat; in the oberek it is the first beat which is accented;

whilst in the kujawiak it is the second beat. The dances also differ in tempo, going from the slowest, kujawiak, to the oberek which is the fastest. The most characteristic feature which unites this group of dances is the *tempo rubato*, which gives the dance a feeling of elasticity and flexibility. It is a 'give and take' within a limited unit of the time-scheme. In other words, if one beat is prolonged, it is at the expense of another beat, which must be shortened to compensate. During the Romantic Period, with its tendency to idealize rural culture, also went an expression of patriotic feeling, of nationalistic fervour, and all three dances came to be adopted by the landed gentry, the aristocracy and the Warsaw Opera Ballet. They truly became 'national' dances, and were danced all over Poland and by all social classes.

Threesomes

In Hungary, from the Upper Tisza region and the Mezőség area of Transylvania comes a threesome csárdás, danced by one man and two women. In Mezőség they call it the 'Szász Tánc (Saxon Dance), after the dances for three persons of the Transylvanian Saxons. One finds related dances among the Romanians of South Transylvania (the 'Invirtita'); among the Bunieva of the Bácska (the 'Momačko Kolo'); and among the Gorals (the 'Góralski Trojka'). The music and the figures of this display dance are those of the csárdás.

A 'Trojak' for two girls and one boy is danced in Poland. First they sing a song about the sowing of wheat, barley, oats, or whatever it happens to be: "From one end of the field to the other we have sown the corn." Then they celebrate in dance. There is an element of flirting, and rivalry between the girls, yet the dance usually ends up with the girls suddenly letting go of the poor boy so that he falls backwards on his bottom. 'Owczarek' and 'Szandor Szatkowy' are variations of the 'Trojak', in which the boy spins round with one girl while the other dances around sulking. The 'Hulan', another threesome dance, belongs to the centre of Poland, and 'Wetrojnik' comes from the Kaszuby region.

Albania possesses only a few dances for three persons, and even these are really only solo dances performed at the same time by three people, and are to be found in the region of Mirdita, where two women with an apple in their hands, and a man take part. In the dance 'Logu' of Malessie e Madhe, Shkodra, the third dancer interrupts the dance of the couple, and the other man or woman then drops out. In the 'Dance of the Hats' from Kukësi, two combattants are reconciled by a third person, and they all end up dancing together.

The 'Llanover Welsh Reel' is a reel for one man and two ladies, and was still performed by members of the Llys Llanover household for the entertainment of their guests in 1887. The fourteen figures of the dance are linked by a *hey*, known as the 'Figure of Eight'. The dance is performed in column formation, and begins with a formal honour or *towards* the music. It has acquired a stylised polish usual in ceremonial dances.

'Pericote' (Little Peter) from the Asturias in northern Spain, is a gay courting dance for one boy and two girls, in which the girls' movements are muted, while the boy displays great agility and variety of step, as he traces a figure-of-eight from top to bottom of a square, the girls weaving their circles from sides to centre with his pattern.

On the Estonian island of Saaremaa, there is a dance for two girls and one boy, with the usual flirting motifs and rivalry between the girls. The dance is called 'Raksi-jaak'. The fact that this is a seafaring community might imply a shortage of boys as dance partners.

Catalonia posseses several delighful and charming dances for one boy and two, three or even four girls. The 'Dansas de Vilanova', performed at Carnival time by dancers wearing masks, has the boy leaping as in a galliard, and there is no element of flirtation. Neither does this element appear in 'l'Espagnolet' which is a very formal and courtly dance with the girls fanning themselves when not dancing. 'Valencia Vella' is for one boy and three girls in which the boy dances with one of the girls whilst the other two dance together, though one of them does not act as 'gentleman'. In 'la Retomba' the boy dances with each of four girls in turn.

Whatever their origins historically, threesomes and multiples of three have become a popular addition to the folk dance scene, and examples can be found in nearly every country. Socially, they may have come into their own during times of war, when a shortage of men made couple dances a difficult choice.

8

WOMEN'S AND MEN'S DANCES

The dance began with ear-piercing shouts as if by a horde of wild beasts. In the middle of the brew-house stood a vat around which the girls danced, from the milkmaid to the swineherd. Their iron-shod clogs made a great clatter on the uneven stone floor. Some shouted, others laughed, altogether making an awful din, and holding hands danced around the vat which contained the beer.

Hans Christian Andersen on Denmark.

A Church council in 692, in Rome, banned the ancient celebrations of Kalends, New Year, Brumalien, as winter festivals, the offering of votive sacrifices, and the honouring of the god of wine on March 1st, as being the remnants of pagan, Bacchic, spring rites, and forbade especially the "public indecent dancing of women".

The chronicle of Abbot Rudolf of St. Tron tells us:

In the year 1133 a ceremonial ship on wheels was hauled from Indra to Aachen, Maastricht and other places in the region of the Lower Rhine. Everywhere it was greeted with jubilation, especially by the women who danced round the ship all night, accompanied by singing.

This dance undoubtedly goes back to those ancient Germanic processions when, each year, a sacred waggon was drawn through the countryside, and dances, in honour of the earth goddess Nerthus, were performed. The wild boisterousness of such women's dances was still to be found at the turn of the nineteenth century in southern Jutland and Holstein: "Then the women ran through the village in wild ecstacy, so that the men ran away from them." If the women caught one of them, he was forced "to dance with them, if he did not wish to have his clothes torn from his body". (Compare the treatment meted out by the *Wilis* to Hilarion and Albrecht in the ballet, Giselle.)

In Saargebiet and in Urexweiler after the beginning of the harvest, the girls danced in the meadow with a loaf of bread formed into the shape of a man. Similarly, in Hessen, they danced around a sheaf of corn, which they called the 'little man'. In Saxony, the slowest of the binders was dressed in the stalks of corn, and the girls danced round him as a 'punishment'. The remnants of this custom of dancing round a man are to be found in those dances in which the girls dance round a straw puppet. So, even today, the women of Obersteiermark who process the flax make a so-called 'Harmandl' out of pussy-willow and bunches of flax, and dance round it. The women harvesters danced round a straw puppet well into the nineteenth century. On occasion, as they danced, they might sing incantations such as: "Waute (the name they used for the straw puppet), Waute, guard your barley well from crows, starlings and wild animals! Waute, Waute, Barleyman, guard it well, so that no harm may come to it!" Often the men were in attendance, though they did not participate directly in the dance.

On St. John's Eve, the girls were wont to roll in the flax and then to jump round it. The jumping may well have taken the form of the Seven Springs – strong fertility magic. The pastor, Florian Daul of Schleswig, in his 'Tantzteuffel', wrote in 1569: "On Ash Wedneday, the old women of Frankfurt am Main jumped high to make the flax grow."

Hans Christian Andersen described a girls' dance from the island of Fyn in Denmark:

> *The dance began with ear-piercing shouts as if by a horde of wild beasts. In the middle of the brew-house stood a vat around which the girls danced, from the milkmaid to the swineherd. Their iron-shod clogs made a great clatter on the uneven stone floor. Some shouted, others laughed, altogether making an awful din, and holding hands danced around the vat which contained the beer. The brewing-girl threw a shiny silver shilling into it and then the girls like demented beings took off their caps and danced in Bacchanalian wildness round the vat.*

82. Dancing to horn and pipe, from an Anglo-Saxon manuscript.

Similarly, when they brewed the special Yule beer in Norway, the women whistled loudly as they span round and round. That this dancing was well known in Germany we can see from a document of 1544 from the town council of Magdeburg in which the dance round a barrel was prohibited. From another document of 1595, we learn that the women of Prussia, before they started to dance, drank the whole barrel of beer.

Girls' circle dances accompanied by love songs are referred to in thirteenth-century Benedictine manuscripts. We find one in the 'Carmina Burana'. One verse reads: "I take a little wreath that a proud man could wear, whose servant I want to be." In Swabia on New Year's Eve, the young men went round serenading their sweethearts, in the hope of being given such a wreath as a token of reciprocal love. In summer time, the girls danced round the wreath, which might be made out of carnations, and whoever danced the best was awarded the wreath.

In Rothenburg, even into the nineteenth century, the girls were wont to dance in a circle while a boy stood in the middle and sang the song to accompany them. The boy in this case was rewarded with ribbons to wear in his hat. Until very recent times in Sweden, a boy or a girl would stand in the middle of a circle making a wreath. All would sing a verse, and the person in the middle would place the wreath on the head of someone in the circle, who would then join the friend in the centre of the circle and dance together. Another person then came into the centre while another verse was sung, and so the dance-game continued until all were paired off.

Another women's dance was the 'Three Leather Stockings'. In this the women pulled the back of their skirt between their legs and twisted it to form a 'third leg'. In Luxembourg, they called the dance the 'Swiss Man', and thus they hopped round, clapping and stamping. Sometimes this dance was performed at weddings or

83. 'Soldiers dancing before the Castle of Kapronica' (at that time in Hungary, now in Yugoslavia), by Justus van der Nypoort, 1686.

christenings, and obviously had phallic connotations. That the Swiss Man was done when the flax was being prepared lends weight to the supposition that it was linked with fertility rites. Similar dances were still to be seen in the 1930's in Germany, where two rows of girls all took their skirts between their legs and danced facing each other. The dance also became a couple dance: the man would put his hands through his legs and take hold of the woman's skirt, and thus they would dance as a couple. On the island of Rügen, two girls danced thus to a song:

Have you seen my man? Yes.
Where was he then? At the market.
What was he doing there? Buying shoes.
What sort of shoes? Panitschen shoes.*

In Falkenburg, children played this as a dance-game until quite recently.

The 'Dance with Lights' (Tanz mit Lichtern), began on the Monday of the village patronal feast, and the girls danced round burning candles. One account tells of a dance round a table on which were placed two burning candles, a bottle of wine, glasses, and a cash machine. A girl came out of the throng, led a boy to the table, poured him a glass of wine, and they drank each other's health. Then the girl gave the boy a ribbon, paid two guilders, and then danced twice round with the boy. This was repeated until all the girls had had a turn. Sometimes the dance was performed round a tree with burning candles. The payment must have had some original significance which is now lost, but the dance is a good example of a 'ladies' excuse-me' when it was permissible for the girl to do the asking.

The shepherdesses of the Grossglockner region performed a dance for eight standing in a line. In Gössl the girls placed their wide-brimmed hats in a row and danced, weaving in and out of them and back again, thus making figure-of-eight patterns.

Medieval texts glorified the 'Reverdies' (the renewal of green growth), when the noble young ladies sang and danced in a circle or chain to celebrate the return of spring. Nothing had changed since pagan times. The 'Rosières' of Thann and the 'Trimazo' of Lorraine were danced still in 1914. In ancient mythology, the Nine Muses danced around Apollo. In the Alsatian Vallée de Munster, up to the seventeenth century, women danced round a goat. In was done on the Monday of Carnival, called 'Monday of the Stag'. This animal seems to have been a survival of the Celtic god Esus, who was transformed each spring into a fertilizing stag. His domesticated successor, the billy-goat, thus conferred on the dancing females his virile qualities and his masculine strength. In effect, on that day, still called the 'Day of the Hat' (Tchapalamandy), these women acquired by subterfuge their menfolk's badge of authority, their hats. They would sit down in the public house and eat meat and indulge in hard drinking in a way normally only done by the men, and then they would dance the 'Schwitzemann' (Sweating Man): they would grasp the back of their skirt and pull it through between their knees (as in the 'Three Leather Stockings' above), and jump with their legs thrown out sideways making

* *Panitschen* was a nonsense word and could be applied to anything.

'scissors'. The dance was highly erotic in nature, and explains the name of the dance – here the Sweating Man rather than the Swiss Man, the two names being very similar. The sweat represented an avatar of sperm. We find it again in the 'Dance of the Smith' (Herr Schmid); he also sweated, working his iron over a hot fire. The symbolism is carried further in the 'Dance of the Nailmaker' (D'r Najelschmitt), the nails made by this person being likened to the seeds (a name elsewhere still given to the smallest nails).

The round dance in Hungary was performed, to song accompaniment, only by girls, and then only after they had reached the age of puberty. If boys came along, and either joined in for a short time or snatched the girls from the circle, it was called 'spoiling the round'. The dance then continued as a couple dance, still using sung accompaniment. The close linking in the girls' round dance inhibits any individual improvisation, even the limited freedom allowed in much Balkan dancing. The song, therefore, is of more importance than the dance.

The Hungarian girls' round dance always remained a close-linked, joined-up circle, variation coming only from the hand or arm holds: simple holding of hands, hands crossed in front or behind the waist of the next dancer, arms linked, or holding the next dancer by the shoulder or waist. What else can you do in a closely linked chain to influence the movement of the dance? The circle can be tightened or slightly opened out by taking steps forwards or backwards. In Sárkőz, this slow rocking movement is called 'babázás' (cradling). By the alteration of size or number of steps to left or right, the circle can be made to move in a clockwise or anti-clockwise direction (in Hungary the circle always travels to the left, only occasionally changing in the leaping or running section), with pauses and recoiling movements interspersed. An age old form still popular in Hungary, as in many other parts of Europe is the 'branle simple'.

Three sorts of tunes may be distinguished which are used to accompany Hungarian girls' round dances: 'Lépő' (stepping), 'Csárdás', and 'Futó' (running). The stepping tunes are usually of the eleven-syllable type. The dance consists of two, sometimes three, parts: csárdás and running; stepping, csárdás and running; a longer slow dance being invariably followed by a shorter quick one. One dance, repeated over and over again, can monopolize the whole evening's dancing and continue for hours.

In Transylvania one finds mixed round dances, the 'Magyar' and the 'Round Csárdás', which are similar in type to the girls' round dance, but also include a

84. 'The Hat Dance' from the 'Quodlibet Tage Buch' by Georgii Schröder. German, 1703.

motif of interplay between the sexes, but often the girls dance on their own, whilst the men perform their special male dances.

Czechoslovakia has several dances just for women or girls. One ancient ceremonial Slav dance is 'Královnicky' (Little Queens), which girls dance in a 'V' formation, casting off and forming chains. They usually go from house to house in a group of nine girls, one dressed as a queen, singing and dancing to bring in the spring. In the 'Vynásení Morany' Slovakian girls carry a straw puppet aloft. It is destined to be taken down to the river and drowned. 'Obzinkové' is a harvest dance, and 'Velikonocní' is danced for Easter.

On St. Lazarus' Day, the Saturday before Palm Sunday, in the district of Leskovac in Serbia, are to be found the *Lazarice* processions, when the girls walk arm in arm singing through the village. In Bulgaria also on this day, girls go about from house to house singing and dancing to bring in the spring. The connection with the raising of the dead Lazarus reflects the springtime rite of the revival of nature. The girls, who should be no older than the age of twelve, usually wear their best finery garlanded with flowers, and have richly-decorated head-dresses, with waving grass surmounting them. The songs they sing have explicit significance. For a newly-married couple they will sing:

85. 'Hallingdans' by Dardel. Norwegian.

For the good health of this house,
For its health and abundance,
Dance for this young bride
And for next year's cradle!

In the fields and vineyards they will sing:

The field we passed,
Exhausting the ground:
From two ears, a basket of corn;
From two grapes a cask of wine!

They receive gifts of money, bread and eggs with which they feast in the evening, when the young men are invited to join them in dancing horos.

The *Peperuda* (Butterfly) ritual is performed in times of drought. An 'orphan' girl, dressed in a chemise and covered in greenery, accompanied by a group of girls, sings and dances from house to house. At each house the mistress douses her with water as she intones a little rain-making charm. Bulgaria possesses other women's dances, usually performed to song accompaniment, which can take the form of a dialogue, with two singers on one side and a chorus answering them. As they chant, they move forwards, and then move back as the others answer. The play is to pull over all the girls from the other side.

'Targa Rehealune' is an Estonian women's, harvest thanksgiving dance. *Rehealune* means threshing floor, and the dance seems to have to do with the threshing of the corn. The dancers move forwards, bend and stamp the whole foot flat on the ground, flexing their knees to keep their heels down, and dance to song accompaniment. 'Kaarasiim' is a stick dance for four girls who each carry two sticks. They grip one stick between the knees and rub back and forth with the other stick, then point across at each other. The dance comes from Setu, a region noted for the fact that the women dance alone. A 'limping' dance from this same place indicates the antiquity of the dances to be found in this region. This 'Setu Kargus' is for two couples, here performed only by women, and limps in like manner to the Russian pivot-step. On the Estonian island of Saaremaa, the women perform the 'Ristpulkade Tants', a crossed-stick dance. In olden times they may have used straw or wattle twigs. In Estonia, the women very often danced as men – with the menfolk absent for long periods either on military service or at sea this was the custom.

In Greece, the 'Trata' or 'Maidens' Dance' is performed by the women of Megara at Easter. They sing their own accompaniment as, with hands joined, their arms crossed in front of their bodies, they circle slowly to right and to left.

During the Turkish occupation of the Balkans, one place where the foreign yoke lay particularly heavily was in Epirus, that region in northern Greece which borders, and overlaps into, Albania. Ali Pasha, an Albanian brigand who had managed to achieve the status of governor or *pasha* under Turkish overlordship, ruled Epirus from his centre in Ioannina with such severity, that the sultan's rule elsewhere

86. 'Hallingdansen' by Waldemar Olsen. Norwegian.

was said to appear lenient by comparison. When the Turks invaded this part of Greece in the fifteenth century, many Greeks withdrew into the mountains, and from their fastnesses, the fortified villages of Souli, carried on a guerrilla war against the Turks. They held out for four years until, in 1803, they were tricked into accepting a safe passage to Corfu. As the menfolk made their way down from their strongholds they were massacred to a man. The women and children remained behind and continued the struggle until their ammunition was exhausted. They then had but one recourse; their fate otherwise would be worse than death. On December 23rd, the women made a suicide pact. The romantic story relates how, led by the daughter of their chieftain, the twenty-one year-old Helena Botzaris, they put on the costumes of crimson velvet and gold which they would wear on festive days, and, in a chain, danced for the last time a Kalamatianós singing:

Farewell, unhappy world, farewell sweet life;
Farewell, farewell our poor country.
Farewell, ye mountain springs, vales, hills and cliffs,
Farewell, farewell our poor country.
The fish cannot live on dry land,
Nor the blossom in the salted sand on the beach,
And the women of Souli cannot live without liberty.
The women of Souli descend into Hades, the free city of death,
With festal dance and songs of joy.

Their villages stood near to the sheer cliff of Zalongo. First the women threw their children over the precipice, and then, one after another, in their death dance, they too cast themselves over the edge. They would never be the prizes of the Moslem bandits.

The Kalamatianós is still sometimes performed to the tragic song of Zalongo, and such is its emotional quality that in many places it is often identified as the national dance of Greece.

Men's Dances

The men's sword, hoop, and morris dances have been dealt with in separate chapters, but, besides these categories, there are other dances which originally were the sole prerogative of men, but some of which are now performed as mixed dances.

There is an almost endless variety of dances: for a man dancing solo, two men, three men, and in larger groups; dances in chains linked by handholds, hands on shoulders, or hands holding belts; dances round certain objects; dances with glasses or bottles on the head; dances in which the performers are armed with batons, brooms, spears; dances which originally were for purely ritual purposes; dances to show off skill; and dances which now are little more than games – tomfoolery, for example, the Swedish Oxendans.

Stilt dances are known in various countries, perhaps none more so than in the Landes on the western Atlantic seaboard of France. But such dances were also known in England at least from the fourteenth century, and in Germany, where, in Unken, they performed a ribbon dance on stilts which raised them 60 centimetres off the ground. For this dance, eight men wore white shoes and white trousers with red stripes, the trousers completely concealing the stilts. Around their waists they wore a wide leather girdle. Their trousers were tied with green garters. For headdress they had wreaths with gold and silver tinsel and flowers, with wide coloured ribbons hanging down to shoulder length, those in front of the face trimmed into a fringe so as not to impede their vision. Large artificial moustaches gave the dancers a grotesque appearance. Thus they performed a maypole dance, interweaving the red and white ribbons which hung down from a central pole.

In some places, Salzachtal for example, the men performed a ribbon dance without stilts. In Schladming in Steiermark, the girls now also participate in a ribbon dance which was formerly performed just by the men. It appears both in summer and in winter; in the early part of the year it is danced round a fir tree, which has been stripped of all but its uppermost branches, which topknot is decorated with candles and coloured tinsel, and long coloured ribbons hang down for the dancers to weave as they move round. Until just before the Second World War, only men danced the ribbon dance in Innviertel in Upper Austria, and in many other regions it was a men-only dance until the turn of the century.

Sometimes the dancers wore masks, especially in the Tyrol-Bavarian border region, and their 'Agattanz' had many figures in common with the sword and hoop dances, with snaking spirals, interweaving, open and closed circles, bridges, and here, interestingly, with a 'turning-wheel' figure. Other figures in the dance

87. 'Jössehäradspolska' by J.W. Wallander. Swedish, 1821-1888.

which contained no fewer than seventeen figures, were finger-wagging, four turn variations, sun-wheel, figure-of-eight, and so on. A similar dance which comes from the Salzburg region is called the 'Maschkerertanz'. As the name implies, the dancers again wear masks, coupled together as: a male and female Moor, gypsies, dairyman and dairymaid, butcher and cook, tailor and seamstress, soldier and maid, coachman and washerwoman, beggerman and his wife. Now again the dance is for men and women, where originally it had been just performed by men, that is, if we accept that masked dances were a sole male prerogative. The fact that the masked characters had much in common with the 'Perchten' or Carnival runners who were male, seems to suggest that these dances once belonged to the male domain.

The 'wheel' figure is very ancient, and is undoubtedly a sun symbol. Often it is performed by eight men, four of whom act as the supports as the others thrust their legs out in front of them into the centre of the circle, and thus they turn, first clockwise then counter-clockwise. In similar manner, the *Sennen* (Alpine herdsmen)

88. 'Taniec Górali' (Goral Dance) by Władyslaw Kuszczkiewicz. Polish.

of Appenzell, Toggenburg, and Central Switzerland dance their 'Mülirad Tanz' (Millwheel Dance). In the canton of Valais, the 'Moulin' is formed by couples holding a hoop aloft above their heads, or by groups of four couples interlocking their hands.

Squatting dances are known in many lands. From Prussia we have a description from the year 1600 of these 'Hocktanzen' or 'Heiduka'. To the accompaniment of song, pipe and drum, and bagpipes, each man, in a squatting position (ill. 84), jumped round his hat placed in front of him on the ground, or round three hats so placed, as in the 'Leuchtertanz'. This was danced round candles or similar lights in holders. The figure-of-eight featured in these dances. The remnant of this dance is to be found in East Prussia, where the men follow each other doing a polka-step, weaving in and out between girls who are sitting on chairs. A similar dance comes from Pomerania, in which there is much turning, stamping, hand-clapping and shouting, first round the girls, and then in couples.

In the region of the rivers Rhine and Main, there is a 'Nettle Dance'. Bunches of stinging nettles replace the girls-on-chairs, and as the dancers are bare-legged, the dance requires a certain degree of alertness, as they weave their way in and out between the clumps. Only after they had done this were the boys allowed to dance with the girls. In Denmark, the men danced around clumps of peat-turf. On St. John's Day, in Lower Austria, they did a sword dance in which they stuck painted wooden swords into the ground and danced between them.

Other dances have degenerated into little more than games, such as the dance in which two or more boys hop round, each holding one of the other's legs off the ground. In many parts of Germany, Russia and the Ukraine, two or three boys will form a wheel, each with his head thrust between the other's legs, and in this way they will trundle over and over together, to the obvious delight of the onlookers.

A 'Dreisteirer', to be found all over the Austrian Alpine region, was originally danced only by lumberjacks. Three dancers in a circle or row made a big jump forwards onto the right foot, a smaller jump backwards on the left, a hop on the left foot, followed by a stamp. Another lumberjack dance called the 'Holzhackerbaum March' from Ruhpolding in Upper Bavaria, for groups of three boys, incorporated Schuhplattler slapping. These dances also sometimes used sawing movements, in which two boys sitting astride a log competed with each other in strength by linking fingers, and trying to pull the other off balance.

The Egg Dance took several forms. We may presume that its time of performance was at Easter. In one dance, the performer, hopping on one leg, had to remove a cup which was covering an egg (ill. 92), dance around in a circle, and then cover the egg up again. In a version from the Inn Valley in Austria, the dancer was required to get several eggs into a basket. Another version was to place an egg into a cup. Egg dances were known in Alsace, Belgium, the Netherlands, and Denmark. In England, the dancer, blindfolded, had to weave his way between rows of eggs placed on the ground, without dislodging or breaking any of them (ill. 94). There is more about egg dances in the chapter on seasonal dances.

Animal dances were also performed only by men. In Stachenwald, they danced a frog dance in which the men, crouching some three metres apart facing each other, hopped towards each other, forwards and backwards, changing places and hopping back to their original places. Chickens and other birds were imitated, the dancers scratching at the ground, bending their heads forwards as if pecking, or they were pigeons shaking bent arms like wings, and, in the Danzig dance, gracefully bowing their heads as the two rows of dancers met each other in the centre. In Schleswig and in Poland today, it is performed as a couple dance in which the two dancers, with hands on their hips, jump their legs ever-further apart and finish off with a polka turning. Bear dances are to be found all over Europe. In Germany, one boy would do a handstand and the other boy grab his legs and swing him back and forth. Then they would do their roll-around figure hugging each other's legs, or they would move around pretending to be growling bears.

The Lithuanians have two hat dances, the 'Skrybéliv Sokiš' and the 'Kepuriné' in which they dance in a squatting position around hats placed in front of them on the ground.

Czechoslovakia has a 'Hajduch' which may be performed with or without axes. It is supposed to have been danced by their seventeenth-century hero-outlaw, Janosikuv, who, like our Robin Hood, lived in the forest with his band of merry men, and used axes for chopping down trees. It can be danced in a circle, and usually culminates in individuals running into the middle of the circle to perform ever more difficult steps to music of increasing tempo. The 'Odsemek' is another competitive dance, originally performed by shepherds round the fire.

Another dance which originally was a men's dance, but is now done by both sexes, is the 'Capucini' dance, in which the dancers dress up as monks (goodness knows where they picked up the habit). They wear false beards and carry a piece of paper,

89. 'La Ceinture' (the Belt). Romanian dance by Théodor Aman, 1831-1891.

which is supposed to represent the breviary which monks would carry. Each monk grabs a partner and they dance. In the middle of the dance, a devil in a sleeveless, torn shirt, and a cow-chain around his body, snatches a couple off the floor and takes them off to blacken their faces. The dance continues until the devil has done his black deeds and everybody's face has been duly blackened. This dance is found in Hessen, the region around Kitzbühl, and in Salzburg. With stylistic variations, the same dance appears in Schwäbian Türkei in southern Hungary, with the dancers dressed as nuns. In this German enclave, it is still performed at weddings. In this, twelve 'nuns' (half boys, half girls) dance with a devil and with a 'nun-father', these last being two boys. In Tschawel in the Batschka, a similar dance has a 'nun-mother' danced by the biggest lad available. The others follow in single file behind him, as he waves a broom back and forth as if giving a benediction, and finish up with all the 'nuns' grabbing a partner from among the onlookers, and dancing a polka round with them.

At weddings in Hessen, the Capuchin dance was performed as a mendicant-monks' dance. Towards nightfall, the door would burst open, and, to march music, dancing with hopping steps, entered a large and a small devil, armed with pitchforks, horns on their heads, black-faced and dressed in black, with tail and huge teeth. Behind them came twelve Capuchin 'monks' with grey cloaks, ropes round their waists, potato sacks on their heads, and begging bowls and sticks in their hands. The leading Capuchin gave a short rhymed speech, then they all hopped around, and the devils rolled around on the floor, and of course begged money from the gathering. Sometimes this dance was followed by the Siebensprung.

90. 'La Jok'. Vlach dance by Auguste Raffet in 'Voyage dans la Russie Méridionale', 1804-1860.

The number nine is for women a special number evoking the nine moons which gestation lasts. In the dance 'D'r Schöffelniner' (Nine of Spades), Alsatian women clasp their hands nine times and make a movement which is called the 'childbirth'. A cave at Lérida in Catalonia has a painting showing nine women dancing around a sort of satyr, and we know from Greek mythology how the nine Muses danced round Apollo. In Provence and Aquitaine, there is a 'ronde de neuf' danced by nine women. For men the magic number is seven. It occurs in initiation rites, and leads to 'seventh heaven', a state reached in the act of reproduction. One of the basic steps in Irish dancing today is the *Seven*, and most northern countries have their version of the Austrian 'Siebenschritt'. In the Romanian 'Hora n'Doua Parti' the dancers circle counter-clockwise and then clockwise counting: "That's one" and so on up to seven. A dance of fertilizing virility therefore could hardly ignore the number seven, and such a dance, the 'Siebensprung', with its seven repeats, proceeds through its seven gestures to take the dancer progressively nearer to the earth in a symbolic fertilizing act. There is a cave painting in Sicily showing a dance in the various phases which bear a striking resemblance to the Seven Springs which has been danced, without interruption, in Alsace to the present day.

The agile and vigorous young men circle round a space sunwise and, without touching, performing no particular steps but waving their arms about, spin and leap like primitive savages, shouting and bellowing like enraged animals. On the musical phrase *cuckoo*, the dancers stand still and stamp the ground once, leap in the air and start their noisy circling once again. On the next musical *cuckoo* the dancers stamp first the right foot, then the left foot on the ground, leap and dance round again. The third time they stamp twice as before and put one knee on the ground. The fourth time they kneel on both knees. Then one elbow is added, then both elbows. The seventh time (which varies from place to place) the dancers either turn a somersault, make a movement to kiss the earth, or a hand-stand with legs waving in the air, before making one final leap as high as possible. The Seven Springs has retained its most pure form among the peasants of Kochersburg and the Outre-Forêt right down to the present time.

This Seven Springs was known as the Harvesters' dance, and was performed also at threshing time. In the Harz region, at weddings, the couples danced seven times in a circle, then shouted: "The Seven-springer is come." Two men tapped the floor with their forefingers and shouted back: "We are the Seven-jumpers." Then, in time to the music, they knocked first with the elbows, then with the knees, the heels, and finally the toes, on the ground. They then fell backwards, rolled over, and tapped their heads three times on the ground. Lastly, they all shouted: "Our Seven Springs is still alive." In Hessen-Nassau, the Seven Springs was performed at Whitsuntide by a 'green man' wearing a leaf-covered mask. In some places the dance was repeated, going through the actions in reverse order. In Taunus, they followed the Seven Springs with a circle dance with a wine-glass balanced on the head.

The Basques do the jumps without the stamping and other movements, counting aloud each number. In the 'Zazpi Jausiak', the dancers wait for a certain bar in the music and then perform one jump high in the air. The second time the tune is played this bar is repeated, and so on until the dancers have completed seven jumps. In the rest of the southwest of France, the jumps have been discarded whilst the other actions have been retained. In Westphalia in Germany, on Easter Day, the dancers circle an oak tree, trying to land their springs in seven sacred holes in the ground. They say that those who succeed will have seven years longer to live.

The words used to accompany the Alsatian version are: "Kännsch dü au de Siwersprung?" (Can you do the Seven Springs?) In Switzerland we get: "Savez-vous comment l'on danse notre joyeux Picoulet?" (Do you know how we dance our merry Picoulet?) A Swiss dance which is closely related is called 'le Picoulet'. In France they sing: "Savez-vous planter des choux . . .?" (Do you know how to plant cabbages?) There is a whole family of dances in which a series of questions is asked of the planter of grain: "Qui veut savoir comm' mon pèr sèm l'avoine?" (Who would like to know how my father sows the corn?) These are now little more than children's dance-games for both sexes. In the dance, the actions of planting are mimed, usually followed by a stamping of the feet, clapping the hands, a turn on the spot, a jump in the air. Other actions follow: cutting, tying, grinding, even eating the grain. It all goes back to fertility magic. The words of the song which accompanies the Liège version exhort the participants to jump high.

A Provençal dance which started off life as a men's dance, but which is now danced by both sexes, is 'la Viajarello' or 'Voyageuse'. It is an adaptation of a sailor's dance from the British Isles, and which the French call 'l'Anglaise'. The English name 'Hornpipe' denotes the instrument which accompanied these jigs, thus giving them the collective name of hornpipe. Italy claims the paternity of this sailor's dance on the grounds that Dante (1265-1321) used the word *giga* by which one named the earliest fiddles, a word which later on designated a dance. Charles d'Albert claimed that the gigue step was already known in England in the time of Chaucer (1340-1400), and that one finds a description of it in 'My Lady Nevill's Virginal Book' dated 1591. The sailors performed this dance before

91. 'Vlach circle dance accompanied by Gypsies and performed by members of the Second Regiment of Prince Ghika, Gospodar of Wallachia' by Auguste Raffet.

92. 'The Egg Dance' by Jan Théodore de Bry. French, 1528-1598.

leaving their native land, and a ritualistic sense may well have been attached to its original form.

The Anglaise is composed of fourteen figures and a finale, and each figure is made up of an *enchaînement* of steps which the dancer performs to the front, back, right and left. The indication of the four directions seems to point to what remains of an ancient ritual act in relation to the four cardinal points, with the intended purpose of protecting the sailor as he ventured forth on the high seas. The Anglaise could be done by one or several dancers. Holding a cane in the hand, the sailor, his torso rigid, and in the most serious manner, danced a suite of steps composed of rocking, pony-trots, scissors, and heel beats, which needed great nimbleness of the legs and especially the feet, which must never be raised from the ground by more than a few centimetres. Under the name Viajarello, the Anglaise came to be the *chef-d'oeuvre* of the dancing master of Villeneuve-les-Avignon, J.B. Duffaut (1850-1932). Today the dance is the examination piece for those aspiring to become *maître de danse*.

The Basques have a men's ceremonial display dance called the 'Aurresku', which means 'First Hand', and which is also the name given to the leader of the dance. He leads his line out and then breaks off, removes his beret, and performs an intricate display of steps. The last man, the *Atzesku* or 'Last Hand' then comes forward and replies in like manner. Thus challenged, the two dancers then strive to outdo each other in the virtuosity of their steps, in much the same fashion as the Portuguese Ribatejo fandango dancers. There then follows the solemn part of the ceremony: four of the *Aurresku's* aides lead out his chosen lady. She stands, while her admirer dances another display of intricate steps, leaping and kicking his legs head high. He then stops and bows, and, presenting her with one end of a handkerchief, leads her into the circle. The music changes to a fandango, and the chain breaks up into couples. The Aurresku is still danced on formal ceremonial occasions such as the opening of the *Semana Vasca* or Basque Week, when the President sends his four aides to the town hall to fetch the mayoress. Then, in top hat and frock coat, he dances with her.

An account of c.1781, describes the 'Rinnceadh Fada' which was performed to welcome King James as he set foot on the sea-shore at Kinsale in Ireland. The dance:

> *... was performed by three persons moving abreast, each of whom held the end of a white handkerchief. They advanced to slow music, and were followed by the rest of the dancers in pairs, each of which held a white handkerchief between them. The music suddenly changing to a quick measure, the dancers passed with a quick step under the handkerchief of the leaders, wheeled around in semi-circles and executed a variety of lively figures before falling back into their original positions.*

The dance was performed on May Eve. The Butchers adopted it, and it was danced until late into the eighteenth century when it was ousted in favour of the new French dances being introduced.

The Hungarian 'Verbunk' or 'Verbunkos' gets its name from the German word *Werben* which means 'recruiting', and is famous as the 'Recruiting Dance'. At the very time that the fashionable dances of the west were seeping into Hungary, and a new Hungarian style began to emerge, so did the Habsburgs use them to attract recruits into their standing armies. In his account of his 'Travels in Hungary' published in 1797, Dr. Robert Townsson wrote of a recruiting dance which he saw at a fair when visiting Pest:

93. 'The Egg Dance' by Pieter Aertsen, 1557.

The recruiting parties, which were not wanting here any more than in our fairs, gave me an opportunity of seeing some Hungarian dances. They are very neat, but, being a kind of hornpipe, very fatiguing. The men wore the hussar dress, and looked well. The rowels of the spurs were very large, some of the size of a halfpenny, but without points, and some had double rowels: these were for the sake of the music, as throughout the dance a great deal of noise is made by striking the spurs against each other, and by flapping their hands against their boots and breeches. They danced to the sound of the fiddle - so are men caught in Hungary!

In 1843, in his 'Athenaeum', Gergely Czuczor wrote:

The men make up a circle, with the corporal at the centre, the uniformed Gypsy Band strikes up a new tune and recruiting is under way. There are no figures during the first verse, they either let their spurs sound, keeping to one place, or they move in a circle, taking a walk, learning the rhythm and the tricks of the tune, so to speak adjusting to the dance. Slow figures follow, their order is generally fixed, if not, the corporal announces them, the dancers keep their eyes on him, as well as on those dancing opposite. This part of the dance is made up of regular steps, without any fancy stuff, when the tune consists of eight beats, two beats to the right, one to the left, again two to the right, one to the left, concluded by two beats of stamping on the spot, all keeping the same time. The fancy stuff starts after five or six such slow verses, it is quicker and fierier, leaps and jumps are in order here, the clashing of swinging swords, and the fluttering of haversacks help to produce the image of a real heroic dance.

There must have been many similarities between these dances and the 'Leaping Dance' of old. Indeed in some regions, Leaping, Swineherds', and Herdmen's dances are called recruiting dances. The recruiting dance entered the repertoire of the people, and in the order of dances performed at peasant dances, it generally came first, by way almost of introducing the couple dance.

The Norwegian 'Halling' is usually a man's solo dance, but it can be danced as a couple, the man going through his repertoire of acrobatic tricks, either on his own or supported by his partner. The favourite trick is to have one's partner stand on a chair, holding a hat high on the end of a broom at arms' length. The man winds himself up for a mighty leap and tries to kick the hat off the broom (ill. 85 & 86). Watching a seventy-year old succeed in putting much younger men to shame, one wonders if it should not become part of the Olympic Games.

The place where you are assured of seeing Greek dancing without having to search for it is the local taverna. The Greek taverna without its dancing is unthinkable, and until tourism, in recent years, demanded the inclusion of women, it had been the sole prerogative of the men. The taverna is the main meeting place for men to get together and talk, and in Greece they do a lot of talking. Television has yet to ruin the social life of the village, at least amongst the older inhabitants, but even the young people like to gather to talk, sing and dance. It is quite usual for one man to dance alone, improvising his steps, lost in his own thoughts. Another may link up with him, with a handkerchief, or clasp shoulders, and dance in tandem with him, or do his own solo quite independently, merely sharing the same music. The music and dance of the village have been adapted to suit the different clime of the urban taverna. The so-called *rebétiko* songs are an amalgam of folk, European and Asian music, and the 'Zeibékiko', 'Hasápiko', 'Karsilamás' and 'Tsiftetéli' are adaptations of older dances.

The Zeibékiko is the dance of the Zeybeks, who got their name from the baggy breeches they wore. Originally a non-Turkic people living in what is today western Turkey, their descendants intermarried with Greek colonists. The Zeybeks gained their reputation and respect as fearsome fighters. The Zeibékiko can be danced as a couple, but *par excellence* it is a man's solo dance, which more than any other epitomizes Greek dance. In it the dancer, lost in his own world, concentrating intensely on his slow and deliberate steps, goes through his repertoire of squats, spins, leaps, his hands outstretched, his thumbs and fingers snapping out the rhythm, or slapping his feet, the whole performance highly charged with emotion. Because the dancer performs with outstretched arms and moves and turns with such power and concentration, the dance has often been called 'Dance of the Eagle'. The meter of the dance is 9/4, not triple-compound but divided as: slow, slow, slow, quick, quick, the rhythm of the most popular 'Zeibékiko' being rather like a habañera with an extra beat, thus: 1̄ &̄ 2 &̄ 3̄ & 4̄ & 5̄ &̄ 6 &̄ 7̄ & 8̄ &̄ 9̄.

94. An English version of the egg dance.

The sight of a dancer, completely oblivious to anything other than his own emotions, can be a very moving sight. The author will never forget standing with his wife, in the early hours of the morning, on the deck of a ship sailing from Italy to Greece. A solitary Greek was up on deck keeping his eyes peeled for a first sight of his homeland to which obviously he was returning after many years. Gradually, almost inaudibly, the sound of cicadas floated across the dark waters, and then a black outline rose slowly from the sea. It was Greece, and suddenly the feeble scratchings of the cicadas were drowned by the roar which surged at full volume from a ghetto-blaster. He was away. Arms outstretched, fingers clicking, his faltering steps interspersed with loud slaps as he bent his legs and clapped the wooden deck-boards, the tears trickling from his cheeks, he gave full expression to emotions that had long been pent up inside him. It was the 'Zeibékiko' which he danced. It was too private a thing to spy on for long, and Odysseus was left to dance for his gods.

The 'Hassapiko' is common to all the countries of the Near East. In Bulgaria it is called the 'Kasapsko oro', in Yugoslavia it is the 'Kasapsko kolo'. Its name comes from the Arabic-Turkish name for 'butcher', but the dance itself was known long before the Turks invaded. It is said originally to have been a 'war' dance, introduced by the returning soldiers of Alexander the Great's army, and was derived from a shepherds' dance of Macedonia and Thrace. The movements of the dance depicted the stealthy approach, contact and then battle with the enemy, culminating in victory, and was used to prepare soldiers for battle, teaching them to move carefully and silently. The final breakneck pace of the dance depicted the victory. The 'Hassapiko' was adopted by the Butchers' guild of Constantinople during the period of the Byzantine Empire, and was known as 'Makellarion choron', *makellario* being the Greek word for butcher. The dance formerly consisted of a slow and a quick section. Today these are danced separately as slow or fast 'hassapiko'. The 'slow hassapiko' is variouly known as 'Naftiko' (Sailors'), 'Ploioritikos' (Stevedores') and 'Peiraeotiko' (after Piraeus, the port of Athens), though it is best known to westerners as 'Syrtaki' or 'Zorba' dance, the name *syrtaki* coming from France, and *Zorba* from the film 'Zorba the Greek' which made it world famous. The 'fast hassapiko' is just called by that name, or sometimes 'Zoero'. It is danced in an open circle to music in 2/4 time, and is lively with fast intricate steps. The leader calls out the step to be performed next. The variations on the basic step are infinite, and new ones are constantly being invented.

The name 'Pentozales' literally means five steps. Though sometimes preceded by a slow section, it is a fast-stepping island dance, and is particularly popular on Crete. Occasionally the line divides into smaller groups, and they do somersaults, leaps and turns. The islanders relate that this too was a war dance which served to train agile footwork both on land and, because they supplied the fighting arm of the navy, on board ship also. When the dance accelerates to breakneck pace, the dance is called *ortsas* meaning full.

The 'Serra' takes its name from the river Serra in the Pontus region. In the dance two men come into the centre of the circle and perform a *Mahera*, a mock sword fight. It is a wildly energetic dance, the dancers' feet appearing to skim over the ground, so fast do their feet move. The arms are held above the head and 'tremble' as if enraged. The weight of the body is back on the heels, which stamp out a rapid rhythm of three beats. The circle of dancers start with their hands clasped and held down at their sides, lifting them to shoulder level and then up high as the dance gathers momentum. The time signature is 7/16, divided thus: $\bar{1}234/\bar{5}67$.

The 'Syrto' is the oldest of all the Greek dances. There are several variations of the dance, but in them all a line of dancers is drawn (the name means to draw or pull) by a leader. Originally the dance was used in religious ritual. It is danced to a 2/4 time signature, the steps giving three beats: slow, quick, quick. The Cretan 'syrto' is rather different, the steps being quick, quick, slow, and the leader shows his skill and energy by performing leaps, turns, and other acrobatic movements, as well as slapping his free hand on his thighs, soles and heels of his boots, while the rest of the line move smoothly and evenly. The half-moon figure made in the dance honoured the Moon-goddess.

The 'Tsamiko' originated in the region of Tsamidon, and became the favourite dance of the Klephts, the mountain fighters, during the Greek War of Independence. It spread from Epirus throughout Greece. It is supposed to symbolize the shepherds climbing and leaping amongst the crags and ledges of the mountains, and is believed to be associated with the 'Geranos', the sacred 'Crane Dance'. The leader performs acrobatic leaps and somersaults, and in a stylized way shows his physical courage and prowess as a fighter. The dance is in 6/8 or 3/4 time, and is divided so that the two steps are performed slow, quick, thus: $\bar{1}234/\bar{5}6$ or $\bar{1}2/\bar{3}$. The Klephts wore the white pleated kilt, the *foustanella*, and the name *tsamika* often referred to the complete costume.

The 'Pedekhto' gets its name form the Greek word *pedo*, to leap, hop or jump, and this well describes it. The dance is Cretan. It starts in a circular formation, but moves diagonally right into a circle and then, almost but not quite, back again, and progressing rather slowly counter-clockwise. Indeed, in some places it barely moves off the spot, and thus performed becomes the fastest and wildest of all Cretan dances, the leader flailing around in all directions, restrained only by the handkerchief which binds him to the second dancer. The dance is in 2/4 divided into slow, quick, quick steps, the basic form being two *pas de grecque* and a step-hop, first moving inwards and then outwards.

The 'Dance of Osman Taka', as the people of the Çamërie region of Albania call this variation of a much older dance, has a romantic story attached to it. Osman Taka, from Konispol, was awaiting execution in the town prison of Ioannina, having taken part in an insurrection against the Ottoman Turks who were ruling Albania at that time. There was a fair taking place in the town, and Osman Taka begged to be granted one last wish, which was to dance his favourite variation, learnt during his childhood at the fair. He was bold, well-built and handsome, and these qualities and his acts of bravery during the war had won him many admirers. His wish was reluctantly granted, and he was led out into the main square, and surrounded by guards with hands linked. Osman Taka's hands were unbound. He calmly went up to the musicians to instruct them what melody to play, and began to dance on a large copper dish. He performed the dance with such skill and charm that the onlookers were entranced, not only because of his expertise, but also for his proud and indomitable stoicism which he showed in his movements. One would like to think that his guards too were sufficiently captivated as to free him, or at least reduce his sentence, but this was not to be, and Osman Taka was duly executed.

The dance has spread to other regions under its new name. The Greeks have 'borrowed' it and given it the name 'Arvanitikó' (Albanian), 'Tchamikó' (Came, from Çamërie), 'Himariotiko' (from Himare), and 'Klephtikó' from Epirus, and it is supposed to have been the dance of the Souliotes. Byron travelled to Albania in 1811 and wrote a description of the dance in his 'Childe Harold'. He described it as the dance in which proud warriors would display their skills, changing the lead dancer so that each could perform his back bends and leaps. The dancers lent their voices to the musical accompaniment and from time to time unsheathed their swords in menacing manner. Here we had the true pyrrhic dance, a dance that mountain fighters, members of a guerilla resistance to the Turkish occupation of their country could be proud to perform – a veritable European Maori hakka. The reference to dancing on a copper shield is reminiscent of the victor dancing on the shield of the vanquished. The 'Dance of Osman Taka' is normally danced by two or three dancers, but only the leader performs the dance, the others being there merely to support him, the second dancer holding the handkerchief tightly. They dance mainly on the spot to a time of 7/8, the rhythm of $\bar{1}23/\bar{4}5/\bar{6}7$ being pounded out on a drum. This is the synthesis of epic heroic dancing, every movement of the body, head, hands, in the dancer's bearing, expressing this inner strength.

9

WEDDINGS

After they've been dancing for a while you'll see a couple of the girls come in and steal away the bride and another girl will take her place. That's to cheat the fairies in case they took it into their heads to steal away the bride themselves. They'll think the bride is still dancing. . ..Then in a minute you'll see the bridegroom look round and find that the bride has vanished, and two or three friends of his will come along and lead him away to where she is, and somebody else will take his place to cheat the fairies again.

Sir Compton MacKenzie: Whisky Galore.

Apollinarius Sidonius, in 460, described a Frankish wedding in his native Gaul, in which the bride and groom were actually married during the course of the dance.

In Germany it was the custom to bring into the house an oak stump on which was laid a decorated spindle, eggs, straw, cakes, nuts, fruit, symbolic of all the things the bride would need in her new home. Sometimes they would dance around the spindle from which radiated lengths of wool or ribbons and dance a 'maypole' dance in which the bride and groom participated.

Greek weddings are a great occasion for dancing. Arranged marriages are rare nowadays, but nevertheless, weddings are still celebrated in much the same way as in the days when the marriage was the culmination of many years of careful negotiations between the families concerned. Professional matchmakers (usually older women of the village) were generally employed to bring about a contract, satisfactory to both parties, to a conclusion. Once an agreement between the respective parents had been reached, the couple were regarded as betrothed, and this was marked by a special party, *gléndi*, with food, drink, singing and dancing. The betrothed couple first dance a 'facing dance', *antikrystós*, and then lead a 'Syrtos'. The dancing goes on all night, and just before the guests depart, the bride-to-be presents her prospective in-laws with gifts of embroideries, socks, kerchiefs, and these they place on their shoulders and dance.

Weddings were frequently spoken of as *chará* (joy). The word itself is not connected with the word for dance, *choro*, but nevertheless it is the *choro* which expresses the *chará* on the wedding-day, and when this arrived it was celebrated in style, however poor the families concerned. The wedding was almost like a play with episodic events, each with its associated songs and dances. 'Weddings' are staged for tourists all over Greece, but, interesting as they are to watch, they cannot capture the spirit of the real thing, like the one which took place many years ago in a remote mountain village, and which the author and his wife were fortunate to witness. However, it is still possible, if rare, to see a wedding conducted in traditional style.

For several days before the Sunday wedding, preparations are made for the feast. Special bread rings, *kouloúria*, are baked, and sweet bread, which the children distribute to the villagers when they invite them to attend the wedding. The girls dance a special dance and sing a special song whilst the dough is left to rise, and end up throwing flour at one another. The young men are probably at this time whitewashing the groom's house, and they too will break off to sing and dance. The next day is set aside for displaying the bride's dowry: embroidered coverlets, blankets and linen, kitchen utensils, furniture, all the things which she will take to her new home. The villagers come to admire and assess the value of the items, and leave money on the items displayed as a token of their esteem. The bridal mattress is filled to the accompaniment of special songs, and then they dance round it and carry it above their heads.

A banner or *flámbouro* is festooned with coloured scarves, embroidered crosses, and apples and pomegranates, again to the accompaniment of special songs, and when it is finished, it is carried by each in turn as he or she dances with it, before setting it up on top of the roof of the groom's house. The bathing and dressing of the bride is, of course, done in private, but once more special songs and dances are performed to mark each act in the ritual. The bridegroom's company now comes dancing in procession behind the best man, *brátinos*, collecting on the way the groom's godparents, the matchmaker and the priest. After they have arrived at the bride's house, she dances a farewell

95. 'The Wedding Dance' after Pieter Brueghel. Flemish, c.1566.

dance with her friends. Then they go to the church for the religious ceremony. When they emerge, it is time for another dance, this time a chain which unites the two families. This is often led by the priest. The bride is then escorted to her husband's house, and shown round by her mother-in-law. Then more dancing, led by the *koumbáros*, the groom's godfather, followed by the bride and groom and the relatives in the strict hierarchical order demanded by protocol. Each in turn dances with the bride. As the evening turns into night, the music gets louder and faster, the atmosphere becomes more relaxed, and the young people perform intricate lively dances in pairs. In olden times, the celebrations used to last until the following Wednesday, but this rarely happens today.

In Hungary, the marriage ceremonies, rituals and jollifications start with the betrothal. One custom, described as early as 1050, is 'buying the bride'. The bridegroom goes with his friends to his intended's parents' house, and, after some difficulties are put in their way, are finally admitted. The poor man first has an old woman, dressed as a young girl, fobbed off on him, or he is given three women, their faces hidden by veils, to choose from. Blessings and drinks follow the 'discovery' of the real bride-to-be, who, by the acceptance of flowers with a coin hidden in them, is thereby 'sold'. The betrothal ceremonies are brought to a close with the dinner, when the young couple eat from the same plate and drink from the same glass. Dancing begins and goes on until morning.

96. 'The Wedding Dance' by Petrus. A. Merica after Pieter Brueghel.

The festivites may last for several days. A *kendöfa* is set up in front of both houses: that of the bridegroom is decorated with farm implements, the bride's with brooms and cooking utensils. Singing and dancing accompany every stage of the ceremony. Great fun is provided by the conveying of the nuptial bed to the couple's new house. Often this is, on the day preceding the wedding day, trundled through the village, with new bedding piled on top of it. When finally it is installed in the bedroom, it is made up, and a small boy thrown onto it, a way of ensuring, by sympathetic magic, that the union will be fruitful, and a baby boy the result. The Bedmakers' Dance follows. In certain districts, the women carry pillows above their heads while others carry the eiderdown. On the morning of the wedding day itself, the invited guests must be collected so that they can dance a farewell to the bridegroom's single status. Then they go to the bride's house, inevitably to find the gate barricaded by a rope. Whilst this has been going on, the bride has been patiently allowing her friends to prepare her. She is forbidden to raise a finger to help. Then she dances the 'Búcsú-túnc' (Farewell Dance) with the best man. She is expected to show great reluctance at parting from her parents. There is much crying and hugging until, finally, the best man signals with his decorated staff that the procession must start. With much shouting, discharging of fire-arms, breaking of crockery, all designed to frighten off the evil spirits, they make their way to the church. Often they perform the 'Paptánc' (Priest's Dance), usually in front of the church, just occasionally inside, a survival from the Middle Ages when dancing in the church or churchyard was customary. More dancing follows the marriage ceremony.

Both family houses serve as venues for the midday meal. Afterwards, the bride is brought to her husband's house. Grain is thrown over her, more fertility magic, and then, after dancing three times round a fire, she goes into her new house, to be received by her mother-in-law. An evening feast is often begun by the 'Becsülettánc (Dance of Honour). Later, masked 'Turks' arrive to dance with the bride, and finally, around midnight, comes the ritual 'Fektelés' or 'putting to bed'. First, the poor bride must dance with every man present, who is expected to give her money for it. In some districts, the 'Kendötánc' (Kerchief Dance) follows, in which each partner drapes a shawl round the bride's shoulders. The 'Vöfély', an important functionary on these occasions, enters bearing three lighted candles between the fingers of his left hand. With his other hand he takes the bride's arm. He gives a speech about marriage, blowing the candles out one at a time as he does so, and then leaves the room quickly with the bride. Elsewhere, the women may accompany the bride to the bridal chamber in slow and mournful procession, the bridegroom being similarly escorted by his friends. The *Vöfély* then lifts the bridal crown from her head, and then all dance nine times round the house before leaving the exhausted couple on their own. All that sympathetic magic hardly seems worth while, does it?

On the following day, the bride, wearing her new woman's cap, is taken in procession to the village square where a bonfire is lighted. They dance around it, and the bride has to jump through the smoke in an act of purification.

An ancient category of dances called 'Leaping Dances' exists. The name differs from region to region as does its composition, that is to say, whether it is for one man, one woman, a couple or a group. It may be called: 'Ugrős', 'Egyugrős', 'Kétugrős', 'Hárumugrős', 'Cinege', 'Dus', 'Tustolő', and many more. These mean:

97. *'Bauernhochzeit' (Peasant Wedding) by Elias Back. German, 1679-1747.*

hopping, one leap, two leaps, three leaps, and tom-tit. Its oldest form is the Recruiting Dance of Somogy. In various regions this leaping dance is performed as a wedding processional dance, a variety of figures linking up the processions, such as the 'leading of the bride through to the departure of the guests'. The women who have done the cooking have their chance to enjoy themselves, dancing, singing, making a deal of noise with their cooking utensils, often whilst the bride's hair is being bound. They will dance with glasses on their heads, and collect money for having amused the guests. The breaking of pots, perhaps more often associated with Greece, may be connected with the making of noise to frighten off evil spirits from the wedding. One of these wedding processional dances is the 'Candle Dance', the symbolic use of the lighted candles taking us back to the ancient consecration and cleansing liturgies and fertility rites.

Among other wedding dances of certain Hungarian regions may be listed the Fox Dance and the Hare Dance. With pantomimic gestures imitating the coupling of animals, they are reminiscent of ancient fertility dances. A Mortar Dance is similarly suggestive in its actions.

A most unusual wedding dance, to be found only in a very few Hungarian villages, is 'Vendel Bene's Dance', a wedding 'funerary dance game'. Danced to a tune called 'Ballad of an Outlaw', it starts with a man lying back in a chair, pretending to be dead. A woman slowly dances round him, wiping his face with her handkerchief and wailing in grief. Suddenly the music increases in tempo, and the man leaps up, twirls round with the woman, before stretching out, once more pretending to be dead. There are references to this dance dating back to the seventeenth century. A similar ritual accompanies Bulgarian weddings. In certain regions they perform a snake-like labyrinthine dance.

In the region through which runs the river Tisza we find the custom observed at weddings of 'sharing-out' dances. It was one of the duties of the best man first to dance with the bride before passing her to the bridegroom. He was then required to perform the same service to all the females present, allotting each an appropriate partner according to family relationships. In this way it was felt that everyone was given an equal share in the festive liturgical dance.

Another unusual wedding dance, now to be found only in Transylvania, calls for a 'dead' bride or bridegroom to be represented by a close friend whose betrothed also takes part in the 'wedding of the dead'. This dance often starts from the cemetry, at the graveside.

Czech and Slovak weddings could last for seven days. On the day before the wedding, unmarried young men and girls prepared crowns of rosemary bound with white ribbons for the girls and buttonholes for the boys. The best man, on the morning of the big day, would set off accompanied by musicians to collect the guests, and then they would all go to bring the bride and groom and his attendants to the church, with much music, singing and discharging of fire-arms. From the church the whole party adjourns to the inn where they fill in the time until the evening meal at the bride's parents's house with dancing. There are special songs and dances suggestive of a fruitful marriage. In 'Kolıbka' (Cradle), the chief bridesmaid stands in the centre of a circle carrying a large plate as if she is nursing a baby, and collects money from the guests. 'Čepení' sees the bride in the middle of the circle, and this is

98. *'Bauernhochzeit' (Peasant Wedding) by Elias Back. German, 1679-1747.*

followed by 'Plaček', in which the bride's mother hands a plaited loaf to the Mistress of Ceremonies who, dancing three times round in a circle, holds it over her head, after which the bread is cut up into pieces and distributed to all the guests. The next day the bride and her belongings are escorted by musicians and guests to her new house. An age-old custom takes place of 'buying the bride', in which coins are spread on a table on which the chief bridesmaid dances, and the bride's wreath is exchanged for her matron's kerchief.

At Czech weddings there is a special dance which they perform as part of the ceremony of removing the bride's veil. The 'Ponad Fl'asku' is danced around the bride carrying sabres. She is asked to take off her scarf, but each time she refuses. After three times, the dancers lift it from her on the points of their sabres, and then perform a number of leaps. The dance is performed to an Odzemek melody. Another dance is the 'Kotek', performed only by the women who join hands in a chain and dance through the house, out of one door and back in by way of a window.

Montenegro in Yugoslavia has some villages where Catholic and Orthodox Christians live side by side with Moslems. Moslem weddings are sometimes attended by several hundred guests, and both Moslem and Montenegrin dances are to be seen. In one Moslem wedding dance a man and a woman dancing alone wave a burning scarf and dash bottles of brandy to the ground. The festivities take place largely out of doors, dancing being done on a level patch of ground called the *gumno*, where the corn is threshed. At Christian weddings a succession of dances, usually *kolos*, are performed by the guests. Two sorts of *kolos* are danced: the 'Lesnoto', which is a light dance, the dancers bending and turning with an easy

99. 'Farmer's Wedding in North-Holland' by Johannes Petrus van Horstak. Dutch, 1745-1825.

grace; and the 'Teskoto', a heavy dance in which the dancers perform slow and deliberate movements. The leader of the *kolo*, the *kolovodja*, must be strong and agile to perform his steps. The women adopt a reserved mien, and take their place in the circle according to seniority, this being gauged, not by age, but by the length of time she has been married.

One dance, the 'Svekrino Kolo' is unusual in that it is led by a woman, the bride's mother-in-law. She dances with a flour sieve and some bread balanced on her head, carries a pitcher of wine, and has a gun tucked into her belt. The bridegroom dances next to her, and later takes over the lead from his mother. In southern Macedonia there is a special dance called the 'Sareno Oro'. It is danced on the final day of the wedding festivities. After sunset, the bridegroom's parents take part in the dancing. The father leads the dance and is joined by the bridegroom and the male members of the family. Then the bride and the womenfolk come into the circle. During the dance, places are changed so that the bride and groom end up between their parents, everyone else being ordered according to seniority. Still led by the father of the groom they all dance into the house, stopping when they reach the hearth where a fire must be kept burning. Then the bride turns towards the chimney-piece and bows three times. She then kisses the hands of her new parents-in-law, thus signifying the end of the ceremony.

Weddings were an occasion for dancing in Scotland too, and often certain dances played a special part. In Roxburghshire and West Berwickshire, the Bonny Briest Knot was usually the first of the dances which followed the bridal supper, and would be led by the bride and groom, and then the best man and chief bridesmaid. In the West Highlands and the Western Isles, it was the Wedding Reel or 'Ruidhleadh na Banais' which commenced the dancing, and which was danced by the bride and groom, and best man and bridesmaid, whilst the rest of the company looked on. It is still performed in the islands of the Outer Hebrides. Further reels follow, in which the bride and bridesmaid dance with other men of the company. It is said that the first man to dance with the bride in the first reel after the Wedding Reel, will become the next to be married. Another special reel was danced as a prelude to the bridal couple being bedded. Again this was danced by the two couples, bride and groom, best man and bridesmaid. Sir Compton MacKenzie in his 'Whisky Galore' described it thus:

> *After they've been dancing for a while you'll see a couple of the girls come in and steal away the bride and another girl will take her place. That's to cheat the fairies in case they took it into their heads to steal away the bride themselves. They'll think the bride is still dancing . . . Then in a minute you'll see the bridegroom look round and find that the bride has vanished, and two or three friends of his will come along and lead him away to where she is, and somebody else will take his place to cheat the fairies again.*

The Kissing Dance at country weddings was invariably the one chosen to end the celebrations.

'Uninvited' guests to a Shetland wedding were the guisers, who would suddenly appear unannounced during the course of the dancing. Often these uninvited guests were, in fact, members of the company who had suitably disguised themselves. J.T. Reid described them in his 'Art Rambles in Shetland':

> *In walks a tall, slender-looking man, called a 'scuddler', his face closely veiled with a white cambric napkin, and on his head a cap made of straw, in shape like a sugar-loaf, with three loops at the upper extremity, filled with ribbons of every conceivable hue, and hanging down so as nearly to cover his cap. He wears a white shirt, with a band of ribbons around each arm, and a bunch of ribbons on each shoulder, with a petticoat of long clean straw, called 'gloy', which hangs loosely.*

The leader of the guisers, the *scuddler*, was armed with a broom, and tried to sweep everything in the room to the bride. He was even known to sweep dirt from outside the house in to her. The rest of the guisers were known as *skeklers* and were similarly dressed. Sometimes they came in dancing a short solo, or they might dance a 'Guisards Reel', which had its special tune. They were then allowed to join in the rest of the dancing, just so long as they did not utter a single word or disclose their identity.

Wedding celebrations, in former times, lasted for three days in Shetland. On the first day, the dancing went on until about one o'clock in the morning, when supper was served. Then followed the ceremony of 'bedding the bride'. She was taken into the bridal chamber by the bridesmaids, who there undressed her and put her to bed, with "dancing about and kicking up a caper". She was then to receive all the women

100. 'A Highland Wedding at Blair Atholl' by David Allan. Scottish, 1780.
By courtesy of the Trustees of Mrs. M. Sharp Erskine's Trust.

present at the wedding and give each a piece of bridescake. This done and the women guests having left the bridal chamber, the young men brought in the bridegroom and installed him in bed next to his bride, whereupon the male guests brought in gifts of money for the bride, receiving in return from the bride a piece of bridescake and from the groom a dram of whisky. Throughout all this, the fiddler sat in a corner of the chamber and played suitable tunes.

On Whalsay, they danced a Shetland reel for three couples. In the first reel to commence the wedding celebrations, the couples were: the bride and groom, best man and bridesmaid, and the 'married folk'. The rest of the company took turns to dance. The need to limit the number of dancers to three couples was sometimes imposed by the lack of space available. A kitchen in a crofter's house, on a tiny island a long way from the mainland, could be minute. Here on Whalsay, was still danced, until quite recent times, a very special dance. Before the bedding of the bridal couple, they danced the 'Bride's Reels', a series of 'auld' reels in which the women only danced in turn. The first of the bride's reels was danced by the bride and the chief bridesmaid, the bride's mother and the 'married woman', the third couple being two of the bride's closest female relatives. Seniority in the community or closeness of kin dictated the order of precedence amongst the remaining womenfolk, when it came their turn to dance. They danced the auld reels throughout: "They grippit arms and keepit two and two thegither, and danced the figure 8 . . . they just keepit goin' on aroun."

101. 'The Wedding in Ojców' showing the Krakowiak by Antoni Zaleski. Polish, 1824-1885.

While the women danced, the men were required to "sweepit the bride" with straw brushes. These consisted of oat straw with the grain removed. The stems were bound with a single ribbon round the bottom half, whilst the tops were tied two or three together by separate ribbons with long ends left dangling. Several men stood round about the dancers waving these brushes over the heads of the dancers, ruffling their hair and tickling their faces, all the while being careful not to touch the bride – "They hadna tae touch the bride". In the bridegroom's reels which followed, the process was reversed, the women having to "sweepit the bridegroom", again being careful to avoid touching the groom himself. This 'sweeping' of the bridal couple appears to be an extraordinary survival of kindred ritual dance ceremonies to be found elsewhere in Europe, the purpose being to sweep away any lurking evil spirits.

The oldest circle dances to be seen in Estonia are often danced at weddings. The chain, holding hands, or in column formation with hands on the shoulders of the person in front, wends its way round the farm led by the fiddle player. This 'Pulmarong' can either be performed to a walking step, a polka, or a little step in triple time. The Estonian bride needed to supply herself with certain gifts to give to relations on the way to the church and back again. Often the route was deliberately barred to force her to pay to continue on her way. Socks, mittens, belts, all had to be beautifully made, and so the bride had helpers to assist her in

102. Peasant wedding dance in Schliersee. German, c.1830.

her preparations. The groom would invite his friends along and all would join in and dance. However, at the wedding reception itself, they would have to ensure first that the pastor had left, for the Lutheran Church regarded dancing as a sin. Even today, some of the old folk would be shocked at dancing on such a solemn occasion. Old feelings linger on. In an old people's home in Sweden, the author saw a ninety-two year-old gentleman leave the room when a local folk dance group arrived to entertain the old folks, as he didn't wish to witness the 'Devil's work', though his ninety year-old wife determinedly stayed to see the fun.

In some parts of Finland, notably in the Swedish-speaking regions, a so-called 'Kryckdansen' (Crutch dance) served as a prelude to the wedding itself. On the day when the bans were read, the couple were said to have 'fallen from the pulpit', and were now 'limping' between their unmarried state and marriage. Dancing played an important part at Finnish weddings. A special 'Alotuspurppuri' or introductory *potpourri* of dance tunes would open the wedding celebrations. Other names for these are, in Finnish-speaking areas, 'Kruusu' or 'Ruusupurppuri', and in Swedish-speaking areas, 'Rospurpuri' (Rose Potpourri). In this, the bridal couple and specially-chosen people danced – polskas, polonaises, minuets and marches were used. There were special dances for each stage of the wedding celebrations. Sometimes the bride and groom were placed on two chairs which had been tied together. They were thus carried into the room to drink a toast with their guests, and then were hoisted aloft amidst cheers. Special dance tunes were used to accompany the ring-dance ceremony in which the bride removed her bridal crown. The dancers would form a circle round the

103. Estonian wedding dance. c.1800.

bride who would remove her bridal crown and have a kerchief tied to cover her eyes. They would then dance round her, and when they stopped, whoever the bride chose to present with her crown would become the next person to get married.

Usually, four distinct circle dances were performed: one each for girls, boys, women, and men: thus the girls would dance the bride out of their circle; the boys would dance the groom out of their circle; the women would dance the bride into their circle; and the men would dance the groom into their circle. Certain dances (*penningdanser*) were also performed in which money was collected for the bridal couple, and a long dance, which gave everyone a chance to inspect the house and surroundings as the chain bounced its way through and round the house. At Ostrobothnian weddings, in the mixed Finnish and Swedish-speaking areas, there is an unbroken tradition of minuet and polska dancing, the minuet always being followed by the polska.

'Nuotakos Šokis' was a Lithuanian bride's dance. The dancers, carrying lighted torches stood in a circle performing little jumps around the bride, who danced with each member of the groom's family and finally with the groom himself. The dance symbolized the acceptance of the bride by her husband's family. 'Sadutė' was the dance which expressed the bride's family and friends' sadness at losing her. On the eve of the wedding they came to visit the bride, with flowers in their hands to bid her farewell, and to place a wreath of flowers on her head as a symbol of her parting with maidenhood. 'Piršlio Šokis' (Matchmakers' Dance) was a humourous wedding dance.

104. Estonian wedding dance. c.1800.

Norway has a 'Kyndeldans' which dates back at least to the thirteenth century, in which girls carry garlands of flowers, the men flaming torches. On the Cantabrian coast of Spain, they too have a special wedding dance. The garlands, decorated with paper flowers, are much bigger than the Norwegian ones, and are held up aloft. The first couple, representing the bridal couple carry white garlands, their attendants coloured ones. They perform various country-dance figures – *moulinets*, *cast-offs* and so on with each person, taking hold of one end of the partner's arch. The dance is known as the 'Floral Dance of the Mayos and Mayas', though it has nothing to do with the month of May, but is a regional expression for young men and girls. Nor have the garlands any connection with those associated with sword or hoop dances. They are merely there for the bridal couple to pass beneath, in a similar way to those in such processions as the 'Treilles' of the Langue d'Oc, where decorated arches are used for such occasions. Another dance to be found in Cantabria is 'La Danza de la Maya de la Copa'. This is not a wedding dance as such, but rather a song-game in which one girl represents the would-be bride choosing her man.

At Breton weddings, a go-between used to appear tricked out in the skin of a goat, and covered in strings of little cakes and all sorts of dainties which he had to guard all day from those who made a grab for them. It was not until the bride had danced the last dance with the final personage that the children were allowed one final assault and to snatch the goodies.

10

MAYPOLES, FIRES AND SPIRITS

I have heard it credibly reported . . . by men of great gravitie and reputation, that of fortie, threescore, or a hundred maides going to the wood overnight, there have scarcely the third part of them returned home againe undefiled

William Stubbes: Anatomie of Abuses, 1583.

Folklore from all over the world tells of the sacred nature of the tree. The tree has been seen as the centre of the world and the support of the universe, as a symbol of life, and of inexhaustible fertility. As the tree put forth new leaves each spring, it was the sign of the renewal of vegetation, the rebirth of the year. Tree 'worship' took many forms. The Holy Thorn at Glastonbury was only one of many thorn trees which were venerated, and as people would gather on old Christmas Eve to watch the holy thorn flower, so at the opposite end of the year, old Midsummer's Day, the people of Appleton in Cheshire would decorate their holy thorn, which was according to tradition an offshoot of the Glastonbury thorn, with flowers and ribbons and would dance around it. They do so to this day. Those dwelling in Aston-on-Clun in Shropshire still decorate their black poplar on Arbor Day, May 29th. They hang flags on poles in the Arbor Tree, enact an eighteenth-century wedding in costume of the period, and do morris and maypole dancing beneath it. Indeed, dancing round trees has always been an integral part of certain rites. In Devon they had special trees for dancing round. In Wales, starting on Midsummer's Day and lasting for several days, they danced round a flower-decked birch tree. In ancient times couples were sometimes married beneath a sacred 'marriage oak'. Even well into Christian times, newly married couples would go to a sacred tree, dance around it and cut a cross in it.

It was the custom, in most countries of Europe, for the villagers to go out into the woods to cut down a tree, to bring it back to the village, and to set it up amidst rejoicing. Cut branches would also be brought back, to be fastened on every house, bringing to each household the blessing of the tree spirits. The custom survives still, and maypole dancing is one tangible relic left over from ancient times. Sometimes they dance round a real tree that has been stripped of its lower branches, or they may use a pole to symbolize the tree, and decorate it with wreaths, garlands, ribbons and greenery. Sometimes the may-tree is carried from house to house to share out the tree-spirits' blessings. Not everywhere is the custom observed in May; early summer and midsummer also provide occasions for maypole dancing.

In his 'Description of Westmeath', Sir Henry Piers, in 1682, wrote:

*On May-eve, every family sets up before their door a green bush, strewed over with yellow flowers, which the meadows yield plentifully. In countries where timber is plentiful, they erect tall slender trees which stand high, and they continue almost the whole year; so as a stranger would go nigh to imagine that they were all signs of ale-sellers, and that all houses were ale-houses**.

In Cornwall, they used to deck their doors and porches, on May Ist, with green boughs of sycamore and hawthorn, and plant trees, or rather stumps of trees, before their houses. In the north of England, the young people would go out after midnight, on the morning of May Ist, and, with music playing and horns blowing, they would gather branches and adorn them with nosegays and floral crowns. Then they would return to the village and fasten the flower-decked branches to the doors and windows of the houses. At Abingdon, Oxfordshire, the morrismen sang:

We've been rambling all the night,
And sometime of this day;
And now returning back again,
We bring a garland gay.
A garland gay we bring you here,
And at your door we stand;
It is a sprout well budded out,
The work of our Lord's hand.

The earliest recorded maypole in England dates from the reign of King John (early thirteenth century), and was erected at Lostock near Bolton, "where the cross was formerly". A further reference, dated 1373, was from Pendleton, another northern village, this one famous for its witches. What the Church condemned was not so much the dancing, as what went on around it. Boys and girls went out into the woods and fields to bring back flowers and greenery, but too many stayed out all night, taking the licence traditionally allowed by pre-Christian festivals of the renewal of nature.

The Puritans greatly disapproved of all this pagan practice. William Stubbes, in his 'Anatomie of Abuses' (1583), vividly expressed his disgust when he wrote:

Against May, Whitsontide, or other time, all the yung men and maides, olde men and wives, run gadding over night to the woods, groves, hils and mountains, where they spend all the night in pleasant pastimes, and in the morning they return, bringing with them birch and branches of trees, to deck their assemblies withall. And no mervaile, for there is a great Lord present among them, as superintendent and Lord over their pastimes and sportes, namely, Sathan, prince of hel. But the chiefest jewel

* A bush painted on the sign-board indicated that this was an ale-house.

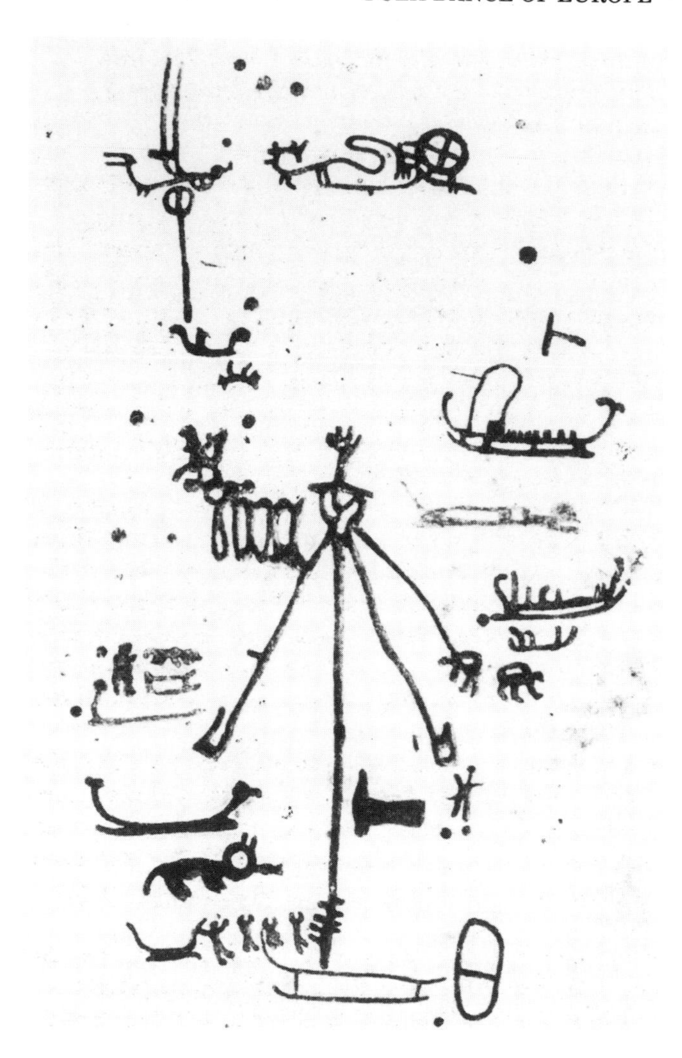

105. Maypole dance? Prehistoric rock painting from Tanum in Sweden.

they bring from thence is their May-pole, which they bring home with great veneration, as thus. They have twentie or fortie yoke of oxen, every oxe having a sweet nose-gay of floures placed on the tip of his hornes, and these oxen drawe home this May-pole (this stynkyng ydol, rather), which is covered all over with floures and hearbs, bound round about with strings, from the top to the bottome, and sometime painted with variable colours, with two or three hundred men, women and children following it with great devotion. And thus beeing reared up, with handkercheefs and flags hovering on the top, they straw the ground round about, binde green boughs about it, set up sommer haules, bowers and arbors hard by it. And then fall they to daunce about it, like as the heathen people did at the dedication of the Idols, whereof this is a perfect pattern, or rather the thing itself. I have heard it credibly reported (and that viva voce*) by men* *of great gravitie and reputation, that of fortie, threescore, or a hundred maides going to the wood overnight, there have scarcely the third part of them returned home againe undefiled.*

Well, of course, it was believed at that time, that Mother Nature needed to be in such manner stimulated herself to be fruitful, and you can't blame folks for trying.

Very little is known of the maypole dances themselves in England, apart from occasional vague references to "people dancing round them wearing oak leaves", and "Men and girls dancing the Maypole dance hand in hand in a ring", and in Elizabethan woodcuts, one of which shows men and women in a hands-all ring round a maypole, with the caption reading, 'Hey for Sellenger's Round'.

In Ireland, hoops wreathed in rowan and marsh-marigolds are carried around some villages. Sometimes balls, said originally to have represented the sun and moon, covered in gold and silver paper, are suspended within the hoops.

The Welsh 'Dawns Blodau Nantgarw' seems formerly to have been a maypole dance. The women carry long trails of wild flowers in each hand, twirling them alternately over their heads or tossing them towards the men as they meet in the dance. In true Welsh fashion, the dance gets wilder and wilder. The women also mime the pulling up by the roots of the flowers. The maypole was more associated with midsummer than with May in Glamorganshire. The *Fedwen Haf* (summer birch) was often highly painted and decorated with rosettes. Ceremonies accompanied the raising of the maypole around which they danced.

The Swedes dance round their maypoles at midsummer. On Midsummer's Eve, the houses are spring-cleaned and decorated with greenery and flowers, and maypoles are garlanded, great care being taken to decorate the poles with garlands made from twigs and foliage of only those trees prescribed by custom: oak, birch, and seven others. Midsummer bonfires also take place on this day, and in Bohemia the poor maypole ends up on the bonfire.

The Latvians combined dancing around their trees with the midsummer fires. At Jani (St. John's Eve), they would set a wooden barrel filled with burning pitch on a pole, where it would be left to burn all night long. Going through the countryside one could see fires burning all around on high vantage points. People would go from village to village singing, dancing and drinking, and then they would go searching for fern blossom, which frequently led to some young girl getting pregnant. The Letts used to congregate in the Elka mountains at holy places to carry out their religious observances and to make their sacrifices. Woods and groves also provided them with sanctuaries to make offerings to their numerous gods. The rituals took place particularly under oak and lime trees, the most holy of all, and offerings to the spirits of the trees were hung in the branches. In 1606, a Jesuit priest, J. Stribingius, observed these rites and left a brief description of them: "In diverse places they set light to pyres and threw into the flames offerings and then began to dance round the trees." In times of drought they prayed to their thunder god, Pērkons, making offerings of a black calf, a black goat, and a black cockerel. They went round the pyre three times, drinking from a goblet of beer and sprinkling the rest on the flames.

In Czechoslovakia the girls carry in a pole decked in white, while the boys bring in a guy, which represents the tree-spirit. In Bohemia, on the fourth Sunday in Lent, the puppet, called 'Death' is thrown into the river. Then the young girls of the village tie a second doll, dressed in white clothes, to a newly felled young tree, and go from house to house singing:

We carry death out of the village,
We bring summer into the village.

In Moravia a maypole goes up in October, moved to that season of the year for political reasons, and the men dance singly, performing high leaps to make the crops grow tall.

The Valais and Tessin cantons of Switzerland see the people dancing round a recently felled birch, beech or fir tree, garnished with flowers and coloured ribbons. In the Tessin, they simply dance round the *Maggiolata* (*Maggio* = May), while in the Val d'Illiez, a valley in the centre of Valais, they plait the ribbons which hang from the tree which has been stripped of its branches. This dance for twelve or sixteen people is called 'la Chevillière' or 'la Danse des Rubans' (Ribbon Dance).

In Swabia in Germany, ribbons are attached to the maypole and the people dance round it holding on to a ribbon. In Saxony, besides the ribbons, they have goodies such as sausages, cakes and eggs, which serve as prizes for the best dancers. In Bavaria, on May 2nd, a tree is put up and danced round by a man dressed from

106. 'Midsummer Dance' by Kilian Zoll. Swedish, 1818-1860.

head to foot in straw. This 'Walber' is also led from house to house bringing luck wherever he is well-received.

French girls go around on the first Sunday in May, singing songs which mention "bread and meal that come in May". If they receive a gift, they fasten greenery to the door: but if not, they wish the household no bread to feed them. Elsewhere, boys called *maillotins* go about singing carols, for which they hope to receive money or a drink. In Alsace, one can find groups carrying may-trees. One of their group may dress in a white shirt and blacken his face; another may carry a basket in order to collect eggs, sweets, or other offerings.

All over Gascony the maypoles go up, fir poles, twenty or thirty feet high, topped with flags, and bottles swinging on strings, the dancers performing *rondes fermées* to the accompaniment of their own voices, or a hurdy-gurdy. In one dance, a boy stands in the middle of the ring, and on a certain bar kisses the girl of his choice at the appropriate moment. In 'la Chouade' the dancers mime the sowing of oats, cutting and tying the sheaves. At Bordeaux, the young people used to dance around the maypole every evening for the whole of the month of May. In Provence, maypole dancing is as popular as ever it has been. The 'Cordelles' is danced, like maypole dances elsewhere, by couples facing each other in a circle round a central pole, holding on to the end of a ribbon which hangs down from the pole, and weaving in and out, plaiting the ribbons as they go. Then, turning, they proceed to unplait the ribbons by dancing in the opposite direction. Originally the 'Cordelles' was reserved for men only, and they in all probability celibate also. An account of 1820 shows that it was still danced only by men. They wore the ritual costume: white clothes, ribbons, headgear decorated with feathers and flowers, and a sword hanging from their side. In some parts of France (Île de France, for example), in addition to having a decorated maypole, they also coat a young man, whom they call 'Father May', in greenery, and lead him about the village, to bring luck to one and all.

In the Basque country, in the province of Guipúzkoa, the men perform, as the last figure of their sword dance, the plaiting of the maypole ribbons. Men and girls are placed alternately, while single dancers stand outside the group performing *pas seuls*. A fool accompanies the dancers. The men wear bells on their legs. In some villages half the men dress up as women for the dance, which is performed at Carnival instead of May.

Catalonia too has the dancers plaiting the ribbons. In Santo Domingo de Silos the dancers perform before the statue of the Virgin, which is carried out into the square. One of the dances is a maypole dance in which the ribbons are plaited. In Almonacid del Marquesando they weave coloured ribbons round the maypole. Spring festivals in Aragon always contain maypole dances. Along the southern coast of Spain they sing verses implying courtship during the dance.

Summer is the time for maypoles in Portugal. In some dances the girls carry fans and promenade round the maypole while their partners bring bunches of flowers, which they present to the girls before joining together in the dance. In another dance the boy places a special bread shaped like a ring over the girl's arm, and after the dance they go off together to eat the bread.

In Russia, they used to go into the woods on the Thursday before Whitsuntide, and cut down a young birch tree. They would then dress it in women's clothes, take it back to the village, and, after singing and dancing, would install it as a 'guest' in one of the houses. When Sunday came, they would take it down to the river and throw it in, flinging garlands into the water after it, certainly as a rain-charm.

In Lithuania, thc prettiest girl of the village is crowned May Queen, swathed in birch twigs, seated beside the may-tree, and everyone dances round her.

The 'Ples pod Trešnjom' (Dance beneath the Cherry Tree) of Yugoslavia is danced only in May. It is the dance of the young men from Punat who have been called up for military service, and who, on the first Sunday in May, perform the ceremony of 'Raising the May'. A cherry tree or pole is erected on the sea-front and secured to the adjacent buildings. The girls present coloured scarves which hang from the pole, around which the young people dance the 'Tanac'. A honey cake is awarded to the best girl dancer, whilst oranges are sent rolling in all directions for the children to pick up. The young men, by participating in the maypole dance, become eligible for marriage.

In many countries, the dancers wore ritual costume: white clothes decorated with ribbons and bells, headdresses with flowers, feathers, greenery, sometimes a sword hanging by the side. In all probability, the handkerchiefs and decorated sticks now carried by Morris dancers were formerly branches of May or other greenery which were waved and struck. The ribbons were the spokes of a wheel, a pre-historic sun symbol. The intertwining of the dancers was seen as the winding of a serpent, symbol of fecundity. The pole was the cosmic tree which joined heaven, earth and the underworld. The spider's web formed by the interlaced ribbons made it also a moon dance, for the Moon-goddess was believed to spin the web of the cosmos, binding all things together.

Fires

Since time immemorial, on certain days of the year, it has been the custom to light bonfires, and to dance round or leap over them. On these occasions, human beings were once sacrificed. Bonfires were bone-fires, the sacrificial victims providing the bones. Fortunately, effigies have long ago replaced that barbaric custom. But sacrifice, whether in human form or effigy substitute, were important, because the fires had a deep significance for those who danced around them, leapt over the smouldering embers, or drove their animals through the smoke.

There were eight great occasions for lighting bonfires, four related to the movements of the moon and four to the sun. The lunar festivals were : Samhain (November 1st), Imbolc (February 1st), Beltane (May 1st), and Lugnasad (August 1st). This last, *Lugh nasad*, commemorates the death of the Goidelic sun-god Lugh. The name was altered first to *Lugh-mass*, and was observed as a mourning feast in medieval times as *Lammas*. *Lammas* is still kept as a fair in parts of Wales, and in the Tailltean Games celebrated in Ireland. It may be that William Rufus was sacrificially killed in the New Forest on this day, the red-haired king being laid on a harvest cart and brought for burial through villages where the inhabitants were mourning the death of Lugh. The last vestiges of Lammas celebrations in England are to be observed today during Lancashire Wakes Week. The sun's festivals were: the winter solstice (on or near December 22nd), the spring equinox (March 21st), the summer solstice (June 22nd), and the autumn equinox (September 23rd).

Thus fires were lit in spring and at midsummer, at the end of autumn and during the course of winter, in particular on Hallowe'en (October 31st), Christmas Day, and on the eve of Twelfth Day. In Belgium, northern France, and parts of Germany, the Lenten fires were kindled on the first Sunday of Lent, Easter Eve, or May Day. The people believed that jumping over the embers secured good crops for the coming year. Young people were promised marriage within the year. Warding off sickness was another reason. In Brabant, men and women disguised in female attire and carrying torches, danced to drive away any lurking evil spirits. In the Ardennes, it was the last person to be married who set light to the bonfire. Cattle and sheep were driven through the smoke as a sure means of warding off sickness and guarding them against witchcraft. In many places, it was believed that the livelier the dance about the fire, the better the crops in the coming year would be.

In Franche-Comte, the final Sunday of Lent is called the Sunday of the Firebrand (Brandons). There are dances special to this day. Sometimes a pole is erected in the centre of the bonfire, and a wooden cock attached to it. In the Auvergne, the people dance and sing around their *Figo*, before they observe their ceremony of the 'Grannas-mias'. The *granno-mio* is a torch of straw carried on a pole. The people light their torches from the fire, and then go round the fields, orchards, and gardens, passing the burning torches underneath the branches of all the fruit trees, singing: "Brando, brandounci tsaquc brantso, in plan pane!" (Firebrand burn; every branch a basketful!) Sometimes they scatter the ashes from the torches across newly sown

107. 'Ronde autour d'un Arbre de Mai' by Pierre van der Borcht. Flemish, 1545-1608.

fields, or in the hen houses, to encourage the hens to lay plenty of eggs throughout the coming year. These are all charms to ensure fertility. Invocations are addressed to 'Granno', after whom the torches are also named. It is tempting to identify Granno with thc ancient god Grannus, the Celtic equivalent of the Roman god Apollo.

In the Eifel region, a huge wheel made of straw is dragged to the top of a hill by three horses. The wheel is set on fire and sent trundling down the slope. In Swabia, the young people hurl blazing discs into the air. The discs are given notched edges to represent the rays of the sun. They also burn straw 'witches' here. The charred remains of both the witch and the discs are later buried in the fields in the belief that this will keep away vermin. Elsewhere it is believed that, wherever the fiery wheel rolls, the fields will not be damaged by storms. In the canton of Lucerne, the people dancing wildly around the fire also crack whips and ring bells. They too send blazing wheels rolling downhill. The greater the number of fires that could be seen, the greater would be the prosperity during the ensuing year, and, of course, the higher the dancers leapt over the fire the higher would grow the crops.

Other fire festivals were held on the Saturday before Easter Sunday. On that day it is customary in Catholic churches to extinguish all lights and relight them from the great Paschal or Easter candle. In some countries, a bonfire is also kindled near the church. Oak, walnut and beech are used. The still-kindling sticks are taken home and placed in the hearth, in the belief that the homestead will thus be protected from fire. If the charred sticks were placed in the roof, the house would not be struck by lightning. Placed in the fields, gardens or meadows, these were protected from blight, hail and storm. Corn and plants would grow better, and would not be devoured by vermin. Sometimes the charred sticks were fastened to the plough, or the wood-ash mixed with the seed at sowing. In parts of Germany, the charred sticks, kept and then planted in the fields on Walpurgis Day (May Ist), would preserve the corn from blight and mildew. Easter fires were common to most parts of central and northern Germany, and the Netherlands, and dancing round them and leaping through the flames are an integral part of the festivities. In Sweden, firearms are discharged, and the noise from these, as well as the flames and smoke from the bonfires, drive away the trolls who are particularly active at this time of year.

The great fires which burned in all the Celtic lands were the 'Beltane' fires. In the Scottish Highlands, they were kindled with great ceremony on May Ist, and undoubtedly human beings were once sacrificed. The Beltane custom of the parish of Callander, in western Perthshire, at the end of the eighteenth century, was described by the parish minister thus:

Upon the first day of May, which is called Beltan, or Baltein day, all the boys in a township or hamlet meet in the moors. They cut a table in the green sod, of a round figure, by casting a trench in the ground, of such circumference as to hold the whole company. They kindle a fire, and dress a repast of eggs and milk in the consistence of a custard. They knead a cake of oatmeal, which is toasted at the embers against a stone. After the custard is eaten up, they divide the cake into so many portions, as similar as possible to one other in size and shape, as there are persons in the company. They daub one of these portions all over with charcoal, until it be perfectly black. They put all the bits of the cake into a bonnet. Everyone, blindfold, draws out a portion. He who holds the bonnet is entitled to the last bit. Whoever draws the black bit is the 'devoted' person who is to be sacrificed to 'Baal', whose favour they mean to implore, in rendering the year productive of the sustenance of man and beast. There is little doubt of these inhuman sacrifices having been once offered in this country, as well as in the east, although they now pass from the act of sacrificing, and only compel the 'devoted' person to leap three times through the flames; with which the ceremonies of this festival are closed.

In the northeast of Scotland, they called their fires 'bone-fires', and lit them on May 2nd. The herdsmen used to dance three times 'southways' around the fire. This probably implied sunwise, because we know that the cattle were driven sunwise round the fires to protect them from murrain. People believed that on that night witches were active, casting spells on their cattle and stealing the milk. To forestall this, they would place twigs of rowan and woodbine over the doors of the cowsheds. The young people danced round the fire or leapt through the smoke, shouting: "Fire, blaze and burn the witches; fire, fire, burn the witches!" In some places, a large round cake made from oat or barley meal was rolled in the ashes.

The lighting of the Beltane fires in Wales varied from the eve of May Day to May 3rd.

108. 'May Dance' by Pieter Brueghel the Younger. Flemish, 1634.

The fire was done in this way. Nine men would turn their pockets inside out, and see that every piece of money and all metals were off their persons. Then the men went into the nearest woods, and collected sticks of nine different kinds of trees. They were carried to the spot where the fire had to be built. There a circle was cut in the sod, and the sticks were set crosswise. All around the circle the people stood and watched the proceedings. One of the men would then take two bits of oak, and rub them together until a flame was kindled. This was applied to the sticks, and soon a large fire was made. Sometimes two fires were set up side by side. These fires, whether one or two, were called 'coelcerth' or bonfire. Round cakes of oatmeal and brown meal were split in four and placed in a small flour-bag, and everybody present had to pick out a portion. The last bit in the bag fell to the lot of the bag-holder. Each person who chanced to pick up a piece of brown meal cake was compelled to leap three times over the flames, or to run thrice between the two fires, by which means the people thought they were sure of a plentiful harvest. Shouts and screams of those who had to face the ordeal could be heard ever so far, and those who chanced to pick the oatmeal portions sang and danced and clapped their hands in approval.

They also danced round fires on Midsummer's Eve in Wales. 'Dawns Gwyl Ifan (Dance of St. John's Eve) came as the culmination of the *Dawnsio haf* (summer dancing). The dance worked up to a breakneck speed, until the music suddenly stopped and the women stood quivering. Then as the music continued slowly, the women made a low curtsy, while the men danced on the spot, their hands clasped above their partner's head. Then the men raised their partners, kissing them on both cheeks.

In Wales also, cartwheels bound with straw and pitch were set alight and sent rolling down the hillside to quicken the powers of the dying sun. If the flames were extinguished before the wheel reached the foot of the hill they could expect a poor harvest, but if the flames burned vigorously then the harvest would be bountiful. To jump over or dance round the glowing embers of a fire was to ensure one's own fertility and good fortune.

Beltane fires were also lighted in Ireland. "Cormac, or somebody in his name, says that 'Belltaine', May-day, was so called from the 'lucky fire' or the 'two fires', which the Druids of Erin used to make on that day with great incantations; and cattle . . . used to be brought to those fires, or be driven between them, as a safeguard against the diseases of the year."

A traveller to Ireland in the eighteenth century wrote:

At the house where I was entertained, in the summer of 1782, it was told me that we should see at midnight the most singular sight in Ireland, which was the lighting of fires in honour of the sun. Accordingly, exactly at midnight, the fires began to appear; and going up to the leads of the house, which had a widely-extended view, I saw, on a radius of thirty miles all around, the fires burning on every eminence. I learned from undoubted authority that the people danced round the fires, and at the close went through these fires, and made their sons and daughters, together with their cattle, pass the fire; and the whole was conducted with religious solemnity.

May-eve fires were lighted in parts of Sweden round which the young people danced in a ring, while the older folk used to forecast the weather according to which direction the smoke blew in: if the flames inclined to the north, the spring would be cold and late; if to the south it would be mild and genial. In Bohemia the fires were kindled on May-eve on top of hills, at crossroads, or in the pastures. The young people danced round the fires and leapt over the embers, even through the flames themselves. They call this ceremony 'burning the witches', sometimes also burning in effigy a witch. This night is the notorious Walpurgis Night when the witches speed though the air on their satanic errands. Kindling fires and burning witches used to be widespread in Saxony, Tyrol, Silesia and Moravia.

Bonfires were also lit to purify and drive out evil spirits. Thus in Germany, incense is burned in the homes and stables during the twelve days of Christmas or, as they are called in Germany, the 'Twelve Smoke Nights', in order to drive away the spectral 'Wild Hunt' on January 5th. In Herefordshire farmers used to light thirteen bonfires on each wheat field to 'burn the witches', for otherwise they would not have a good crop. In many places cattle were driven between bonfires so that the smoke would purify them and protect them against witchcraft.

The midsummer fire festivals are generally held on either Midsummer's Eve (June 23rd) or Midsummer's Day (June 24th). The name St. John's Eve gives a veneer of Christianity to what was one of the most celebrated days in the pagan calendar. As with so many pagan festivals, the Church took it under its wing, and today the feast day of St. John the Baptist is more immediately recognized than Midsummer's Day. This is the summer solstice, when the sun has reached its highest point in the sky. From this day, the days begin to shorten, the nights to lengthen. Early man had long observed this phenomenon. To him the sun had reached the zenith of its power, and now its strength was on the wane. No country in Europe has failed to observe this festival when Man, however feeble, attempted to exert his influence and assist the sun to renew itself. By means of bonfires, flaming torches, and the rolling of burning wheels, he has sought, by sympathetic magic, to safeguard himself at this season.

One medieval writer relates how youths burned bones and filth of various sorts to make a foul smoke what would drive away the noxious dragons which, excited by the heat of the midsummer sun, copulated in the air, poisoning the wells and rivers by dropping their seed into them.

In most countries, the bonfires were lighted on Midsummer's Eve, and everyone passed most of the night away, singing and dancing about the fires. The people wore chaplets of mugwort and vervain, and, as they left the fire, they threw their chaplets onto the dying embers saying: "May all my ill-luck depart and be burnt up with these!" Again, cattle were driven through the smoke to cure any animals that were sick, and to protect their herds from pestilence through the year, and, again, the height of the flames was believed to condition the abundance of the harvest. Whoever was able to leap over the burning embers would not suffer backache when reaping the corn at harvest, and the higher he leapt, the higher would grow their

109. 'Peasant Dance round the Lime Tree' by D. Kandel. Alsace, 1546.

crops. Sometimes as they jumped over the fire, they shouted: "Flax, flax, may the flax this year grow seven ells high!"

The Bulgarian midsummer fire festival is called 'Enyovden' The people believed that this was the day when the sun reached the farthest point of his journey and then forgot which way he should go. Fortunately, his young sister, the Morning Star, was on hand to point him in the right direction. Before he continued his journey the sun took a bath. On this day everyone was encouraged to bathe. Even bears are said to bathe on Midsummer Day.

In Norway, the fires were lighted to banish sickness among the animals, and to drive away witches, who were thought to be flying from all parts to Blocksberg that night. In Sweden, they danced round 'Balder's balefires', and discharged fire arms. Just as the maypoles must be decorated with nine different sorts of wood, so must nine sorts of wood be used for the bonfires. Certain kinds of toadstools were thrown on the flames to counteract the power of the trolls and any other evil spirits which are thought to be lurking that night, for at that mystic time of the year, the mountains open up to release from their cavernous depths those restless spirits which are allowed, for a few brief hours, to dance and disport themselves. If the peasants see a goat in the vicinity of a bonfire, they are convinced that it can be no other than Old Nick himself. In Brittany, a girl who dances round nine midsummer bonfires, will marry within the year.

Midsummer fire-festivals were the most widespread throughout Europe, but, for the Celts on the western fringes of Europe, the two main festivals were on May Eve, and six months later on Hallowe'en, (October 31st), that is, the day preceding All Saints' or Allhallows' Day. These two days, or rather nights, are quite independent of the two solstices and two equinoxes. Nor do they coincide with the principal seasons of the agricultural year, spring sowing and autumn reaping. The explanation for this seems to lie in the importance of these two times of the year, not to the agriculturalist but to the pastoralist. In many parts of Europe, not merely in those designated 'Celtic', May and November were turning points in the year of equal importance to the herdsman. In May, on the approach of summer, he drove his cattle out into the open to allow them to feed on the new crop of fresh grass. On the approach of winter, he saw to it that his beasts were back in the shelter of their stalls. In regions of hills and mountains, these would be the times when the animals would be taken up to their summer pastures, and brought back down again for the winter (transhumance). Walpurgis Night and Hallowe'en, (we may call them terrestrial divisions of the year) had more significance for him than the celestial solstices.

For all that, the ways in which Man chose to celebrate his fire-festivals, at whatever time of the year, or in whatever place, bore a striking similarity. And so, on the eve of May Day, or on the eve of All Souls, we find the young people again dancing round their fires, leaping through the smoke and flames, trundling wheels coated with burning straw down the hillside, scampering round the fields and through the orchards with burning torches, and driving their cattle through the smoke.

The Celts regarded Hallowe'en as the beginning of their year, and therefore presumably as more important than Beltane. Until the close of the nineteenth century, the Manx looked upon November Ist (old style) as New Year's Day. This was the time when Manx mummers went round singing their 'Hogmanay' song which began: "Tonight is New Year's Night, hogunnaa!" In ancient times, the Irish kindled their fires from the sacred fire which every year was lighted anew on Hallowe'en or the eve of Samhain. It was to Hallowe'en fires that the dead souls came to warm themselves and comfort themselves from the good cheer provided for them by their kinsfolk.

Midwinter was the second great turning point of the sun's apparent course through the sky. At midsummer he kindled fires to assist the sun in maintaining its strength; at midwinter his fires were lighted to help the sun renew its strength. They were kindled indoors, perhaps because of the inclement weather, when snow and rain might well have thwarted attempts to get a good blaze going outside. We have many references to the practice in England, France, and Yugoslavia, of bringing into the home, with great solemnity, the Yule log which would burn throughout the festive season. Its ashes would, at a later date, be scattered on the fields to promote the growth of the crops. In Westphalia, it used to be the custom to tie up the Yule log in the last

110. 'Midsummer Dance' by Anders Zorn. Swedish, 1897.

corn-sheaf to be cut at harvest time. Elsewhere, the Yule log protected the house and its occupants from fire and lightning, and chilblains in winter. It could cure the cattle from various maladies, and a piece put into their drinking water helped them to calve. As many sparks as they could strike out of the burning log, so many would be their hens, calves, pigs or whatever.

Spirits

Green-men are to be found in the folklore of most European countries. Some are mentioned in connection with maypoles, but many others existed independently of the maypole.

On St. George's Day (April 23rd), in Carinthia, they carry a newly-felled tree in procession, singing and dancing as they go. Their green-man is called 'Green George', and is covered with birch twigs. An effigy of him is later thrown into the water. If the young man disguised as Green George does not change places with the effigy quickly enough, he risks being thrown into the water himself. This is another instance of a rain-charm, to ensure green meadows in the time to follow, and to provide fodder for the animals. In some places they sing a song which says:

Green George we bring,
Green George we accompany,
May he feed our herds well.
If not, to the water with him.

In some parts of Russia and Slovenia, Green George went out into the corn fields, carrying a lighted torch in one hand, and holding a pie in the other. The girls followed singing. A circle of brushwood was placed around the pie and set alight, and then the pie was divided among themselves.

Elsewhere, one used to find a 'Little Leaf Man', a child who had been covered in leaves and twigs by his young friends, and with song and dance, led from house to house, asking for gifts of food such as eggs, sausages, cream and cake. The leaf-man is then sprinkled with water, before they feast off the food they have collected. In Switzerland, the leaf-man is set upon a horse, led back to the village, and ducked in the pond. He thereupon retaliates by sprinkling water on all and sundry. In England, this character is called the 'Jack-in-the-Green'. He used to lead a motley gang of chimney sweeps and others, dancing and play-acting to raise a few pennies. Other similar characters may bear the names of May King, or Queen, or Whitsuntide King. In Ireland, the May Queen retained her title for twelve months, and presided over the dances and festivities, which took place during her year of office, though her reign was cut short if she married during that period. Other characters who appeared on these occasions and may once have represented tree-spirits are, the lord and lady, bride and groom. In Slovakia the custom was to burn the straw doll, judging the abundance of the following harvest by the height of the flames.

We have seen how it was believed necessary for the sacrificial king, or his substitute, to meet a violent death, in order to ensure a fruitful harvest and prosperity for the tribe. It seems that, in the same way, some present-day customs find their origins in the sacrificing of the tree-spirit (or spirit of vegetation). And so the King of the Wood, or whatever name was given to him, had to be killed, to forestall otherwise inevitable decay. A king could hold office only so long as his strength held up, but when that strength began to fail, then he must be replaced by a stronger king, so that his decrepitude should not entail a corresponding weakening of the community, their animals, or their produce.

In Bavaria, the Whitsuntide representative of the spirit of vegetation or tree spirit, the *Pfingstl*, is completely covered in alder and hazel leaves, twigs and flowers. He wears a tall pointed hat, so large that the brim rests on his shoulders, and holes have to be cut in it to enable him to see out. The cap is covered with water-flowers and a wreath of peonies. His sleeves are also covered with water-plants. On either side of him march two boys carrying swords, as do others in the procession. At each house they stop, bringing good luck and soliciting gifts, and the *Pfingstl* is liberally doused with water. His 'death' comes, when he wades into the river, where he is 'decapitated' by one of the boys standing above him on a bridge.

On Whit Monday, in Swabia, boys dressed in white trousers, shirts and red scarves, carrying swords, and led by trumpeters, ride out to the woods, and there cover one of their number in oak branches. He is given a long artificial neck and head with a face on it. A may-tree, usually a birch or aspen, is cut down, decorated with ribbons and flowers, and brought back to the village in procession. Some of the participants would be familiar to any English mummer: there is a Moorish king with blackened face and wearing a crown, a doctor Iron-beard, a soldier and an executioner. Each character in turn makes a rhymed speech. The executioner announces that the *Pfingstl* has been condemned to death, and promptly cuts off his head.

Elsewhere, in Saxony and Thuringia for example, there is the Whitsuntide ceremony of 'fetching the wild man from the wood'. A 'wild man', covered from head to toe in greenery, is found hiding in the wood, captured and fired at with blank muskets. He falls dead to the ground, but revives after being bled by a doctor. He is then taken in the usual manner from house to house, receiving gifts on his circuit.

The *Feuillu* of Cartigny near Geneva, has 'la Bête' (the Beast), covered in fir and beech branches and bedecked with ivy and flowers. The young men, wearing garlands, dance around it.

Each village in Galicia in northwestern Spain has its variation of the Dance of May. The *maio*, a man dressed up in straw and crowned with flowers, dances with characteristic springing steps in the middle of a circle of boys and girls. These copy his springing steps, occasionally one of them, usually one of the girls, going into the circle to taunt the *maio*, who eventually leads the line of jumping and skipping dancers in a winding path.

On St. George's Day, in the district of Turopolje in Serbia, it is still possible to see the 'Festival of Youth and Greenery'. A boy or girl called 'Zeleni Juraj' is covered in greenery, the twigs interwoven basket-fashion to conceal the head and shoulders. As usual the procession makes its way from house to house, the participants receiving gifts in exchange for bringing good luck to each household. On the eve of St. George's Day, the villagers dance and sing around bonfires, the young people leaping over the embers.

In Bohemia, at Shrovetide, a wild man, wearing round his body a bladder filled with blood, is chased round the village until he stumbles, falls to the ground and is captured. The executioner runs his sword though him (that is, through the bladder), so that the blood reddens the ground. On the following day, a straw puppet, dressed up to look like the wild man, is carried in procession to the pool or river, where he is thrown in. They call this ceremony, 'Burying the Carnival'.

On the last day of Carnival, in Italy, they also bury the Carnival. At Frosinone, about half way between Rome and Naples, a crowd, furiously dancing the saltarello, accompany a gigantic figure, representing the Carnival, which is enthroned on a huge chair, and taken in procession through the town. Everyone carries a root or leaf of the aloe or agave plant, which gives the festivity its name, 'Radica'. If an aloe or agave leaf cannot be procured, then a bunch of plaited grass on the end of a stick is an acceptable substitute. After much singing, dancing and drinking, the effigy is stripped of its finery, laid on a pyre and burned, the roots being thrown onto the fire also. In the Abruzzi, an effigy of the Carnival is carried by four 'grave-diggers'. A weeping wife of the Carnival, dressed in mourning, walks in front. From time to time they stop, to allow the wife to solicit sympathy from the onlookers, and the gravediggers to snatch a drink from the wine-bottles, which they carry on their shoulder-belts. The effigy, to the accompaniment of wails from the women and a roll of drums, is laid on the pyre and burned, while chestnuts are scattered among the crowd. Sometimes a man, lying in a coffin, personifies the dead Carnival. One of the accompanying onlookers acts as a priest, and dispenses 'holy' water from a bath tub.

On Ash Wednesday, in Provence, a figure representing the Carnival, and called 'Carementran' is put on trial, found guilty, and sentenced to death. He is then stoned, and his battered remains thrown into the sea. Also on Ash Wednesday, throughout the Ardennes, an effigy representing the Carnival is burned. 'Carrying out Death' and 'Bringing in Summer' are further relics of ancient pagan ritual still observed in various parts of Europe.

Often Death is represented by a straw effigy, which is sometimes burned, sometimes thrown into the water. In Upper Silesia, the effigy representing death is called 'Marzana'. In Bohemia, it is carried to the village boundary, the villagers singing:

We carry Death out of the village,
And the New Year into the village.
Dear Spring, we bid you welcome,
Green grass, we bid you welcome.

111. 'Elddans' by Olaus Magnus. Swedish, 1555.

The effigy is then burned, and they return singing:

We have carried away Death,
And brought Life back.
He has taken up his quarters in the village,
Therefore sing joyous songs!

On the third Sunday in Lent, the young people of Moravia make a straw man, which they dress up, hoist on a pole, and carry into the open fields. There they set the effigy down, and dance round it, before tearing it to pieces with their bare hands. The pieces are set alight, and they continue the dancing merrily round the bonfire. In Bohemia, in those parts where the effigy is drowned rather than burned, the girls go into the woods, cut down a young tree, and attach to it a doll dressed as a woman. They then decorate the tree with green, red and white ribbons, and return to the village collecting gifts and singing:

Death swims in the water,
Spring comes to visit us.

On Maundy Thursday or Good Friday, the 'burning of Judas' takes place in villages in southern Poland. An effigy of Judas is first hanged on a tree, then thrown down on the ground, dragged to the limits of the village, flogged thirty times as a punishment for the thirty silver coins Judas received for his betrayal, and finally his effigy is burned and thrown into the river. In other regions of Poland, the custom of burning or drowning a straw doll, called 'drowning the Marzanna' or 'killing of Death' takes place on March 21st.

In the Eifel mountains in France, on Shrove Tuesday, they dance around a pyre on which they have set a straw-man. The effigy has previously been put on trial, accused of having committed various thefts and other misdemeanours, and condemned to death. He was then paraded round the village, shot, and burned. It is the custom for the newest bride to leap over the smouldering embers.

Another way of celebrating this age-old custom of welcoming the summer, was by enacting a battle between summer and winter, in which summer naturally always emerged triumphant. These 'battles' are to be found widely scattered across Europe. In various towns in Sweden, summer and winter confront each other in the persons of two opposing troops of young men on horseback. The representatives of winter are clad in furs, those of summer are covered in flowers and fresh greenery. In some places in Germany, the representatives of summer are clad in ivy. Winter is clad in straw, and, after being vanquished, is stripped of his straw covering, which is torn to pieces and scattered. Sometimes winter is ducked in the village pond. Inevitably, those enacting the battle go from house to house collecting gifts of eggs, cake, or fruit.

In Russia, they used to enact funeral ceremonies, both in spring and at midsummer. One such was 'Kostrubonko'. A girl would lie on the floor as if dead, while mourners would circle her singing:

Dead, dead is our Kostrubonko,
Dead, dead is our dear one.

Then the girl would suddenly jump up, and the mournful dirge would change to a joyful chorus:

Come to life has our Kostrubonko,
Come to life, come to life has our dear one.

There is a dance very similar to this still in England, though here it has degenerated into a children's game. In 'Old Roger is Dead' the children sing verses and mime the actions suggested by the words:

Old Roger is dead and laid in his grave,
Laid in his grave, laid in his grave,
Old Roger is dead and laid in his grave,
Hey, hi, laid in his grave.

There grew an old apple tree over his head,
Over his head, over his head,
There grew an old apple tree over his head,
Hey, hi, over his head.

The apples grew ripe and they fell off,
They fell off etc.,
Hey, hi, they fell off.

There came an old woman a'picking them up,
Picking them up etc.,
Hey, hi, picking them up.

Old Roger jumps up and gives her a knock,
Gives her a knock etc.,
Hey, hi, gives her a knock.

He makes the old woman go hippety hop,
Hippety hop etc.,
Hey, hi, hippety hop.

In this dance-game, the children first join in a circle, their arms folded, and sway from side to side as if in mourning. One boy lies on the floor in the centre of the circle, a handkerchief over his face. A girl goes into the centre and stands next to the boy, her arms raised like tree branches. She then lowers her arms, and another girl (pretending to be the old woman) mimes picking up apples. The boy jumps up and starts to beat her, and finally all circle round limping and hobbling while the boy chases the 'old woman' round the outside of the circle.

In another celebration, the Russians used to combine several elements to be found in a variety of other customs. On Midsummer's Eve, an effigy called 'Kupalo', made of straw, was dressed in women's clothes, complete with necklace and floral crown. The doll was then placed next to a newly-felled tree, which had been decorated with ribbons, and set up on a chosen spot. They called this tree 'Marena' (winter or death). A table with food and drink was placed by the tree. Then they lit a bonfire, and, in couples, the young people jumped over it, holding between them the straw doll. On the following day, the tree and the doll were stripped of their decorations and thrown into the water.

The Spirit of the Corn, or the Corn-Mother, was believed to be present in the last sheaf of corn left standing, when the harvest was all but complete. When this last sheaf was cut, so was she caught, driven away, or killed. In the first case, the sheaf would have been joyfully carried home, and treated as an honoured divinity. Placed in the barn, the corn spirit appeared again at threshing time. In the region of Hanover, the reapers would beat the last sheaf with sticks, ordering the corn-mother to leave it. They beat it until the grain was threshed out of it, believing that thus they had driven away the corn-mother. In Holstein, the corn-mother was dressed in women's clothes, carried home, and then drenched in water, a further example of a rain-charm. Often the corn-mother was placed in the centre of the floor, when all who are gathered for the harvest supper danced around it. Then, the sheaf hung in the barn until the threshing was over.

In Gdansk in Poland, the person who cut the last sheaf made it into a doll, and this corn-mother, or old woman, as it was called, was brought home in the last cart.

112. 'Das Sommerspiel in der Pfalz' by C. Roux. German, 1865.

Still, in some places, the grain is rubbed out of the last sheaf, and is scattered among the new corn, so that the spirit of the corn can rise from the dead with the spring corn. Elsewhere, the wreath, which had been made from the last sheaf, was placed in the manger, to make the cattle thrive. Sometimes, the grain was saved until the following spring, so that it could be mixed in with the seed corn. In parts of France, the puppet, made out of the last sheaf, is called the 'Ceres'. It is set in the middle of the dancing floor, and the boy who reaped the fastest is able to choose the girl he considers the prettiest to be his dancing partner. After the dance, the doll is pulled apart, adorned with flowers, and placed on a pyre. In Belfast, the reapers cut the last handful by throwing their sickles at it. In Wales, the reaper who suceeded in cutting it down was rewarded with a jug of ale. In County Antrim, the reapers were blindfolded for the purpose of the game. The winner hung the plaited sheaf above his door.

In Cracow, Poland, the corn doll, if bound by a man, was called the 'Grandfather', if bound by a woman, the 'Baba' or Grandmother. In Lithuania, the last sheaf is similarly called the 'Boba', and is drenched with water before the people dance around it. In Russia, the sheaf, shaped and dressed as a woman, was accompanied home with singing and dancing. In Bulgaria, the poor Corn-queen, as they called it, ended up in the river, to ensure a plentiful rainfall for the next year's crops. Sometimes, instead, it is burned, and the ashes strewn on the fields. The harvest-queen appears also in England. Thus Milton wrote in Paradise Lost:

Adam the while
Waiting desirous her return, had wove
Of choicest flow'rs a garland to adorn
As reapers oft are wont their harvest-queen.

In the north of Scotland, the corn-doll or maiden, was kept until yule morning when it was fed to the cattle, "to make them thrive all the year round". Sometimes the corn was given to the chickens for the same reason. The supper at which the reapers danced was also called the maiden.

Yet another appellation for the corn-doll was the 'bride'. In parts of Germany, a couple were swathed in straw, and danced together at the harvest feast. In Saxony, the oats-bridegroom was gradually stripped of his straw by the dancers, and, despite his efforts to preserve his modesty, usually ended up naked, and the object of much unkind mirth. The oats-bride, usually a man in woman's clothing, was left unmolested. In Silesia, the oats-king and oats-queen celebrated a 'wedding' with rustic pomp.

Sometimes the corn-spirit takes the form of an animal. Either the sheaf is fashioned into the shape of an animal, or a person is dressed in straw, greenery, and animal skins. Thus in Poland at Christmas-time (midwinter), when the lengthening days herald the approach of spring, a man with a wolf's skin over his head is led round the village to collect money or gifts. Sometimes the corn-spirit appears in the form of a wolf, cock, hare, or cat, but most popular of all is the corn-goat. Occasionally the last sheaf to be cut is called the goat. Straw goats are a popular Christmas decoration in Scandinavia, and Christmas loaves are baked in the shape of different animals. Often these are made from the corn taken from the last sheaf to be harvested. Sometimes part of the bread is kept until the next sowing-time, when it is crumbled up into the seed-corn, some also being given to the plough horses or plough oxen. A Christmas custom in Sweden is for a man to be disguised as an animal, carrying a whisp of straw in his mouth. He is then 'sacrificed' by an old woman with blackened face. In Estonia, on Christmas Eve, a cake, which they call a Christmas boar, is baked. It sits on the table until New Year's Day, when it is broken up and fed to the animals.

Well Worship

Natural springs, pools and wells were, like mine shafts, seen as entrances penetrating into the body of the Earth Mother, and early Man cut ritual shafts, pits and wells deep into the earth (one near Stonehenge is over thirty metres deep), and threw votive offerings of pottery, bones, even human skulls, into these shafts. Still today we throw coins into wishing wells for good luck.

Well worship survived into the twentieth century in the form of well-dressing. Once common throughout Britain, it now survives only in Staffordshire and Derbyshire. Up to the 1830s, the villagers of Rorrington, on the border of Shropshire and Wales, would gather on Ascension Day at the holy well, would decorate it with a bower of greenery, rushes and flowers, erect a maypole, and dance to fife and drum. In West Glamorgan, the people living in the vicinity of Gellionen Well, performed a ritual at the well whenever they suffered drought. They used to dance, scattering flowers and herbs over each other, sing old ballads and play 'kiss-in-the-ring'. The combination of these elements can only be construed as the degenerate remains of a fertility ritual. The leader then cried out three times: "Bring us rain!", and the people filled bowls with water from the well, splashed it about, and took the rest home to sprinkle on their gardens. They claimed that rain always came, though, given the British climate, this is not altogether surprising. As late as the nineteenth century, fertility rituals were practised at the well of Melshach in Grampian, Scotland. Women gathered to dance around the well, hands joined, whilst an old woman sprinkled them with water from the well. The dancers were married women who had remained childless, and had come in the hope that the holy water would make them fertile.

11

SEASONAL, WORK AND ANIMAL DANCES

Beat, beat the year,
A joyful year,
Big ears of corn in the field,
Red apples in the orchards,
Yellow corn on the cobs,
Large bunches of grapes on the vines,
A house full of children,
A purse full of money,
May we live happily until next year,
Until next year, Amen.

Bulgarian sourvakari song.

There are certain dances which do not conveniently belong to any particular category, but as some of them seem, like whips and tops, to have made their appearance in their own special season, they are included here.

The ancient Greeks possessed the whole repertoire of dances which folk dancers all over Europe perform today: circles, chains, garland dances, *pyrrhic* dances, dances imitating animals and wearing animal masks, and one particularly intriguing harvest dance. On the so-called 'Harvester Vase' in the Herakleion Museum on Crete, is a scene depicting a harvest festival with song and dance. A body of men moves in line four abreast, carrying over their shoulders what appear to be long tools, weapons or flails. Three girls are singing and a man is shaking a rattle to accompany them. One dancer is in a crouching position, striking the ground (as they still do today on Crete) to stir the earth into renewed effort. One can hardly fail to compare this with harvest dances performed throughout the continent to this day.

Illustrations 38 & 39 depict groups thus armed who are indulging in a fight, and who presumably represent the forces of summer and winter. That these battles occasionally became violent is attested to by the number of prohibitions on indulging in these pastimes which litter city archives across Europe from early medieval times, and from the accounts of bloodshed to which these 'games' often led. The picture by Hans Sebald Beham (ill. 39) shows a severed hand lying on the ground, the result apparently of over-exuberance. Such dances would be performed not only in spring but also at church and village fairs, and harvest-home celebrations. It should be born in mind that country people only had a limited repertoire of dances, and the tendency was to perform the same ones irrespective of the time of the year (exceptions being

113. Vintage dance. Asia Minor, Roman period. © Photo R.M.N.

midwinter sword and springtime morris dances). And so we get 'harvest' dances also performed at spring sowing, and the whole repertoire trotted out to dance in conjunction with May-day festivities, midsummer fires and weddings.

Medieval Germany had plays, akin to the mummers' plays, in which the characters of Summer and Winter harangued each other, speaking lines of mutual recrimination and self-justification and praise. Summer was dressed in green leaves and jubilantly received by the onlookers; Winter was dressed in rags and chains. He was sometimes put on trial, found guilty and driven out (like the scapegoat), or he admitted defeat and promised to become the obedient servant of Summer. Songs welcoming the cuckoo (herald of summer) date back to about the year 1000. The cuckoo appears again in these plays, praised by Summer for his song, branded a thief by Winter. Summer accuses Winter of making the milk too cold, but Winter retaliates by accusing Summer of turning the milk sour. Summer says how much jollier it is to dance outside in the sunshine; Winter tells how much cosier it is to sit indoors in front of a nice warm fire. So they rail at each other through a long list of arguments for and against.

Variations on these fighting games feature peasants *versus* nobles, the fat *versus* the thin, one faction of rich folk against another, and, yes, a Moorish king occasionally plays a part in the proceedings. The 'battles' were fought out to the accompaniment of bagpipes and song, and the participants were armed with pitchforks, flails, scythes, rakes, in short, any implement which came to hand.

A dance performed in Piedmont in Italy called 'la Lachera' re-enacts a traditional tale. Sometime during the Middle Ages, there lived in Roccagrimalda a despot named Isnardo Malaspina, who claimed for himself the *jus primae noctis*, the right to spend the wedding night with the bride. The story goes as follows:

All wedding ceremonies were preceded by a procession in which two friends of the bridegroom, dressed in Longobard costumes, accompany the couple through the town dancing and skipping all along. These two men were called lacheri. *One day a young horse trader on the eve of his wedding is informed that the Sire of the Castle is infatuated with his bride-to-be and that he is planning to abduct her during the wedding procession. The bridegroom, with the help of friends, draws up a plan to protect his bride: in the procession, two* zuavi *armed with scimitars, walk on either side of the couple, and a soldier with a* durendal *walks near the bridesmaid. As if not enough, the couple are surrounded by a number of* mulattieri *(mule drivers) in their typical round hats adorned with flowers and by other youths called* trappolini, *who wear their working clothes inside out, showing a vast number of coloured patches similar to Arlecchino's suit. They all wear round their waists the mules' collars with bells and walk at the end of the procession keeping the crowd away with whiplashes. This show of strength and the noise produced frighten the Malaspina bravoes, who leave without accomplishing their horrid task. The whole town rejoices and the wedding feast goes on for many days with banquets and balls.*

Thus does an ancient spring rite attract like a magnet a tale to explain the reason behind the ritual.

The French 'l'Estacada' from Breil-sur-Roya has been handed down from generation to generation since time immemorial. When the original purpose for which it was performed became blurred, the Brellois similarly applied to it the odious practice of the *droit de cuissage*, the lord's right to spend the wedding night with his vassal's bride, and thus the May Queen became the bride. In the 'Estacada' the bride is accompanied by the *Couret*, who is King of the May, herald of spring, who brings fertility and fecundity. Dressed in white, crowned and garlanded with spring flowers, he carries a staff covered in multi-coloured ribbons (reflecting the colours of the rainbow). By his prodigious leaps and energetic display, it is his function to promote the growth of plants by sympathetic magic. Such have been the limits to which the dancers' energies have been tested, that some, we are told, have been known to have had to take to their beds for several days afterwards, and it has been reported that some have even given their very lives.

In order sufficiently to build his strength in preparation for this outburst of energy, the *Couret* must eat nothing but hard-boiled eggs, entities which are regarded as biologically complete in themselves, and possessing the germ of life and all the constituent elements of a new individual.

The young bride (Queen of the May) also ushers in the renewal of spring, which explains why, during the ball which is held in the afternoon, she must refuse all invitations to dance, and dance only with the *Couret*. To mark the start of each dance a blunderbuss is fired, and the *Couret* salutes the huge talismanic flag which, despite the barricades which had been raised all along the processional route (to retain its beneficial influence), had been paraded through the streets without once having been lowered. Now the *Couret* strikes the ground with his foot to awaken Nature from her winter slumber, and concludes his *variation* with a *tour en l'air*. At the ball he must dance in the opposite direction to the rest of the couples whom he separates with his staff as they move forwards with a springy polka step. He then dances crosswise between them three times as if to transfer his powers of fecundity to them. Each time he has moved between three couples they must turn three times to the left, hands on hips. Having passed all the couples in this fashion, the *Couret* again salutes the flag. The ball continues with the *Couret* dancing with each of the distinguished ladies in turn before opening the general dancing which concludes the festivities.

The third main character in this performance is the *Tambour-Major* who carries on his chest, held by a grille, a special cake called the *creschenta*. We can turn to Spanish folklore to explain this item. At Taüll in Catalonia, on the feast of St. Isadore in July, the corresponding personage goes about the whole day carrying a bottle of wine and a cake in the form of a crown. His job it is to guard these from all the youngsters who try to snatch them from him. If he is successful it presages a good year to come – here we have the spirit of vegetation fighting off the forces of evil. In the 'Estacada' the bottle of wine is carried by a *cantinière*, a female cook who is actually a man dressed in travesty and who wears a huge sun on her bolero.

Another game which belonged to the same category as the 'Kegelschieben', which concludes the chapter on mythology, and which was played in Medieval Germany and, indeed, in Brandenburg up until the end of the nineteenth century, was the 'Brautball'. It was the custom for young people to go, on the afternoon of Maundy Thursday, to the houses of those couples who had married in the previous twelve months, to collect a large ball made out of pieces of coloured leather. They used this to play a game on the village green. It was competitive and was accompanied by singing and dancing. Herbert Oetke has advanced the hypothesis that these 'ball' dances and songs which told of the epic deeds of gods and heroes were the origin of the ***ball***ads and ***ball***ades.

The *báire* was a session of dancing at which a cake was awarded to the couple who were deemed to have provided the best performance. A description of the custom in Westmeath in 1682 related:

> *On the patron-day in most parishes, as also on the feasts of Easter and Whitsuntide, the more ordinary sort of people meet near the ale-house in the afternoon, on some convenient spot of ground and dance for the cake. Here to be sure the piper fails not of diligent attendance; the cake to be danced for is provided at the charge of the ale-wife, and is advanced on a board on the top of a pike, about ten foot high; this board is round, and from it riseth a kind of a garland, beset and tied round with meadow flowers, if it be early in the summer, if later, the garland has the addition of apples set round on pegs fastened unto it; the whole number of dancers begin all at once in a large ring, a man and a woman, and dance round about the bush, so is this garland call'd, and the piper as long as they are able to hold out; they that hold out longest at the exercise. win the cake and apples, and then the ale-wife's trade goes on.*

The Basques have a *charivari* or a punishment-play, very much in the fashion of their 'scapegoat' mummeries. In this, any offenders against village morals are brought to justice. Pots and pans, whistles and drums, crackers and anything else that will make a noise are used. Dancers are brought in to disguise the fact that this is a traditional punishment and to obtain permission from the *Préfet* to stage it. The police may not be fooled, but tend to turn a blind eye to the proceedings because "it is traditional".

The 'Trescone' is an Italian dance for four couples forming a square and has been known since the Middle Ages. The girls step lightly in their places while the boys dance with lively steps from one girl to the next, trying to outdo each other in the bravura of their performance. It is still danced at certain times of agricultural work, such as the picking of hemp or the stripping of corn cobs. In former times the 'Trescone' was danced at weddings, when it would be performed by four couples in the middle of a circle of singers.

Dances for four couples plus one to make an odd number we have already met elsewhere and are to be found in various countries. The 'Moirrey ny cainle' was performed on the Isle of Man at Candlemas (February 4th), the women carrying lighted candles while the men had unlit ones. The extra person, always a woman, was called the *Moirrey*. Another Manx dance, 'Yn mheillea' is a circular harvest dance. The *mheillea* queen sat in the middle and cradled in her arms a *babban*, a straw baby in swaddling clothes, while the others danced around her.

The 'Danza de Santa Maria de Toras' comes from Galicia and is believed to be of great antiquity. The women hardly move at all in the dance. They have their bodies leaning forwards, and as their right foot is placed in front, so their right arm comes forwards and down as if to touch the foot, and the left arm is placed behind the body in a similar bent position. The body turns slightly away from the front foot. The men dance a normal 'Muiñeira'. This movement is also to be found on the island of Madeira, here performed by both men and women. The dance starts off in a longways set, further figures forming a circle or a line in single file, each boy facing his partner. One figure has the line of boys following a leader as he snakes in and out of the file of girls. The final figure has the couples moving in a double circle, girls on the inside, in an anti-clockwise direction.

114. Procession of the Nürnberg carpenters. German, 16th century.

The Cerdaña of the Spanish Pyrenees (the Sardana or Serdana of Catalonia) is a harvest dance performed in honour of the barley-goddess Cerdo. In Welsh mythology she is Caridwen or Cerridwen who was also a grain-goddess. The valley of Cerdaña, dominated by the town of Puigcerdá, Cerdo's Hill, is the best corn land in the region. Cerdo was the White Goddess who, after disguising herself in the form of a bird or beast, destroyed children. The hawthorn which was sacred to her might not be brought into the house in case she destroyed the children inside. In England it is still considered unlucky to bring May-blossom indoors. Though the Cerdaña varies from place to place, the steps remain very simple. The 'Saltiro de la Cardina' of Perpignan, for example, consists of a point in front followed by a *pas de bourrée under*, done in four straight counts and going across the melodic phrase, without elevation, though with a lilting quality, hands held with the arms in a low 'V'. It can be varied by doing a point in front, closing the foot next to other foot, repeating with the other foot, *pas de bourée under*, this time with arms lifted to head level and a little in front of the body, and with a more springy step, so that the step in front becomes a tap and lift with bent knee raised in front, at the same time hopping on the supporting leg, and the *pas de bourée* having a 'running on the spot' quality.

Still in Catalonia, the 'Ballet de Folguerolles' has hand movements indicative of the picking of bunches of grapes from the vines, in similar fashion to the Mateixas of Majorca, where it was the picking of figs which was being mimed.

In Lithuania, on St. John's Day and at Whitsuntide, the growing seed corns were ritually inspected. Several families would walk through the rye fields and feast out in the open. The young people would make wreaths of flowers and dance in the fields. They also danced the 'Dobilélis (Clover), and 'Aguonéle' (Poppy), which imitated the growing plants.

In Finland at harvest time, the villagers would often thresh the corn by dancing the 'Säätö Polska' on the threshing floor, and when the hay had been stacked in the loft they had a special dance for packing it down.

On the island of Lewis in the Western Isles, dancing used to follow the rituals to encourage the washing ashore of sea-weed. Elsewhere along the coast of Scotland, men used to walk into the sea chanting:

O God of the sea,
Put weed in the drawing wave,
To enrich the ground,
To shower on us food.

The Portuguese also know the value of seaweed as a fertilizer. The seaweed gatherers perform their dance dressed in a costume which is reputed to have been worn since Roman times; the hat is shaped like a Roman soldier's helmet, and the short tunic which he wears to enable him to wade into the water without getting his clothes wet, is also very reminiscent of that worn by Roman soldiers.

Another occasion for dancing was to celebrate the completion of marling. This mineral-rich clay used to be dug out of marlpits and spread on the land. At Little Crosby in Lancashire in July 1712, they danced round the maypole to mark the occasion.

The Dutch have a dance, 'Donder in't Hooi' (Thunder in the Hay), whose title seems to indicate some remote and forgotten belief. The dancers sing and circle together, their claps and stamps perhaps representing the thunder and lightning which would ensure the arrival of the rain so essential for the growth of their crops.

We have already met egg dances in an earlier chapter, but they were not exclusive to men, and there are several reports of them having been performed by girls as well as couples. Easter and Carnival time were their seasons, though we also find them being danced for entertainment and amusement at other times of the year. An egg dance was performed by two couples on the occasion of the wedding of Margaret of Austria and Philip the Handsome, duke of Savoy, which took place in 1498. We are told that over one hundred eggs were laid out on the ground, and the couples danced around and over them. Their reward for completing this dance without breaking any eggs was permission to marry. Apparently it took three attempts before they were able successfully to complete the feat. Do we here have the last vestige of an ancient ritual where a test before marriage was set?

An English reference to an egg dance comes from 'The Longer thou livest, the More Foole thou Art' by the Elizabethan playwright, William Wagner:

Upon my one foote pretely I can hoppe and daunce it trimley.

In the Netherlands, a chalk circle was drawn on the ground and flowers and greenery as well as a pile of eggs were placed within it. The dancer was then required to manœuvre the eggs to the outside of the circle with one foot while performing a dance; the one who could complete the task in the fastest time was rewarded with a basket of eggs. In 1828 at a fair in Utrecht, a blindfolded young girl danced between fourteen eggs without treading on any.

Dr. Johnson witnessed an egg dance while sojourning in Paris in 1775, but unfortunately and uncharacteristically he has left us no account of what he saw. Laborde, in his 'View of Spain' in 1809, was more forthcoming in describing an egg dance which he witnessed in Valencia:

In the first they place on the ground a number of eggs, at small intervals from each other; they dance around the eggs in these intervals; it seems as if they must crush them every moment, but notwithstanding the celerity and variety of the steps they display, they never touch one of them.

In "The Sports and Pastimes of the People of England" published in 1801, Strutt described a similar dance:

This performance was common enough about 30 years back, and was well received at Sadlers Wells; where I saw it exhibited, not by simply hopping round a single egg, but in a manner that much increased the difficulty. A number of eggs, I do not precisely recollect how many, but

I believe about 12 or 14, were placed at certain distances marked upon the stage; the dancer, taking his stand, was blindfolded and a horn-pipe being played in the orchestra he went through all the paces and figures of the dance, passing backwards and forwards between the eggs without touching one of them.

This account of course refers to a display on stage at the Sadlers Wells theatre, but was undoubtedly not invented by a dancing master but taken from country pastimes.

A similar form of egg dance was adopted by the Danish Royal Ballet in Copenhagen, and used to sharpen up the dancers' footwork. In one Danish 'Aeggedans' an egg was set on top of a goblet which was placed upside down on a pile of sand or earth. The dancer was required first to dislodge the egg from its perch and then to replace it with his feet, all the while performing a dance. On the island of Amager, in 1758, we hear how the egg had to be knocked from its perch on a goblet, this then having to be made to cover the egg. The dance may well have been introduced by Dutch farmers who had been invited to settle on the island of Amager (now a district of Copenhagen) in 1521.

The German writer Goethe gave a detailed description in his novel 'Wilhelm Meister' of an egg dance in which a girl, having spread a number of eggs out on the floor:

. . . tied a band about her eyes, gave a signal (for the musician to begin) and like a piece of wheel-work set a-going, she began moving the same instant as the music, accompanying her beats and the notes of the tune with the strikes of a pair of castanets. Lightly, nimbly, quickly, and with hair breadth accuracy, she carried on the dance. She skipped so sharply and surely along between the eggs, and trod so closely down beside them, that you would have thought every instant she must trample one of them in pieces, or kick the rest away in her rapid turns. By no means! She touched no one of them, though winding herself through their mazes with all kinds of steps, wide and narrow, nay even with leaps and at last half kneeling.

Constant as the movements of a clock, she ran her course; and the strange music, at each repetition of the tune, gave a new impulse to the dance of recommencing and again rushing off as at first . . . The dance being ended, she rolled the eggs together softly with her foot into a little heap, left none behind, harmed none; then placed herself beside it, taking the bandage from her eyes, and concluding her performance with a little bow.

In the Pieter Aertsen painting (ill. 93), we can see the chalked circle on the floor, the upturned bowl and egg, a litter of broken egg-shells, garlic, leaks and other greenery, and empty mussel shells – all these were symbolic of fertility because of their supposed aphrodisiac properties.

The egg dance is used in a German expression to mean: Why all this silly nonsense? – "Warum dieser Eiertanz?" An unknown Flemish writer wrote:

It's all a silly business, as you can see.
As the old folk sing and make music
The foolish youngsters prance over the eggs.

115. Procession of the Frankfurt carpenters. German, 1659.

Work dances

There are basically two categories of work dances: there are those connected with certain trades, which the guilds adopted into their ceremonials, and those which through pantomime portray certain work actions. In the first category we find various guilds displaying mainly the kind of sword and hoop dances already referred to in the relevant chapter: sword dances can be seen to be suited to trades making swords or knives, hoops in the case of barrel makers, and even flag-waving dances in the case of weavers or cloth makers.

It is as well to bear in mind, when one talks of urbanization killing off the folk dance, that the vast majority of town dwellers belonged to various trade guilds, and all these had their own ceremonial dances. There is no reason to believe that opportunities and occasions for dancing were any fewer in an urban environment than when living out in the country. In many countries, the older villagers would probably only dance on the annual feast day of their patron saint, or on certain (and quite few) special occasions such as weddings, the completion of harvest, or whatever occupation they were involved in.

The list of trades' guilds is almost endless: besides those of the sword and knife and barrel makers already mentioned, there were guilds of workers employed in the various branches of cloth production: weavers, fullers, tenters, dyers, shearers; there were gold and silversmiths, butchers, bakers and candlestick makers – the list would fill several pages. On the various occasions that guild members came together, for initiating new members or conferring master's status, meetings to decide policy or for socializing, dancing played an important part. In Germany, one of the earliest references relating to the *Schembartlaufen* (Carnival running) of the artisans, comes from the year 1349, when the Nürnberg butchers danced a chain dance, the knifesmiths a sword dance and the barrel makers a hoop dance. The dancing took place at Whitsuntide. The dancers were masked; they wore white tight-fitting pants, short boots, two-coloured clothes from top to bottom, gloves, hats or bonnets adorned with feathers. Collars, belts and sleeves had little bells either singly or in rows. On the right side of the participants they carried a bag in which to put the gifts they collected from the onlookers. Leading the procession were jokers carrying rattles who acted as whifflers. Someone else threw nuts into the crowd. Another bombarded the women and girls watching the procession from their doorways or balconies with eggs filled with rose-water which, on breaking, left a pleasant smell. Accompanying the musicians was a man carrying a small tree adorned with various decorations. Also participating in the merriment was a group of hobby-horses. Later, after having had a drink at the house of some notable, they would share out the money and gifts they had collected.

From 1521 to 1560, the 'Storming of Hell' was one of the items in such a procession (ill. 43). In this, a fully-rigged ship-on-wheels was trundled along. The 'ship' was crewed by a motley assortment of personages: in between a priest and a joker sat a doctor, this last resembling a most unpopular doctor, Andreas Osianer, much to the amusement of the crowd but not to the doctor, who objected and managed to have the *Schembartlaufen* abandoned. The ship also contained a castle manned by old soldiers in rusty armour. Soldiers attacked the ship, the defenders resorting to spraying their attackers with water. The Reformation at this period was taking a hold, and priests came in for much criticism. In one procession, a 'priest' was clothed in indulgences complete with red papal seals.

Of the rites relative to work, those to do with sowing and harvesting are the most numerous, but by no means the only ones. Giraldus Cambrensis in the twelfth century, in his 'Itinerarium Cambreiae' (Journey through Wales), described how men and women danced while they sang, first in the church, then in the churchyard, and later in a chain round the church, miming actions of work activities which would not have been allowed on the Sabbath. Some pretended to be ploughing, one wielded a whip as if goading oxen along, another mimed a shoemaker preparing the leather for his shoes, while a woman mimed spinning wool and weaving.

Sailors' and fishermen's dances were to be found not only in coastal regions but inland also. Fishermen's dances sometimes showed the actions of mending nets, and, as sailors' sea-shanties were sung to accompany their work, there is every reason to suppose that their dances also mimed such things as weighing the anchor, hoisting the sails, swabbing down the deck and so on.

Shoemakers' dances are amongst the most familiar of dances which display work actions: preparing the leather and the twine which had to be strengthened with a tar-like substance, biting off the thread or hammering nails.

Weavers' dances both mimed work actions and also imitated the shuttle plying back and forth across the warp of the loom. The dance often ends with a snail figure, usually interpreted as showing the winding of the thread round a bobbin, but perhaps this could be the ancient spiral which used to feature in the chain dances of old. The Hebridean Weaving Lilt is only the best known of many weaving dances, to which group also belongs the Foula Reel from the Shetland Islands. The Latvians have a weaving dance, 'Kamoliņš' in which they both mime the winding of wool, and make weaving patterns, passing over and under their raised arms. Further examples are to be found in Denmark, Norway and Sweden. These work dances were freely improvised and lacked in the early years set figures and patterns. Gradually some of them found their way into the popular entertainments of the period, and, certainly by 1716, we find in Gregorio Lambranzi's 'Neue und curieuse theatralische Tantz-Schule' illustrations showing sailors', shoemakers' and stone-masons' dances stylized for the stage.

Sometimes association of ideas credits certain crafts with dances. For example, we get millers' dances or wine-pressers' dances, so-called merely because of their 'turning-wheel' figures, which probably had no connection with grinding corn or pressing grapes, but, by association, were adopted by these trades. Woodcutters' dances are also well-known. We read of one performed in Germany by five boys, one of them being the tree standing in the centre, whilst the other four performed wood-cutting actions around him, as they circled first one way and then the other. They then crouched down making sawing actions, crossing over arms. The 'tree' was thus felled and the dancer lay down on his back. The others then pruned the branches before the tree was eventually set up again. You have no doubt heard of grape-crushing dances (ill. 113), but what do you think about the 'Krauttreter' from the Böhmerwald – a sauerkraut pressing dance? Yes, when the cabbage is put into the barrels with salt it has to be packed down, and what better way to do it? Other dances display preparing clay by stamping on it (East Prussia), or miming the sinking of piles into the ground in preparation for dyke building (Netherlands).

Many miners' dances exist still (in the Saar region of Germany for example), in the form of sword or hoop dances, but incorporating work actions. We read accounts of miners dancing in their work clothes, wearing feathers in their helmets, holding miners' lanterns in their right hand, in their left hand a walking stick with silver handle, whilst the girls who now join them wear the colourful folk costume of the region. Such dances with both sexes are of course of much more recent provenance, but nevertheless, many of the dances have adopted what can only have been much older motifs coming directly out of their occupation as miners. Some climbing or bending steps appear to indicate postures used in their work, in particular when the dancers go down on their haunches or knees one can imagine them moving down the cramped narrow mine shafts and galleries. Other actions are indicative of constructing the scaffolding to hold up the roof of the gallery. Often these miners' dances use the tools of their trade rather than swords, for example, the rappers used by the short-sword dancers in England. Times were also when work in the mines was short, and the miners had to supplement their incomes by other work. Occasionally

116. Procession of the Nürnberg coopers. German, 1835.

they took to wood carving, and also earned a little extra by performing their dances, often then carrying the tools used in their woodcarving.

Some of these dances belong to the sword-dance or Carnival-play categories rather than to work dances. For instance, one description is of ten to twelve dancers with long, wild, black beards, white pants with red stripes, red waistcoats with white and gold belts, red caps adorned with white bands and green tassels, swords on their shoulders, always with a fool in their company. He is dressed in a red jacket with a green belt with little bells on it, short red pants, striped garters and buckled shoes. On his head he wears a gold trimmed cap with bells, and carries in his hand a Harlequin's wand. The dancers commence standing in two rows confronting each other and then form themselves into a circle, the fool jumping over their linked swords. The two rows are reformed, and the leader challenges one of the dancers to a fight. The one challenged comes forward, is killed and falls down dead. The fool then starts his 'business', sitting on his back, blowing into his face, calling him back to life, but, failing to revive him, strikes him hard with his wand, which does the trick, for the dead man comes back to life again. They then perform the usual hilt-and-point figures. Eventually they surround the fool and threaten him: "Either you pay us 3000 guilders or we cut off your head." The fool who obviously cannot pay kneels down, and they put their swords onto his shoulders, all except the leader, who jumps onto the fool's back and shouts:

Da bin ich heraufgestiegen,
Wär besser, ich wäre unten geblieben.
Der Fasching ist ein vertuelicher Mann,
Hat all sein Hab und Gut vertan.
Er hat verloren sein Hab und Gut
Bis auf einen alten zerrissenen Hut,
Er reist da Land wohl auf und nieder,
Was er bekömmt versauft er wieder.
So spring ich aus dem grünen Kranz,
Spielmann mach auf den lustigen Schwerttanz!

"I have climbed up here, better had I stayed down there. Fasching is a poor man – he has lost all his belongings and is left only with an old torn hat. He travels through all the lands. If he gets any money he only spends it on drink. So I spring out of the green wreath, musicians give me a jolly sword dance!"

At Biot in the French Alpes-Maritime, on the feast of the Labourers, celebrated on October 23rd, everyone gathered in the main square with their various agricultural implements, and there, on the command of their leader who was wearing a traditional garb, the 'angel's coat', and to the sound of fife and drum, they went through the pretence of their work: some scattered the seeds, dug the ground, or hoed, while others raked and mowed. In Haute-Provence, the harvesters, before they hired themselves out, mimed the harvest. For the feast of St. Antoine, January 17th, at Valensole, carrying sickles and sheaves of corn, the dancers went about the streets miming the work actions of the harvesters, and the people would give them oblations in the hope of a good harvest. In the afternoon, during the procession, they acted out the work actions of preparing the ground. They danced on the newly-worked earth to encourage germination. At Treto on the day of Pentecost (Whit Sunday), called the 'Ramado', the young people solemnly mowed the communal meadow on which the girls danced, garlanded in flowers and greenery.

The harvest closed with dancing round a large column made out of the last sheaves. The dancers, with bells on their garments, performed the work actions from sowing to harvesting the corn. La Sinse had a betrothal ceremony between the reapers and the girls binding the sheaves, which ended the communal work. The young girls danced a farandole round a huge stack of corn set up in the square by the church, and then ran to hide their faces in the stack of corn. The boys came out of the church, danced around the corn-stack, hoping to find the girl of their choice, and then dashed towards them to draw them into a big chain around the corn-stack. In the valley of Ubaye, during the long winter evenings, the peasants danced the 'Ronde de la Civaïa', imitating the cultivation of the oats. They threw their rough homespun shawls into the middle of the circle and danced round, stopping after each couplet to perform the successive actions of: digging, sowing, harvesting, binding and so on, singing:

Quand mon paire semenava la Civaia, Fasié aco emai aco,
Aussava la chambra, aussava lou pé . . . Raou.

"When my father sowed the oats, he did this and then that, he lifted his leg, lifted his foot . . . Raou."

In this mime, common to the whole of western France, are to be found all the elements of a ritual of fertility: the jump from foot to foot, the imitation of the pawing of a horse by the beating of the heels, the noise to frighten off evil spirits, the clapping of hands, and shouts of "Oats, oats, Raou!"

Before he ever became an agriculturalist, Man tended herds of cattle and flocks of sheep and goats. In just the same way that later he danced to ensure the abundance of his harvests, so formerly he danced to ensure the well-being and fruitfulness of his animals. In Provence they still dance to a song called 'la Lano' (*la Laine* = Wool) while miming the various work actions of shearing the sheep, washing the wool, carding, spinning and so on. Another dance, the 'Bergères' (Shepherdesses) or 'Pastourelles' has become almost a sort of courtship dance, in which the couple mime various actions. The boy carries a shepherd's crook and the girl, adorned in flowers, holds a spindle. This dance is mentioned frequently in the pastoral ballads of the troubadours.

The most popular of the Provençal 'work' dances are: 'les Jardinières' (Gardeners), 'les Cordelles' (Warps), 'les Tisserands' (Weavers), and 'la Matelote' (Sailor's Dance). For a long time these have been seen as 'work' dances, but it is clear from different aspects of these dances, that they in fact belong to the older category of ritual dances which date back to time immemorial.

In Estonia, the men do the 'Kingsepapolka', a Shoemakers' dance in which they polka for eight bars, hammer, pull the thread, and then lick their fingers to make the

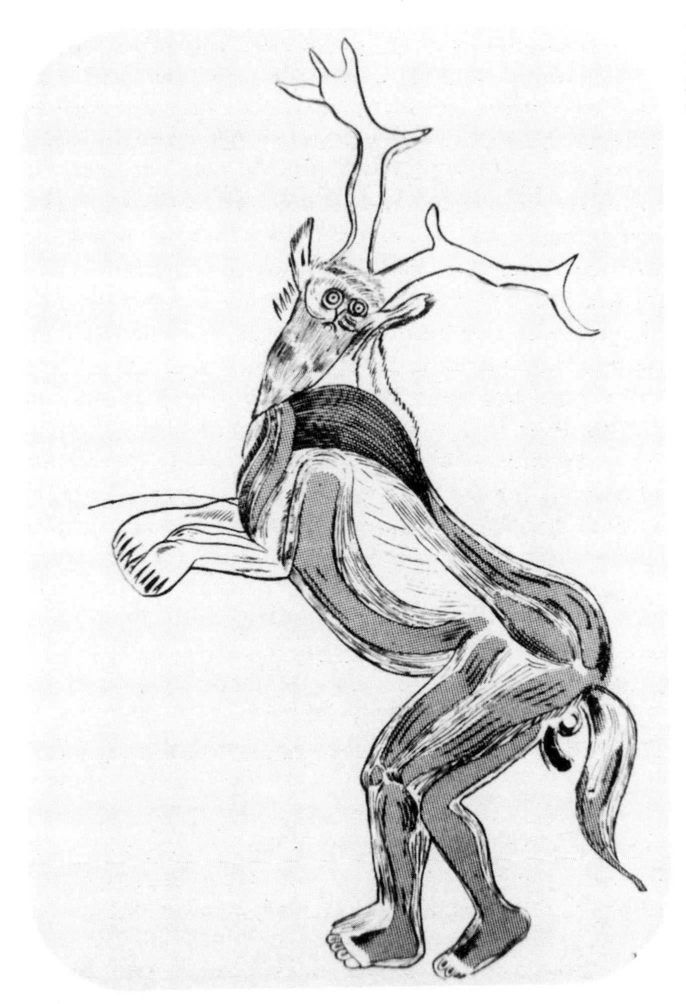

117. Masked dancer. Prehistoric cave painting from the Trois Frères, Arriège, France.

thread pointed. Couples dance the 'Voor-sahkadi', a wood-cutting dance, the name indicating the noise made by the saw. 'Kalames' is not so much a work dance as an after-work dance. The fishermen, stiff after rowing their boats, dance with difficulty but gradually loosen up. Similarly 'Kivikasukas' which means 'beaten by a stick', has the workers limping home with real effort, but as the music quickens so does their dancing become livelier. *Talgud* was the occasion when communal work was done. When certain jobs such as the preparation of flax, the drying and spinning, required more hands than the farm could provide, girls from neighbouring farms would help out with the work, often taking their own spinning wheels with them. Getting feathers ready to stuff eiderdowns was another occasion for communal work, when the boys would come along later to dance. These however were occasions for dance rather than work dances.

The Lithuanians have various dances which imitate work actions: 'Malūnas' (the Mill) depicts rhythmical movements, 'Rugeliai' (Rye), 'Piovéjai' (Mowers),

'Gyvataras' (Hedgerow), 'Audéja' (Weavers), 'Kubilas' (Wash-tub), are all expressive of various activities, whilst 'Jungas' (Yoke) is a men's dance showing ploughing with oxen.

'How Black Pepper is Sown' was once, in Bulgaria, a men's ritual dance, now performed usually at weddings for amusement. In it, the men, ten or more in number, stand in a semi-circle, and while they sing they mime the actions of sowing, gathering, pounding, and threading the peppers on strings to dry.

Czechoslovakia has a Poppyseed dance in which the dancers mime preparing the soil, sowing the seed, treading it down, watering it, seeing it grow, harvesting it, and finally popping it in the mouth and eating it. One interesting aspect of this dance is the use of the limping step, a smooth dipping step, which they make as they circle round miming the work actions. The girls also have a dance with flails and rhythmically mime threshing. A similar dance with bats for beating the washing is also done.

Poland too has a Poppyseed dance. In 'Mak' it is grandmother who sows the poppy seed. The Poles also have a Shoemakers' dance (Szewc), and a Sweeps' dance with besoms (Miotlarz).

The Irish have various dances with pantomimic actions. One called 'Droghedy' was described as being of a very objectionable nature. We do not know what sort of actions were performed in this dance, but in the 'Maide na bPlanndaí', a solo dance from Connacht, tilling, planting and digging potatoes were mimed.

In Hungary there is a weaving dance, 'Takácstánc' in which the dancers imitate the passing of a shuttle on the loom by pulling a hat through their legs. Other seasonal-work dances to be found here are those associated with preserving plums, preparing hemp or tobacco, spinning, and building. Dancing in Hungary is a highly organized affair. Whenever a special occasion comes along, be it a wedding, completion of a building project or seasonal work, or to celebrate the harvest, *kezes* ('bosses') are detailed to make all the necessary arrangements. They hire the musicians, collect the money to pay them, hire a dance place, and arrange the course of the celebrations. Guest strangers must be offered the best dancers amongst the girls as partners. If the dance place is to be paid for by mowing, for example, the Gypsy musician moves along each furrow at the end of the meadow fiddling 'a pair' or a dance – 'a pair' is a dancing section which goes uninterrupted from one break to another without changing partner. The mowers thus pay in kind for their dancing place.

In Russia, the girls mime the whole process of the corn planting and growth: making the furrows, planting the grain, stamping and smoothing the soil, clapping to mime the thunder which will bring rain and, finally, indicating with their raised arms the height to which the corn should grow. The name of the dance, 'Moonshine', would seem to denote its ancient origins. The planting must be done with the new moon so that, as the moon waxes full, she will pull up the new corn with her. More sympathetic magic; without realizing the deeper significance of their actions, many farmers today plant with the new moon.

Animal dances

There are dances which are imitative of the movements of various animals and birds which probably developed from those magic rites performed by early Man to bring him luck in the hunt. Cave and rock paintings exist all over Europe, showing man in pursuit of animals, and it seems clear that these were painted as sympathetic magic to ensure an abundant food supply.

'Danza do Galo' (Rooster) is an ancient dance from the region of Rianxo in Galicia, Spain. It is danced by a boy and six, eight or ten girls. He imitates the movements of a rooster playing with the hens, jumping and hopping round them with quick and exaggerated steps. The girls dance more sedately, holding their skirts with their hands and moving them in the same direction as the front foot.

Many countries have dances in which the dancers imitate the movements of the bear, which, coming out of its winter hibernation, heralded the coming of spring. There was a bear dance in Alsace right down to the nineteenth century. Czechoslovakia's bear dance, the 'Medvědka', has the dancers squatting, doing press-ups, and acrobatically jumping over each other. To the Finns this animal was 'Lord of the Forest', and when one was killed, its spirit had to be appeased by the observance of special rituals. Faint traces of these remain in some of the hopping and jumping dances still to be found. These relics of shamanistic rites link the Finns to their distant cousins who live yet in tribal communities spread eastwards into and across Siberia. Still in Finland, we read in a seventeenth-century account of another animal dance which landed its performers in a court of law charged with an indecent act; they had been caught performing a dance which depicted a couple of copulating capercaillies. The movements of the seal are incorporated into a present-day Finnish folk dance.

Eagle dances are to be found amongst many mountain people: in the Caucasus, Albania and Montenegro for example. There is a partridge dance performed in Turkey, though no record of a turkey dance. Lithuania has dances imitative of cocks, racehorses and kids; the Karelians have a bullocks dance; and 'Gusachok' (gosling) is a favourite humorous parody amongst the Russians.

In Estonia the men imitate the movements of bears, frogs, and birds. In the 'Kiitsakatants' (Magpie Dance), two men dance a polka and then jump, clapping their hands in front and behind. Because of the prevalence of wolves the men often carried sticks, and this led to many stick dances being performed. 'Karutants' imitated a bear on its hind legs. The 'Konnatants' imitated frogs, the men squatting and leaping, or bouncing around in a 'press-up' position, rather like the Swedish bear dance.

Latvian pigs were singularly fortunate in having their very own patron saint. St. Tenis would dance at the back of the pig sty, and, according to the number of footprints he left behind, so many would be the piglets born in that sty. On his saint's day, January 17th, it was the custom to let the sow and the piglets dance so that they would become strong and healthy. In the evening, everyone went to the inn to dance with the swineherd and the children, again to ensure the growth and health of the pigs. They danced in a circle, sprinkling water over each other – the usual rain charm. On St. Bārbalas's Day, December 4th, Latvian shepherds hopped in a crouching position through the rooms of the farms, copying the movements of

118. Dancers wearing bird masks and costumes. Greek oenochoe. Reproduced by Courtesy of the Trustees of the British Museum.

the animals. Mārtiņš Day was connected with the end of the agricultural labour in autumn. On this occasion the children put on masks and dressed up, and performed the Mārtiņš dance in which they imitated birds.

Old Lithuanian sources mention the 'Blezdingėlė' (Swallows) as being widely known in the country. A nineteenth-century Danish author wrote:

"I saw this dance one summer evening in a little birch grove. Couple behind couple take up positions in two sets facing each other, they swing around, bend down and pass through quick as a flash so that really in a way it reminds one of the swallows' twisting and rapid flight." The dance is the girls' farewell to the swallows flying off to warmer lands. The men have a ceremonial bear dance which they perform at Carnival time, and the 'Gaidys' (Rooster).

In the Austrian 'Schuhplattler' the boys circle the girls, crowing and flapping their arms like wings in imitation of the black cock's mating dance.

Some dances do not so much imitate animals as derive their inspiriation from them. The Poles, for example, have a great affinity with horses, and in several of their dances they make horse-like movements or recreate the sound of horses' hooves. 'Konik' is such a dance, with the boys, jingles on their costumes and plumes in their hats, high-stepping like prancing horses, and forming a 'cart' for the girls to ride in. They dance the krakowiak galop, using the *hołubic* (cut step) and turning with outstretched arms.

Similarly, in the dance 'la Llarga' from Ibiza, the girl follows a figure-of-eight with small steps getting quicker and quicker, while the boy makes large semi-circles round her, moves nearer, and then with big jumps and rapid turns, moves to her side. He finishes the dance by raising his arms above his head, a sign of possession. This dance is always performed at weddings. In the 'Goignade' from the Auvergne in France, in the Russian 'Ruskaya', and in the German 'Hasenschlager', the girl turns round and round modestly, while her partner dances clapping his hands, beating his feet, slapping his thighs, before finally lifting her in the air.

The Bretons have a wolf dance, but this is in no way imitative of the animal, but is used to scare them. Safe inside their houses, they dance in the hearth, stamping noisily so that the din will echo up the chimney and frighten off any wolves that may be lurking in the vicinity.

— 12 —

CHURCH, HEALING, ECSTASY AND DEATH

There was dancing one minute on the green round the church, and the next minute wounded and unfortunates circled the church seeking cures.
Giraldus Cambrensis: Itinerarium Cambreiae, 1188.

Many of the pagan rites found a benefactor in the Church, which sensibly harnessed them to its own service. Well-dressing and Rogation processions, both pre-Christian in origin, now have the well-dressers singing hymns and dancing in religious procession. In England, dancing in the churches was common until the Puritans put an end to it in the seventeenth century, though down to the nineteeth century, the villagers of Batford and Wishford had the right to dance in Salisbury Cathedral. In York, the apprentices claimed a similar right in the Minster on Shrove Tuesday. Even today, many of the ceremonies are still under the wing of the Church. The Abbots Bromley Horn Dance leaves from the church, where the horns are housed for the rest of the year, after a short service.

In the cathedral of Seville on Corpus Christi, boys dance in the chancel, singing and clacking their castanets. Dancing in two lines or linked in a chain, they perform ten figures. This 'Dance of the Seises' is first mentioned in 1508, though it is undoubtedly far older than that. The story goes that, in 1685, the newly consecrated bishop of Seville decided to suppress the dance. The cathedral chapter appealed to the Pope, who ruled that the dancing might continue, but only as long as the boys' clothes lasted; when they wore out the dance must cease. By careful and regular repairing the life of the clothes has been prolonged, and the dancing continues. Until the middle of the nineteenth century, the Corpus Christi procession also included sword dancers and dancing 'giants'.

In the mountain village of Yebra in Spain, the 'Paleotada' is danced in honour of Santa Orosia, who came to Aragon in the eighth century, to convert the heathen, and had her head cut off by the Moors. The dancers, complete with bells, ribbons and flower-decorated hats, holding a stick in each hand, spend June 26th, dancing and singing, eating and drinking.

The 'Farsa de Damas e Galáns' is danced in Vigo, Galicia, at the Feast of the Assumption, Santa Cristina de Lavadores, and in the Romeria de San Roque. It is a dance for men, four of them dressed as women, with coloured skirts and straw hats covered in ribbons and gold chains, and wearing gold necklaces around their necks and on their chests. They wear gold rings on their fingers, from one of which hangs a handkerchief. The others are dressed in white, with red scarves, and tall hats decorated with coloured ribbons. They have two coloured handkerchiefs pinned to

119. Ring dance from the Lesnovo Monastery. Yugoslavia, c.1345.

the buttonholes of their lapels, and these hang down and are tucked into their belts. The leader has short red trousers, coloured striped stockings, white jacket, and a silk handkerchief held by two rings, a straw hat with a ribbon and a red feather, and carries a handkerchief in his left hand. All carry castanets. The first part of the dance is like a *contredanse*, danced without castanets, very slowly and ceremoniously. The second part is a 'Muiñeira' with castanets, and the third part is very quick, like a 'Ribeirana'.

In Braga, north Portugal, the 'Dance of King David' forms part of the St. John's Day procession. The Portuguese town of Pedrogão Pequano preserved a 'mourisca' until late in the nineteenth century. On St. John's Day, seven men dressed in skirts, with ribbons on their jackets and flower-decorated conical hats, danced and played instruments. Two of the dancers carried wands with bunches of carnations tied to them. The 'King' wore a crown and carried a sword and shield, on which St. John's lamb was painted. The dance was performed before the altar of the chapel.

The sword dancers of Zumarraga perform their dance before the altar in the church of Santa Maria la Contigua. Larramendi, in the middle of the eighteenth century wrote: "The sword dance is for grave occasions such as Corpus Christi processions. The dancers enter in silence, without shouting or noise other than their music; nor do women take part in the dance, nor any other thing which might make it less worthy of the Church or the presence of the Lord."

The festival of Corpus Christi seems to have been particularly associated with the sword dance. This festival forms a link between the Church and the guilds, for it was the guilds which were responsible for furnishing and equipping the various parts of this day's procession. At Onate near Zumarraga, a sword dance performed by skirted dancers is still today a feature of the Corpus Christi procession.

In the French Basque town of Arbéroue, a 'regiment' wends its way towards the church. The dancers have ribbons and mirrors on their white clothes, and wear large busbies. They are led by a band. The *Sapeurs* (sappers) come first, the *Voltigeurs* (light infantrymen) bring up the rear, and all dance into the church. They mount the steps to the raised sanctuary, and remain there throughout the Mass, and then, at the Elevation of the Host, instead of kneeling, the regiment dance, thudding their rifle-butts on the floor.

At Lequeitio on the Biscayan coast, St. Peter himself dances. The members of the Fishermen's guild, on June 29th, used to elect their officers for the coming year, and then would carry round the town a statue of St. Peter, which they took down to the sea. They then beat the statue as a threat of what the saint might expect should he fail to provide good catches of fish. The statue has now been replaced by a dancer, who carries a banner bearing St. Peter's keys to denote his origin. He is carried through the streets by the officers of the guild, and dances before the houses of the mayor and other notables of the town. He is more fortunate than his predecessor and escapes the beating.

In Commillas on the coast near Santander in northern Spain, St. Peter is borne in procession, preceded by young men, dancing backwards, two by two, carrying castanets and streamers. They are accompanied by the *pandereteras*, girls playing tambourines and singing.

If Carnival is the time when anything goes, Easter is quite the reverse. This is the time for formality and piety. Easter in the Greek Orthodox Church is the most holy time of the year, more so even than Christmas. The Resurrection was, in many parts of the country, the only Christian celebration allowed by the Turks when they ruled Greece, and so Easter became especially an occasion for feasting. The dance was often led by the priest, and in some villages the priest even started the dance inside the church, leading the congregation out at midnight as he intoned "Christós Anésti" (Christ is risen). After the liturgy for Matins on Easter Sunday, the faithful throng the church forecourt, and the men and women dance in their separate circles, all in order of descending age. The dances are accompanied by Easter songs, which are slow and sedate. If the priest is leading the dance, he it is who always sings the song, often an adaptation of a hymn. The dancing commences with a slow 'syrtos' sometimes in a circle round the church, if there are sufficient people to link up. Later they go to another place to dance livelier dances, sometimes being specially for Easter.

One of the most beautiful buildings in the fortified medieval town of Kotor in Yugoslavia is the cathedral of Sveti Tripun (St. Triphon), patron saint of Kotor and the gulf. According to legend, on January 13th, 809, the relics of St. Triphon, which had been carried by Venetian merchants from Asia Minor, were returned home to Kotor. Around the relics the sailors danced a 'kolo' which was later named 'Kolo

Svetog Tripuna' (St. Triphon's Kolo). Every year on St. Triphon's feast day (February 14th) the members of the Boka Marine, a society which was supposedly founded on the day the saint's relics were brought to Kotor, danced in front of the church. The dance consisted of twelve figures, the fifth figure being the one in which the dancers formed an anchor, a symbol of its origin as a sailors' dance. The society of the Boka Marine still exists, though the dance is now rarely performed.

The province of Vojvodina is particularly rich in folk dance, for here, side by side, live Serbs, Croats, Slovaks, Ruthenes, Hungarians, and Romanians. Among the Bunjevci (Croats), they celebrate the *Dužijanca*, a holiday which follows the harvest, usually on a Sunday in August. In former times, the boys and girls of the villages made a wreath from the last sheaf of corn to be harvested, and carried it to the church. Nowadays, a crown is made and carried by a boy and girl, the *bandaš* and *bandašica*, who ride through the village in a cart decorated with greenery and sheaves of corn, and when they reach the church, the corn from the crown is distributed round those present. Here we have a relic of an ancient pagan custom of sacrificing to the harvest gods.

The *Slava*, a feast day originally set aside for ancestor worship, survives still in Serbia, but now it is the celebration of the name-day, the name deriving from a saint, and passing from father to son. Much ritual merry-making and a banquet attend the celebrations. The 'Moravač', 'Kačerac', 'Čačak', 'Djurdjevka', 'Žikino' and 'Devojačko' kolos are some of the popular dances performed on these occasions.

At Echternach in Luxembourg, pilgrims dance to the shrine of St. Willibrod. They set out from the surrounding villages, to reach the shrine on the Wednesday of Whitsuntide. The parish priests accompany their flocks, dancing the 'Pilgrims' Step' of one backwards and two forwards, four abreast and linked by sticks or handkerchiefs, until, approaching the shrine, they change the step to one back, one forwards, and three jumps; all this exhausting step being done in honour of St. Willibrod "who cures calves of St. Vitus' Dance".

Provence, in the south of France, can boast many dances and processions which have been taken under the wing of the Church. For much of the Middle Ages, the Papacy found refuge in Avignon, and the Church became intimately bound up with the life of the people. It served as temple, school, place of reunion, and the meeting place for the guilds. Religious ceremonials were embellished with rounds danced to the accompaniment of hymns, and theatrical scenes to inspire the devotion of the congregation.

One of these is the 'Branle de Saint Marc' or the 'Danse de la Souche'. In Limoges, as the people danced a round in the church, they used to sing: "Saint Martial, pray for us and we will dance for you." In the same spirit, since the eleventh century, the Confraternity of Wine Growers have solicited the protection of their patron, Saint Mark, by lively branles. The Feast of Saint Mark is celebrated on the Sunday nearest to April 25th. On the eve of the feast, certain members of the confraternity go in solemn procession out into the vineyards to uproot the best root-stock plant, the *souche*, which they can find. On the day of the feast, the souche, decorated with greenery, flowers, and a few ears of corn, is carried in triumph to the church by a young wine-grower, followed by the members of the confraternity.

After Mass, the priest blesses the souche, and all leave the church to begin the 'Promenade de la Souche' through the village, stopping from time to time in front of the houses they wish to honour. Here, the carrier of the souche performs his dance. Members of the confraternity go into the house to present 'la fougasse ou tourtihado', and receive in return refreshments and presents. Before departing, they finish with a song, a curious mixture of French, Provençal and Greek, the 'Grâces de Saint-Marc', which is accompanied by mimed gestures. The *promenade* reaches its conclusion in the evening in front of the church, where a pile of faggots has been set in preparation. The dance is performed once more with couplets from the 'Grâces'. Then one of the wine-growers steps forward to recite a prayer to Saint Mark, and the priest lights the fire, intoning a benediction. The carrier of the souche throws it into the flames, and then leads the members of the confraternity in a branle, punctuating it with high leaps and cries of: "Vivo la souco, vivo lou maiou." Two *baïle*, armed with *fourcaù* (rakes), stand on either side of the smouldering embers, making an arch with their rakes, underneath which all pass in a farandole, to seek the magical blessing and protection of the souche. The prayer addressed to St. Mark leaves no doubt regarding the sacred nature of the dance:

O, grand Sant Marc, que nostro vigno
Nous doune d'aboundous rasin,
Que lou soulas que la grafigno
L'escaufo e nous doune lou vin,
Lou bon vin que nous reviscoulo
Tau lou bon pan de cade jour,
Adounc, Sant Marc, fai que la vigno,
Coumo lou blad, creissoun toujour.

120. 'Cain's Descendants' from the Dečani Monastery. Yugoslavia, c.1345.

"Oh, great St. Mark, let our vines give us grapes in abundance. Let the sun which touches them, ripen them and give us the wine, the good wine which cheers us, like the daily bread. Therefore, St. Mark, make it so the vine, like the corn, ever increases."

The vine has always played a symbolic rôle. This extraordinary plant which produces the 'water-of-life', has been called the 'grass of life' or the 'herb of life', and has represented in man's mind: light, wisdom, purity, immortality; as the wine has remained the symbol of youth and eternal life. Its leaf was the Sumerian symbol of life, and Christianity chose the vine as the 'Tree of Redemption'. It has frequently been looked upon as being the immense cosmic tree on which the grapes themselves were stars. In the ceremony at Villeneuve-lès-Avignon, it is as a cosmic tree, giver of fertility, that the souche is burned in a ritual of regeneration, aimed at strengthening the growth of the new plant, and to hasten, and commemorate in advance, the arrival of a good harvest. The Provençals have a saying: "Emé de pan e de vin, poudès pas mouri de fam." (With bread and wine you cannot die of hunger.) Often, therefore, they will decorate the souche with a few ears of corn.

Provence seems to have preserved her ancient dances to a greater degree and in a less adulterated state than many other parts of Europe. Here is another dance-ritual, which, with little doubt, was in origin a part of a bull-worshipping cult. Various legends surround the Feast of St. Marcel at Barjols (Var). Some say, it is to commemorate the miraculous appearance of a fat bull which saved the people from the famine, that now, every year, they roast a whole ox which has been ritually sacrificed, in the main square. Another tradition relates how an ox, stubbornly halting in front of a prickly bush, indicated, by striking its hooves, the resting place of St. Marcel's remains, and where subsequently, in 1050, they built the chapel of Notre-Dame de l'Espinas. This connection between an ox and the relics of a saint seem to imply the former existence of an ancient cult.

The most widespread version is that on January 17th, 1350, during the sharing out of the goods of the Templars, the people of Aups and Barjols quarrelled bitterly over the relics of St. Marcel, the fifth-century bishop of Die, which were buried in the convent of St. Maurice. Advised by the people of Tavernes, the canons clandestinely seized the relics. Escorted by all the people, they were carrying them in triumph back to their collegiate church, when they came across some down-and-outs who were washing beef tripe in the stream. (The tripe was distributed annually as alms to the very poor.) These people joined the procession, carrying their baskets full of tripe. The solemn instalment of the relics in the church of Barjols brought the crowds to the heights of enthusiasm, and, without regard for the holiness of the place, they started jumping and dancing for joy. The memory of these exalted moments was so vivid that every year, on January 16th, the day of the Feast of St. Marcel, the same transports of joy are indulged in, and the tradition has come to be named the 'Danse des Tripettes' (dance of the strips of tripe). The dance is still performed in church.

At Barjols, as at Saint-Tropez, and indeed in many places, including Siena in Italy, the crowd does everything it can to impede the progress of the saint's procession, believing that the longer it takes the better will be the year to come. The next evening, the ox, garlanded with flowers, in a torchlight procession, is led around the public fountains of the town and allowed to drink its fill, and then taken to the place of sacrifice. Afterwards, it is set on a waggon and brought to the main square, accompanied in their traditional costumes, by the guilds of Butchers, Tripe-makers, Tanners, and Cooks. Whilst it is roasting, the people take up the 'Danse des Tripettes' once more, and the feast is terminated by a great farandole.

This ancient custom of bull sacrifice is a relic of a bull cult, where the bull symbolized fecundity, the revitalizing force of the sun, and the regeneration of nature. According to Apollodorus, the second-century B.C. historian, the cult was introduced into Provence in 542 B.C. Thus the sacrifice of the bull at Barjols predates St. Marcel by a long way. The eve of January 17th is the day of St. Antoine of Winter, and is the feast day of both cultivators and herdsmen. As the feasts often used to run into several days, the two feasts have become somewhat confused, especially when we find the guild of Butchers chanting: "Nous, nous fêterons Saint Antoine, Saint Antoine." It is even possible that the name of the feast has become confused with that of the saint. The word *macellum* signifies a meat-market. The Provençal word for abattoir is *masèu*, and when the Provençals pronounce the name of their saint they say "Macèu", not "Marcèu".

'Les Tripettes' may also have stemmed from another source – the Provençal word *trepa* signifies to dance or to jump, whilst *faire tripet* in Provençal signifies to kick up a shindy. In Old French, the terms *treper*, *trepeter, trepiller*, were the equivalent

121. 'Un Aurrescu à Begona' from 'Espana Artistica'. Spanish Basque.

of to jump, skip, hop. The Barjols ceremony, with the parading of the sacrificial bull, garlanded and with horns and hooves gilded, through the streets before it is roasted and eaten, retains all the ancient aspects of a pagan cult, a cult taken up by the guild of Butchers, and performed in honour of their patron saint, and still to be seen in the streets of Barjols to this day.

An interesting aspect of the 'Dance des Tripettes' is its use in the curing of epilepsy (see also Tarantella and St. Vitus' Dance). St. Marcel was held to have been able to cure epilepsy, and in the same way that in southern Italy they will dance to sweat out certain disorders, so the leaps of the 'Danse des Tripettes' are employed in church, sometimes for hours on end, to cure the malady. The evil spirit of the illness is literally sweated out. Thus this dance is also a remedial dance.

The towns of Provence were also celebrated for the magnificence of the processions which they mounted. Elaborately costumed, their parades rivalled the spectacle of Carnival. The most famous was (and happily there are plans afoot to revive it) the 'Procession de la Fête-Dieu d'Aix' (ill. 50). It took place at the season of the summer solstice. Tradition acknowledged King René as being the instigator of this festival, though without doubt King René merely gave form and order to the ancient folk dances which the people held so dearly. The fame of the Aix procession spread far and wide. No less a personage than Catherine de Médici came with her retinue to Aix to witness the splendours of the occasion: the plays or games of the Devils, of the Cat, the *Reino Sabo* (la Reine de Saba), the Beautiful Star, the *Tirassoun*, the Apostles, the *Chivau-frus* (hobby-horses), the Great and the Small dancers, the *Razcassèto*, St. Christopher, Death, and many more besides.

St. Christopher had much in common with the giants promenaded in the Pyrenean processions. The *Tirassoun* formed a band of urchins, dressed in linen shirts, who, at a signal given by a blast from a blunderbuss, splashed around in the gutters – possibly a survival of a mystical lunar ritual. The Great and Small dancers were made up of four youths and four younger children richly costumed in white silk, with short breeches, and gold epaulettes on jackets covered with embroidery. Their hats were decorated with precious stones and large multi-coloured plumes, and they wore little bells on their garters. In the left hand they carried large handkerchiefs, and in the right a beribboned stick with which they marked the beat of their dance. Perhaps this stick served also the same purpose as the whip elsewhere, frightening away evil spirits. Ritualistic aspects of their costumes were the white clothes, the bells, ribbons, plumes, and large kerchiefs. These dancers were followed by a troupe of Big and Little Devils dressed in black, with skull-caps with red and black horns, and bells hanging from belts.

The *Reino Sabo* (Queen of Saba) was a Carnival-type character; richly costumed and wearing a gauze veil, she conducted herself with exaggerated nobility. A dancer with little bells on his garters, and carrying a sabre tipped with a gold castle with four weather-vanes on top, represented King Solomon. He approached the queen, bowed low before her, and performed a very lively dance. The third time round, he was replaced by three of the queen's attendants who, having made their reverences, danced a minuet, holding a cup in their hands. The weather-vanes on King Solomon's gold castle were there perhaps to attract the four cardinal winds, and the cups to catch the rain which they could bring. So many of these processions and other rites were rain-charm rituals. In these hot, sun-drenched regions of southern Europe, periodic rainfalls were literally a matter of life or death.

The 'Reine de Saba' was in fact a derivative of the Earth Mother who, from paleolithic times, had watched over the harvest, the well-being of the herds and flocks, and man's fruitfulness. The Romans had their *Magna Mater* whom, on March 27th, they set in a car pulled by oxen decorated with spring flowers. She was taken down to the river, where the chief priest ceremoniously washed the image of Cybele, her car and other sacred objects in a ritual of purification, before returning her to her sanctuary on the Palatine. Similarly, the vessel, mounted on wheels (ill. 50 & 51), which carried the Germanic goddess Nerthus, displayed her effigy, placed in a niche resembling a house, which only the priest had the right to touch. This car was followed by a herd of oxen. Perhaps the house which sheltered the goddess is to be seen in the castle presented to the 'Reine de Saba' by King Solomon. In Catalonia, one finds a house similarly impaled on the stick carried by a shepherd. The herd of oxen came to be replaced in the procession at Aix by shepherds carrying batons, on top of which were round plates bearing various attributes of the goddess, one of which was a golden calf.

The *Rascassèto* were four dancers, each carrying a fruit in the left hand. Three of them wore skull-caps to give them the appearance of being bald, and carried in their right hands a comb, a brush, and sheep-shearing scissors (lazy tongs). The fourth one, wearing a copious wig, jumped one way and then the other, as if to avoid being combed and brushed by the others. The symbolism of this piece of play-acting was of course to do with vegetation: the long hair, combs, brushes, tongs and fruit. The *Chivau-frus* or *Chibalet* were the principal attractions of the procession. Dressed in white, with a helmet decorated with a crest of feathers, their legs were placed through the back of the horse which they wore around their waists, suspended on straps which went over their shoulders. They carried in their right hands a sword, a banner, or maybe a small baton decorated with ribbons, whilst they held the reins in their left hands. The horses' heads were decorated with plumes, their bodies enveloped in ornamental trappings which hid the riders' legs. There used to be some twenty cavaliers, led by a herald or Harlequin, making equestrian-like looking manœuvres of such skill as to make their mounts look almost real. The *Chibalet* was made up of an uneven number of dancers surrounding a 'horse', the dancers wearing little bells

122. Bacchanalian dance. Wall painting from the Villa Pamphilii, Rome. 1st century A.D. Reproduced by Courtesy of the Trustees of the British Museum.

on their legs. One made as if he were giving oats to the horse, another cracked a whip, a third twitched a fly-swat. Following behind, a farrier wielded blacksmith's tongs and a hammer.

The 'Course de la Tarasque' (ill. 51) is another famous Provençal procession which takes place at Tarascon. It was St. Mamert, bishop of Vienne, and St. Césaire, archbishop of Arles, in the fifth and sixth centuries, who established the Rogation processions which replaced the ancient pagan feasts. In the course of these processions, they played out the battle which finished with a victory for the Christians over the pagan spirits, represented in those places down the valley of the Rhône by the *Tarasque*, and at Draguignan by a dragon. The amusements of Tarascon, as set out by William of Tilbury in the twelfth century, were regulated by King René who, in 1474, in order to try to appease quarrelling factions, instituted the order of the 'Chevaliers de la Tarasque' or *Tarascairés* who took the motto: "Anèn Béure" (Let us Drink).

The participants, who were recruited from the oldest families, undertook to preserve piously this spectacle and "to perform it at least seven times a century". They had to receive strangers aimiably, and not interrupt the 'horse' plays, jollifications and dances for forty days, make a great racket, celebrate weddings, dance farandoles, and provide banquets in order to regale their guests "willingly and without reason". At one time the celebrants would start their festivities one month before the special day, and go on for one month after, with "farandoles from time to time", especially after Sunday lunch. On Ascension Day, the *Tarascairés* would 'try out' their *Tarasque* (ill. 47), the huge dragon with smoking mouth, and talons which the men manœuvred from inside the beast. Surrounded by its attendant knights, in their ceremonial dress of red silk, their hands gloved, a red cockade in their hats, it swept its tail from side to side, knocking over anyone who got in its way, bellicose behaviour which contrasted sharply with its meekness and docility when it took part in the procession for the feast of St. Marthe on June 29th, when it reappeared, led by a young girl, representing the saint who had tamed it.

A lively description of the grand parade which took place on Whit Monday, 1792, is to be found in Mouren's 'Relations de la Course de la Tarasque':

> *The Tarascairés were ready for the off, the drummers had assembled by the fountain in the square and were beating out the rhythm of the farandole, the rigaudon, and everyone was dancing, when the Tarasque was taken and gently led to the square, to the corner by the town hall. There they placed two rockets in his nostrils, the men squeezed themselves into position, whilst the little business of the drummers rat-a-tatting now the rigaudon, now the farandole or whatever it happened to be, when the dancing finished and everyone drew back feigning fear and then a moment later the beating of the rigaudon started anew and everyone recommenced dancing . . . they danced until midnight before the feast was finished. Sometimes they keep at it thus all night.*

The *Tarasque*, as with dragons or other beasts or puppets to be found scattered all over Europe, was made the scapegoat of the city. All the ills and evils of the people could be heaped on the scapegoat and driven out of the town, or exorcised in some way. We have seen repeatedly that one of the most effective means to keep out evil spirits and protect oneself from them was to dance round with hands joined, and, in a farandole, this is exactly what the people of Tarascon and elsewhere did. We know from texts written between 1465 and 1478, that the *Tarasque* was destroyed and thrown from the Pont de Jarnègues into the Rhône.

St. Hermentaire overcame the dragon which was terrorizing the region around Draguignan by thrusting a ball of resinous pine down its throat and choking it to death. In her memory the citizens of Draguignan created a procession in which different groups would evoke events from the history of the town: that of the Druids recalled the time when the *Pèiro de la Fado* (Rock of the Fairy) served for sacrifices; the Corybantes, clashing cymbals, danced round the young Jupiter; the Company of Chivau-frus enacted the battle between the Centaurs and the Lapiths; behind the effigy of the dragon came the Saracens dragging along slaves in chains. Bringing up the rear of the cortège came companies of soldiers dressed in the uniforms of successive periods, the porters of the relics, the town dignitaries, and members of the various guilds, shepherds dancing the 'Olivettes', and lastly the 'Danse des Cordelles'.

One comes across the 'ship-on-wheels' again in the Fréjus procession. The story of the origin of this procession relates how Louis XI, gravely ill and hoping for a miraculous cure, sent for the saintly François de Paule to come to France. François arrived in Fréjus not knowing that the plague was raging there. He found the streets deserted, but finally he came upon an aged woman and asked her why there was no-one to be found in the town. She told him about the plague. When he heard this, he threw himself on his knees and prayed to God to drive away the pestilence. His prayers were granted, and Fréjus thenceforward annually commemorated the miracle by a High Mass, in which the *Chivau-frus* had a place of honour at the foot of the altar, and by a procession in which figured a fully-rigged ship mounted on wheels, in memory of the saint's arrival in France, and filled with children to attract good fortune. After the procession, the effigy of the saint was set up beneath a triumphal arch of boxwood, erected in the square, and in front of which they mimed the dialogue between St. François de Paule and the old woman. Then the soldiers and the sailors discharged their muskets, the *Chivau-frus* capered about the statue, whilst the crowd plucked twigs from the box-tree arch to protect themselves, they believed, from fire.

In ancient times, there were close links between Fréjus and Ostia, the port of Rome. Today, in the Vatican Museum, there is preserved a mausoleum from Ostia, which shows a car in the form of a rigged-ship mounted on wheels, and drawn by children in white tunics. It would seem that, in a Christian form, the procession of Fréjus preserved a much more ancient rite.

The festival of Sant Brancaï (St. Pancras) at Manosque in the alpine region of Haute Provence, which lasts from Easter to May 12th, has a curious dance performed around the effigy of their saint. Strangely costumed, the dancers are called the *dansairé de Sant Brancaï* (dancers of St. Pancras). On the eve of the festival, at eight o'clock in the evening, the people came together at the chapel, where was kept the effigy of the saint. In the church and during the procession the dancers of St. Brancaï, wearing strange cocked hats, and dressed in white trousers, loose tunics which formed a skirt finishing at the knees, and a bolero, danced a wild and noisy Sarabande about their patron saint.

The dancing around a sacred object, we know, goes back deep into prehistoric times. Appianus, the Greek historian who, in the second century A.D., wrote a number of special histories of the several lands and peoples until the time they fell under Roman domination, described such a pagan festival. He told how the young people, who formed the processional pageants, encircled their heads with golden wreaths, and danced with trained precision. Martialis, the Roman writer, who was born in Spain in the mid-first century A.D., and went to live in Rome, sought the origins of this form of processional dance in Italy, from whence, he claims, it spread to Spain, where it was still danced in his day, as also in Portugal where, he writes, the people were particularly fond of it.

On the island of Majorca, the statue of the Virgin is carried in procession on August 15th, and is accompanied by six dancers called *els Cosiers*. They wear white clothes which are decorated with multi-coloured ribbons, and flower-decked hats. They carry in their hands a kerchief and a fan. One of the dancers, called 'la Dama', is dressed as a woman. A Devil leads the cortège, making a way through the crowd with his fork. They continue their frolics even in the church. The word *cossier* is derived from *cos* (course – race), because only the winners of the races, having shown themselves to be the strongest, had the right to perform the dance. Six in number, they are led by 'la Dama', who has on either side two devils armed with sticks, dressed in patched sackcloth, their heads covered with bull-hide, complete with ears and horns.

The dance varies from region to region. In that of Alaro, the dancers stand in two lines linked by kerchiefs. The last two dancers pass, one after the other, between the dancers opposite, finishing at the top of the set. The second figure, called the *processo* has them going round the statue of the Virgin, first in a counter-clockwise direction, then, after a turn to the right, they end with a big jump, bringing feet together to face the statue. They move towards it with three hops on the right foot, three on the left, and three on both feet. Then they make two jumps backwards to their places, and repeat this figure ending with a quarter-turn to reform their lines. When the statue has been returned to its place in the church, the *cossiers* do

123. Funeral dance. Wall painting from the tomb of Ruvo, Naples. Etruscan, 4th century B.C.

a dance called 'gentil Senyora' in her honour. Surrounding the statue, they perform jumps and turns alternately. Then they sing an ancient hymn, before moving round the statue, first counter-clockwise and then clockwise. In the fourth figure, called *l'Ofrena* (the Offering), the 'Dama' presents the priest with white doves, while the *cossiers*, in single file behind, repeat the steps.

At Mallocor, the 'Dama' wears small bells which tinkle as 'she' marks the main beat with jumps. The other dancers, carrying wooden swords and shields, perform a mock combat, striking their swords against their shields.

The number three which occurs in the jumps on each foot and on both of the *cossiers* may be compared with the dance of the Salian priests in Rome. They, dressed in a short tunic, armed with a shield and a short sword, sprang to a triple rhythm. Seneca, writing to Lucilius in the early years of the 1st century A.D., compared their jumps repeated three times (*tripudium*) with the march on the spot of the Fullers. And similarly to the *dansairé* of the Aix procession, they were divided into two groups, the *juniores* and *seniores*. They performed their dance in March and October, in honour of the god Mars who, before becoming the god of war, had originally been a god of vegetation, who fought to keep away the evil spirits.

The *dansairé of Sant Brancaï* originally carried swords (still to be seen in the tiny chapel of Gars (Haute Provence). In time, they came to replace the swords with sticks, and to attach a handkerchief to the stick to form a sort of flag. Their costume, with its short skirt, is found in similar form elsewhere: in Majorca, Spain, Portugal and

124. 'Jota round the Dead Child' by Gustav Doré. Alicante, Spain, 1832-1883.
© Photo R.M.N.

Romania. We know that the fisherfolk of Marseilles kept their costume for a long time; the seaweed gatherers of Portugal certainly trace their present costume back to Roman times; and, of course, the Romans left their influence, language, and much else in Romania.

Other forms of processional are those in which a sacred object, usually a statuette of the Virgin or a local patron saint, is taken from the church and given an 'outing'. Thus, at Tarascon, the Virgin, called 'la Belle Briançonne', is taken out in procession. In the pilgrimage processions of the Saintes-Maries, which take place in May and October, a boat, symbolizing that in which the holy Marys landed in the Camargue, is taken down to the sea; at Martigues, it was essential that those carrying the statuette of 'Notre-Dame de la Mer' did not stop; St. Maxime at Callian, draped with bunches of grapes, was taken to a fountain and immersed. In Italy also one finds similar processions. In Siena, the thronging crowds do all in their power to impede the progress of the saint, believing that the longer it takes to cross the square round which the Pallio horse race is held, the longer period of prosperity they will enjoy.

In the pilgrimage of St. Gens, the people of Monteux take their saint up the mountain in an unbridled procession which lasts for an hour and a half. On the eve of the festival, walking behind a banner carried in relay by two children at a time, the saint is carried by men wearing traditional short trousers and white gaiters. At each halt, four more men take up the statuette, until they arrive at the village of Saint Didier. When they reach the chapel the pilgrims perform a mock fight, before forming a file and walking three times round the statuette of the saint. The next day, the 'Black Penitents', carrying a figure of Christ hidden under a cloth, run up the same track to the chapel. Following the interdictions by the Church on such processions, the inhabitants, to keep the tradition going, put St. Gens on a cart, and as long as he remained concealed from view under a barrel or whatever, they were allowed to continue their outings.

In times of drought, it often happened that the local saint was taken down to the sea and plunged into the water. He was not taken out until someone, the priest in Christian times, shouted out: "N'a proun, Sèbo!" (He's had enough, stop!) This dunking of an effigy in water is a relic of ancient rain-charms.

Numerous outings have existed and still do far and wide. In Provence, often these took the form of races – the French word *course* covers both an outing and a race. At Arles, in the fifteenth century, for the festival of St. Madeleine, they held a race for young girls, giving a prize to the best runner. This may go back to the cult of Flora, in whose honour the courtisans of Rome would race round the stadium, the magistrates awarding the honours. And were not the chief priestesses of various cults thus chosen, the office of Chief Priestess going to the winner of a race? In Athens, in ancient times, a few days after the birth of a child, they used to race around the hearth, carrying the child, to influence benevolent forces to strengthen the infant and endow it with all good things. (It is to be hoped that this activity didn't make the infant sick.)

Healing

The 'Căluş Dance' belongs to southern Romania, and is performed during Whitsuntide, a period known as Rusalii. Spring comes to replace winter and the weather turns warmer. Early fruit appears, and at this time spring-cleaning is done. Spring-cleaning originally was done to sweep out of the house any lurking evil spirits, for on Whit Sunday the dead were supposed to visit their former homes. The malevolent fairies, called *ieli*, come out at night to dance and sing. They leave behind them a circle where their dancing has scorched the grass, and the ground afterwards remains barren. They can 'possess' you, causing paralysis, deafness, blindness if you offend them in any way, or if you observe their dancing or hear their singing. You can try to protect yourself by wearing garlic or wormwood, but the only cure for anyone who becomes possessed is the Căluş dance.

The dance is performed by a group of men called Căluşari (the name means little horses). The dance leader knows the secret healing charms. The group consists of seven, nine, or eleven performers. Originally they all wore women's dress; white veils hid their faces and they spoke in *falsetto* voices, although they also used to carry swords. A hobby-horse was probably an original feature of the occasion (hence the name *Căluşari*), though it is rarely seen nowadays. Today they wear long white tunics with embroidered patterns, crossbands and decorated hats. They may wear bells on their legs, or jingling spurs. The noise helps to drive away evil spirits. They chew garlic and wormwood for the same purpose (and this probably keeps away more than a few evil spirits). They also carry sticks. One of their number is a fool. He is masked, and wears a grotesque costume, usually with a woman's skirt or apron, and he provides the bawdy buffoonery which alternates with the intricate dancing of the remainder of the group. They are accompanied by musicians and a flag-bearer.

Today, it is the dance which is the all important element of what once was a complete mimed ceremony which included 'mutes' who carried swords or whips with which they lashed out to drive away evil spirits, mimed obscene actions with the Căluşari, and, in some districts, were killed and revived. In the eighteenth century, they wore masks like storks' heads, working the beaks with strings, and film shot in 1939 shows a mute wearing a goatskin mask, the tail forming the beard. The play was long and involved, the main protagonists being a Turkish overlord, a bride, a Russian and a priest. After much knock-about action, wooing and fighting, the Turk was killed and borne away for burial. There was no revival, but it is probable that this had been lost, and that originally the play followed the usual format of death and subsequent revival.

In other regions, characters included a hobby-horse, a Jew, a bear, a Gypsy, a bride and groom, and others who mimed harvesting. The hobby-horse danced with the Jew, the bear with the Gypsy, and the bride with the groom. The bear died and was revived. In one village, one of the mutes soused himself with water from a pot which he then threw high in the air. This was to ensure that there would be no drought. A pyramid was formed by the dancers clambering on one another's shoulders to represent the stacks of corn obtained from a bountiful harvest.

One feature of the performance was the enclosure of a space by linked performers to represent a 'marriage-house' where the newly-weds set up home. This idea of a 'marriage-house' is ancient. In Mesopotamia in the days of the early kingdoms, the king and his daughter themselves often played the leading parts in a sacred marriage which took place inside such a bower, and indeed it was the sacred marriage which was one of the rituals in the annual cycle of Dionysos.

The Căluşari meet privately on Whit Saturday to take their solemn oaths to their leader and to raise their flag. The next day they tour the village, dancing in the yards of the houses, bringing good luck and expelling evil spirits. It is believed that those who can pull garlic from the belt of one of the dancers will keep their husbands faithful, whilst a woman struck by the wooden phallus, carried by the fool, will soon bear a child. It is customary for the villagers to place salt, wheat, garlic, wool, and a bowl of water where the Căluşari dance, to ensure good crops, rain, and health for the animals for the coming year.

If anyone becomes possessed by the *ieli*, the Căluşari can exorcize the evil spirits. This is not for public amusement. The rite is performed away from the village, and onlookers are kept at a distance. The one possessed has to lie on the ground whilst the Căluşari dance round and jump over the prone body. Then one of the dancers falls down in a trance, and the leader smashes a pot and kills a chicken, at which the patient is helped up, supported by two of the dancers. The dancer who, by falling into a trance has given health to the one possessed, is now recalled from his trance. To complete the healing, the whole procedure is repeated twice more. The payment for their services is to be fed at the patient's expense for the days of the *Rusalii* for the next three years, and to dance a special dance with them when they perform one of their healing ceremonies. It has been claimed that the *ieli* themselves taught the Căluşari to dance so fast that their feet barely seem to touch the ground, but now the performance is done to keep the *ieli* from harming people.

Throughout southern Macedonia the ancient rite of the *Rusalije* was once observed. Today it is to be found in only a few villages of the Djevdjelija region, where it is performed between January 8th – 19th. The special dances, the 'Rusalijska ora' are performed by men wearing a costume only worn on this occasion. It consists of the *fustan*, a gathered white kilt, and two scarves tied crisscross front and back. The men dance singly, one hand placed on the waist, the other holding a wooden *yataghan* (a sword with a double-edged curved blade) which has presumably replaced the sword once used. The *yataghans* are waved in various directions as the dancers perform their complicated figures and balances. Starting in their own village, the dancers later visit neighbouring communities. Formerly they danced in front of every house in the village, bringing good luck to man, beasts and crops. As in Romania, the *Rusalije* were once believed to have the power to cure sickness and prevent disease. Their dances are performed with dignity and in silence.

The *Rusalii* of Bulgaria appear at Whitsuntide. Like their Romanian counterparts, they can cure a sick person by their magical healing while dancing round the patient. They also bring fertility and general prosperity. Their name is derived from the Latin *Rosalia*, when garlands were hung up during the festival of 'Rosales Escae'. They dance in rapid tempo with little stamping steps and carry small staves.

Ecstasy

Dance manias, similar to the ones which were to sweep over Europe in the Middle Ages, appeared in ancient Greece during the Mycenaean period. There are many accounts describing them. One concerned the daughters of Proetus, king of Tiryns. We are told that when the three princesses had grown to womanhood and were attracting suitors from all over Greece, they suddenly went mad. They dashed outside and, tearing their garments and singing weird songs, they ranged over the countryside unable to stop their frenzied dancing. Some versions of the story state that the princesses were afflicted with a leprous disease which disfigured them horribly. One died, but the others were cured by Melampus and Bias who "ran them off their feet" until they dropped from exhaustion. This compulsive dance frenzy seems to be brought on by hysteria, which itself can be induced by pestilence, famine and war, and can spread through the community, often running unchecked until many have succumbed.

'St. Vitus' Dance' is not a fable, though some of the descriptions are, to say the least, fantastic. According to the Chronicle of the Monastery of Kolbik, in the bishopric of Halberstadt, St. Vitus' Dance originated in the year 1021, in the time of Emperor Henry II. There was, runs the story, a miracle which occurred in that church. During the feast of Christmas Eve, some peasant people began to sing and dance in the churchyard of Kolbik, and made so much noise that the priest could not perform the service. He scolded them, telling them that it was not God's will that they should behave thus. The peasants numbered fifteen men, two women and a girl, the churchwarden's sister. As the priest's words had no effect, he uttered these words: "Now I hope God and St. Magnus will punish you, that you will have to sing and dance for a whole year." The churchwarden wanted to tear his sister away from the dancing, but succeeded only in wrenching her arm from her body. Then they danced for a whole year. They wore deep ruts in the ground, but their clothes and shoes did not become worn out, hair and beards did not grow, nor did rain or snow fall on them.

> *When the year was past, two bishops from Cologne and Hildesheim came to Kolbik and prayed earnestly to God that he should lift the curse from these unfortunates. After they had ceased to dance, they slept for three days and three nights. Four died, but the others went into church and thanked God for their deliverance. Amen.*

The message is clear: the commands of the priests must be obeyed, otherwise terrible things will befall the offenders. Anyway, such was the original story which, passed by word of mouth from person to person, gradually became changed in certain details.

It is believed that the St. Vitus' Dance was derived from a Wendish pagan dance from Pomerania called the 'Pomwitzeltanz'. The story relates how these Wends, coming to the church on Christmas Eve, but finding it locked, danced in a circle, as round an altar, in the churchyard. The combination of heavy drinking, sweating through the exertions of their dancing, the bitter cold of the December night, the priest's curse and, finally, the superstition which existed that anything which occurred on a certain important date in the calendar would have to be repeated throughout the following year, all added up to a similar story. The story which was written in Latin in a Saxon monastery, and purported to be the *verbatim* account of a Wendish peasant witness to the scene, gave the chronicler great scope for colourful embroidery. Again, the girl's arm was wrenched from her body, though the chronicler added that not a drop of blood was spilt, their dancing wore a rut knee deep, and only the bishop of Cologne was able to loosen their hands.

No more is heard about this dance mania until 1278 when, on July 18th, at Maastrich, two hundred peasants danced on a bridge spanning the river Maas, missing the church service on acount of it. The bridge collapsed, and all but one were drowned. The next reference comes from a Limburg chronicle from the year 1347. In the middle of summer, the people of the region of the Rhine and the Mosel began to dance and rave. They danced for half a day on one spot and often fell down, allowing themselves to be kicked, which they believed cured them. They went from town to town and church to church, and got money from the people who felt sorry for them. The mania spread to such an extent that in Cologne alone there were more than five hundred such dancers. It lasted for sixteen weeks in Germany.

During the reign of Emperor Charles IV, in the year 1373-4, whole masses of men and women, young and old, together danced from one town to another, one village to another. Some danced from the Rhine and the Mosel to Flanders, others from Antroff through Hennegau to France. They could not help themselves. It was believed that it was because their christening had not been properly carried out that they were thus being punished. So at this time, the priests went about in fear for their lives for not having attended to their duties as they should. In 1374, St. Vitus' Dance appeared in Lüttich and Utrecht. The fourteenth century saw the dance become a dance of zealots. The relics of St. Vitus were highly honoured at this time, and the people would dance on this saint's day.

Dr. Felix Plater, in an account written in Basle in 1624, remembered from his youth how, in order to cure a girl smitten with the plague, the city guardians had to dance with her day and night a whole month long. In 1518 in Strasbourg, men and women in their hundreds danced like souls possessed. The priests called it the devil's work, and tried to exorcize it by uttering incantations in the name of St. Vitus. Another explanation why the dance was so called is that it was danced for the first time on St. Vitus' Day (June 15th), and, needing the intercession of a saint to help them, the people chose St. Vitus.

In Italy, in the year 1233, occurred what has come to be called the 'Great Hallelujah'. The people, in a state of ecstacy, followed after the penitential preachers, carrying with them burning candles and branches. One particular instance, which may have given rise to the Pied Piper of Hamelin story, immortalized by Byron, comes from Erfurt in Germany where, in 1237, more than one hundred children, following some irresistible urge, left home and set out on foot for Arnstadt. Many are reported to have died on the way while the rest were ever afterwards afflicted with palsy.

Other tales tell of young girls who loved to dance too much depite warnings that they risked being abducted by the devil. One Finnish girl danced the *Melkutus* step (*coupé sauté forwards and back*) for several days until someone suddenly noticed too late that her partner had hooves – the devil had danced her to death.

The story usually associated with the tarantella is that of the spider, whose bite caused the victim to indulge in frenzied movement. The Puglian spider, also known as the tarantula (after the southern Italian town of Taranto, or others say after the river Thara), must have spent most of its life preying on unsuspecting human beings, so many seem to have been afflicted by its poison.

A treatise by E. Fransisci, written in Nürnberg in 1663, goes into considerable detail regarding the appearance and nature of the spider, its nasty habits and its effect upon its human victims. So we learn that some tarantulas are grey with white and black, or red and green spots on their backs; larger ones are black with grey and red stripes. Their favourite haunt is the hot plain in the extreme south of the country. Their bite might only feel like a bee-sting, but the poison spreads throughout the body and soon has the victims running, laughing, shouting, crying, sleeping and so on. Besides dancing, the victims love brightly-coloured objects which they are wont to gnaw and bite like hungry bears. In Taranto, it happened in the presence of Cardinal Cojetani, that a Capuchin monk who had been bitten exchanged his habit for the cardinal's bright red cassock, which he then kissed, and started to dance with it like one possessed. The sick also like to play with naked swords and indulge in serious manœuvres with them (so here we have the tarantula as responsible for the origins of sword dancing also). After about a year, through the heat of the sun or the harmonious sound of music, the poison is activated and the victim starts to dance, losing all sense of decency or decorum. He dances until his sweat drains the poison from his body.

The poison, he goes on to explain, stays with the victim only so long as the spider is alive, there being a magnetic interaction between the spider and its victim. The best cure is to kill the spider and rub its body on the bite, so acting as an antidote to the poison. One sure cure is sweet melodious music. However, a word of caution: if the music is sour, the victim's condition will be worsened. He will roll his eyes, head, neck, and generally writhe in anguish. Each poison requires its own special music, and in order to discover what this is, it is recommended to send musicians out to play to the spiders, which will then respond to their favourite tune by hopping about and dancing. So, if the patient knows what colour of spider bit him, then the musicians will know what music to play to effect a cure – make of this what you will!

In Sicily, a dance by flagellants has survived. On the second Sunday in May, at Villafranca Sicula, the 'Riattate' is danced during the festival of the Madonna of the Myrtle, the dancers ecstatically waving branches of laurel and myrtle.

Fire dancing, while becoming rarer, still exists in Bulgaria, where, on May 21st, the feast day of Sts. Constantine and Helena, the 'Nestinary' take place, with the performers dancing barefoot on burning coals to the accompaniment of bagpipe and drum. A procession, in which sacred icons are carried, precedes this, and horos are danced. The dancers believe that by dancing barefoot on burning embers they can commune with the dead, and under their guidance protect themselves and their community from disease and danger. May is the only month when this can be done, and nowadays they communicate with two Christian saints. Two villages in the Burgas region still observe these rites. The clergy perform the church liturgy on the morning of May 21st, and then the icons of the two saints are taken in procession to a holy spring. The water is duly consecrated and the people drink it, or bottle it to use at some later date in cures. A fire is lighted, and the *nestinari*, 'possessed' by the spirits, the deafening beat of the drums and the blowing of pipes increasing their ecstasy, leap about on the embers. The dancers are reputed to suffer no ill effects – maybe it is because they plunge their feet into a cool mud pool immediately after they have finished dancing, which prevents blisters, or maybe their state of ecstasy makes them immune from blistering.

Death

In the villages of Zvižd and elsewhere in eastern Serbia where Wallachian ethnic groups have settled, they observe special funeral rites in memory of the dead. On All Souls' Day, the *pomane* takes place. The dancers perform a *kolo* round a table on which various dishes have been laid. They wear, hanging from their backs, long white towels decorated with flowers and tiny mirrors. They hold lighted candles stuck into small bouquets of flowers. The rest of the costume is brightly coloured, and their smiling faces contrast strangely with the mournful music which accompanies the dance. Afterwards, the food is carried to the graveside and, to song which is not at all melancholy, they 'invite' the departed souls to supper.

On August 2nd, on top of Mount Željin, they celebrate Elijah's Day with loud music and a *kolo*. Friends and relatives from far afield are united on this day. If, since they last met, a friend or relative has died, they express their condolences by forming a circle, arms round each others' shoulders, and slowly dance the 'Žalosno Kolo', moving clockwise, that is, contary to the direction usually taken in Serbia.

The most striking feature of Romanian funerals is the *bocet*, the keening, that is the weeping and wailing, done by the dead person's family, friends and neighbours. The *bocet* is an improvised lament, in some regions a 'conversation' with the dead person. The funeral wake is sometimes accompanied by masked dancers. In Moldavia and the Vrancea Country until quite recent times, the masked figures performed an ancient dance, in which they jumped over a fire as a sign of purification. Ancient traditional songs, such as 'Dawn' and 'Fir Tree' are sung in Oltenia, southern Transylvania and the Banat, during the different stages of the burial ceremony, a ceremony which prepares the deceased for the last journey, and the occasion for family and friends to take their leave and pay their last respects. 'Pohřebni Tance' is a funeral dance from Czechoslovakia. Some funeral dances have survived in Hungary. There are those which follow funeral feasts, and others where the deceased was young or unmarried, which are danced round the grave. Hired mourners dance carrying wine flasks on their heads.

In Jatea in the south of Valencia in Spain, they perform a dance around the coffin (ill. 124). They believe that if a child dies under the age of six, it goes straight to heaven, not to purgatory, and so it is not a sad occasion.

Wulfstan, the ninth-century Anglo-Saxon missionary, wrote that the Prussians danced at wakes, and other Lithuanian references from the thirteenth to the sixteenth centuries mention dances as part of ceremonial rites, but unfortunately do not give any descriptions.

Until recently in the Hebrides, before they danced on St. Michael's Day, September

29th, the crofters rode round the burial ground in a clockwise direction. They made a cake of each sort of grain on the farms, and then celebrated with games and horse-races. At the dance in the evening was performed the 'Cailleach an Dudain', the 'Old Wife of the Mill Dust'. In it the woman falls down as if dead; the man mimes grief, but then revives her by touching her with a magic wand, and they dance joyfully once again.

Veļi was the name the Letts gave to their All Souls' celebrations, when the dead souls were invited back to participate in a feast. A fortnight after a person's death, family and friends used to get together to 'let the deceased go'. Should a person die before marriage, then a 'marriage' between the dead person and a 'bride' was celebrated.

A dance popular at Irish wakes is described by the English traveller, Dunton, thus:

> *Sometimes they follow one another in a ring (as they say fairies do) in a rude dance to the music of a bagpipe . . . At these meetings the young frye appear as gay as may be, with their holyday apparrell, and with piper, harper, or fiddler revell and dance the night throughout, make love and matches.*

13

COUNTRY DANCING AND DANCING MASTERS

Daunces, Carols and Somour games,
of many swych come many shames.

Church censure, 1303.

Country dances are not ceremonial dances, fixed to the festal calendar, but social dances done purely for recreation. They have always been subject to the whims of fashion, and have been brought into the ballrooms, or discarded, at the dictates of current taste.

Country dance is a term which covers a wide spectrum of social dance. In England, some of these dances are genuinely traditional, that is, they evolved through country usage, but many have been invented. Back in the seventeenth century, there was money to be made from the publication of country dances, and John Playford, a

125. 'De Kermis van St. Joris' by Pieter Brueghel. Flemish, 1564-1637.

music printer, edited a series of collections, only the earliest editions containing anything like original, traditional dances. All the later works are choreographies in the idiom of traditional dance. Fortunately, England was rich in folk-dance tradition, and did not have to rely solely on the 'Playford' dances – nor indeed on those collected by Cecil Sharp. Country dance and the age-old country customs were largely and successfully suppressed by the Puritans, to the extent that, when more lenient times were reintroduced with the Restoration in 1660, few of the old customs crept back in, though of the old country dances there were still many which survived. Cecil Sharp began to search the countryside for these survivals, but he abandoned his search too soon, resorting to plundering the Playford collections instead. Only his 'Country Dance Book I' records the traditional dances he found.

Since the Second World War, when close ties were forged with America and Canada, the square dance has won widespread popularity. And so, in modified form, have many of the country dances, lost to the 'Old Country' following the Puritan suppression, been reintroduced. Back from the Kentucky Mountains have come the progressive rounds; returned too are the formal quadrilles from New England and Quebec, whence they were taken in the nineteenth century by English and French settlers.

The French *contredanse* dates back no further than the seventeenth century. It is not mentioned by Thoinot Arbeau in his 'Orchésographie' (1589), nor for that matter by any other writer on the dance. However, we are fortunate enough to have two references which leave us in no doubt but that the country dance as we know it originated in England. John Weaver, in his 'History of Dancing' (1712) writes that: "Country dances . . . is a dancing the peculiar growth of this nation, tho' now transplanted into almost all the Courts of Europe, and is become in the most august assemblies the favourite diversion." John Essex in his 'Treatise on Chorography, or the art of dancing Country Dances' (1710), says: "This which we call Country Dancing is originally the product of this nation." France adapted one of the forms of the English country dance known as a 'square dance for eight', and gave it the name *contredanse*, in which form it returned to England. The quadrille is one of its numerous varieties. Before long the English quadrille found itself in competition with the *contredanse* in France, according to an article in 'The Times' of January 12th, 1820: "It would appear that *Contredanses* are revived in Paris, to the discountenance of Quadrilles." Such is the perverse nature of changing fashion.

In the eighteenth century, the grand-ball programme would commence with the minuet, and country dances would follow. In the nineteeth century, the valse elbowed out the minuet, though not the country dances, and when the quadrille came in, valse, country dances, and quadrille lived on together. In fact, the new French quadrille was really only an English square country dance under a different name. Then followed a host of couple dances: polkas, mazurkas, csárdás, and so on, originating out of the folk dance of different countries, and becoming universally accepted and popular. These popular couple dances hit country dance hard, particularly in the urban environment, though in the country, where fashion lags behind and things are less susceptible to change, country dance survived, to flourish anew today. In fact, village dances have never totally disappeared, and even now one can go out into the Yorkshire Dales or into Northumbria and find a programme of dances very much like that described by a Mrs. Hall of Newcastle-upon-Tyne in 1929:

> *The programme consisted of 'Circassian Circle', 'Morpeth Rant', 'Corn Rigs', 'Drops of Brandy', 'Roxburgh Castle', 'Call of the Pipes', and 'The Spanish Waltz' . . . There was a good selection of old time dances, also 'The Valeta', 'St. Bernard's Waltz', 'Eva Threestep', 'Boston Twostep', and an uproarious version of 'The Lancers'.*

Of the country dances, the oldest and simplest form is the round, a descendant of the medieval carole, which was a singing dance. Originally, the carole was a ritual dance; the dancers might circle (wassail) a fruit tree to encourage its fruitfulness, or dance round a maypole to bring in the spring. In ancient Greece, as in several countries today, the dancers would circle the village threshing floor, in celebration of a bountiful harvest, and sometimes even stamp on the grain to separate the husks. Of course, it all brought censure from the Church; these lines were penned in 1303:

> *Daunces, Carols and Somour games,*
> *of many swych come many shames.*

When the carole grew into a round country dance, it usually took its name from the tune to which it was danced.

By the sixteenth century, the carole became the round, singing being replaced by instrumental accompaniment. 'Sellenger's Round' is the earliest we know by name, this being derived from Sir Anthony St. Leger who was a noted dancer in court circles in the time of Henry VIII and who became Lord Lieutenant of Ireland. In

126. 'Behold this Peasant Folk' by David Vinckboons. Dutch, 1576-1629.

1548, Scottish Lowland shepherds were seen to "dance in a ring; every old shepherd led his wife by the hand, and every young shepherd her whom he loveth best". From the round developed the square for three or four couples, the men facing the women. Elizabeth I's maids-of-honour, we are told, loved 'Trenchmore' and the old 'Cushion Dance', finding them a light relief from court pavanes, courantes and galliards. James I called for "only Country dances" as they did not know the French ones, and Pepys tells us how Charled II delighted in his native figures, and describes how he led 'Cuckolds all Awry', the "dance of old England". This dance appears in the first edition of Playford's 'Dancing Master'. The next development was the 'Longways for as Many as Will', the men facing the women as in 'Sir Roger de Coverley'. This particular dance retained its popularity up until the Second World War. It became the traditional finale to the party – when the hostess announced 'Sir Roger de Coverley' it was always understood to be the last dance and time to go home.

From 1651 to 1728, the seventeen Playford editions provided a host of new dances for the eager ball-goer. But out in the country, the old dances retained their popularity well into the nineteenth century. Thomas Hardy's Dorset folk enjoyed their 'hands-six-round', and the Elizabethan 'Cushion Dance', thanks largely no doubt to the kissing which lingered long in Cornish and Cotswold villages. Other dances were popular up to the mid-nineteenth century: the jig and the hornpipe, which however lost popularity in England, along with the reel, but which were adopted by the Scots and the Irish, and enjoy a new lease of life.

Country dancing spread from England to Ireland. An English traveller, Thomas Dineley wrote in 1681:

127. 'Kermesse at Hoboken' by Pieter Brueghel the Elder. Flemish, 16th century.

> *They are at this day much addicted (on holidayes, after the bagpipe, Irish harpe, or Jews harpe) to dance after their countrey fashion, the long dance one after another of all conditions master, mrs, servants.*

Country dances and figure dances based on the jig and reel were popular in the early part of the nineteenth century in Ireland, and ousted for the most part the older country dances. The reel of three and the reel of four or common reel were later followed by the eight-hand reel (High Caul Cap) and the sixteen-hand reel (Humours of Bandon). Other dances, derived from the quadrille which was very popular in the Paris of Napoléon's time, were introduced into England and Ireland on their return by Wellington's victorious soldiers. The dancing masters adapted these new dances, substituting Irish steps for those of the ballroom, and speeding them up to match the time of the jig and common reel. The sets of quadrilles, called 'sets' when four couples danced, and 'half-sets' when only two couples danced, became popular all over Ireland. Adapted to suit Irish traditional tunes, they retained their popularity for over one hundred years, until they in turn were elbowed out by revivalists, who regarded them as 'foreign', and who regarded only *céilí* dances as acceptable social activities.

Céilí means a gathering of neighbours in the evening at some house, to talk and gossip. Originally no music or dancing took place, and, in fact, the first *céilí* as we know it today was organized, not in Ireland but in London, by the newly founded *Conradh na Gaeilge* or Gaelic League, in October 1897. A form of group dancing, in which men and women faced each other in two lines, where they performed the

128. 'Kermesse Flamande' by Nicolas de Bruyn after David Vinckeboons.

double jig, was devised. By a linking movement, the couple changed places between each step, which meant that only every second step was performed in the dancer's original place.

Reels, country, square and circle dances made up the repertoire of dances in Scotland. Today, the distinction between these categories has become blurred, but formerly each had its special characteristics. The 'reel' proper consists of 'setting steps' danced on the spot, alternating with a travelling figure. This last usually remains the same throughout the dance, while the setting steps can be as varied as the dancers wish. A change in the musical rhythm in the course of the dance is an unusual feature of the dance, which may begin to a strathspey and change to a reel. The Scotch or Highland reel is commonly known as the 'Foursome Reel'. The setting steps are performed by the dancers in lines, the travelling step following the pattern of a figure-of-eight with a third loop added. The 'Eightsome Reel' differs in its construction from the true reels, though its style of performance is similar.

The country dances were performed in two parallel lines, each couple progressing down the set in turn, the change of place being only one remove, as in Petronella, or from the top to the bottom as in Strip the Willow. The Scots understand 'Square Dance' as a type of quadrille, four couples standing in a square – Lancers is a typical example. The term circle dance did not signify a round dance, but a dance in which the couples progressed round the dance floor in a circle. Also popular in Scotland were the polka, schottische and varsovienne. Outside these classifications came a miscellany of other dances such as the 'Bumpkin', 'Spanish Waltz' 'Circassian Circle', 'Dashing White Sergeant', 'Ninepins', and a kissing dance variously known as 'Babbity Bowster', 'Bee Bo Babbity', or the 'White Cockade'.

Of all these dances, only the reels can be said to be truly indigenous to Scotland. These were danced in all regions and by all classes of society. Often performed in barns or croft-house kitchen, the reel, with its compact travelling figures and alternating vigorous stepping, was well suited to the confined dancing space available. Country, square and circle dances came to Scotland from about 1700 onwards, though rapidly the Scots contributed their own figures inspired by native reels. The dances originally were introduced for the amusement of the upper classes, but before the end of the eighteenth century, they had become popular with ordinary working people also in the Lowlands and southern Highlands, though not until about 1880 in the remoter Highlands and islands.

If the country dance came from England, the square dances (quadrilles) were introduced directly from Paris by the soldiers returning from the Napoleonic Wars. The circle dances also came from the continent, the valse being introduced in the early years of the nineteenth century. The mazurka followed, and towards the middle of the century, the polka. Others flooded in soon afterwards, whilst barn dances were introduced from America towards the end of the century.

The hiring fairs, where people both sought work and workers, provided a popular venue for dancing, for the hiring fairs were also fairs in the more conventional sense, with travelling salesmen and stall-holders plying their wares. Custom demanded that a man having several dances with a girl should present her with her 'fairin', usually a box of sweets bought from one of the stalls. A girl who managed to collect several such boxes during the course of the fair could boast of her popularity. 'Penny reels' were a feature of some fairs, where the fiddle player would charge the dancers a penny per dance to provide the musical accompaniment. The 'harvest home' or *kirn* provided another occasion for dancing, which took place in the barn or granary of the farm. *Ceilidhs* in the croft houses or outside on moonlit nights were further opportunities for dancing to the fiddle or the pipes, as also were the annual balls given in some parts of the Highlands by the laird for his tenants and neighbours.

The kissing dance was once very widespread throughout Scotland. In it couples were paired off, having alternately selected a partner by a kiss, sometimes kneeling on a handkerchief whilst the piper or the fiddler played a special 'kissing' phrase. One finds in Denmark the fiddler scraping his bow across the bridge of his instrument to indicate that a kiss should be given. Formerly the couple knelt on a pillow. (Playford described a similar dance in which a cushion was used and which was very popular in Elizabethan court circles.) The Scottish name 'Babbity Bowster (Bob at the Bolster) relates to the time when a bolster was used instead of a handkerchief, and is probably an oblique reference to the bridal bed. The tune 'Pease Strae' to which the dance was sometimes performed had this little verse:

The best bed, the feather bed
The best bed ov a'
The best bed i' wor hoose
Is clean pea straw.

129. 'Country Dance' by Pieter Bloot. Dutch, 16th century.

In Northumberland, these words were actually sung by the dancers of the kissing game, which here was known as the 'Cushion Dance' or 'Pease Straw'.

There are many references to traditional dancing in Wales in old manuscripts. The reputation that Welsh dancing acquired for being boisterous and energetic was already apparent from the remarks of Giraldus Cambrensis, when, concerning a feast celebrating St. Almedah's Day in Brecon in 1188, he wrote: "There was dancing one minute on the green round the church, and the next minute wounded and unfortunates circled the church seeking cures." In 1284 the dancing, which followed a tournament at Nefyn, was so energetic that the floor collapsed.

The Rev. Richard Warner, in 1798, made a journey through Wales. He described attending a Welsh ball:

> *'Tis true there is no great variety in the figures of them, but the few they perform are so complicated and long that they would render an apprenticeship to them necessary in an Englishman. We therefore contented ourselves with looking on, and were really astonished at the agility and skill which these rusticks displayed. Our surprise, however, was still more excited by the performance of a custom which, as it is not practised at the Bath Balls we were not prepared to expect. On a sudden the dance ceased, and the harper, running his finger rapidly down*

130. 'Récreation Flamande' by Jean Moyreau. Flemish, 17th century.

the chords of his instrument, gave the accustomed signal on which every gentleman saluted his partner three or four times with considerable ardour. The dancing then re-commenced with such spirit as convinced us that this interlude had added to the energies of all the parties concerned. The ball was concluded by a contest of agility between two brothers, who danced two distinct hornpipes with so much power and muscle, variety of step and inflexible perseverance as exceeded everything of the kind we had seen.

In 1892, William Williams, in his Antiquities and Traditions of Llanberis and the Surrounding District, refers to the "immoral and corrupt customs before the coming of Non-Conformity and the light of the pulpit and the Sunday school". He expands further: "Young people on a Saturday night had *nosweithiau llawen* (merry nights) where they entertained themselves singing and dancing to the harp until daybreak on the Sabbath." The Welsh suffered more than most from the fervent zeal of the religious revival which took place in Wales during the latter part of the nineteenth and the early years of the twentieth centuries, and which persecuted and exiled old traditional dances practically out of existence. Almost but not quite, for two collections of dances, the 'Llangadfan' and the 'Nantgarw' were set down to ensure their survival.

The Llangadfan dances were noted by William Jones (1729-95) of Llangadfan, Montgomeryshire. The three dances which make up the collection are for three couples, and are in three parts: the first for the men (and called the *leading* part)

131 'Fête dans une Auberge' by Jan Steen. Dutch, 1626-1679. © Photo R.M.N.

is followed by a men's hey; the women's is the *tracing* and is followed by a women's hey; and finally comes the *turnings* followed by *cross keys*, the dance being concluded by a progressive round. 'Aly Grogan' (Lumps of Pudding) should, he tells us, "be performed as simple buoyant walking steps, with a double hop for the Heys".

There are nine dances in the Nantgarw collection, remembered from the 1880's by Margretta Thomas of Nantgarw, Glamorganshire, two being solos, the rest being for four couples. Nantgarw in the 1880's and 1890's was a typical Welsh rural community, the only industry being the pottery works. Old customs were fostered by the Men's Club, despite the stern puritanism which viewed games and dancing with abhorrence. After their annual fête at the nearby village of Y Groeswen, dancing, chiefly solos, to the accompaniment of a harp took place. Also on fairdays at Caerphilly and Tongwynlais, a dance floor or area was set up for the dancers from outlying villages to amuse themselves and also to collect the customary donations from the onlookers. One of these dances, the 'Rali twm Sion' is described as being for twelve dancers who lead round, dance heys, lead round once more, cast out, weave up, before marching to the corners and serpenting back, much in the manner of a processional morris. The men and women did not link as partners, being unable to take hands as they were carrying bells on their fingers.

Dance knows no frontiers. Fashion carries it from one country to another. Often a dance can turn up in a foreign country, long forgotten in the land of its origin.

132. 'Sunday Evening in a Dalecarlia Cottage' by Amalia Lindegren. Swedish, 1860.

Different countries at different times have set the fashion. Sometimes dances crop up elsewhere under different names, quite unrecognizable from their original name. Thus the Dutch today dance 'Anna van Duinen', a corruption of a French quadrille figure *en avant deux*. The French who gave the name *contredanse* to the country dance also termed it the *vis à vis*, and this the Alsatians turned into 'Wisewi'. In Hessen in Germany, the 'Siciliano' is known under the name 'Zisseljänner.

The country dance may well have originated in England, but, if not, the English certainly made it their own, and contributed most to its development and elaboration. In his 'Recueil de Contre-danses' (1707), Feuillet states that the English were the 'first inventors' of the country dance, and one can recognize the English 'Greensleeves' in his 'Les Manches Vertes'. When Robert Walpole was in Florence in 1740 he exclaimed that "Italians are fond to a degree of our Country dances", and at about the same time, the Romans were dancing 'Piselli al Burro', none other than the English 'Buttered Peas'. In Portugal too in the early nineteenth century, a writer described how "in many societies, particularly in the provinces, the English Country dances are still in use". In Vianna do Castello in Portugal today they still dance 'O Pretinho' which is identical to 'Strip the Willow'. The dance seems to have travelled widely throughout Europe. In France, for example, it is to be found under the name of 'la Boulangère' (the Baker's Wife) in which the plaiting figures of the dance reflect the plaited loaf of bread. In Norway, the 'Sekstur' is a purely English country dance. English country dances also travelled across the Atlantic, and have sometimes returned to England under a changed name, when the original was long forgotten in the old country.

Sea-borne commerce has spread English country dances all over northern Europe. Sometimes the host country has superimposed elements belonging to their own children's games, such as hand-clapping, finger-wagging, bowing, kissing, and chucking under the chin, as in the Dutch 'Drickusman', the English 'Sweet Kate', the Swedish 'Klappdans', or the Czechoslovak 'Judentans'. In Latvia, country-dance figures are found in 'Ackups', 'Sudmalinas' and 'Jandalins'. In Austria in 1717, an English lady described the Viennese ball as always concluding with English country dances.

Dancing masters

Many countries employed dancing masters in their armies and navies. Indeed, for a Jew in the Imperial Russian Army it was the only way of gaining a commission. For the officers it was a chance to learn (or brush up on) the social graces, for, even when on campaign, not all the time was spent on the battlefield, and there was ample opportunity for the officers to socialize in high society, and for the ranks to fraternize with the locals. Thus did Napoléon's troops learn foreign dances at two levels, court and peasant, and spread them to those parts of the Continent they had yet to reach. In this way the polonaise, mazurka, and many other dances travelled across the face of Europe. From the seventeenth to the nineteenth centuries, when they were not engaged in training the military or the marine, the dancing masters would be out and about in the provinces, teaching the townsfolk and villagers all the latest fashionable dances and the skills required to dance them.

If the French dancing masters borrowed their steps from the Basques, they amply repaid their debt by giving to the Provençals, whose dance today is a reflection of the dancing masters' instruction and art. The Basques are quite adamant that their dance came first, and, as Classical Ballet had to have its roots somewhere, there seems no good reason to dispute the Basque claim. It was in the wake of the visit of Louis XIV to the Basque Country to meet the Spanish Infanta, when he saw and was duly impressed by Basque dancing, that court dancing masters were sent south to learn from the Basques.

Basque dance is full of the repertoire of steps which now we associate with Classical Ballet. However, the picture is complicated somewhat by the fact that we do know that dancing masters were active in the Basque Country during the eighteenth and nineteenth centuries, and the question which arises is, did their presence in any way affect the existing dance there? No doubt it did, even if it was only to hone and polish the steps that the Basques were already performing. Certainly Basque dance looks, and is, highly trained. It is not a form of dance one picks up casually at college, or in adult life. Boys from an early age (girls too nowadays) attend class and work hard to attain the refinements and skill demanded by their dances.

The Provençal situation is somewhat different. In this part of France, civilized by Greeks and Romans, and enjoying all the trappings of that civilization in the form of buildings, social amenities, and the arts, this land was less affected by the fall of the Roman Empire and the Barbarian invasions, and retained much that, in other regions and countries, was destroyed. Here, the dance provides us with a unique link between ancient times and modern. Chain dances no doubt existed long before the Phoenicians, Greeks and others set up colonies here, but, watching a line of dancers performing the 'Pas Grec', transports one immediately to a little square in some Greek village, where the steps and feeling for the dance are not all that

133. 'Dancing Master Öberg giving a Lesson'. Swedish.

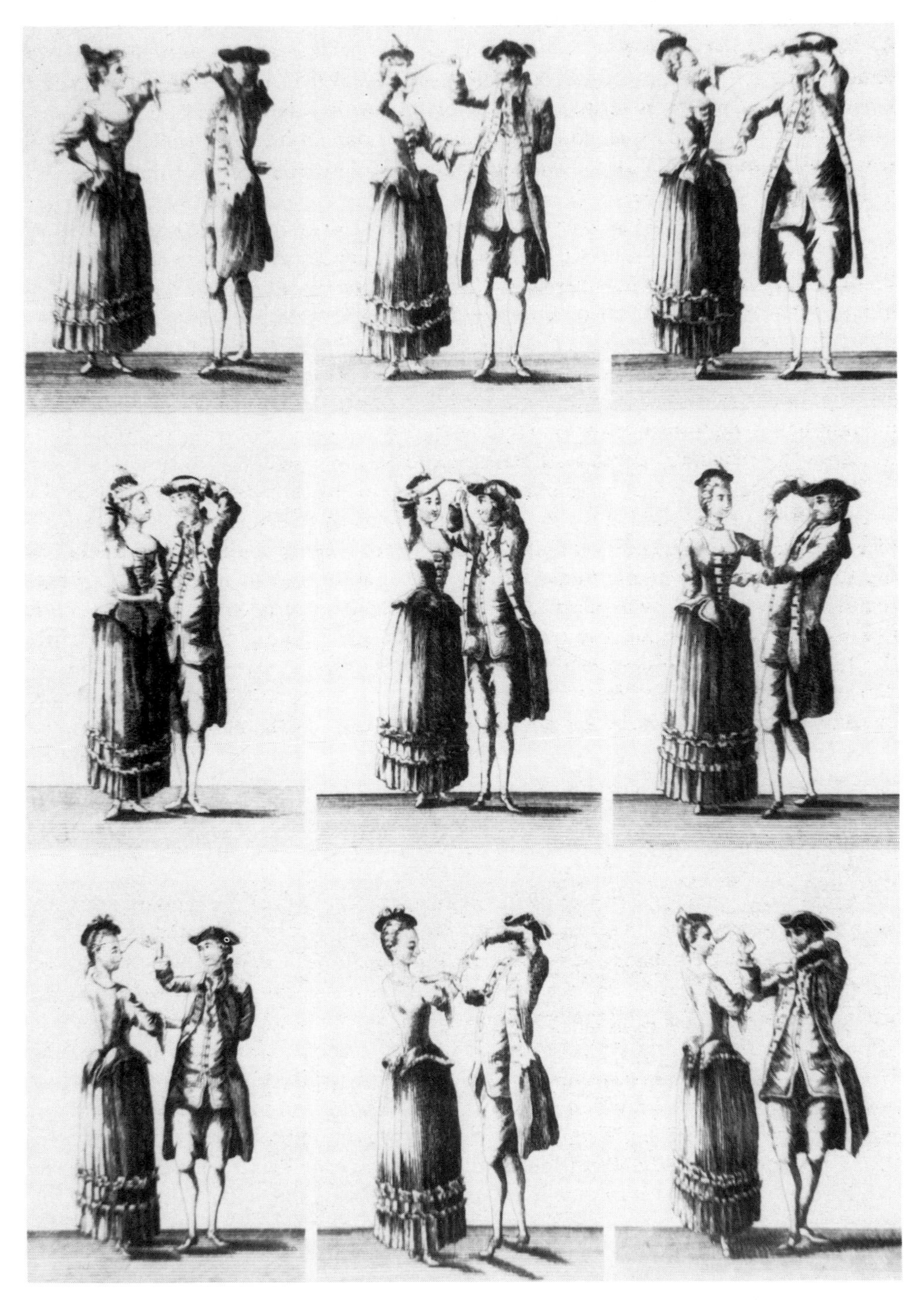

134. 'Nine Figures from the Allemande' from 'Positions et Attitudes de l'Allemande'. Paris, 1768.

far removed. The 'Pas Grec' is not so much the invention of the dancing masters as an adaptation of existing folk dance, the steps now becoming more defined and regulated. Nevertheless, here we have a dance which we can recognize and classify as folk dance. It is a transitional dance of transitional difficulty. Here are the steps learned in Barbentane, one of the leading centres of the dancing masters:

> 1st *enchaînement*: Step forwards on the R.F., & close L.F. to R.F. Step forwards on the R.F., at same time throwing the L. leg out to the L. side in a high kicking movement. *Coupé* over with the L. leg, ending with R. leg in *jeté derrière* position. Extend R. leg in a high kick to the R. side, *assemblé* over. Repeat in reverse.
> 2nd *enchaînement*: *Sissonne doublé* under to the R. side. Hopping on L.F., place R. heel to 2nd, place R.F. with inverted toe to 2nd, jump feet together. Repeat to other side.
> 3rd *enchaînement*: Travelling forwards, *coupé* under with the R.F., and step forwards on the L.F. Close R.F. to L.F. Repeat with other foot. 2 *grands pas de basque* making a full turn on each, travelling backwards and commencing each with the R.F. Repeat.

The Provençals refer to *batterie* rather than *enchaînement*, and use a very different terminology. Here is another version of the 'Pas Grec' as it appears in a French teaching manual:

> *1re Batterie: Pas russe, terre à terre, pas russe, ange perdu à droite, à gauche,*
> *2e – Passer la jambe devant, derrière, devant et pirouette à droite et à gauche,*
> *3e – Brissé devant, glissade et brisé en arrière, glissade et terre à terre, balancement de jambe,*
> *4e – Pas russe sur les 4 faces, brisé, entrechats 2 fois.*

We can now watch a series of dances which become ever more demanding, ever more the product of the dancing masters, and whilst still based on the traditional dance, are leaving traditional dance far behind. Waiting for us on the next to the top rung of the ladder is the 'Gavotte'. This is the test piece for those aspiring to become *prévôts* of the dance, second only to the master's diploma.

The gavotte started life off as just another branle, one performed by those people living in the alpine region around Gap, and who were nicknamed 'gavot' or 'gavotte' by the Provençals. Stuck indoors for much of the long hard winter, these mountain dwellers danced in their barns and stables to song accompaniment. As happens everywhere, the young people vied with each other in the swiftness, intricacy and pyrotechnics of their variations, and, come the patronal feast day, they would be there, in the village square, pitting their skills against their rivals. Competition was enhanced by the best couple being chosen to display their dancing skills for all to enjoy, the right to kiss all the boys or girls, and to present the *bouquet* to the organizers of the next year's festival (rather like being chosen to carry the flame at the Olympic Games).

135. Sailor's dance from 'Neue und Curieuse theatralische Tantz-Schul' by Gregorio Lambranzi, Nürnberg. German 1716.

As pedlars, the 'gavots' went as far afield as Paris, Flanders, and even up into Scandinavia. It is not improbable that, in order to earn a few extra pennies, they displayed their dancing talents, giving rise to their springing step being named *pas de gavotte*. The *pas de gavotte*, amalgamated with galliard steps, in course of time became a 'courting' dance, and, because of its subtle changes from lively and gay to slow and serious, it became a model of grace and delicacy, and a great court favourite. It was already known by the time Thoinot Arbeau described the gavotte as:

> *a miscellany and mixture of several* branles doubles *which the performers have chosen and which they have composed into a suite . . . to which they have given the name* gavottes, *which they dance in duple time with little springs in the style of the Haut-Barrois, and which consists of a* double *to the right and a* double *to the left, like the common branles, except that the dancers interrupt these aforementioned* doubles *to right and to left with passages taken at pleasure from the galliardes . . .*

In court ceremonial, the gavotte became the branle of the young people, and followed the more reserved branle double of the older members and the livelier and gayer branle reserved for the middle aged or married couples. The gavotte remained in favour at the courts of Louis XIV, Louis XV, and Louis XVI, and was still *à la mode* during Napoléon's Consulate. It passed into the theatre, where it mimed a scene of courtship between two dancers, became a favourite of star performers, and was immortalised by the two Vestris, father and son. It incorporated all the steps of Classical Ballet: *jetés*, *pas de basque*, *pas de zéphyr*, *pas de bourrée*, *entrechats*, *ailes de pigeon*, *brisés*, and so on, and became a veritable concert piece, far removed from its humble beginnings as the branle from Gap. In the hands (or feet might be more appropriate) of the famous dancing master, Jean Baptiste Duffaut (1850-1932), it was given incomparable nobility.

Nevertheless, the pinnacle of the dancer's achievement was to perfect the Gigue Anglaise, and thus earn one's master's diploma. Try this J.B. Duffaut version before breakfast:

> *La grande promenade à droite, à gauche,*
> *Marcher en avant, en arrière, 3 mesures de talons,*
> *La boiteuse à droite, à gauche, rappel final,*
> *Rappel final en avant, en arrière, 3 mesures de talons,*
> *Les ciseaux en tournant à droite, à gauche,*
> *Pas de cheval en avant, en arrière,*
> *Les ciseaux à droite, à gauche,*
> *La petite promenade à droite,*
> *Les terre à terre à droite, à gauche et pirouette en six temps,*
> *La petite promenade à gauche,*
> *Terre à terre à droite, à gauche, les grands écarts,*
> *Les ciseaux en avant, en arrière,*
> *Les ciseaux en tournant, à droite, à gauche,*
> *Ciseaux, pas de farandole, brisé, balancement (se fait sur place),*

136. Sailor's dance from 'Neue und Curieuse theatralische Tantz-Schul' by Gregorio Lambranzi, Nürnberg. German 1716.

Ciseaux, changement de talon, pas tombé (deux fois),
Rappel, glissade et brisé à droite, à gauche, pas de bourrée,
Rappel et final sur place double,
Final à droite, à gauche, sur place,
Les triolets en avant, en arrière, rappel final,
Terre à terre, à droite, à gauche et pirouette en six temps, Les grands écarts doubles et entrechat en avant et en arrière.

All this had to be performed with a rigid torso and plenty of *balon*. Often the dancer was required to carry a baton, sergeant-major fashion under one arm, to keep the upper body quite still.

The earliest references to Irish solo or step dances date from the late eighteenth century, since which time they have been honed and polished and brought to the heights of technical perfection. They undoubtedly owe their existence to the dancing masters. That the dancing masters did not need to look far for their pupils is evidenced by a seventeenth-century account, which relates how the people of Cork would bring their children up to be able to dance, play the fiddle and to fence, even if they could afford nothing else.

Dancing masters appeared on the Irish social scene during the second half of the eighteenth century. They taught rich and poor alike. Indeed, such was the passion for dancing among the poor, that cottars, living in their mean hovels, were prepared to pay the dancing master to teach their children dancing. It was usual for the dancing master to stay several weeks in one place, hiring a barn or the use of a kitchen from a farmer, or the villagers might even erect a temporary shelter for the purpose. The master might be housed by the farmer, whose children he would teach without payment, or else he would rest the night with each of his pupils in turn. It was deemed a great honour to host the dancing master.

He had his territory, respecting his rivals' territory as he expected them to respect his. Meetings between rivals at some country fair or sporting event often led to challenges, and, to the public joy, they would dance in competition with one another, even putting up their territory as the stake. To make it more difficult, it was even known for them to compete, dancing on the soaped top of an upturned barrel.

The dancing masters, besides teaching the native dances, would also give lessons in the valse or quadrille. They might also instruct their wealthier clients in deportment and fencing. They were expected to invent new and intricate steps, and because they required the most skill and practice, it was the solo dances which were held in greatest esteem. His less able pupils were given less demanding round and group dances to maintain their interest, but, as all had been instructed in the basic steps of jig and reel, we may suppose that the standard of performance was unexpectedly high.

The 'jig', 'reel' and 'hornpipe' are the principal dances in the category of solo or step dances. The most popular of these is the 'common' or 'double' jig, performed by one or more couples. It starts off with the 'rising-step', the pupil's first step taught. In this the right foot is thrown forwards a little way off the ground, a hop made on the left foot while the right foot is drawn back to tap the floor, before tapping left, right, left. This is done to one bar of music and is repeated three times. On the fourth bar of the music, the boy does the 'grinding step' (the girl the 'shuffle') on the left foot. To perform the grinding step, the ball of each foot alternately strikes the floor to the six notes of the bar. It was considered unladylike for the girl to perform the boy's steps, so the girl would follow the rising step and shuffle with graceful sliding steps. As the dance progressed, each step would become more elaborate, each time rounding off with the shuffle. The men's steps were made ever more intricate by introducing grinding, battering and drumming steps in various combinations. In a contest between rival dancing masters, one performed a total of thirty-six distinct steps, only to be outdone by the other who managed a further six.

The 'hop' or 'slip' jig is performed to a tune in 9/8 time, and is considered the most graceful of the step dances. Two couples together usually perform this dance, which consists of light hopping, tripping and sliding actions, though as each couple dances independently of the other, the number of couples is really not important. The dance alternates between more complex steps *sur place* and promenading round with a light skipping movement before returning to one's place. The 'reel' also alternates steps and promenade, though a side step may be substituted.

The 'hornpipe' was a man's dance. The steps required a vigour and sound which it was felt only a man could bring to them. However, the ladies of Cork insisted on dancing the hornpipe, as also the heavier steps in jigs and reels.

The special feature most instilled into the pupil, who wished to be a respected step dancer, was the control and restraint exercised, although the performance required vigour and speed. The good dancer must keep his body rigid, arms extended straight down at the side, and only moving from the hips down. The hands must not be flung about wildly or be flourished head high. It was said that the good dancer should be able to dance on eggs without smashing them, and balance a pan of water on his head without a drop being spilled. Neither did the dancer need to travel, a small table top providing adequate space for his performance.

The English traveller, John Carr, in his 'Stranger in Ireland' (1805) wrote: "A Sunday with the peasantry in Ireland is not unlike the same day in France. After the hours of devotion, the bagpipe is heard, and every foot is in motion." Every countryman is said to have had his halfpenny to pay the piper on a Sunday afternoon.

Scotland too had its professional dancing masters who, however, unlike the Irish itinerant dancing masters, had their studios in the bigger towns, but would teach also in the neighbouring villages and smaller towns, pupils coming in from the outlying crofts on foot and walking several miles there and back to learn the 'Reel of Tulloch', 'Flowers of Edinburgh', 'Haymakers Jig', 'Rory O'More', 'Blue Bonnets', 'Cumberland Reel', or any of the country, square and circle dances becoming ever more popular. Most children took dancing lessons by the end of the nineteenth century, and dancing masters and pupils participated in the Highland Games, dancing being held at least in equal esteem to sports and other arts. The dancing master would besides all these teach a variety of 'step' dances to include Highland solo dances.

Aberdeen had its official public dancing master at least as early as 1695, when we hear that one of his duties was to arrange the public balls which were a feature of the town's social life. Aberdeen, where the Kirk never had absolute control over the running of affairs, was the centre of much counter-reformation activity, and dancing seems always to have played an important part in the life of the people.

Francis Peacock was one of the most revered teachers to have held the post of official dancing master here. In 1747, he was appointed "to be sole dancing master within the burgh during his good behaviour." His conduct must have been exemplary, for he held the post until his death in 1807. The influence of the dancing masters was to be felt well into the twentieth century.

Francis Peacock was greatly impressed by the footwork of the Highland dancing which he found already waiting for him, when he left his native Edinburgh to take up his new appointment. He wrote:

> *I once had the pleasure of seeing, in a remote part of the country, a Reel danced by a herd boy and two young girls, who surprised me much, especially the boy, who appeared to be about the age of twelve. He had a variety of well chosen steps, and executed them with so much justness and ease, as if he meant to set criticism at defiance.*

'High' dances, that is solo and step dances, *pas de deux* and *pas de trois*, were composed especially to display the individual skills of the pupils, and these compositions often employed very intricate and balletic steps. Into the repertoires of the dancing masters, now arranged, adapted and undergoing considerable change to suit girls as well as boys, came: the 'Highland Fling', 'Lochaber Broadswords', 'Highland Laddie', the 'Ghillie Callum' and 'Sean Trubhais'. An Irish spectator at one of these exhibitions was heard to remark: "I never saw children so handy with their feet."

We can learn much about the social history of the time through the description of the lessons taught in the early nineteenth century from the pen of Elizabeth Grant, who in her 'Memoirs of a Highland Lady' delightfully evokes the social life of the period with great skill. She describes how:

> *A dancing master taught us every variety of wonderful Highland step – that is, he taught me, for William never could learn anything, though he liked hopping about to the fiddle – and we did 'Merrily danced the Quaker's wife' together, quite to the satisfaction of the servants, who all took lessons too, in common with the rest of the population, the Highlanders considering this art an essential in the education of all classes, and never losing an opportunity of acquiring a few more flings and shuffles. The dancing master had, however, other most distinguished pupils, the present Duke of Manchester, and his elder sister Lady Jane Montague, who were then living in our close neighbourhood with their grandmother the Duchess of Gordon.*

So we see that the grandees and the ordinary folk not only shared a dancing master to learn additional 'flings and shuffles', but shared the ballroom too. She continues:

> *We children sometimes displayed our accomplishments on these occasions in a prominent manner, to the delight, at any rate of our dancing master. Lady Jane was really clever in the Ghillie Callum and the Shean Trews,*

I little behind her in the single and double fling, the shuffle and the heel-and-toe step. The boys were more blundering, and had to bear the good-natured laugh of many a hard-working lass and lad who, after the toil of the day, footed it neatly and lightly in the ballroom till near midnight.

The Highland dances continued to remain popular, but the new quadrilles rapidly came to sweep away the old minuet, which might not have been so popular as those who bemoaned its decease gave it credit for. It is but natural that the older generation gives up with reluctance the things that are familiar, and is unwilling to accept the introduction of new-fangled ideas. The dancing masters had a living to earn, and were not averse to giving their pupils what they wanted. Elizabeth Grant wrote:

We young people were all bit by the quadrille mania, and I was one of a set that brought them first to notice. We practised privately with the aid of a very much better master than Mr. Smart. Finlay Dunn had been abroad, and imported all the most graceful steps from Paris; and having kept our secret well, we burst upon the world at a select reunion at the White Melvilles, the spectators standing on chairs and sofas to admire us . . . People danced *in those days; we did not merely stand and talk, look about bewildered for our vis-à-vis, return to our partners either too soon or too late, without any regard to the completion of the figure, the conclusion of the measure, or the step belonging to it; we attended to our business, we moved in cadence, easily and quietly, embarrasing no one and appearing to advantage ourselves. So well did we all perform, that our exhibition was called for and repeated several times in the course of the evening. We had no trouble in enlisting co-operators, the rage for quadrilles spread, the dancing master was in every house, and every other style discarded.*

It was thanks to the dancing masters that there was a common bond in dancing. Thus the middle and upper-working class elements of the towns learned together their quadrilles, mazurkas, valses, polkas and so on in public halls and dance studios. Out in the country, the youth gathered in a farm kitchen, schoolroom or barn or, occasionally, they would take their lessons at the laird's 'big hoose' along with his family.

At the end of the season the dancing master would organize a ball to show what his pupils had achieved, and to which all were cordially invited, with the proviso that "anyone under the influence of liquor, or using bad language, or annoying the pupils or the parents will be expelled from the Room and their Tickets cancelled". A typical programme from the north of England, towards the end of the nineteenth century, would have consisted of: 'Polka', 'Square Eight Reel', 'Hoop Dance', 'Quadrille', 'Clog Dance', 'Circassian Circle', 'Skirt Dance', 'Schottische', 'Highland Fling', 'Clog Hornpipe', 'Lancers Quadrilles', 'Waltz', 'New Highland Reel', 'Dancing through the Hoop', 'Varsoviana', 'Skipping Rope Dance', all liberally interspersed with a variety of 'Hornpipes', performed by the star pupils whose names were individually listed in the programme.

Stepping

Chain and round dances were popular in Wales in the Middle Ages. The *jongleurs* entertained their audiences with their acrobatic antics, and their tricky footwork may well have influenced the 'fancy' steps to be found in Welsh clogging. In the middle of the nineteenth century, one writer described Welsh dancing as being "exceedingly energetic and boisterous with its toe and heel clicking, in perfect time with the music . . .there was no slithering, sliding and walking, as in the modern fashionable *quadrille* dancing to be seen in other parts of Britain." Clogging or stepping seems to be an unbroken tradition in Wales.

Step dancing or clogging has long been part of the life of northern England, where clogs have been worn by workers both in town and country. Building upon the basic vocabulary of steps, the individual dancers create their own improvisations, often giving rise to a competitive spirit. Regionally the style and method of placing the steps can differ slightly, but overall the 'look' of the dance remains the same, with a quiet upright carriage, all the energy being channelled into the footwork.

Whilst nowadays no-one associates step dancing with the rather balletic style of Scotland, in Nova Scotia, the descendants of the Scottish immigrants dance a form of step dancing almost identical to the Irish.

It is in Ireland and amongst Irish communities abroad, however, that step dancing is really to be seen in its most developed form. It has been highly polished for competitive dancing, and today thousands of people from children to adults attend classes to perfect their technique. This development has given rise to a new costume for the competitive occasion. The girls wear a short dress, usually of velvet, and heavily embroidered with Celtic motifs. The colours owe little to tradition, and range widely according to individual taste. The old Kerry cloak, in which the wearer could literally wrap herself up, has given way to a very short and purely decorative cape. The boys wear the traditional kilt with shirt and jacket.

In Portugal, the fandango gives us another example of men's competitive step dancing. Here, like the Irish dancing masters, two men will compete in displaying their virtuosity and originality. An interesting feature is how, while each takes his turn in display, his opponent 'prowls' up and down, dancing a basic fandango step.

CONCLUSION

It is still possible to assemble an impressive collection of folk customs, though now few, if any, are observed with regard to their original purpose. Where masks are donned and 'fancy' costumes worn, it is no longer to drive out the evil spirits of winter but rather for amusement only and, maybe, an ever underlying, lurking belief that if age-old customs are not observed then ill fortune might visit the community.

A few remnants still remain with us, taking on a different guise to fit in with present-day life. Spring cleaning, if done at all nowadays, is for the practical reason of taking advantage of the warmer, dryer weather after the cold and damp of winter. Now it seems sensible to open all the doors and windows wide, to clean away the dust and cobwebs, and to let light and fresh air into the house. Winter and summer, darkness and light – perhaps somewhere in a deep folk memory we are still hedging our bets.

If Europe were still partially living in an age of innocence at the close of the nineteenth century, then the two world wars of the first half of the twentieth century rapidly changed all that. In fact, greater changes took place in that period than at any other time in our history. War affected neutrals and combatants alike, and the peoples of Europe were forced into rapid maturity. Folk customs appeared to have less and less relevance in the lives of populations reeling from the effects of global strife, and who were intent merely on survival.

Yet, hanging on to ancient ways, preserving folk tales, songs, costumes, customs and dances, however irrelevant at first sight it may appear to our present way of life, is important beyond measure. These are our very roots, things which have been with us for thousands of years, and to lose them now would be an act of criminal neglect. Fortunately for all of us, this is now unlikely to happen, as more and more people interest themselves in all the various aspects of folk culture, and join societies to sing and dance, and to come together at the numerous international festivals which take place in nearly every country of Europe. It is on occasions like these, when the peoples of the world unite in a common passion for their folk heritage, that one realizes that it really is most relevant to our lives. Here, at such gatherings, we can join hands in the dance and learn the futility and ignorance of intolerance and suspicion - long let us dance together in peace and friendship!

Appendix A
The Sun, the Moon, and the Dance

Why do some dances move clockwise and others counter-clockwise? It is to do with whether one is dancing in honour of the sun or of the moon. Early Man observed how the sun, the moon and the stars moved in the sky. He saw how, when he stood facing south, as the sun rose in the east and set in the west, it traced a path which took it in a clockwise direction (the most suitable term to use since we have made the hands of our clocks follow the path of the sun). A dance honouring the sun would therefore travel sunwise. But we know that in some societies it was the moon which took precedence over the sun, and dances honouring the moon are supposed to travel counter-clockwise. Yet the moon travels in the same direction as the sun. There is one explanation which in the absence of a better one will have to do, though it is not possible to prove whether it is valid or not.

As has already been said, our forbears spent more time than their modern counterparts in watching heavenly bodies (the only ones we watch today are on television). They saw that when the moon appeared each day it came up further to the left and rose to ever decreasing heights in the sky. If one plots this movement out on a piece of paper and continues the progression full circle, the line of dots will move in a counter-clockwise direction.

Sunshine and rain, as has been pointed out elsewhere, were the two most important elements in man's existence. The south-east of Europe, parched dry by long hot summers, cries out for rain, and it was the moon, they believed, which replied to their entreaties by sending this cooling, life-giving element. They had sun enough, and it was thus natural that they should first turn to the moon for help and dance their rain-charm dances to the right in her honour. Northern Europe on the other hand needed all the sun it could get – it had rain a-plenty without asking for more, and so they turned to the sun for help and moved sun-wise in their dances. This is a sweeping generalization because rain-charm rituals and dances are to be found in profusion all over Europe and not necessarily travelling to the right. Also this explanation will not suffice for the south of France, most of Spain and Portugal, where they have an abundance of sun, but not always as much rain and at the right time as they might wish, and yet whose dances travel sun-wise.

The subject is too wide and dance too ancient to be fitted neatly into any generalization. We have seen something of the endless tribal movements ebbing and flowing over the face of Europe, and all tides leave some flotsam and jetsam. We have also come to recognize that the history of dance is merely the tip of the iceberg, and that beneath that tip lies the history of mankind and the vast amount of dance which has been with us since the very dawn of life on this planet.

So we must accept that the ancient Greeks danced to the right, and that even when they abandoned their matriarchal religion they continued to dance to the right, and

137. 'Witches' Sabbath on the Brocken'. German, 17th century.

are still dancing to the right to this day. All forms of life have undeniable primitive instincts stemming from time beyond our ken. Why do hedgehogs defiantly follow ancient tracks, imprinted into their beings long before the dawn of killer highways with their traffic, and birds continue to migrate across areas where modern man, more greedy than his ancestors, awaits them with lethal gunfire?

Another interesting hypothesis worth considering might be that the left has always had *sinister* connotations (Latin *sinister* = left), and maybe people, if they were not consciously setting off on the left foot round in a circle in honour of the sun, might have been reluctant to move left foot first, and travelled to the lucky right instead. The left foot was also the foot of aggression. Aetolian warriors were famous for campaigning with only the left foot shod. Jason (of Argonaut fame) similarly went into battle with his right foot bare. According to Thucydides, this enabled soldiers during the Peloponnesian War to gain a better purchase in the mud, while at the same time being able to strike out at an opponent with the left foot. Thus the left foot should never be set on the threshhold of a friend's house, and even today soldiers set off marching with the left foot foremost.

That this 'left foot first' has always to have been a conscious effort is underlined by the fact that the overwhelming number of people are right handed. Set any group of children in motion to galop in a circle and they will instinctively move first to the right.

It would be too glib to say that all western European dances travel clockwise and all eastern European dances travel counter-clockwise. For example, most Russian circles move to the left (clockwise), but there are examples of old dances which reverse this. In Yugoslavia, the Orthodox Christians and the Moslems travel to the right while the Catholics progress to the left. However it is true to say that the circles and chains of Greece, Romania, Bulgaria, Albania, parts of Yugoslavia and Czechoslovakia move to the right (counter-clockwise) and most western European dances move in a clockwise direction. An interesting exception to this rule is the Basque Country where the circles travel to the right, and maybe this gives us a clue to the origins of this enigmatic race and suggests that they came from the east. Not so the Normans. Today, many folk-dance groups from Normandy make their circles go to the right, but this is for the most disreputable of reasons. In the early years of this century, a lady dance revivalist in Normandy insisted, for no other reason than that this pleased her, on the circles going to the right – she was wrong, and now we are left with them going to the right – right? The same thing nearly happened in Provence where the revered dancing master, D.B. Duffaut, believing that the farandole was descended from the Greeks and knowing that the Greek dance travelled to the right, also taught his dances going to the right. Fortunately, the others did not follow suit and continued to dance as before clockwise.

Mistakes can easily be made, and in all innocence. Filming a folk dance group in a mountain village in the Savoy Alps, I watched intrigued as the chain snaked its way in a counter-clockwise direction. Questioned about this at the end of the dance a shame-faced leader admitted the mistake. They had started off on the wrong foot, but knowing that they were on camera they did not like to stop and start again. Presumably, had I not asked for clarification, I too might now have been writing that dances in this part of the world go to the right. One must be careful.

In the preamble to the chapter on sword dancing we referred to the connection between mines and Mother Earth, and the magical significance of miners dancing in honour of the moon. It would make good mythical sense therefore for all sword dances to travel to the right. Many do, in Spain and Czechoslovakia and some Flemish ones for example. Unfortunately this does not hold good for England where the overwhelming majority of sword dances travel sun-wise. Handsworth is one exception, dancing counter-clockwise as they do, but their close neighbours, Grenoside, move clockwise. Of course, it is always possible that, like our lady in Normandy, someone has misunderstood the significance of the dance, and sent everybody off in the wrong direction.

Funeral dances usually go in the direction opposite to that which is the norm of the country. In Yugoslavia we find limping dances moving clockwise – perhaps a memory of an ancient sacrificial king's demise. Witches' dances also are reported to move in opposition to the norm, and witches with their black magic are synonymous with evil.

In general, couples progress round the floor in a counter-clockwise direction. There seems to be no logical reason why they should do so and no satisfactory explanation is forthcoming. Again, one can find numerous instances where the dancers reverse this direction, having the lady either on the inside or the outside of the circle, and with the lady holding the gentleman by the left or the right hand. Golden rules are there for the breaking.

Appendix B
Flamenco

A detailed study of Flamenco and Spanish Classical dance is beyond the scope of this book. They have both grown out of the folk dance, but have become as technical and as stylised as classical ballet, and have thus developed into an art form uniquely their own, deserving (and receiving) a special study in their own right. Suffice it to say that Flamenco today is generally (but wrongly) associated with Gypsy culture, although Gypsies do not hold anything like a monopoly of this dance form.

Let us first sum up the argument put forward by those who seek the origins of Flamenco in Gypsy culture.

The home of Flamenco is Andalusia, in that part of the south of Spain which was colonized by Arabs and Berbers from North Africa from 711 until they were finally conquered by the Christians in 1492. Even then, the Moslems did not by any means all leave the country, many staying on, either having converted to Christianity or taken to the hills. It is hardly surprising that Moorish culture should deeply have impregnated the very roots of all the arts which grew up in Spain. Eight hundred years of occupation is bound to have had a profound influence. In that time classical Moorish music and dance developed, especially in the highly civilized Moorish court. Indeed, it was Moorish culture which maintained a brilliant civilization through the period of the Dark Ages, when in the rest of Europe, outside the Byzantine Empire, culture and literacy were reduced to little islands of monasticism in a sea of cultural apathy.

Having said that, we are told that Flamenco is by nature oriental. Experts in Indian Kathak dancing have observed many close parallels between the two, with their forceful styles and rhythmically complex foot beats combined with elegant and graceful arm movements. We know that the Gypsies came out of India, and we are therefore not to be surprised to find musical and dance affinities between Indian court dance and the dance form which evolved in Spain. The origins of Flamenco, we are led to believe, are to be found in the music and dance of the highly civilized Moors as these were adopted, adapted and developed by the Gypsies into an expression of fiery and passionate independent temperament.

The question which remains to be answered is, how did the Gypsies, living a semi-nomadic existence on the fringes of society, come into contact with the classical court art which existed in Andalusia? It would seem that, following the fall of Granada in 1492, all those refusing conversion to Christianity were forced to leave the country. Many were driven into exile, but some accepted baptism, while the rest, Moors and Jews who clung tenaciously to their religions, sought refuge in the mountains, notably the Alpujarras, where they joined into bands for mutual support. The Gypsies too were put under great pressure to leave, or otherwise to conform, that is to abandon their semi-nomadic independent existence, and to settle down and take up suitable occupations in conformity with the rest of society. Many joined the Moors and Jews who had gone into hiding, and it is here, we are told, that contact was made. For 350 years, the Gypsies kept themselves and their supremely expressive music and dance much to themselves, until they were 'discovered', in the nineteenth century, by the great Romantic Movement which swept across Europe. The exotic, be it Gypsy, Hungarian or Scottish, was seized upon, to be incorporated into operas and ballets to be performed in the theatres of all the capital cities of Europe and America. Non-Gypsies now learned the arts of the highly idiosyncratic Flamenco singing and dance.

But there are problems with this argument, and an equally convincing case can be made out by those seeking non-Gypsy origins to Flamenco.

Traders have been visiting Spain's southern shores for thousands of years, attracted by the ores to be found there in abundance. Phoenicians, Greeks, Carthaginians all established colonies before Rome incorporated the Iberian Peninsula into her mighty empire. By this time, a lively cosmopolitan community, which drew on peoples from all over the eastern and southern Mediterranean, enjoyed a rich mix of cultures, with their music and dance. The musicians and dancers of Tartessus were, apparently, so prized by the Romans living there, that, according to Pliny the Elder, when an edict for the expulsion of all foreigners was made, the musicians and dancers were allowed to remain. These will have come from the far-flung reaches of the empire and, as war booty, from further afield still. Thus, long before the Moors conquered Spain, exotic eastern dancing was one of the popular entertainments, and it was this which provided the foundations on which the unique Andalusian style was based.

We must now try to account for the Gypsy involvement in Flamenco music and dance. Gypsies first made their appearance in Spain during the fifteenth century, only a few years before the fall of Granada. The first reference we have concerning them comes from the year 1427, which relates that they came by way of France. They too sought refuge in the Alpujarras along with Moors and Jews, but they were expelled even from here in 1609, very little time for them to make Flamenco their very own. Flamenco was undoubtedly developed by the Spanish themselves, but performance in the taverns, where it was not respectable for nice girls to go, let alone dance, had to be provided by the 'no-gooders', the Gypsies, who had re-infiltrated by the nineteenth century. The phenomenal growth of tourism following the Spanish Civil War and the Second World War created a demand for local colour, and it was the Gypsies who responded by making Flamenco almost their own, to the extent that many today regard Gypsies and Flamenco as inseparable.

The foot stamping and sinuous arm movements of Flamenco are not the result of the marriage of Moorish and Indian court dance, solemnised by the Gypsies. A unique and exotic style of dancing existed in Andalusia long before Gypsies (or Moors for that matter) set foot in the land. Flamenco grew out of this, undoubtedly influenced along the way by Arab culture, which itself drew upon the same eastern exotica that had so captivated the Romans. It is in Persia, Egypt and Arabia, not among a few wandering Gypsy nomads who had left their original homelands in India centuries before (c. 1300 B.C.) where the origins of Flamenco are to be found.

Be all that as it may, Flamenco is one of the most thrilling and captivating art forms it can be one's good fortune to experience. Today, it is to be found not only in theatres, *tablaos* (floor-shows), and the *cafe cantante*, but also it is to be enjoyed in the streets and plazas of southern towns in both Spain and France, where bands of Gypsies may break into spontaneous display, and improvise an exciting and colourful performance.

Flamenco is basically an intricate combination of four elements: singing, dancing, guitar-playing, and *jaleo,* which is rhythmic hand-clapping and shouts of encouragement. *Cante jondo* is profoundly sad and serious singing, though not necessarily an expression of the oppression suffered by a people over many centuries, as some will have us believe. It may be *soleá*, singing of unrequited love. It is contrasted by the *cante chico* which is gay, light and often humorous. Occasionally, an 'Alegrias' dance (*jondo*) may finish with a coda in the comic and satirical *chico* style of a 'Bulerías'. The 'Siguiriyas' is the most profound and emotional of all *jondo* pieces, and sometimes presents an evocation of death. The majestic 'Taranto' reflects the fusion of middle-eastern and Moorish influences in the arm movements of the dancers. The 'Martinete' is usually performed to the accompaniment just of hammers and anvils, and is said to stem from the time when the Gypsies, forced into 'useful' occupations, took to blacksmithing. Flamenco gives unlimited scope for displays of unbridled bravura. In a 'Farruca', the combined virtuosity of singers, musicians and dancers, the fiery rhythms, the stamping, clapping, foot tapping (*taconeado*) like drum-rolls, and finger-snapping or castanet playing, are exciting beyond belief.

Gypsies, wherever they have settled, have adopted whatever music and dance came their way. Hungary is a prime example, for here they have developed their own unique style of dancing, but which is in no way reminiscent of Spanish Gypsy dancing. In Spain, it was not only 'Moorish' but also Galician music which was brought to Andalusia, and these *cantinas*, improvised, cheerful songs, have been transformed into light-hearted songs and dances of great charm.

Appendix C
Musical Instruments

Accordion (International) Accordions come in all shapes and sizes, with or without a piano keyboard, and are ideal instruments to accompany folk dancing, which is why their use is so widespread. It is almost inconceivable not to find at least one accordion in an ensemble, and as this instrument can trace its origins back to the *handaoline of* 1822, one must suppose that it may now be regarded as a traditional instrument. However, its over-exploitation has driven out many other traditional instruments which is a great pity.

Adufe (Portugal) (ill. 139) A square hand-drum or tambourine held upright by one corner and drummed with the fingers of both hands. Sometimes has pieces of tin inside the rim to make a jingling sound, and sympathetic strings to increase the resonance.

Alboka (Basque Country) Small horn. Rather like a pair of cow's horns stuck into a central hollow block of wood with finger holes, so that one horn is blown and the sound comes out of the other. The player puffs out his cheeks to enable him to keep playing as he takes another breath, so making a continuous sound like a bagpipe.

Baglamás (Greece) A small bouzouki with three strings.

Bagpipe (International) (ill. 138) Under a variety of names and in a variety of types, with or without drones, the bagpipe is among the most popular and most suitable instruments for accompanying folk dancing. Basically it is a reed instrument, with a bag filled with air and either being mouth-blown or by use of bellows. The bag is tucked under the left arm, pressure of the arm squeezing the bag and feeding air into the pipes - the melody pipe or *chanter*, and one or more drones. The bagpipe has been widely popular for centuries. One of the earliest references to it in western Europe tells us that the Emperor Nero could "play the pipes, both by means of his lips, and by tucking a skin beneath his armpits".

Balalaika (Russia) A triangular intrument with three strings.

Bandoura (Ukraine) (ill. 141) Usually played in ensembles, this is a type of *zither* with numerous double open strings, and a certain number extending over a short fretboard. The strings are plucked or strummed.

Bandurria (Spain) A type of guitar.

Biniou (Brittany) Bagpipe.

Bodrán (Ireland) The traditional Irish drum, like a large tambourine without jingles, though small bells may be attached to two crossed pieces of wood by which it is held. The instrument is struck by a short stick, called a pin, tipper or kippeen, which is held like a pencil, the wrist being twisted to strike the drum with both ends.

Bombarde (Brittany) Shawm.

Bombo (Spain) Large drum.

138. 'Bauerhochzeit' by Elias Back. German, 1679-1747.

Bouzouki (Greece) Has eight strings often tuned in pairs, used to accompany the *rebétika* or urban folk song.
Burczybas (Poland) A bass viol, used especially to accompany songs from the Kaszuby region of Pomerania on the Baltic Sea.
Caramella (Spain) A pipe.
Castanets The instrument most associated with Spanish music is the castanet. It derives its name from the wood from which it is fashioned - chestnut. The people of the Auvergne in France claim the origin of the manufacture of castanets for themselves, for here the chestnut grows in profusion. But then so it does in the northern climes of the Iberian Peninsula, where festivals of the chestnut are occasions for celebration and dance. Castanets made from ivory and bronze were known in ancient Egypt. Castanets are commonly played in pairs: a male, deeper sounding, which strikes the beat; and a lighter female, which plays the embroidered rhythmic pattern. In Flamenco (if they are used at all), they are usually tied by looping the string on either side of the thumb joints, but in other forms of folk dance they are tied to the middle fingers.
Caval (Romania) A flute.
Chicotén (Spain) (ill. 67) See Pyrenean drum.
Chistuak (Basque Country) A small flute played with one hand.
Chitara (Italy) A type of guitar.
Cimbalom (Hungary) See cymbalon.
Cláirseach (Ireland) A harp with the sound box made from a hollowed-out block of sally or willow. The oldest surviving harp, the 'Brian Boru' harp, dates from the fourteenth century.
Cobza (Romania) Type of lute with ten to fifteen strings.
Concertina (International) Dating from 1844, the concertina was originally a very limited instrument. Between the buttons of both hands a chromatic scale could be played. In time the range was extended so that each hand individually could play chromatically.
Curle (Albania) A type of flute.
Cymbalon (Hungary) A stringed instrument, the strings being struck by hammers. Gives to Hungarian music its very distinctive character.
Dalmatian bagpipe (ill.141) A *musette*, the air to the bag being fed by bellows. The chanter and the drone curve up at the ends rather like a tobacco pipe, and decorated with an animal head.
Défi (Greece) A tambourine.
Diabelskie Skrzypce (Poland) Literally devil's violin, a kind of fiddle ornamented with a devil's head.
Doedelzak (Netherlands) Bagpipes.
Draailier (Netherlands) (ill. 143) A hurdy-gurdy. See *Vielle à roue.*
Duda (Hungary) Bagpipe.
Duduk (Serbia) (ill. 142) Shepherd's flute.
Dudy (Bohemia) Bagpipes, inflated by bellows worked by the elbow.
Dulzaïna (Spain) A type of shawm.
Dvoinïtza (Yugoslavia) Double flute fitted to a single mouthpiece and pipes may be played separately or together.

Ferrena (Spain) A tambourine without a skin.
Fiddle (International) A violin that the Scandinavians have particularly made their own.
Flahutet (Provence) A three-holed flute held in left hand.
Flaviol (Spain) A pipe.
Floyéra (Greece) A type of flute.
Fluier (Romania) A primitive pipe.
Fluviol (Catalonia) A flute played with one hand.
Forgólant (Hungary) Related to the hurdy-gurdy.
Friscaletta (Italy) A very short flute, no more than 20 cms. long, with seven holes on one side and two on the other.
Fujara (Czechoslovakia) Enormous pipe akin to a bassoon.
Gadoulka (Bulgaria) A rebec.
Galoubet (Provence) A three-holed flute held in left hand.
Gaída (Greece) (ill. 142) A bagpipe with one single drone. The finger pipe has six or seven holes and is mainly to be found in Greece, Macedonia and Thrace.
Gaita (Spain) (ill. 142) Bagpipe.
Gajde (Yugoslavia) (ill. 142) Bagpipe.
Gajdy (Moravia, Slovakia) Bagpipe, like the Bohemian dudy.
Goč (Serbia) A bass drum.
Gousla (Bosnia) A one-stringed fiddle played with a bow. The soundbox is covered

139. Granada, 1615.

with a skin. The neck is often carved with the head of an animal or a man on horseback.

Gratille (France) A six-holed pipe of boxwood.

Guitarra (Portugal) A lute-like instrument with a rounded soundboard and six double strings of wire which are plucked with a piece of tortoiseshell.

Gusla (Bulgaria) A rebec.

Hardingfele (Norway) The Hardanger fiddle has four extra 'sympathetic' strings. These are not played with the bow, but begin to vibrate 'in sympathy' when the other strings are played, the result being a fuller and quite different sound to the normal fiddle.

Hommel-vlier (Netherlands) A type of dulcimer, having a flat soundbox which can sit on the player's knees or on a table, the strings being plucked with a plectrum.

Jew's harp (International) Examples of this instrument dating back to the Middle Ages have been excavated in Denmark. It has a tongue enclosed in a frame of wood, metal, or occasionally bone. The frame is supported by the teeth, and the tongue of the instrument is plucked either by the fingers or with a plectrum. The mouth acts as a resonator, and the sound may be varied by the use of the tongue, lips and cheeks. The term *jew's* is considered a corruption of *jaw's*.

Kannel (Estonia) A dulcimer, rather like the Finnish kantele. Usually the strings are plucked, but may also be bowed.

Kantele (Finland and Finno-Karelia) A type of dulcimer. It is made of wood, with chip ornament, in the shape of a long triangle, originally with five strings.

140. 'Orsapolska'. Swedish.

Karadouzéni (Greece) A medium sized bouzouki tuned an octave higher.
Kaval (Bulgaria) Shepherd's flute.
Kementsés (Greece) A three-stringed instrument played with a bow. Being a small instrument it is usually held upright in front of the player who keeps close to the dancers, encouraging them with exhortations as he plays.
Köcsogduda (Hungary) A rumble-pot.
Langeleik (Norway) A type of dulcimer.
Laoúto (Greece) An eight-stringed lute which has moveable frets. The strings are tuned in pairs and are plucked with a plectrum.
Launeddas (Italy) A double flute made of canes of different length and blown like a recorder. It gives a curious 'twittering' sound and is used to accompany the Ballo Sardo.
Lijerice (Dalmatia) Also **Lirica** A three stringed instrument played with a bow.
Lodër (Albania) A type of drum.
Lučec (Czechoslovakia) A type of hurdy-gurdy.
Lyra (Crete) A stringed instrument played with a bow. About 50 cms or so in length, the body and neck are carved out of a single piece of wood. It has three strings, the melody usually being played only on the high string, the other two acting as drones.
Mandoline (Italy) A small lute-like instrument with strings tuned in pairs. Played with a plectrum.
Mandoúra (Greece) A type of flute.
Maniura-arpa (Basque Country) Like a Welsh harp.

141. Folk musicians by William Donachie.

Maranzano (Sicily) A jew's harp, also used by bandits to warn their comrades of the approach of police or soldiers.
Mešnica (Croatia) Also **Mišnice** Bagpipe, the bag being of goat or sheepskin.
Mouth music This style of singing, often in imitation of instruments, is to be heard all over Europe. In some countries, Sweden and Finland for example, the singer fills the cheeks with air, to continue making a sound whilst breathing in, that is acting as one's own bagpipe. The sounds made by Albanian and Bulgarian singers are highly distinctive.
Mundgige (Denmark) See jew's harp.
Naiu (Romania) Several flutes joined together.
Northumbrian smallpipes (England) See uileann.
Nyckelharpa (Sweden) A keyed-fiddle, almost like a cross between a fiddle and a hurdy-gurdy, but played with a bow and not by rotating a handle. Gives to Swedish music a highly distinctive sound.
Oúti (Greece) A lute without frets. Introduced into Greece with the exchange of populations between Greece and Turkey in 1922. It has five pairs of strings which are plucked with a plectrum.
Pandero (Spain) A square drum or tambourine.
Pyrenean drum (France) (ill. 67) A six-stringed drum, shaped like a dulcimer, and very much looking like one, held by left arm and tapped with a stick held in the left hand. Played by flute player at the same time.
Rebec A three-stringed instrument used during the Middle Ages. It was played with a short curved bow.

142. Folk musicians by William Donachie.

Rommelpot (Netherlands) The 'rumble-pot' is a type of friction drum. A pig's bladder or similar membrane is stretched over a pot or small jug, and a stick is inserted through the middle. To make the distinctive *grunt*, moistened fingers are rubbed up and down the stick.
Salterio (Spain) See Pyrenean drum.
Santoúri (Greece) (ill. 141) Akin to a cymbalon it can have up to 140 strings, and is played with two small wooden hammers. The instrument usually rests on the player's knees or a table, but he can also carry it in front of him, hanging from a strap around his neck.
Shawm (International) (ill. 138) The forerunner of the oboe, it is a reed instrument held like a recorder.
Silbotia (Basque Country) A large flute.
Siringa di Pan (Italy) Panpipes.
Sopele (Croatia) Also **Sopile** A wind instrument related to the oboe.
Sourávli (Greece) A type of flute.
Šupeljka (Macedonia) Primitive flute.
Sulittu (Sardinia) A pipe with a wedge-shaped mouthpiece usually played by shepherds.
Syrinx (ill. 141) Panpipes especially associated with Romania. A series of pipes of graduated length bound in a row and played by pressing the lower lip against whichever pipe is to be blown.
Tabalet (Spain) A drum.
Ţambal (Romania) A cymbalon.

143. Folk musicians by William Donachie.

Tambura (Yugoslavia) A banjo-like instrument.
Tambourin (Provence) Drum hung over left arm and struck with a *masseto*, drum stick, held in right hand.
Tamburica (Croatia) Akin to a mandoline.
Tekerölant (Hungary) Related to the hurdy-gurdy.
Tenora (Catalonia) A sort of oboe.
Tilinca (Romania) A flute without stops.
Tiun-tiunak (Basque Country) A small drum hanging from the left arm. The player stikes this with a stick held in the right hand, at the same time playing the chistuak (see above).
Torupill (Estonia) Form of bagpipe.
Toumbáno (Greece) (ill. 142) A cylindrical drum with skin covering both faces. Played with two drum sticks of differing size, this, combined with the differing tensions of the skins, gives two different sounds. The toumbáno hangs by a strap over the left shoulder of the drummer, and he beats the main rhythm with the thicker stick, *kópanos*, and a quicker repetitive sound with the other, *vérga*. It is these two distinct sounds which determine the dancers' steps. It is said that the dancer with less experience listens to the *kópanos*, whilst the accomplished dancer converses with the *vérga*.
Toumbeléki (Greece) A percussive instrument made in pottery or metal, covered with a skin at one end and played whilst gripped between the knees or held under the arm or around the neck.
Tupan (Macedonia) A large drum.

144. Folk musicians by William Donachie.

Träskofiol (Sweden) Clog-fiddle. A type of fiddle.
Tsamboúna (Greece) A bagpipe without a drone, but with two pipes with finger holes, both pipes being played with both hands as though they were one. Now largely confined to the islands of the Aegean.
Ttun-ttun (Basque Country) See Pyrenean drum. Also ttunttuna, the six strings are struck with a *baguette* or stick covered in leather.
Txistus (Basque Country) Drum.
Uileann (Ireland) These bagpipes, like the Northumbrian smallpipes, are not mouth-blown, but the bag is filled by means of bellows strapped to the right arm. The other arm squeezes the bag. The chanter has a range of two octaves, and up to three drones on a modern set.
Vedel (Netherlands) An old-fashioned fiddle.
Vielle à roue (France) (ill. 143) Literally means *wheel-fiddle*, and this is an apt name, for instead of a bow being drawn across a string as with a fiddle, a boxwood wheel with a resinated rim, mounted on an iron axle, is cranked with the right hand by means of a handle to make the strings, melody and drone, resonate together to provide a continuous sound. The process of fingering is also mechanized, the string being stopped to provide the required notes by wooden blades mounted on transverse wooden keys, activated by the player's left hand. Hurdy-gurdies date back in Europe over eight hundred years. Its forerunner, the *organistrum*, later known as the *symphony*, required two people to play it, one to crank the handle and the other to operate the keyboard.
Viola da França (Portugal) Spanish guitar.
Whistle (Ireland) The humble whistle in skilled Irish hands gives a new dimension to whistle-playing. Aileann, chief of the Tuatha dé Danaan was able to lull the defenders of the royal residence at Tara to sleep by playing fairy music on this instrument.
Xirolarru-cornamusa (Basque Country) A one-drone bagpipe.
Xirula (Basque Country) Flute with three finger holes.
Zarrabete (Basque Country) A hurdy-gurdy.
Zé pereira (Portugal) Large drum held by a cord round player's neck, played on both faces.
Zoumás (Greece) A type of shawm mainly to be found in the Peloponnese and Macedonia. Elsewhere it is being replaced by the clarinet. It is usually made of walnut, beech, olive or cherry, and has seven finger holes, one at the back for the thumb. It is blown through a reed rather like an oboe. A skilled player can keep the sound going by filling his cheeks with air and forcing the air through the instrument whilst taking another breath. Thus he is his own bagpipe.
Zourna (Bosnia) A shawm.
Zurla (Macedonia) Primitive shawm.

Appendix D
Leading Festivals

Country	*Place*		*Month*	*Frequency*	*Type*
Albania	Gjirokaster		Oct	5years (1993)	national
Belgium	Jambes	*	Aug	annual	international
	Schoten	*	July	annual	international
Bulgaria	Burgas	*	Aug	biennial(even)	international
	Koprivshtitsa		Aug	5 years (1991)	national
	Sofia	*	Jan	annual	Koukeri
Czechoslovakia	Košice	*	Jun/Jul	annual	regional
	Strážnice	*	July	annual	international
	Vychodná	*	July	annual	regional
England	Billingham	*	Aug	annual	international
	Morecambe		Aug	annual	international
	Sidmouth	*	Aug	annual	international
Estonia	Tallinn	*	June	4 years (1994)	Baltic
Finland	Helsinki	*	June	annual	international
	Kaustinen	*	July	annual	international
	Tampere	*	June	biennial(even)	international
France	Bayonne	*	Jul/Aug	annual	international
	Confolens	*	Aug	annual	international
	Etaples		July	annual	national
	Gannat	*	July	annual	international
	Lorient		Aug	annual	inter-Celtic
	Martigues		Aug	annual	international
	Nancy	*	Aug	annual	international
	Nice	*	July	annual	farandole
	Rochefort sur Mer	*	July	biennial(even)	international
Germany (East)	Karl-Marx-Stadt	*	July	4 years (1993)	international
Germany (West)	Bitburg	*	July	annual	international
	Ludwigstein	*	July	annual	international
	Marburg	*	July	biennial(odd)	international
	Scheessel	*	July	biennial(odd)	international
	Schlitz	*	Jun/Jul	annual	international
Greece	Athens		May/Sept	annual	national
	Lefkada		Aug	annual	international
	Naoussa	*	July	annual	international
	Rhodes		May/Oct	annual	national
Hungary	Kalocsa	*	July	3 years (1993)	Danube lands

	Szeged	*	July	biennial(odd)	international
Ireland	Dublin	*	Aug	annual	international
Italy	Latina	*	July	annual	international
	Rome		July	annual	international
	Tarcento	*	July	annual	international
Latvia	Riga		July	4 years (1994)	Baltic
Lithuania	Vilnius	*	July	annual	Baltic
Luxembourg	Mersch	*	July	biennial(odd)	international
Netherlands	Bolsward	*	July	annual	international
	Brunssum	*	July	4 years (1992)	international
	Heijen	*	July	annual	international
	Warffum	*	June	annual	international
	Zandeweer	*	June	annual	international
	Zelhem		July	annual	international
Norway	Bergen	*	May	biennial(odd)	international
Poland	Lublin	*	July	annual	national
	Plock	*	Jun/Jul	annual	national
	Sosnowiec	*	Sept	annual	national
		*	Sept	biennial(odd)	international
	Zakopane	*	Sept	annual	international
	Zielona Góra	*	Sept	biennial(even)	international
Portugal	Braga		July	annual	international
	Bragança (Miranda do Douro)		Aug	annual	men's dances
	Gulpilhares		July	annual	international
	Madeira (Monte)		Aug	annual	regional
	Mafra		Sept	annual	national
	Santarem	*	June	annual	international
	Praia de Rocha		Sept	annual	national
Romania	Mamaia/Sinaia		Aug	annual	national
	Mount Găina		July	annual	regional
Spain	Burgos	*	Jun/Jul	annual	regional
	Córdoba		May	annual	Flamenco
	Granada		July	annual	international
	Murcia	*	Sept	annual	international
	Ronda	*	Sept	annual	international
	Seville	*	June	annual	national
Sweden	Rättvik	*	June	biennial(even)	international
Switzerland	Fribourg	*	Aug/Sept	annual	international
	Martigny	*	Aug	biennial(even)	national
	Neuchatel	*	Aug	biennial(even)	regional
Wales	Llangollen		July	annual	international
Yugoslavia	Dubrovnik		July/Aug	annual	national
	Kopar		July/Aug	annual	national
	Maribor	*	Jun/Jul	annual	international
	Ohrid	*	July	annual	Balkan

Sarajevo		July/Aug	annual	national
Split		summer	annual	national
Zagreb	*	July	annual	international

The Europeade takes place in July every year in a different location.
Details from: Secretariaat, Bouwcentrum, Jan Van Rijswijcklaan 191, 2020 Antwerpen.

The Festival Mondiale is held in a different republic of the Soviet Union every other year (even), in August.

* = C.I.O.F.F. organized festival. Full details may be had from:
Le Conseil International des Organisations de Festivals de Folklore et d'Arts Traditionnels (C.I.O.F.F.), Boîte postale no. 14, 16500 Confolens, France.
C.I.O.F.F., Festival Office, Town Centre, Billingham, Cleveland TS23 2LW, United Kingdom.

Embassies, consulates, and travel bureaux are generally most helpful in supplying the necessary information.

Acknowledgements

I owe a deep debt of gratitute to literally thousands of people: researchers, experts, specialists and teachers, who have all been most generous in sharing with me their knowledge, and dancers who have been unstinting in their co-operation, dancing, demonstrating steps, and patiently answering my endless barrage of questions. Space does not permit every name to be mentioned, and I just hope that they will forgive the omission and accept here my undying thanks for all they have done for me. Undoubtedly there will be errors in the book, and I should be grateful to the reader for drawing my attention to these. Any mistakes I have made, however, I claim for myself alone; they in no way reflect on those kind persons whose names I must find space for, and who can now run away, shouting:

Don't lay the blame on me
You awful villains all,
I'm sure its none of I
That did this bloody act.

Thank you: Håkan Andersson; Egil Bakka of Trondheim University; A.M. Bassery; A. Belmontet; Dr. Ëva Benkő; Maurice Berthier; Thomas Bjerre; William Bland of the Anglo-Albanian Society, London; Professor Dr. Jan-Petter Blom of Bergen University; M.C. Bonamy; André Botineau; British-Bulgarian Friendship Society, London; Gunnar and Kirsten Broust; Roger and Martha Brun; Dr. José and Isabel Maria Calejo; Janine Capet; Olivier Chabroux; Alain Charlet; Rómulo do Patrocínio Marreiros Chucha; António N. do Carmo Cláudio; Rita Conroy; Maria Matilde Ferraz Péreira Viana Côrte-Real; Hans Deibel; Emilio Sotelino Domarco; Femke van Doorn-Last; Daniël and Reine Dost; Rikus Draijer; Jean and Danielle Duc Martin; Aili Eistrat; Bjørn and May Engebretsen; Leif Epel; Estampas Burgalesas; Jean-Pierre and Jacquie Fauche; Louise Fayolle; Hedy Fromings; Bo Godsk; Cristina Mora Fernandez; Fritz Frank; F. H. Geens of the Vlaams Dansarchief; José-Manuel Lozano González; José Maria Villavoy González; Viktors Grigulis; Jean-François Gueganno; Roberto Díez Gutiérrez; Werner and Hermien Halbach; Svend and Anna Hamborg; Robert Harrold; Dr. Ben and Geno Hartman; Betty Harvey; Juhani and Sari Heikkilä; Professor Dr. Karl Horak; Marcel and Nicole Houillon; Jaap and Mariëlle van der Hout; Lise Jaussiomme; Patrick Jehanno; Jens Skjold Jensen; Rhodri Jones; Tecwyn Vaughan Jones of the Welsh Folk Museum, St. Fagans, Cardiff; Ana Jordá; Claus Jørgensen; Rolf Karlberg; Thomas and Lotta Karlson; Kendalc'h; Elsche Korf-Schröder; Gonzalo Rey Lama; Jean-Louis and Annette Lamolie; Professor Dr. Roderyk Lange; Dr. Jan Krzysztof Makulski; Jo and Gre Maljers; Raymond-Yves Martinez; Bernard and Annick Meyer; Jan and Wouda Minet; Kathy Mitchell; Jean Nesprias; Louis and Eliane Neuville; Astrid

Njøs; Theo and Elly Olderaan; Marucha Osuna; Tore Pedersen; Gunnar and Siv Persson; Dr. Valeria Cottini Petrucci; Alain Pierre; António Lopes Pires; Børre Qvamme; Professor Dr. Stoyan Radev; Professor Dr. Alkis Raftis; Carmen Ramos; Esko and Pirkko-Liisa Rausmaa; Martina Relihan of Le Rincí Gaelacha; Dr. Cyrill Renz; Jean and Anne-Marie Ricard; Dr. Miloš Ríha; Alexander Sagys of the Lithuanian Folk Dancers, Cleveland, Ohio; Anna-Liisa Sallavuori; Svend and Lisbeth Sandkvist; Hans Schijffelen; Richard Schneider; Henry Sjöberg of the Danmuseet, Stockholm; Society for Cultural Relations with the U.S.S.R., London; Dr. Bernd Steinbrugger; Lasse Svahnström; Flemming and Henny Thomsen; D. Manuel Touza Toja; Henning Urup of Copenhagen University; Alain Vaquette; Ove and Else Viberfeldt; João Francisco Rosado Nunes Vidal.

For their kind permission in allowing me to reproduce the illustrations in this book my grateful thanks go to:
Herakleion Museum, Crete: 1;
Kestner Museum, Hannover: 2;
Antikensammlungen, Munich: 3;
Museo Municipale, Corneto: 4;
Worcester Art Museum, Worcester, Massachusetts: 5;
Louvre, Paris: 6, 113, 131;
Garnstone Press, London: 7, 8, 9, 10;
Antikvarisk-Topografiska Arkivet, Stockholm: 11;
Museo Capitolino, Rome: 12, 13;
British Museum, London: 14, 15, 118, 122;
Soprintendenza alle Antichità, Florence: 16;
Nordiska Museet, Stockholm: 17, 23, 34, 64, 66, 85, 87, 111, 133, 140;
Bibliothèque Nationale, Paris: 18, 19, 81, 124;
Kupferstichkabinett, Berlin: 20, 38, 92;
Narodni Musej, Beograd: 21, 22, 120, 121;
British Library, London: 24;
Bodleian Library, Oxford: 25, 36, 42, 82, 137;
Kunsthistorisches Museum, Vienna: 26, 58;
Zentralbibliothek, Zürich: 27;
Bibliothèque Royale Albert Ier, Brussels: 28, 67-74, 89-91, 107, 121, 128, 130;
Stadtbibliothek, Nürnberg: 29, 32, 41, 43, 114;
Germanisches Nationalmuseum, Nürnberg: 30, 46, 97, 98, 102, 112, 115, 116;
Tanzarchiv, Leipzig: 31, 52, 84, 105, 135, 136, 138;
Victoria and Albert Museum, London: 35;
Schlossmuseum, Gotha: 39;
Robert Lépine: 40;
Tiroler Landesmuseum Ferdinandeum, Innsbruck: 45, 60, 65, 108;
Musée Arlaten, Arles (photographs: M. Lacanaud): 47-51;
Kungl. Bibliotheket, Stockholm: 53, 139;
Staatliche Kunstsammlungen, Dresden: 54, 57, 96;
Collection Rothschild, Paris: 55, 56;
Gripsholm Castle, Sweden: 59;

Vest-Agder Fylkesmuseum, Kristiansand: 61;
Universitetsbiblioteket, Oslo: 62;
Norsk Folkemuseum, Oslo: 63, 86;
Museu Nacional de Soares dos Reis, Oporto: 75;
Muzeum Naradowego w Krakowie, Cracow: 76, 88;
Biblioteka Narodowa, Warsaw: 77-80, 101;
Magyar Nemzéti Múzeum, Budapest: 83;
Rijksmuseum, Amsterdam: 93;
Hull Daily Mail: 94;
Detroit Institute of Arts, Detroit, Michigan: 95;
Het Nederlands Openluchtmuseum, Arnhem: 99, 126;
National Galleries of Scotland: 100;
Kansallismuseo, Helsinki: 103, 104;
Nationalmuseum, Stockholm: 106, 110, 132;
Museo Nazionale, Naples: 123;
Koninklyk Museum voor Schone Kunste, Antwerp: 125;
Courtauld Institute of Art, London: 127;
Galleria Nazionale d'Arte Antica, Rome: 129;
Felix Rosenstein's Widow & Sons Ltd., London: 141-144;

For help in translation my thanks go to: Joachim Duebelt, Mariëlle van der Hout, Renée Lawrence, Lut Ongenaet, Pauline Schenk-Levick and Lisa Thenen; and to my wife and Stephanie Phillip for reading the typescript and making innumerable corrections.

Bibliography

ALFORD, Violet The Hobby Horse and Other Animal Masks. The Merlin Press, London. 1978.

Sword Dance and Drama. The Merlin Press, London. 1962.

& GALLOP, Rodney The Traditional Dance. Methuen & Co. Ltd., London. 1935.

ALLENBY JAFFÉ, Nigel and Margaret Denmark. Folk Dance Enterprises, Skipton. 1987.

The Netherlands. Folk Dance Enterprises, Skipton. 1982.

ANDERSSON, Otto Folkdans. Finlands Svenska Folkdiktning, Turku. 1964.

ARBEAU, Thoinot Orchésographie. Langres. 1589. (Trans. Cyril W. Beaumont. C.W. Beaumont, London. 1925; also by Mary Stewart Evans. Dover Publications Inc., New York. 1967.)

ASSEN, Nicoloff Bulgarian Folklore. Cleveland, Ohio. 1975.

BAKKA, Egil Danse, Danse, Lett ut på Foten. Noregs Boklag, Oslo. 1970.

BAKKA, Egil SELAND, Brit and VÅRDAL, Dag Grunnbok i Folkedans. Noregs Boklag, Oslo. 1986.

BLAKE, Loïs Traditional Dance and Customs in Wales. The Gwynn Publishing Co., Llangollen. 1972.

BOGDANI, Ramazan Sur la Structure de la Danse Populaire Albanaise.

BRAGAGLIA, Anton Giulio Danze Populare Italiane.

BREATHNACH, Breandán Folk Music and Dances of Ireland. The Mercier Press, Dublin. 1971.

BROWN, H.M. Catalogue des Danses de la Renaissance. 1965.

CHAVET, Luís Danças & Bailados. Lisbon. 1944.

Coreografía Popular Portuguesa. C. Bermejo, Madrid. 1945.

CONTE, Pierre Danses Anciennes de Cour et de Théatre en France. Association 'l'Ecriture du Mouvement', Paris. 1974.

COON, Carleton Stevens The Races of Europe. The Macmillan Co. Harvard University. 1939.

CZERWINSKI, Albert Geschichte der Tanzkunst bei den Cultivirten Völkern. Verlagsbuchhandlung von J.J. Weber. 1862.

FLETT, J.P. & T.M. Traditional Dancing in Scotland. Routledge and Kegan Paul, London. 1964.

Traditional Step-dancing in Lakeland. The English Folk Dance and Song Society.

FRAZER, Sir James George The Golden Bough (abridged edition 1922). The Macmillan Press Ltd., London.

GALANTI, B.M. La Danza della Spada in Italia. Rome. 1942.

GEIPEL, John The Europeans. Longmans. 1969.

GRAVES, Robert The White Goddess. Faber & Faber Ltd., London. 1960.
The Greek Myths (vols. 1 & 2). Penguin Books. 1960.
GROVE, Lilly Dancing. Longmans, Green and Co., London. 1895.
GUILCHER, Jean-Michel La Tradition Populaire de Danse en Basse-Bretagne. Mouton & Co., La Haye. 1963.
La Contredanse et les Renouvellements de la Danse Française. Mouton & Co., Paris. 1969.
HARITSCHELHAR, Jean Être Basque. Editions Privat, Toulouse. 1983.
HELM, Alex The English Mummers' Play. D.S. Brewer and Rowman and Littlefield for the Folklore Society. 1981.
HENRIKSEN, Vera Christmas in Norway, Past and Present. Tanum-Norli, Oslo. 1981.
HOLDEN, R. & VOURAS M. Greek Folk Dances. Folkraft Press, Newark, N.J. 1965.
HOLT, J.C. Robin Hood. Thames and Hudson Ltd. 1982.
HOLM, R and VEDEL, K. Folkedansen i Danmark. Copenhagen. 1946.
HOMEM DE MELLO, Pedro Danças de Portugal. Livraria Avis, Porto.
HOOD, Evelyn M. The Story of Scottish Country Dancing. William Collins Sons and Co. Ltd. 1980.
KENNEDY, Douglas English Folk Dancing Today and Yesterday. G. Bell and Sons Ltd., London 1964.
LAWLER, Lillian B. The Dance in Ancient Greece. Adam and Charles Black, London 1964.
LIESTØL, Knut & SEMB, Klara Norske Folkedansar. Noregs Boklag, Oslo. 1961.
LOUIS, Maurice A.-L. Le Folklore et la Danse. Editions d'Aujourd'hui. 1963.
LOUTZAKI, Rena The Traditional Dance in Greece. Hellexpo, Thessaloniki. 1985.
LUCIAN The Dance. (vol. 5 in Collected Works), translated by A.M. Harmon. Harvard University Press. 1955.
MARTIN, György Hungarian Folk Dances. Corvina Press, Budapest. 1974.
MELLOR, Hugh Welsh Folk Dances. Novello & Co. Ltd., London. 1935.
MENIL, F. de Histoire de la Danse à Travers les Ages. Editions Slatkine, Geneva. 1980.
MICHALIKOWA, Lidia & CHRZASTOWSCY, Zofia & Stanislaw Folklor Lachow Sadeckich (Poland). Centralny Osrodek Metodyki Upowszechniania Kultury, Warsaw. 1974.
MOURGUES, Marcelle La Danse Provençale. Marcel Petit, Raphèle-lès-Arles. 1985.
NAVARRO, Juan Antonio Urbeltz Dantzak. Caja Laboral Pupular Lankide Aurrezkia.
NIELSEN, H. Gruner Vore Aeldste Folkedanse. Copenhagen. 1917.
NOSAĽ, Štefan Choreografia Ludového Tance (Slovakia). Slovenské Pedagogické Naklad Atelstvo, Bratislava. 1984.
OETKE, Herbert Der Deutsche Volkstanz (2 vols.) Heinrichshofen's Verlag, Wilhelmshaven. 1983.

PETRIDES, Ted Greek Dances. Lycabettus Press, Athens. 1975.
PETRIDES, Theodore & Elfleida Folk Dances of the Greeks. Bailey Brothers & Swinfen Ltd., Folkestone. 1974.
PHILLIPS, Patricia The Prehistory of Europe. Pelican Books. 1981.
PIRENNE, Henri A History of Europe. (Fall of Roman Empire to c. 1550). George Allen & Unwin Ltd. 1967.
POHREN, Donn E. The Art of Flamenco. Musical New Services Ltd., Shaftesbury. 1984.
PREVITÉ-ORTON, C. W. The Shorter Cambridge Medieval History (2 vols: European history from late Roman Empire to 1500). C.U.P. 1971.
RAFTIS, Alkis The World of Greek Dance. Finedawn Publications, Athens. 1987.
Tradition and Folklore in Greek Dance. Kanonaki. 1984.
RAUSMAA, Pirkko-Liisa Ilokerä. Suomalaisen Kirjallisuuden Seura. 1984.
RIBAS, Tomaz Danças do Povo Português. Direcção-General do Ensino Primario, Lisbon. 1961.
RIPLEY, William Z. The Races of Europe. Kegan Paul, Trench, Trübner & Co. Ltd. 1899.
RIPPON, Hugh Discovering English Folk Dance. Shire Publications Ltd., Aylesbury. 1981.
SACHS, Curt World History of the Dance. George Allen and Unwin Ltd. 1938.
SCHNEIDER, Richard Extraits de l'Encyclopédie de l'Alsace. Editions Publitotal, Strasbourg. 1983.
La Tradition en Alsace. Editions S.A.E.P., Strasbourg. 1975.
SEIDEL, Jan & ŠPIČÁK, Josef Zahrajte mi do Kola! Tance Českého Lidu (Czech). Nakladatel'stvi L. Mazác, Prague.
SESTAVILI, Vybrali, KOS, Bohumil, & STRUSKA A. František Mužské Lidové Tance (Czech). Naše Vojsko, Prague. 1953.
SHARP, Cecil J. The Sword Dances of Northern England. Novello and Co. Ltd., London. 1951.
SILIŅA, Elza Latviešu Deja (Latvia). Latviešu Folkloras Krātuves Izdevums, Riga. 1939.
SIMPSON, Jacqueline European Mythology. Hamlyn, Twickenham. 1987.
TKACHENKO, Tamara, USTINOVA, T.A., RUDNEVA, A.V., POPOVA, T. Large Soviet Encyclopaedia.
TOOMI, Ullo Eesti Rahvatantsud (Estonia). Eesti Kiiklik Kirjastus, Tallinn. 1953.
TRUMP, D.H. The Prehistory of the Mediterranean. Pelican Books. 1981.
VAN DER VEN-TEN BENSEL, Elise and VAN DER VEN, D.J. De Volksdans in Nederland. A. Rutgers, Naarden. 1942.
VERSTRAETE, Eugeen Zwaarddansen in Vlaanderen. Stadsbestuur Sint-Niklaas. 1984.
VOSS, Rudolph Der Tanz und Seine Geschichte. Verlag von Fr. Bartholomäus, Erfurt. 1868.
WILLIAMS, Alice E. A Welsh Folk Dancing Handbook. The Welsh Folk Dance Society.

WILLIAMS, Huw Welsh Clog/Step Dancing.
WOSIEN, Maria-Gabrielle Sacred Dance. Avon Books, New York. 1974.
ZÁLEŠÁK, C. L'udové Tance na Slovensku (Slovakia). Osveta, Brastislava. 1964.
ZEROMSKA, Olga Tance Polskie Narodowe i Regionalne (Poland). Alma Book Co. Ltd., London. 1963.
ZUNIC-BAS, Leposava Folk Traditions of Yugoslavia. Izdavacki Zanod.

Dance Studies ed. Roderyk Lange. Centre for Dance Studies, Jersey.
Der ältere Paartanz in Europa - Konferenzbericht. Arkivet för Folklig Dans, Dansmuseet, Stockholm. 1980.
Folkdanser ed. Dagmar Hellstam. Stegelands. 1981. Svenska Folkdanser. Svenska Ungdomsringen för Bygdekultur, Falun. 1975.
Traditional Dance ed. Theresa Buckland. Crewe and Alsager College of Higher Education.
A General History of Europe (multi-vol.). ed. Denis Hay. Longman, London/New York.
Fontana History of Europe (multi-vol.). ed. J.H. Plumb. Fontana/Collins.
The Penguin Atlas of World History (2 vols). Penguin Books. 1974.

INDEX